D1423013

# GROUSE IN SPACE AND TIME

## The Population Biology of a Managed Gamebird

THE REPORT OF THE GAME CONSERVANCY'S
SCOTTISH GROUSE RESEARCH PROJECT

&

NORTH OF ENGLAND GROUSE
RESEARCH PROJECT

PETER J HUDSON
UPLANDS RESEARCH GROUP
THE GAME CONSERVANCY

The printing of this report has been made possible with support from
THE FAMOUS GROUSE Finest Scotch Whisky in the interests of conservation

Copyright©The Game Conservancy Ltd 1992

Published by
Game Conservancy Limited
Fordingbridge
Hampshire
SP6 1EF, UK

All rights reserved. Except for the quotation of short passages
for criticism or review, no part of this publication may be reproduced, stored
or transmitted in any form without the prior permission of the publisher.

Printed and bound in Great Britain by BAS Printers Ltd

Page make-up/typesetting by
McKenzie Clark Creative Agency

Front cover: Red Grouse (*Lagopus lagopus scoticus*), by Stanley Todd.
Reproduced from Matthew Gloag, The Famous Grouse Finest Scotch Whisky Collection,
by kind permission.
© Matthew Gloag & Son

The vignettes of grouse within the book are also by Stanley Todd
and were specially commissioned by Matthew Gloag and Son for this report.
© Matthew Gloag & Son

Photographs by the author unless otherwise acknowledged.

ISBN  0 9500130 1 3

# CONTENTS

# FOREWORD

In central Scotland, grouse numbers were reasonable in the mid 1970s, but after poor weather conditions during 1975 and 1976 they started a decline which many people feared to be terminal. By the early 1980s a high proportion of those connected with grouse moors felt in their heart of hearts that grouse shooting in Scotland was a thing of the past. However, stimulated by the most generous gift from HH Sheikh Hamdan al Maktoum, The Hon. Jamie Bruce, then Scottish Chairman of The Game Conservancy, initiated the creation of the Scottish Grouse Research Project and the fundraising for it. Through the combined enthusiasm and effort of many contributors, a half million pounds was raised by Sir Robert Spencer Nairn's Appeal Committee during the six year life of the project, which has resulted not only in the production of this report by Dr Peter Hudson and his team, but also the long term establishment of a Game Conservancy Upland Research Unit in the Scottish Highlands. I would also remark that Peter Hudson's vast knowledge of his subject resulted in his quickly gaining the confidence of many moor owners and their staff, and indeed re-establishing morale and hope in many areas.

We live in a period of fast moving change in rural Scotland; unlike the first half of this century, there appears to be no shortage of finance for major developing industries such as forestry and fish farming. However, traditional land uses have been challenged and in some instances dislodged by these changes. In the light of such pressure, the Project Steering Committee guided Peter Hudson to establish the facts behind the collapse of grouse during the late seventies and to look in detail at some of the problems facing the low density grouse populations in Scotland.

In many western areas of Scotland, managed moorland has either been overtaken by blanket forestry or made impractical by its close proximity. Not only has this resulted in the loss of grouse but also a wide range of other moorland birds considered of national and international conservation value. Even in prime areas of grouse moorland, large areas of once productive moorland, for example Aberfeldy to Dunkeld, have gone under the forester's plough and we have lost grouse, sheep and the people involved with their management. As such it has become imperative first to establish a case for the continuance of traditional moorland management by way of grouse moors and hill farming and second to identify the problems and determine what needs to be done to improve the viability of grouse management.

The work undertaken by Peter Hudson has exposed the role of parasitic worm disease and also the problems of louping ill in certain areas. Even so, it is clear from this Report that the decline in grouse was also influenced by the combined effects of increasing predation and particularly the adverse effects of the Scottish weather. While spacing behaviour of grouse was previously believed, in scientific circles at least, to be the main cause of changes in grouse numbers, the fascinating experiments described in this Report show that spacing behaviour is unlikely to be limiting many of the low density populations. Predation is an important cause of mortality which must be addressed by managers of grouse moors and others interested in land management. At times I marvel at the incredible powers of the grouse to survive the harsh winter storms and at their parenthood in rearing young. Surely it is within the birds' fortitude and the art of their management that the fascination of grouse lies.

Hitherto, the major 'in depth' report on Scottish grouse was the Lovat Report of 1911, 'The Grouse in Health and in Disease', although there was also a report on the decline of red grouse produced by the then Nature Conservancy, sponsored by the Scottish Landowners' Association, in 1959. Since the 1911 report we have come a long way. Advances in technology have given us radio-tracking equipment and computers, while the knowledge of grouse held by keepers has expanded our understanding of grouse management. Peter Hudson's research on strongylosis has built on much of this earlier work and I am pleased to say resulted in the development of new techniques for parasite control including both direct dosing and medicated grit. Louping ill has been identified as an important problem whereas the impact of ticks in conjunction with louping ill was dismissed in the 1911 report. While we can now solve this problem in some areas, the new techniques do not appear to have helped some of the Moray moors that suffer from the worst effects of ticks.

In comparison with the 1911 findings it is interesting to note that this current Report emphasises the importance of predation and places less emphasis on heather management. Even so, the importance of habitat management is stressed and in particular the localised effects of heavy grazing which is such an important problem in parts of England and Southern Scotland. There has also been a clear and dramatic increase in predators in Scotland: much greater than on the English moors. Not only have foxes and crows increased at an alarming rate over the past 10 years but Scottish grouse face a wider spectrum of predators, ranging from those that can be legally controlled such as fox, crow and mink, to the protected species including pine marten, wild cat and several species of raptor. Coupled with this increase in predator numbers has been the decline in grouse, so the pressure of predation on grouse in Scotland often seems inordinately high. Because of this I am not surprised Peter Hudson's research has led him to look at this problem. I should emphasise that he was not instructed at the outset to investigate predation; there were no preconceived ideas; but the results of the scientific studies clearly indicated this was a problem that needed researching in detail.

One of the main problems facing our understanding of grouse populations is the importance of spacing behaviour. Do grouse determine their own breeding density in autumn or is mortality through predation and other causes important in determining density? Such a question may seem of little importance to those directly involved in the day to day management of grouse where the keepers decide the level of fox control that will run during the winter months. However, testing this idea is of fundamental importance to grouse management. On the one hand, if grouse determine their own spring density in the autumn, winter predator control is not necessary because then the predators take surplus non breeding individuals and keepers can be employed on other tasks. On the other hand, if predation is an important cause of death, as I believe this study shows, then to maintain grouse shooting as a viable form of land use, incentives are needed for the control of predation. These issues have become so important that the whole problem was debated in a constructive atmosphere with other scientists at Imperial College in December 1989. The chairman, Professor John Lawton FRS, produced a most readable booklet summarising his views entitled 'Red Grouse Populations and Moorland Management'.

I believe that moorland sporting estates are under- represented in the political arena. Government agencies such as the Scottish Natural Heritage and non- government conservation bodies such as the RSPB continually stress the importance of grouse management to the conservation of moorland areas. However, it is important to realise that unlike heavily subsidised farming and forestry, grouse shooting attracts no financial support but is in fact penalised in Scotland by sporting rates. Moorland owners in England have formed a Moorland Association to consider the political initiatives of open access and changes in grazing pressure. A representative body of moorland estates who would consider and protect the plight of moorlands in Scotland is needed. Given the different legislation in Scotland and the recent autonomy to Scottish Natural Heritage this would clearly have to be a Scottish based organisation.

In the second part of this Foreword I would like to express my personal views on the future management of Scotland's open moorland as opposed to deer forests, stimulated by the belief that this moorland is unique for the specialized bird life and wildlife it supports and therefore of international importance.

For tourists to drive through open heather country, and maybe to stop, listen to and to see all the bird life that Scotland's moorland supports, must provide an exhilerating experience in comparison to driving through unthinned juvenile plantations. As the Report shows, the greatest diversity of upland bird life is found in the central Highlands. I believe the reason we have such an asset and the only way of retaining this resource is through the traditional management methods. Thus I would like to see a meeting of minds between those who live on and for the grouse moors, those conservation organisations which often appear single minded in their preservation attitude and the ramblers who are so vociferous in demanding rights of access. These latter interested parties often fail to acknowledge the responsibilities (financial and otherwise) and achievements that traditional land management has created and retained in the very countryside they admire.

The conservation and management inputs of moorlands are continually changing and we must all consider these changes so as to conserve the wildlife in a balanced state while maintaining the social structure of upland communities. Traditional land management in Scotland has an admirable record. On the other hand, if increased public control of land management were ever to come I have no doubts of the disaster and costs attached that would befall our own wildlife. This has already been shown in other European countries such as Hungary, Czechoslovakia and Portugal.

Recent parliamentary activity against legal predator control threatened rural conservation with a deadly blow. The snaring of foxes (essential around forestry) and the bolting of foxes by terriers from their cairns on the hills are just two examples of procedures which some politicians aim to make illegal. Yet without these controls the uplands might as well be abandoned for sheep and grouse production. It is clear that our interests must be defended with the utmost vigour. I believe this Report, aided by the Strathclyde University report on the economics of grouse shooting, will greatly assist us.

Since a large proportion of Scotland's habitat has been lost to forestry, the surviving dependent bird life from that area must either die or move on to such moorland as is left. Conservation bodies and traditional land users have a common interest in preserving the remaining Scottish open grouse moorland. All interested parties should have an opportunity to debate whether traditional moorland management is the best form of preservation in a fair minded manner and without the need to score political points. If this can be achieved, it is only reasonable that SNH (Scottish Natural Heritage) should preside over the debate. Indeed, under the terms of the 1981 Wildlife and Countryside Act, SNH has authority within Scotland to put before the Secretary of State such changes as it considers necessary to the Act and to review the status of all species every five years.

There is still looming before us the possibility that some of what remains of our Scottish moorlands may revert to total or partial afforestation, as encouraged by the Government's planting target of 30 000ha per annum. My apparent critical stance of *upland* confierous forestry is based upon my experience over the past 35 years in attempting to manage sheep and produce grouse in close proximity to large plantations. Many commercial plantation owners both public and private do not comply with the traditional aspects of 'good neighbour' predation control despite the provision in the rules of good estate management as set out in the Fifth Schedule of the Agricultural Scotland Act (Part 3, Sections 39/41). Within this Report there is clear evidence of an increase in fox numbers and crows which are associated with this increase in afforestation.

Scottish hills must be managed and the control of foxes and crows are important to most upland land users. Yet the onus for this control has fallen increasingly on private sporting interests while the forestry areas harbour many of the problem species. Added to the problems of predation, forestry also limits burning practices and the erection of deer fences causes further heavy bird mortality, particularly when grouse move into wintering areas which have been recently planted. I have personal experience, when erecting deer fences which I thought well under grouse flight lines, of picking up 20 dead grouse after one winter storm.

In conclusion, I hope that those who read this Report will find in it both good value for all the effort put in, and an encyclopaedia of knowledge of day to day life on a grouse moor. I believe it justifies widespread support for traditional moorland management.

Last but not least, I must convey all our thanks to Mary, Peter's wife, for putting up with 'grouse' to the extent she has over these years; and to Eira and John Drysdale for providing Crubenmore and their adjacent moors for major study areas. I must also thank the many moor owners and keepers for allowing Peter's staff access to their ground and grouse throughout the year. I would like to convey my warm thanks to our Steering Committee for the time they have given to this project and to all those generous people who have spent so much of their time raising the necessary funds and finally to Colin Stroyan and the Trustees for looking after the finances so admirably.

**C. R. CONNELL**
**Colqhalizie, Perthshire**

# STEERING COMMITTEE OF THE
# SCOTTISH GROUSE RESEARCH PROJECT

C.R. Connell (Chairman)

The Rt Hon. The Marquess of Linlithgow

The Rt Hon. The Earl of Mansfield

The Rt Hon. The Earl Peel

The late Lord Biddulph

The Hon. Philip Astor

The Hon. Charles Pearson

Major Colin Mackenzie

Capt. A. Farquharson

John Drysdale

David Laird

Kenny Wilson

## Ex officio:

Sir Robert Spencer-Nairn (Chairman, Fundraising)

Patrick Gordon-Duff-Pennington (Scottish Landowners' Federation)

Richard Van Oss (Director General, Game Conservancy)

Dr. G.R. Potts (Director of Research, Game Conservancy)

Dr. Peter Hudson (Upland Research Manager, Game Conservancy)

David Newborn (Project Scientist, North of England, Game Conservancy)

Ian McCall (Regional Director, Scotland, Game Conservancy)

# STEERING COMMITTEE OF THE NORTH OF ENGLAND GROUSE RESEARCH PROJECT

The Rt. Hon. The Earl Peel (Chairman)

J. Archdale

D.T.C. Caldow

J.A. Currer-Briggs

C.J. Dent

P.W.T. Duckworth

J.D. Morley

P.W.D. Roberts

Dr. D. Wise

## Ex officio:

Sir Anthony Milbank Bt., (Moorland Association)

L. Waddell (Moorland Gamekeepers Association)

Richard Van Oss (Director General, Game Conservancy)

Dr G. R. Potts (Director of Research, Game Conservancy)

J. D. Jackson (Advisor, North of England, Game Conservancy)

Dr. Peter Hudson (Upland Research Manager, Game Conservancy)

David Newborn (Project Scientist, North of England, Game Conservancy)

# SCOTTISH RESEARCH TRUST

C.S.R. Stroyan (Chairman)

The Hon. J.M.E. Bruce, CBE

C.R. Connell

R.F. Gibbons

The Rt. Hon. Viscount Slim, OBE

P. De Vink

J. Drysdale

R. Douglas Miller

Sir Charles Morrison


# SCIENTIFIC ADVISORY COMMITTEE

Dr J.C. Coulson, D.Sc. (Chairman), University of Durham

Dr R. Connan, University of Cambridge

Dr A.P. Dobson, Princeton University

Professor D. Jenkins, D.Sc., FRSE, University of Aberdeen

Dr B.T. Grenfell, University of Cambridge

Professor D.L. Lee, D.Sc., University of Leeds

Dr I. Newton, D.Sc., Institute of Terrestrial Ecology

Dr D.B.A. Thompson, Nature Conservancy Council Scotland

Dr D. Wise, University of Cambridge

# RED GROUSE RESEARCH TEAM
## (as at January 1992)

Dr Peter Hudson    Upland Research Manager

David Newborn    Project Scientist, North of England

Flora Booth    Field Research Worker, England

David Howarth    Field Research Worker, Scotland

Caroline Hunt    Secretary

Dr Andrew Dobson    Research Associate, Princeton University

Martha Hurley    Research Student, Princeton University

Anne Wakeham    Research Student, Strathclyde University


**Past research workers:**

Dr Stephen Redpath    Research Student, Leeds University

Dr Harold Watson    Research Student, Leeds University

John Renton    Field Research Worker

Graeme Dalby    Field Research Worker

Joan Goddard    Computer Assistant

Peter Moore    Field Research Worker

Ilona Furrokh    Computer Assistant


**The dogs:**

Fennell, Quill, Fly, Bell, Fergie, Rowan, Peely Wally, Max, Domino and Lady.

# PREFACE

Grouse research and the problems of grouse management first started for me in the Panamanian rain forests, just north of the Columbian border in the spring of 1979. I was studying the flowering biology of a tree known as *Brownea rosa-de-monte*, pollinated by the long-tailed hermit hummingbird. One day, at the end of the dry season, a colleague arrived from the coast after a day's walk and brought with him some news and the magazine New Scientist. Within this magazine was an advert seeking a research worker to investigate the population dynamics of red grouse in Northern England. The rains were starting so I arranged a trip back to Britain. After the formalities of an interview and discussions at Fordingbridge with Dick Potts of The Game Conservancy I met Lord Peel in Swaledale. Field studies were initiated which resulted in the production of the book, *Red Grouse: The Biology and Management of a Wild Gamebird* in 1986.

In 1983, the Scottish Landowners Federation held a meeting on grouse and sheep in Edinburgh and asked me to present a paper on the role of research in identifying and developing management solutions. During the conference a whole series of questions were raised about the cause of the fall in the Scottish grouse population and what needed to be done to improve the situation. One outcome of this meeting was the formation of the Game Conservancy's Scottish Grouse Research Project in 1984. Initially, Dr Richard Barnes collected and analysed data on the bag records and David Newborn spent the summer of 1985 in Scotland collecting information on grouse breeding production. One thing led to another and eventually to a meeting with John and Eira Drysdale and the establishment of a research base at Crubenmore in the Highlands of Scotland.

This book summarises the research findings from the period 1985 to 1991 in Scotland and research supervised by me but undertaken by David Newborn in England. The research was guided by two Steering Committees, one in Scotland and one in England. I would like to express my sincere thanks for the excellent discussion and contributions of the chairmen, Lord Peel and Mr Charles Connell. Many of the members of these committees have become good friends. Lord Peel, a great friend and a man with a deep understanding and intuition about the behaviour of grouse provided wonderful support throughout these studies. Jim Briggs provided helpful enthusiasm and drive; I wish there were more people like him. Sir Robert Spencer-Nairn's kindness in welcoming us to Scotland made him a firm favourite with my family.

This Report would not have been possible without the support of a series of field workers. Special thanks must go to David Newborn and John Renton for their support throughout the studies. I also wish to thank Flora Booth, Graeme Dalby, David Howarth and Peter Moore for their help and guidance in the field work. They were in turn helped by trainee keepers and a series of visiting research workers from various countries as far apart as China and South Africa.

Working in isolation in the Highlands of Scotland means that there are few academics to discuss ideas, techniques and approaches to unravelling the life of the grouse. A number of scientists have either visited us at Crubenmore or I have visited them. First, I wish to express my gratitude to my close friends and colleagues: Andy Dobson, Bryan Grenfell, Mick Crawley, Charles Godfray, Steve Redpath and Tim Birkhead. Throughout the studies encouragement and advice have been given by some notable ecologists including Bob May, Roy Anderson, John Lawton, Mike Hassell, Chris Perrins, John Coulson, Kate Lessells, Ian Newton, Doug Wise, Roger Connan, David Jenkins and Des Thompson. Several people read and commented on the manuscript in detail and I would specially like to thank David Jenkins, John Coulson and Doug Wise for their interest, speed and efficiency.

Friends and colleagues in The Game Conservancy provided support in almost every way possible and naturally I wish to express my warmest thanks to Dick Potts. Dick carries a fantastic enthusiasm for wise use conservation of game and the wildlife resources of this country and his energy and drive frequently resulted in productive discussions. We both enjoy such discussions and remain firm friends and colleagues after 11 years. I hope he agrees that grouse are at least as interesting as his beloved partridges. The project would never have reached fruition without the dedication and drive of Richard Van Oss who was instrumental in obtaining and managing the funding of this research project.

Almost everyone in The Game Conservancy has helped in one way or another but I should like to thank Caroline Hunt, Ilona Furrokh, Joan Goddard, June Chapman, Pam Mataitis, Michelle Treblico, Lorraine Josling, Patsy Hitchings, Corrine Duggins, Wendy Jefferd and Brenda Carwardine for their help and good sense of humour. The research department of The Game Conservancy is a happy place in which to work and I thank Nick Sotherton, Peter Robertson, Dave Baines, Steve Tapper, Nicholas Aebischer and Nick Giles for their contribution. Charles Nodder remained his normal calm and sensible self during the gestation and birth of this publication. Karen Blake was a great help with the figures and Judy Pittock did the last minute corrections.

My family and close friends need a very special thanks for their support. My warmest thanks to my wife Mary, and my wonderful children Tom and Kitty. The families of the other research workers and our friends have always understood and been interested in the work and I would like to thank the Newborns, the Howarths and the Rennys for their support over the years.

Finally I express a very deep gratitude to John and Eira Drysdale. The contribution made by them to the research programme is difficult to measure in anything but superlatives. Not only did they provide us with a place to live, offices and study areas, they also interacted daily with the research and the problems we faced. Few people could show such remarkable confidence and dedication to the importance of our grouse research and the role of shooting as a form of land use. I know I speak for my whole family and the Steering Committee in thanking them and their estate staff, Ken Dakers and Alistair Lyon, very warmly for their encouragement and support.

**Peter Hudson**

# SYNOPSIS

**The distribution of red grouse in Britain is limited by the availability of heather-dominant moorland, a habitat currently being lost through overgrazing, poor burning and afforestation. The abundance of grouse within this habitat varies according to mortality caused by predation, nematode parasites and the disease louping ill. Emigration is proportionately greater at high autumn densities and, for a given density, greater on isolated moors.**

The distribution of red grouse within Britain is severely limited by the availability of heather dominant moorland. Loss of this habitat has been one of the main factors that has caused the long-term decline in numbers and particularly in the wetter areas, where the heather vegetation is less tolerant of grazing and burning. In a limited number of cases, high stocking densities of sheep and the consequent overgrazing of heather during the winter months have caused heather loss. Even on many areas that carry an acceptable or low stocking density of sheep, heather is still being lost. In these areas sheep (and in some instances deer or cattle) are concentrated at winter feeding sites and rapidly destroy localised areas of heather (Chapter 35).

## Variations in numbers shot between grouse moors

The density of grouse and the number of grouse shot varies greatly throughout Britain. Areas of the Pennines and eastern Scotland produce larger bags of grouse than areas to the north and west (Chapter 3). Three features account for most of the variation in average bag size, not only at the present time but also during earlier decades. Grouse bags are greater in areas with higher June temperatures, where the conditions for heather growth are good (high summer temperature and low summer rainfall) and on estates which carry the greatest number of moorland gamekeepers per unit area (Chapter 4). June temperature and heather growth are related to the geographical location of the population, while the distribution of keepers is a function of estate management. The effect of keepers is mainly through predation control rather than the pattern of heather burning.

Grouse density is greater in populations with high chick survival rates. While predator control and weather conditions may influence the survival of chicks, the over-riding factor associated with poor chick survival is the disease louping ill (Chapter 9). This disease causes high mortality, with 80% of infected birds dying and an overall reduction in chick survival of about 50% (Chapter 33). In some populations the disease appears to be endemic with high levels of infection maintaining high mortality, in others the disease is epidemic with only occasional outbreaks. Chicks in the endemic areas carry higher tick burdens than chicks in the epidemic populations. In epidemic areas the disease may be maintained by the sheep population and could be reduced or even eliminated through vaccination but in endemic areas the grouse and ticks may be able to maintain the disease (Chapter 34). Further research is needed on this disease.

## Year to year variations in low density populations

The processes which appear to operate on low and high density populations differ, although in both, year to year changes in grouse abundance reflect changes in the loss of grouse during the winter months (Chapter 8). In high density populations, parasites are frequently associated with the death of the grouse, while in low density populations predation is the principal cause of death (Chapter 11). The main predators of the adult grouse are the fox and the peregrine but in low density populations these predators do not appear to be catching individuals selectively according to condition or territorial ownership (Chapters 11 and 18). The number of grouse taken by these predators remains constant irrespective of grouse density, such that the proportion taken falls with grouse density (Chapter 12). This inverse density dependent predation rate appears to keep grouse populations in a 'predation trap' whereby high predation rates prevent the grouse population from increasing. Where this occurs, management activities should operate to reduce these predation losses by the careful and legal control of foxes during the winter months.

Heavy chick losses can be caused by a wide range of factors including louping ill, the indirect effects of the parasitic trichostrongyle worm, lack of food and predation. Crows, foxes and a range of predators, including hen harriers, will take grouse chicks during the summer months. At low densities of less than five grouse pairs km$^{-2}$, harriers may take significant numbers of chicks and these losses, coupled with heavy winter predation, may be sufficient to prevent the grouse population from increasing (Chapter 21). Such effects are far less important at higher densities, when harriers and other predators take relatively few grouse. The relative importance and interaction of these predators continues to be studied.

While gamekeeper density and predator control are important aspects of management on each estate, the relative density of grouse on neighbouring areas can also influence the movement and subsequent abundance of grouse. Movement in the autumn is density dependent, with immigration in to low density populations and an increase in the proportion of young birds leaving populations with high grouse density (Chapters 12 and 14). On moors where management has provided a high density of young grouse, there could be a significant loss of birds to neighbouring low density populations where management investments have not allowed numbers to increase. Alternatively, where density is high on neighbouring estates then overall losses may well be less. In this respect predator control through keeper employment on a series of contiguous estates provides the most effective way of producing grouse.

### Year to year variations in high density populations

When predation control is sufficient to allow grouse numbers to increase, grouse populations start to suffer from periodic crashes in numbers caused by heavy infestations of the caecal threadworm, *Trichostrongylus tenuis* (Chapter 25). The increase in these worms on wet moors reflects increased grouse density, whereas on the drier eastern moors worms only increase during periods of damp weather (Chapter 20). Inside the grouse the worms burrow into the caecal wall, causing internal bleeding, a reduction in condition and in some cases the death of the bird. However, the most significant effect of the worm is in reducing the condition of the female grouse and her subsequent breeding success (Chapter 27). Control of the parasite can be achieved through either the application of medicated grit or through direct dosing (Chapter 30). Medicated grit is effective in reducing parasite intensities and probably acts best in the long-term reduction of worms. Direct dosing is effective in the short-term and should be applied when worm burdens are increasing.

### Synthesis

Long-term maintenance of red grouse populations must pivot on the care of their habitat. Balanced grazing and careful burning of heather are needed to prevent the degradation of the moors and the spread of coarse grasses and bracken. Given a suitable habitat, legal predator control is essential to limit the effects of predation and to achieve a sufficient density of grouse for driven shooting. Only then will the economic, social and conservation benefits of grouse managment be fully realized. In some localities, even where keepers are present, heavy winter predation by foxes and peregrines may keep grouse densities low. The effects of such predation are greater where there is already a heavy mortality of chicks caused by the disease louping ill, and in some instances by hen harriers. When all the above factors are favourable, grouse density rises to a level at which parasitic worms can cause periodic crashes in numbers.

In conclusion, habitat management, and the control of predation and parasites are all essential to producing a yield of grouse which is realistic both in terms of economics and conservation.

Grouse shooting maintains the multiple land use system and provides important financial income in upland Britain (Chapter 1). *The Earl Peel*

In the region of 450 000 grouse are shot each year in Britain from about 460 grouse moors (Chapter 2).

An August density of more than 60 grouse per square kilometre is required to produce driven grouse shooting and to realise a sustainable economic return (Chapter 1, Appendix 3). *The Earl Peel*

The lack of grouse during the late seventies resulted in several grouse moors being sold to alternative forms of land use such as commercial afforestation. Forestry on ground neighbouring moorland can act as a refuge for predators and can limit heather burning activities (Foreword, Chapter 5). *Charles Connell*

# GROUSE SHOOTING: ECOLOGY & ECONOMICS

# INTRODUCTION: HISTORY, OBJECTIVES & ACHIEVEMENTS

**Grouse shooting indirectly conserves heather moorland, benefits other wildlife and maintains a multiple land use system. With the decline in grouse numbers between 1975 and 1983, these advantages were threatened in Scotland. The object of this work was to examine the biological factors influencing changes in grouse numbers.**

## 1.1 Grouse management and land use

Grouse management as a form of land use serves three important functions:

(i) *Grouse shooting maintains a multiple land use system in the uplands of Britain:* Grouse management provides the labour and management skills needed to maintain the heather habitat. By and large, only estates with grouse shooting interests care for the heather moorland and in so doing maintain the multiple land use system. Heather moorland provides winter feed for sheep and deer, a relatively rich habitat for important species of wildlife and an aesthetic quality which tourists find attractive. Without grouse shooting, the habitat would probably be replaced by a single land use practice such as sheep ranching or commercial afforestation. These tend to be intensive forms of management which regularly conflict with the objectives of conservation and invariably support fewer people than a multiple land use system.

(ii) *Grouse shooting indirectly supports the objectives of conservation:* Heather moorland is a habitat of international importance, much of it centred in the uplands of Britain. This semi-natural environment exists largely as a consequence of the tradition of grouse shooting and the management of the habitat for grouse production. Sporting interests and the economic importance of grouse shooting are the prime reasons why the uplands hold a significant proportion of the European population of several bird species with high conservation value (Chapter 6).

(iii) *Grouse shooting provides important financial income and community support in impoverished areas:* Approximately 450 000 grouse are shot in Great Britain each year, if all were shot on driven days and let at the current value of £70 per brace this would generate a gross income of £35 million to upland areas. In reality the amount is much less than this although the people who come and shoot usually spend money on hotels, goods and travel all of which generates a significant income in impoverished parts of the country. The report by Strathclyde University on the economic value of grouse shooting to Scotland (Appendix 3) estimated this indirect expenditure at greater than £9.5 million and the total expenditure at almost £21 million.

## 1.2 The decline in grouse numbers

Given the important role of grouse shooting as a form of upland land use there was general concern amongst Scottish landowners and others involved in grouse and moorland management when grouse numbers fell during the mid 1970s and failed to show signs of recovery (Figure 1.1). This was an unprecedented decline which resulted in many traditional grouse moors being sold to alternative forms of land use, mainly commercial afforestation.

While the change to afforestation was worrying, two important points should be noted. First, such ground would never have been sold from grouse shooting if the grouse bag numbers had not fallen and the original landowners been able to retain a healthy stock of grouse. Second, when the land was sold it was sold to forestry because of tax incentives at that time. If grouse numbers had not fallen, some potentially good grouse ground in both the Southern Uplands and the Highlands would never have been afforested.

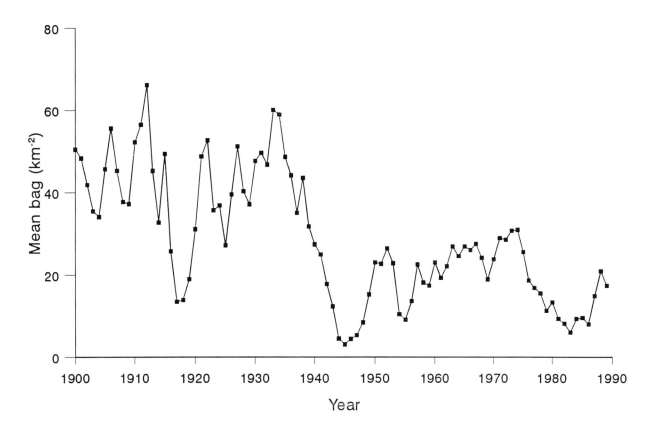

Figure 1.1 Changes in numbers of red grouse shot in Scotland on managed estates, showing the decline in grouse numbers during the 1970s and the problem which led to the formation of the Scottish Grouse Research Project. The decline was greater than represented here because these results were collected from estates which continued grouse shooting after the decline.

### 1.3 Objective and history of current research programme

The aim of the Scottish Grouse Research Project was to describe the decline in the grouse population in Scotland and assess the various factors that were keeping many of the Scottish grouse populations at a low density.

The project was launched in 1985 and started with a dual approach. First Dr Richard Barnes wrote to many estates and obtained initial information on bag records and management procedures. He subsequently described the decline in numbers of red grouse[1]. Second, David Newborn, working on red grouse in England, moved to Crieff, established study areas and conducted an initial comparison of the breeding performance of grouse in different parts of Scotland.

Using the information gained from the initial studies of bag records and breeding performance we then designed intensive and extensive studies in Scotland and established a main research base at Crubenmore near Newtonmore. Strathspey was chosen as the central point for this work because there were large variations in grouse density (ranging from 3 to 60 pairs km$^{-2}$), variable climatic conditions, variable habitat structure on nearby estates and easy access to estates throughout Scotland. While these intensive studies concentrated on 6km$^2$ (1500 acres) of ground in Badenoch, comparative observations were taken on study areas in Strathspey, Sutherland, Deeside, West and East Perthshire, the Angus glens, the Borders and in various parts of England. Special projects were also initiated to examine additional problems including the interaction of hen harriers and grouse in 1985 (Dr Steve Redpath with a University of Leeds Scholarship), the control of invasive grasses on heather moorland in 1990 (Miss Anne Wakeham with sponsorship from Rhone-Poulenc), and dispersal behaviour of red grouse in 1991 (Miss Martha Hurley, Princeton University with a National Science Foundation Fellowship).

### 1.4. What has grouse research achieved?

The grouse moor manager frequently asks what grouse research has achieved for grouse shooting and management. The simple answer to this question is "An insight into the workings of grouse populations, identifying what management should be done, when and where, and thus making grouse management efficient".

The ten most significant achievements of our grouse research have been:

1. Establishing the role of predation in determining grouse numbers and evaluating the role of spacing behaviour at low grouse density.
2. Establishing the effect of parasitism and its role in causing cyclic changes in grouse numbers.
3. The development of medicated grit as an aid to long term reductions of the trichostrongyle worm.
4. The development of the catch and treat technique for short term reduction of the trichostrongyle worm.
5. Describing in detail the interaction between predators and grouse, especially the relationship between hen harriers and grouse.
6. Describing the benefits of grouse moor management for other kinds of wildlife which inhabit British moorlands.
7. Investigating the epidemiology and control of louping ill.
8. Developing techniques for re-establishing heather dominant vegetation on over-grazed moorland.
9. Understanding the role of invertebrates in chick diet and development of insect-rich areas for chicks during early life.
10. The application of selective herbicides to control invasive grasses and bracken.

All in all this amounts to a significant progress in providing the basis for the conservation and sensitive management of red grouse in a sustainable manner.

## 1.5 How to read this report

This report has been written so it may be read at several different levels:

*Level 1: Recommendations:* These can be obtained by reading summary sections within the report or the short abstract at the beginning of each chapter.

*Level 2: Management suggestions:* This report is not designed to suggest management options but included at the end of a number of chapters are management recommendations.

*Level 3: The grouse manager:* To avoid scientific details but to obtain the main gist of the report, the interested reader should read in each chapter the Introduction and Summary and examine the figures and tables.

*Level 4: The scientific reader:* Details of statistical tests and key references are presented at the end of each chapter and referred to in the text with relevant notes. Most of this is either published or being prepared for the scientific press.

### 1.6. Notes

*a. Areas referred to:*
The report refers to grouse densities as grouse $km^{-2}$ which should be read as grouse per square kilometre. One square kilometre is 247 acres, so as an approximation multiply each square kilometre by four to estimate every 1000 acres, i.e.:

| Square Kilometres | Acres (Approximate) |
| --- | --- |
| 1 km² | 250 acres |
| 2 km² | 500 acres |
| 3 km² | 750 acres |
| 4 km² | 1000 acres |
| 5 km² | 1250 acres |
| 10 km² | 2500 acres |
| 20 km² | 5000 acres |
| 40 km² | 10 000 acres |

### 1.7 References

1. Barnes, R.F.W. (1987). Long term declines of red grouse in Scotland. *Journal of Applied Ecology*, **24**, 735-742.

# CHAPTER 2

# GROUSE SHOOTING, KEEPERS AND ECONOMICS

**In Scotland there are estimated to be 583 upland estates comprising 35 104km² (8.7 million acres) which have a major sporting interest. Of these 296, comprising 13 979km² (3.5 million acres) are considered to be grouse moors. The average annual bag in Scotland is 250 500 grouse, the total for Britain being 450 000. The number of keepers employed on estates still producing grouse has remained relatively stable, whereas the overall number in upland counties of Scotland has fallen by 85% since the turn of the century.**

## 2.1 Introduction

The uplands of Scotland and England have been dominated by the three main land use practices of farming, forestry and game shooting. Currently, sheep farming is the primary land use practice and it supports the majority of people, assisted through a financial support system. Forestry also receives fiscal support but grouse shooting attracts no financial support even though it has probably done more than other land use practices to conserve and maintain natural habitats in the uplands.

The economic significance of grouse shooting to the Scottish economy has been reviewed by Professor McGilvray and Dr Perman of Strathclyde University[1] and is summarised in Appendix 3. This chapter estimates the number of estates, area of estates and number of grouse shot in Britain, the basic economic breakpoints in relation to management inputs and the long term change in the number of keepers.

## 2.2. Extent of grouse shooting

The extent of upland ground in Britain is about 66 000km² (16 million acres), 29% of the total land surface. A total of 46 000km² (11 million acres) has

been estimated [2,3] as hill pasture, bog and moorland (20.8% of Britain, Table 2.1).

The area of heather dominant moorland within upland Britain has been estimated by a number of workers as between 14 000 and 17 000km² (3.5 - 4.2 million acres) with approximately two-thirds centred in Scotland. The Merlewood Land Classification System classified 21 categories of upland cover, three of which were characteristic of grouse moor management and produced an estimate of 4890km² (1.2 million acres), 28.9% of the total area of heather moorland and 6% of the total area of upland Britain. According to this system, land classified as deer forest was estimated at 10 740km² (2.7 million acres), producing a total sporting area in the uplands of 15 630km² (3.9 million acres), 23% of upland Britain.

As an independent assessment of the area of grouse moorland, we obtained detailed information on land use practices from 353 upland estates comprising 11 521km² (2.8 million acres; Table 2.2). This information is not a complete coverage although an estimate of the total area can be obtained from detailed mapping of upland estates[5,6] producing an estimate of 746 estates and a total land area of 37 888km² (9.4 million acres: Table 2.2). This includes ground both classified as deer

**Table 2.1.** Extent of Upland Britain (after Ratcliffe & Thompson[4] derived from Ball and others[2])

| Altitude (metres) | Land Type | Total | Thousands of square kilometres Scotland | England | Wales |
|---|---|---|---|---|---|
| 123-244 | Marginal | 54.3 | 19.9 | 28.9 | 5.5 |
| 245-610 | Pasture & Moorland | 47.3 | 27.0 | 12.4 | 7.9 |
| 611-914 | Mountain | 5.3 | 4.6 | 0.4 | 0.2 |
| >915 | High Mountain | 0.4 | 0.4 | 0.0 | 0.0 |

forest as well as grouse moor but is more than twice the estimate produced through the Merlewood Land Classification System (15 630km²).

Excluding the regions of Scotland where deer stalking is the primary land use, the estimated total number of grouse moors is 459, comprising 16 763km² (4.1 million acres: Table 2.2). This is almost four times the area estimated through the Merlewood Land Classification System (4890km²) but such differences probably reflect errors in both techniques. The estimate produced in our assessment will include ground that would not be classified as heather dominant moorland. The Merlewood technique was probably too rigorous in the classification of grouse moor and excluded some areas which were used as grouse moor, including much of the blanket bog, a highly productive habitat for grouse. The frequency distribution of estate size differs between the Scottish Highlands, Southern Uplands and Northern England, with not surprisingly a predominance of larger estates

in Scotland[a] (Figure 2.1). Average estate size was 52km² in the Highlands, 20km² in Southern Uplands (36km² in Scotland) and 20km² in England.

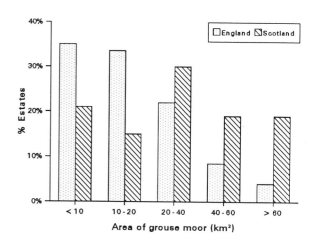

Figure 2.1. Frequency distribution of estate size in Scotland and England. England has significantly smaller estates than Scotland.

**Table 2.2.** Area and number of upland estates where grouse shooting was recorded in Britain and an estimate of the total number and area in each region. (Regions shown in a map in Figure 3.1.)

| Region | Sample Estates | | Total Estates | |
|---|---|---|---|---|
| | No. | Area (km²) | No. | Area (km²) |
| 1. North Highland | 26 | 1442 | 66 | 5258 |
| 2. N.W Highland | 21 | 1002 | 102 | 9383 |
| 3. Argyll | 27 | 882 | 79 | 4483 |
| 4. Monadhliath | 15 | 542 | 41 | 2904 |
| 5. Moray & Nairn | 14 | 493 | 22 | 967 |
| 6. Buchan & Donside | 11 | 247 | 17 | 636 |
| 7. Rannoch | 17 | 1032 | 21 | 1334 |
| 8. Cairngorm | 11 | 795 | 14 | 1198 |
| 9. Atholl | 15 | 518 | 19 | 667 |
| 10. Angus & S.Deeside | 19 | 659 | 41 | 1925 |
| 11. S. Tayside | 21 | 548 | 45 | 1980 |
| 12. Trossach | 9 | 110 | 11 | 323 |
| Highland Total | 206 | 8270 | 478 | 31058 |
| 13. Pentlands Moorfoots & Lammermuirs | 19 | 323 | 31 | 863 |
| 14. Borders | 32 | 683 | 74 | 3183 |
| S. Uplands Total | 51 | 1006 | 105 | 4046 |
| Scotland Total | 257 | 9276 | 583 | 35104 |
| 15. N. Dales | 29 | 778 | 47 | 1120 |
| 16. N.York Moors | 12 | 438 | 21 | 477 |
| 17. S. Dales | 29 | 359 | 45 | 503 |
| 18. Bowland | 10 | 152 | 13 | 174 |
| 19. Peak District | 11 | 118 | 27 | 430 |
| N. England Total | 92 | 1845 | 153 | 2704 |
| 20. Wales | 5 | 39 | 10 | 80 |
| Overall Total | 353 | 11521 | 746 | 3784 |

### 2.3 Number of grouse shot in Britain

Detailed information on regional and temporal changes in numbers of grouse shot are presented in later analysis but within this section an estimate is made of the total number of red grouse shot throughout Britain.

Not all moors approached during this survey provided information on both area of estate and the total number of grouse shot in each year. From the 361 estates that supplied bag information, the sum of the average annual bag shot by region between 1970 and 1989 was 291 225 birds. This does not include all grouse shot, since an estimated 98 estates were not included within the analysis. Taking the regional estimates of mean bag shot per square kilometre and correcting for area produces a total mean number of grouse shot per annum between 1970 and 1989 in Scotland of 250 500, in England and Wales a figure of 200 000 grouse and a total mean bag of 450 500 for Britain (Table 2.4).

There is large variation in the number of grouse shot per square kilometre in both England and Scotland (Figure 2.2) although England is more productive overall. In Scotland the majority of estates shot less than 25 grouse km$^{-2}$ while about one third of English estates shot more than 100 grouse km$^{-2}$.

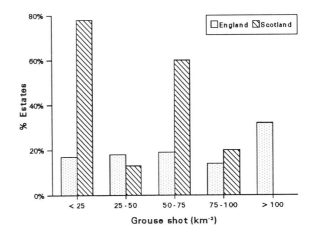

Figure 2.2. Frequency distribution of average number of grouse shot km$^{2}$. Greater numbers of grouse shot are in England and the majority of Scottish moors shoot less than 25 grouse km$^{2}$.

**Table 2.3.** Area and number of main grouse producing estates from various regions of Scotland and northern Britain.

| Region | Sample Estates No. | Area | Total Number No. | Area |
|---|---|---|---|---|
| 4. Monadhliath | 15 | 542 | 41 | 2904 |
| 5. Moray & Nairn | 14 | 493 | 22 | 967 |
| 6. Buchan & Donside | 11 | 247 | 17 | 636 |
| 8. Cairngorm | 11 | 795 | 14 | 1198 |
| 10. Angus & S.Deeside | 19 | 659 | 41 | 1925 |
| 11. S. Tayside | 21 | 548 | 45 | 1980 |
| 12. Trossachs | 9 | 110 | 11 | 323 |
| Highland Total | 100 | 3394 | 191 | 9933 |
| 13. Pentlands Moorfoots & Lammermuirs | 19 | 323 | 31 | 863 |
| 14. Borders | 32 | 683 | 74 | 3183 |
| S. Uplands Total | 51 | 1006 | 105 | 4046 |
| Scotland Total | 151 | 4400 | 296 | 13979 |
| 15. N. Dales | 29 | 778 | 47 | 1120 |
| 16. N.York Moors | 13 | 438 | 21 | 477 |
| 17. S. Dales | 29 | 359 | 45 | 503 |
| 18. Bowland | 10 | 152 | 13 | 174 |
| 19. Peak District | 11 | 118 | 27 | 430 |
| N. England Total | 92 | 1845 | 153 | 2704 |
| 20. Wales. | 5 | 39 | 10 | 80 |
| Overall Total | 248 | 6284 | 459 | 16763 |

## 2.4 Economics of grouse shooting

On the majority of grouse moors, shooting is let commercially[1] but this is principally done to help cover the fixed costs of keeper employment. This section examines the relative costs and income that could be generated from the letting of grouse shooting in order to determine at which point costs could be balanced. This information is then extended to estimate the optimal keeper density needed to shoot sufficient grouse to cover costs.

The fixed costs, variable costs and revenue from grouse shooting are summarised in Table 2.5 and were entered into a simple model in which shooting pressure was described according to the average relationship between keeper density and grouse bag (Section 2).

**Table 2.5** Fixed and variable costs of grouse management used within the economic model.

**Fixed Costs:**

| | |
|---|---|
| Keeper wages and vehicle costs etc. | £13 000 p.a. |
| Additional costs per keeper | £ 2 000 p.a. |

**Variable Costs:**

| | |
|---|---|
| Beaters wages | £15 per day |
| Beaters employed | £20 per day |
| Driven bag | 150 birds per day |
| Shooting rates | £ 10 per brace |

**Income:**

| | |
|---|---|
| Driven grouse shooting (when grouse density $> 60$ birds km$^{-2}$) | £ 70 per brace |
| Walked up shooting (when grouse density 15-60 birds km$^{-2}$) | £25 per brace |
| Grouse carcass sale: old birds | £1.00 per brace |
| young birds | £3.50 per brace |

**Table 2.4.** Estimates of number of estates, area, average grouse bag and total bag per annum between 1970 and 1989 from regions of Scotland, England and Wales.

| Region | No. | Sample Area | Shot /km$^2$ | Total Area | Total Bag | Estimated Bag |
|---|---|---|---|---|---|---|
| 1. North Highland | 26 | 1442 | 5 | 5258 | 26290 | 15000 |
| 2. N.W Highland | 21 | 1002 | 3 | 9383 | 28149 | 10000 |
| 3. Argyll | 27 | 882 | 8 | 4483 | 4491 | 1500 |
| 4. Monadhliath | 16 | 542 | 11 | 2904 | 31944 | 10000 |
| 5. Moray & Nairn | 15 | 493 | 13 | 967 | 12571 | 12000 |
| 6. Buchan & Donside | 11 | 247 | 29 | 636 | 18444 | 15000 |
| 7. Rannoch | 17 | 1032 | 7 | 1334 | 9338 | 9000 |
| 8. Cairngorm | 11 | 795 | 22 | 1198 | 26356 | 25000 |
| 9. Atholl | 16 | 518 | 17 | 667 | 11339 | 10000 |
| 10. Angus & S.Deeside | 19 | 659 | 29 | 1925 | 55825 | 40000 |
| 11. S. Tayside | 21 | 548 | 33 | 1980 | 65340 | 40000 |
| 12. Trossachs | 9 | 110 | 18 | 323 | 5814 | 3000 |
| Highland Total | 209 | 8270 | . | 9933 | 295901 | 190500 |
| 13. Pentlands Moorfoots & Lammermuirs | 20 | 323 | 61 | 863 | 52643 | 35000 |
| 14. Borders | 34 | 683 | 14 | 3183 | 44562 | 25000 |
| S. Uplands Total | 54 | 1006 | . | 4046 | 97205 | 60000 |
| Scotland Total | 263 | 9276 | . | 13979 | 393106 | 250500 |
| 15. N.Dales | 29 | 778 | 82 | 1120 | 91840 | 90000 |
| 16. N.York Moors | 13 | 438 | 60 | 477 | 28620 | 25000 |
| 17. S. Dales | 29 | 359 | 115 | 503 | 57845 | 55000 |
| 18. Bowland | 10 | 152 | 53 | 174 | 9222 | 9000 |
| 19. Peak District | 11 | 118 | 94 | 430 | 40420 | 20000 |
| N. England Total | 92 | 1845 | . | 2704 | 227947 | 199000 |
| 20. Wales. | 6 | 39 | 50 | 80 | 4000 | 1000 |
| Overall Total | 361 | 11521 | . | 16763 | 625053 | 450000 |

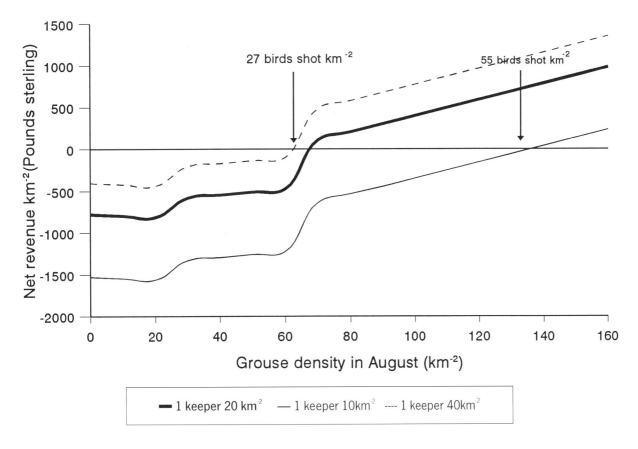

Figure 2.3. Outputs of an economic model encompassing the essential costs and income summarised in Table 2.5. The increase in net revenue at grouse densities above 60 grouse km$^2$ relates to the change from walked up to driven shooting. The financial breakpoint for one keeper 40km$^2$ (1 to 2500 acres) is 27 brace shot km$^2$ (109 brace per 1000 acres). For one keeper 10km$^2$ (1 to 10 000) it is 55 brace km$^2$ (222 brace per 1000 acres).

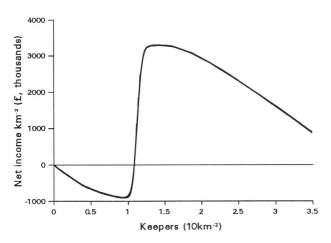

Figure 2.4. Net revenue in relation to density of keepers employed on grouse moors; income is estimated through the increase in grouse density with keepers and the costs with keepers as per Table 2.5. Within the errors that such an estimate would produce, the optimal keeper density would be in the region of one keeper to 10km$^2$ (1 to 2500 acres) of moorland.

The net revenue per square kilometre of let grouse shooting in relation to grouse density is shown in Figure 2.3 for three levels of keeper density. When keeper density is one keeper 10km$^2$ (one per 2500 acres) and all grouse shooting is let, then costs and income are balanced when 55 birds are shot km$^2$ (550 brace on 2500 acres). At lower keeper densities of one to 20km$^2$ (5000 acres) or one to 40km$^2$ (10 000 acres) at least 27

birds still need to be shot per square kilometre. This bag will only be produced when the grouse density in August exceeds 60 grouse per km$^2$, equivalent to a density when there are sufficient grouse to drive. Most Scottish moors failed to reach this density of grouse between 1970 and 1989, implying that on many estates grouse management and heather conservation were subsidised by private individuals because income from shooting was insufficient to cover costs (see Appendix 3).

In Section 2, we investigate the variables associated with the average number of grouse shot between estates. Climatic conditions and number of keepers appear to be the important variables, such that estates with more than one keeper per 15.5km$^2$ (one keeper to 3850 acres) tended to produce grouse at a suitable density for driven shooting. Incorporating this into the basic model and examining net income in relation to keeper density produced an optimal grouse keeper density of one keeper to every 10km$^2$ (one to every 2500 acres) of heather moorland (Figure 2.4). This estimate assumes that all grouse shooting is let and the general trends seen across the country apply to all types of moors. For the future, this model needs further ecological inputs which could determine the benefits of keepering on different types of estates.

## 2.5 Changes in numbers of keepers

Numbers of keepers employed in grouse management have decreased during this century as employment costs have risen and land use practices have changed from sporting to forestry. On areas which have remained as grouse moors to the present date, there has been a small fall in numbers of keepers employed in both England and Scotland. In England, on moors still managed for grouse, the density of keepers has remained relatively constant and has tended to be above the calculated optimal keeper density of one keeper to every 10km$^2$. In Scotland, on moors still managed for grouse, the average keeper density has remained below one keeper per 10km$^2$ (Figure 2.5). This is probably a reflection of the larger average size of estate in Scotland (36km$^2$ as opposed to 20km$^2$ in England). Examining the regional differences in keeper employment (Figure 2.6) shows that in the productive areas of eastern and southern Scotland, keeper densities have remained relatively stable and higher than in western and northern Scotland.

These figures of changes in keeper density are taken from grouse moors which are still producing grouse and do not include estates which have been sold to other forms of land use. A national figure for Scotland can be estimated by extracting the total number of keepers that are registered in the National Population Census. The use of the census figures has some drawbacks: First, grouse keepers cannot be distinguished from either stalkers or lowland keepers. Second, there has been a change in the style of recording the employment of keepers in the Census; since 1961 keepers have been classified as agricultural workers. To correct for this, a sample set of figures was used to estimate what proportion of agricultural workers were indeed keepers and this estimate was then extrapolated to other years. The figures since 1961 are therefore estimates and not total counts and so contain some level of error.

The total number of keepers in Scotland fell by 86.5% between 1901 and 1981 and by 66% between 1951 and 1981 (Figure 2.7[a]). These figures include both upland and lowland keepers in Scotland, but by selecting counties which are mostly upland we can obtain a rough estimate of the change in upland keepers. In the counties of Angus, Inverness, Nairn, Moray, Banff, Aberdeen, Kincardine, Perth, Lanark, Peebles, Selkirk, Roxburgh, Dumfries and Berwick the number of keepers declined by 85% between 1901 and 1981 and by 67% between 1951 and 1981 (Figure 2.8). These estimates are similar to those for the overall decline of keepers throughout Scotland.

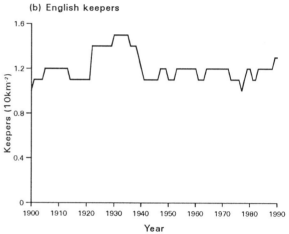

Figure 2.5. Average density of keepers employed on estates in Scotland and England which are currently still managed grouse moors.

It is interesting to examine these two sets of figures in more detail. First, the number of keepers employed on estates still managed as grouse moors has remained relatively stable. Second, the number of keepers in upland areas has fallen by 85% since the turn of the century. This implies that estates which have maintained grouse shooting as an important part of estate management have retained keeper employment and the overall fall in keepers was from estates which no longer produce grouse.

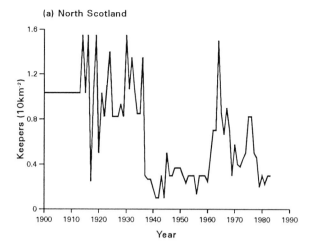

(a) North Scotland

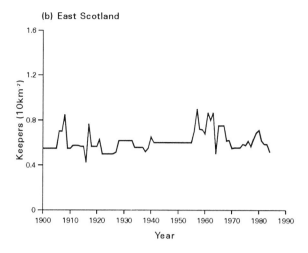

(b) East Scotland

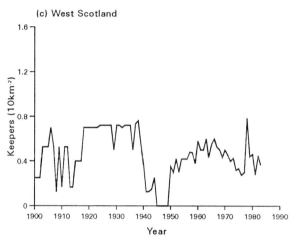

(c) West Scotland

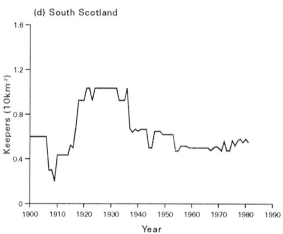

(d) South Scotland

(a) Total keepers in Scotland

Figure 2.6. (Above) Average density of keepers employed in regions of Scotland which are still managed as grouse moors. This information does not include estates which were once grouse moors but have changed to forestry or other land uses.

Figure 2.7. (left) Number of keepers employed in Scotland according to the National Population Census, (a) total number and (b) number in each region.

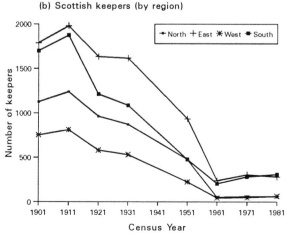

(b) Scottish keepers (by region)

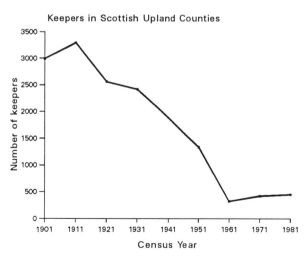

Keepers in Scottish Upland Counties

Figure 2.8. Total number of keepers employed in upland counties of Scotland recorded by the National Census.

## 2.6. Summary

In Scotland, there are estimated to be 583 upland estates comprising about 35 104km$^2$ (8.7 million acres), which have a major interest in sporting returns from either grouse and/or deer. About 296 of these estates comprising 13 979km$^2$ (3.5 million acres) are considered grouse moors. Within Britain as a whole, there is an estimated total of 459 grouse moors occupying 16 763km$^2$ (4.1 million acres). The average annual grouse bag in Scotland was estimated at 250 500 grouse with a total of 450 000 for Britain. At current driven letting values, this would be worth £31.5 million per annum.

Modelling estate economics for grouse shooting indicated costs would be covered when grouse density exceeds 60 grouse km$^{-2}$ or 27 birds shot km$^{-2}$. This is equivalent to the lowest density for practical driven grouse shooting. An optimal density of keepers for financial returns would be one keeper to 10km$^2$ (2500 acres) if shooting is let. If shooting is not let, a density of one keeper to 15.5km$^2$ (3800 acres) would allow driven grouse shooting and minimise costs. The density of keepers on estates still managed as grouse moors has not fallen greatly, however the total number of keepers employed in upland counties of Scotland has fallen by 85% since the turn of the century.

## 2.7 Notes

a. Estate size was significantly larger in Scotland, $X^2 = 29.23$, d.f. = 4, $P < 0.0001$.

## 2.8 References

1. McGilvray J. & Perman, R. (1991). *Grouse sporting shooting: an economic analysis of its importance to the Scottish Economy.* Unpublished report, Strathclyde University.

2. Ball, D.F., Radford, G.L. & Williams, W.M. (1983). A land characteristic databank for Great Britain. Occasional paper No. 13, ITE, Bangor.

3. Bunce, R.G.H. & C.J. Barr (1989). The extent of land under different management regimes in the uplands and the potential for change. In: *Ecological change in the Uplands.* Ed M.B. Usher & D.B.A. Thompson, pp. 415-426. Blackwell Scientific Publications, Oxford.

4. Ratcliffe, D.A. & Thompson, D.B.A. (1989). The British Uplands: their ecological character and international significance. In: *Ecological change in the Uplands.* Ed M.B. Usher & D.B.A. Thompson, pp 9-36. Blackwell Scientific Publications.

5. McEwen, J. (1981). *Who owns Scotland?* Polygon Books, Edinburgh.

6. Mountaineering Council of Scotland & Scottish Landowners' Federation (1989). *Heading for the Scottish Hills.* Scottish Mountaineering Trust

# CHANGES IN NUMBERS OF GROUSE AND OTHER MOORLAND ANIMALS

# CHAPTER 3

# REGIONAL VARIATIONS IN NUMBERS OF RED GROUSE SHOT

**Numbers of grouse shot on managed estates have declined this century in most parts of the country, although the rate of this decline has varied between regions. Overall, populations in the north and west of the country have fallen at a greater rate than populations in the east and south. English grouse moors are generally more productive for grouse than Scottish moors.**

## 3.1 Introduction

One of the principal objectives of an ecological study is to understand why the density of the animal studied varies both through time and from one area to the next. This may appear a simple objective and yet in few studies can sufficient information be obtained. In the case of the red grouse, like many gamebirds, the bag records provide an invaluable source of information. They can be used to estimate both changes in numbers over the past 100 years and how these changes differ in various parts of the country.

Bag records do have a number of drawbacks and these should be borne in mind during any analysis. First, they may reflect the density of grouse present on an estate during the autumn months when the population includes both the adults that have attempted breeding and also the young they produced; as such the bag reflects both breeding density and breeding success (the relationship between bag records and grouse present is examined in Chapter 5). Second, the size of the bag will be influenced by a range of factors other than grouse density and will include the sporting policy of the estate and the extent to which the grouse are harvested. Some estates may attempt to maximise the numbers of grouse shot, aim for several big days of over 100 brace and shoot a large proportion of the population. Others may wish to maximise financial returns from a hotel or house and provide many days of shooting even when the daily bag is not large. Other sporting activities may carry priority over grouse shooting, for example fishing or stalking and thus limit the time spent harvesting the

grouse bag. Finally, the shooting accuracy of individual sportsmen can vary greatly.

The objective of this chapter is to describe changes in the numbers of red grouse shot in various parts of Britain and to determine which areas have shown a decrease in the numbers shot this century. Some of this work has already been published in previous reports for parts of northern England[1] and Scotland[2] although this current analysis updates these previous studies to 1989 and provides a different type of analysis.

## 3.2 Bag record information

Information on numbers of red grouse shot and the size of the estates was obtained through three postal questionnaire surveys. The first in the north of England and north Wales was conducted in 1979, repeated in 1983 for Scotland and then updated for all parts of the country in 1989. Such a survey could only obtain bag records from managed estates and there was a tendency for well-managed and productive estates to respond. Estates which no longer shot grouse or on which the major land use practices had changed (for example from grouse to forestry) were less likely to respond because records had been lost or remained with the previous owner. As such, the bag records tend to over-emphasise the average number of grouse for a particular part of the country. They also tend to under-emphasise the extent of any decline, since the estates where grouse shooting fell to a level where the sporting part of the estate ceased or the estate was sold for other land uses would not be included.

Bag records are expressed as number of birds shot per square kilometre. For each series of records we have also estimated a rolling ten year average around each year. This is the average number shot over a combination of the previous five years, the year in question and the subsequent five years. These running averages provide a clearer description of population trends since they remove the cyclic nature of many of the bag record series. (Analysis of cycles in bag records is examined in Section 8). A total of 362 sets of bag records were considered suitable for analysis.

## 3.3 Grouse moor regions

The moorland areas of Scotland, England and Wales fall into a series of distinct geographical areas separated mostly by areas of white ground (upland grass), low ground or forestry blocks not utilised by red grouse. Such divisions provide suitable blocks of grouse populations for analysis. Some of these divisions are too small to carry a suitable sample of estates and in these cases neighbouring areas were combined to provide a sample of between 10 and 20 estates.

Any division would be arbitrary but the divisions used tend to reflect natural breaks in the grouse population and as such are considered more meaningful than County or Scottish Region divisions. A total of twenty such regions were determined and are shown in Figure 3.1.

Bag records were analysed from estates in each of these regions and then amalgamated in a series of four tiers:

1. The national grouse bag for all estates
2. Scotland and England
3. Each of four Scottish regional groupings: North, West, South and East Scotland
4. The twenty moorland regions

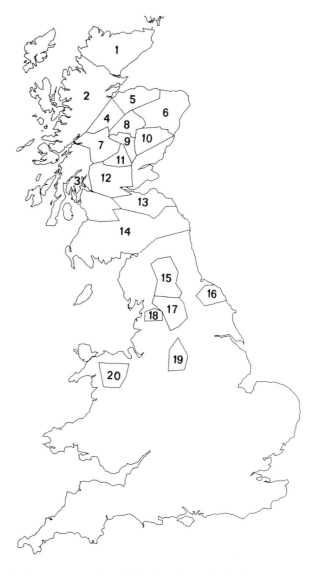

**REGION**

1.  CAITHNESS, SUTHERLAND
2.  OUTER HEBRIDES, E. ROSS, W. ROSS, W. HIGHLANDS, LOCHABER
3.  ARGYLL, ISLAY, CUNNINGHAME, S. CLYDESIDE
4.  MONADHLIATH
5.  MORAY & NAIRN
6.  BUCHAN & DONSIDE
7.  RANNOCH, TUMMEL & BREADALBANE
7.  CAIRNGORM
7.  ATHOLL
10  ANGUS & S. DEESIDE
11. S. TAYSIDE
12. TROSSACHS, OCHIL, CAMPSIE
13  PENTLAND, MOORFOOT, LAMMERMUIR
14. BORDERS, LOWTHER, DUMFRIES & GALLOWAY, NORTHUMBERLAND
15. N. DALES
16. NORTH YORK MOORS
17. S. DALES
18  TROUGH OF BOWLAND
19. PEAKS
20. WALES

**REGIONAL GROUPINGS**

| | |
|---|---|
| 1,2 | N.SCOTLAND |
| 3,4,7,12 | W. SCOTLAND |
| 5,6,8,9,10,11 | E. SCOTLAND |
| 13,14 | S. SCOTLAND |

Figure 3.1. Geographical areas of moorland referred to in the text, each relates to blocks of moorland rather than administrative boundaries and consequently relates to areas of grouse management.

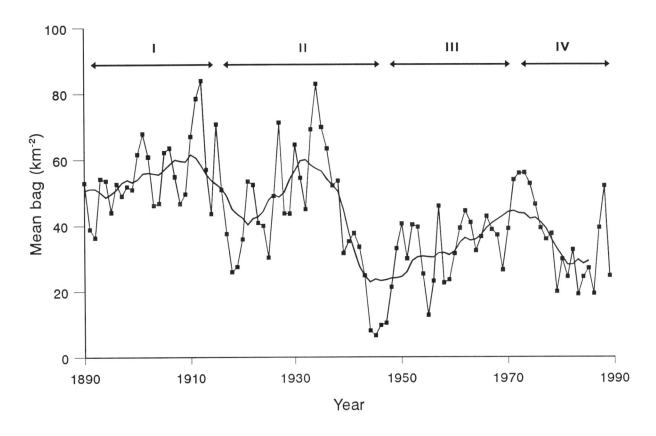

Figure 3.2. National grouse bag showing four periods of grouse shooting: I Prior to the first world war, II Between the two wars, III Post war recovery and IV Recent decline.

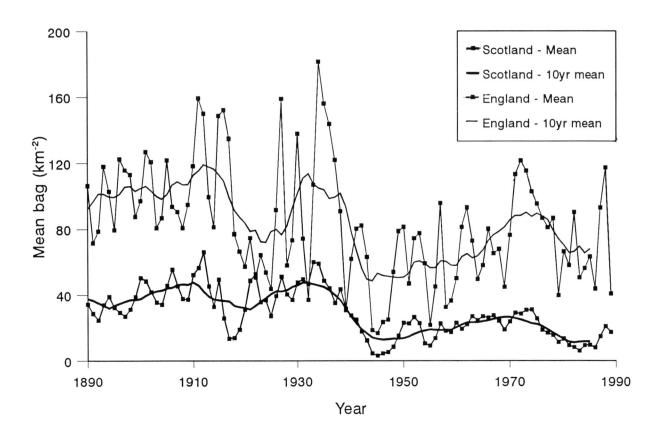

Figure 3.3 Average grouse bag for Scotland and England. In all years more grouse were shot per unit area in England than Scotland, although there were variations both between and within years.

Multiple land use is essential if people are to be employed in the uplands and conserve heather moorlands (Chapter 1).

A red grouse flying towards the butts on a shooting day. The bird provides a challenging shot and attracts sportsmen from all corners of the world (Chapter 1, Appendix 3). *The Earl Peel*

Walked-up shooting provides enjoyable sport but seldom attracts sufficient income to support high levels of grouse management (Chapter 2). *Game Conservancy*

Upland estates in Scotland have a range of interests including grouse shooting, deer stalking, sheep farming and forestry. The revenue from grouse shooting is important to these estates, allows the employment of staff and in turn ensures the conservation of large areas (Chapter 2).

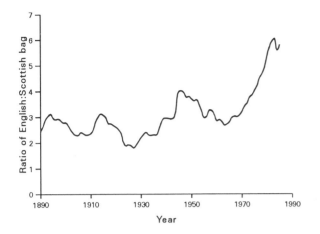

Figure 3.4. Ratio of English to Scottish grouse bags showing that up until the 1970s English estates shot on average between two and three times the Scottish bag per unit area, but this has increased since 1970 to nearly seven times the Scottish bag, principally because of the relative decline in the Scottish bag.

### 3.4. National grouse bag

The national grouse bag shows four distinct periods of grouse shooting (Figure 3.2) as first noted by Barnes[2]:

Period I: A period before the First World War whengrouse shooting was productive and average numbers fluctuated but remained relatively stable. Numbers fell during the First World War as management inputs and shooting pressure decreased.

Period II: A period between the two World Wars when average numbers recovered after the First World War and returned to previous levels. Numbers fell again during the Second World War.

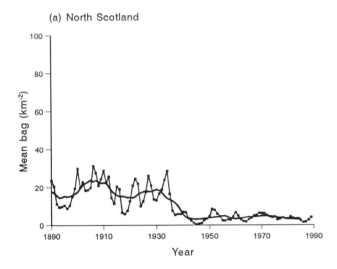

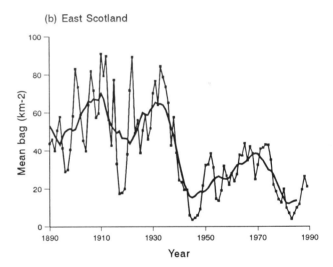

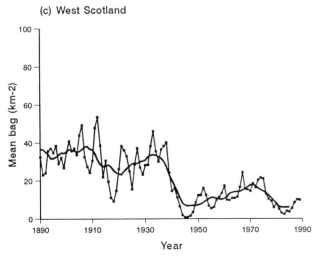

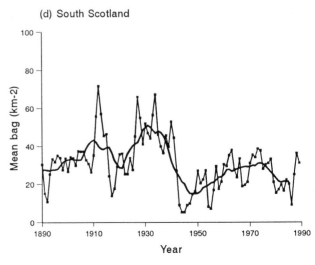

Figure 3.5. Average grouse bag for four regions of Scotland. While the eastern and southern regions were more productive for grouse than the western and northern regions, each exhibited the general pattern of four periods of grouse shooting.

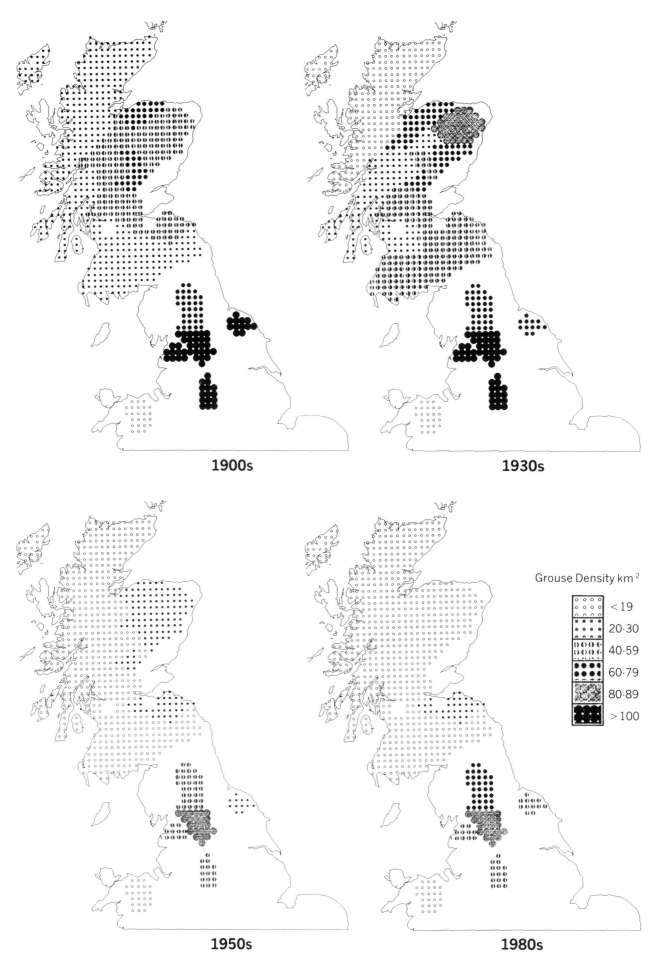

Figure 3.6. Geographical variations in numbers of grouse shot per square kilometre in each of four periods of grouse shooting. The Southern Dales have been consistently high while there was a general pattern of numbers falling in the northern and western parts of Britain.

18

Period III: A period of recovery following the Second World War when average numbers increased from 1950 to a peak in 1970. This post-war level was not as high as the pre-war levels.

Period IV: A period when numbers showed a general decline in the mid-1970s to a low in the mid 1980s followed by a more recent recovery.

3.5. Scotland and England

This general pattern of four periods is more clearly observed on most of the individual moors in Scotland than on those in England (Figure 3.3).

Scottish estates shot less grouse per square kilometre than English estates in every year for which records exist, although there was a great deal of variation between estates within both countries (Figure 3.3). Prior to the Second World War, English estates shot from two to three times as many grouse per square kilometre as Scottish estates but since the War, Scottish estates have shot progressively less and the ratio of the English to the Scottish bag has increased (Figure 3.4).

### 3.6. Scottish regions

Within Scotland, more grouse were shot per square kilometre in eastern, central and southern Scotland than in the northern and western regions (Figure 3.5). Each of these regions, with perhaps the exception of northern Scotland, exhibited the general pattern of four periods of grouse shooting described for the national grouse bag.

### 3.7. Moorland regions – geographical variations in density

The geographical variation in grouse density during each of the four periods of grouse shooting is best illustrated through a series of four maps (Figure 3.6). The general pattern is for the lowest density to be found in north Wales and north-west Scotland but the extent of this low density increases in each of the four periods of grouse shooting.

### 3.8. Moorland regions – variations this century

The rate of population decline is usually estimated in biological populations from the assumption that the decline is exponential, i.e. the proportion of the population lost each year remains constant. High grouse bags were reached for most regions around the 1930s (Figure 3.7), so the rate of decline for each region was determined as the rate of exponential decline from the 10 year average bag in 1930 to the 10 year average in 1980.

The exponential decline assumes that the populations exhibit a constant rate of decline. This is biologically reasonable. However most populations showed a recovery after the Second World War leading to a post-war peak in the early 1970s and then a subsequent fall, so that in reality there has not been a constant decline since 1930. The rate of change in the numbers of grouse shot was determined for:

1. 1930 to 1980
2. 1930 to 1950
3. 1970 to 1985
and for the period of increase:
4. 1950 to 1970

It should be noted that these rates of change (Figure 3.8) provide only a rough comparison between regions and cannot be used to estimate past or future bag records.

Borders

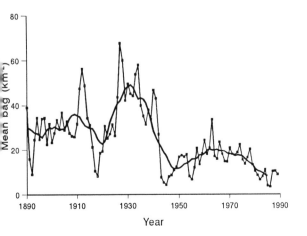

Pentland, Moorfoot and Lammermuirs

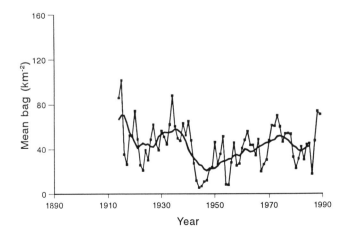

Figure 3.7. Numbers of grouse shot in each of 20 geographical regions of Scotland and England. (Continued overleaf)

## Moray and Nairn

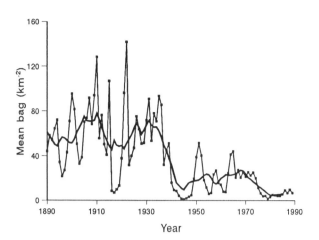

## Buchan and Donside

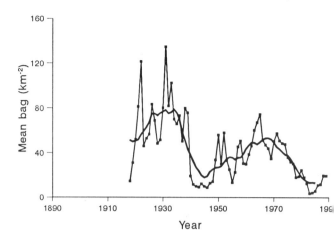

## Cairngorms

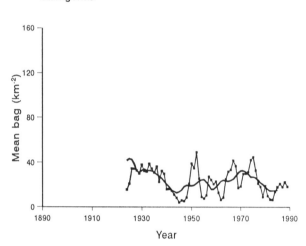

## Angus and S. Deeside

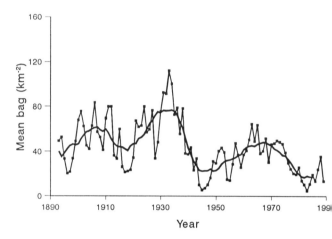

## South Tayside

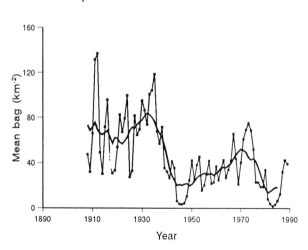

## Atholl

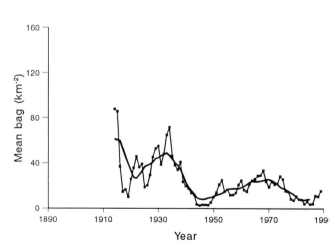

20

## North-West Highlands

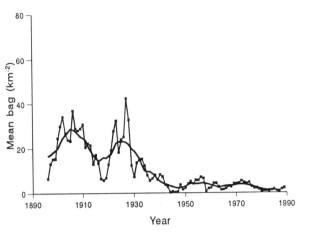

## North Highlands

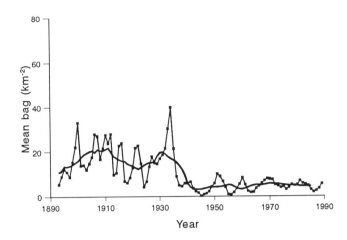

## Monadhlaiths

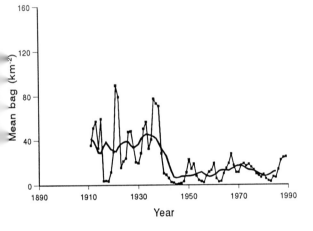

## Rannoch, Tummel and Breadalbane

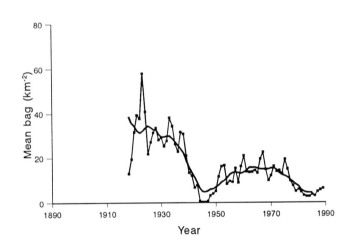

## Argyll and the South-West

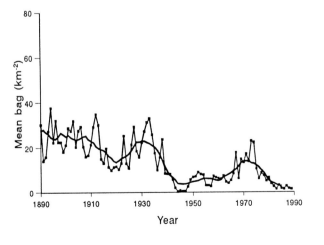

## Trossachs, Campsie and Ochils

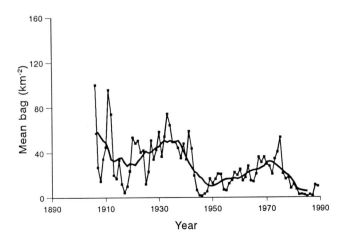

## South Dales

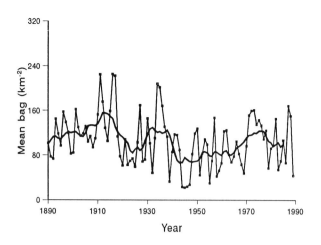

## North Dales and Cumbria

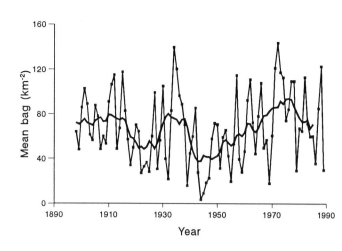

## Trough of Bowland

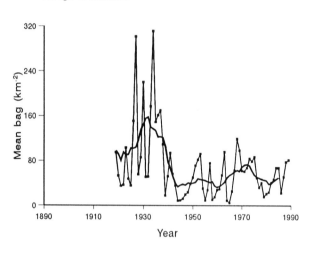

## North York Moors

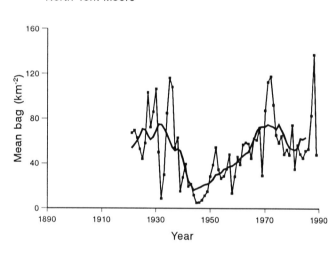

## North Wales

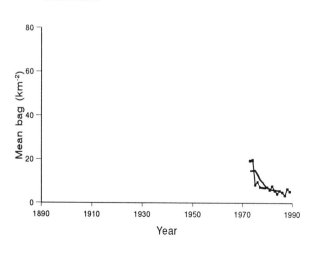

## Peak District

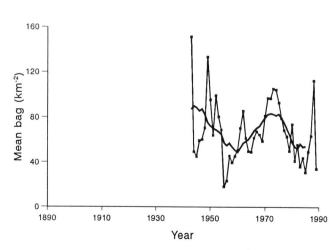

22

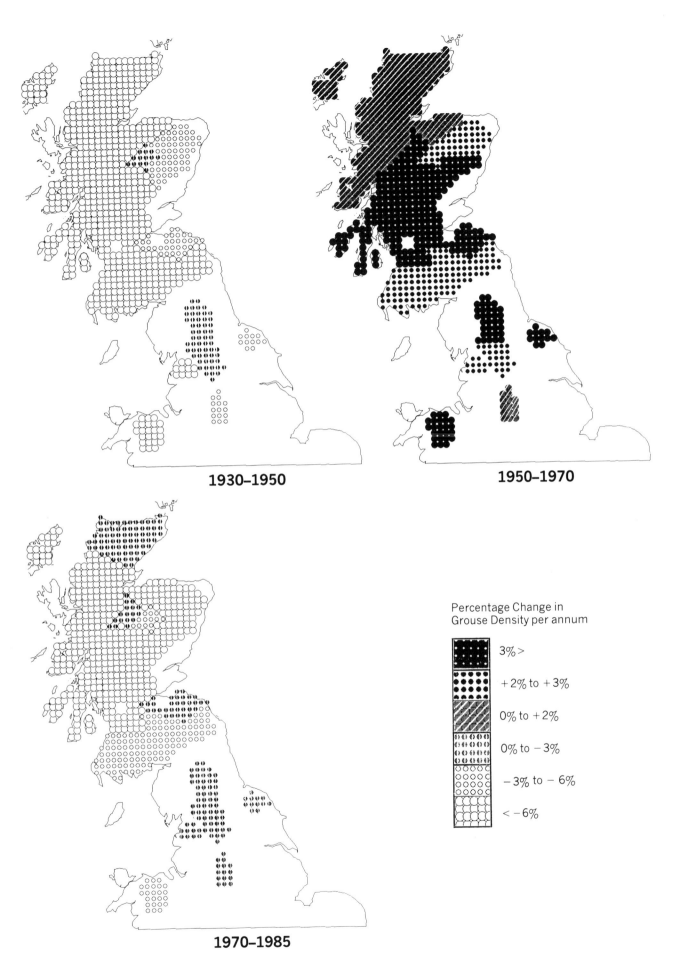

**1930–1950**

**1950–1970**

**1970–1985**

Percentage Change in
Grouse Density per annum

3% >

+2% to +3%

0% to +2%

0% to −3%

−3% to −6%

< −6%

Figure 3.8. Geographical variations in the rate of change in grouse numbers during three periods of grouse shooting. Numbers generally decreased between 1930-1950 and again during 1970-1985 but increased between 1950 and 1970. Those regions suffering a high rate of decline in the 1930-1950 also showed a high rate of decline between 1970 and 1985.

23

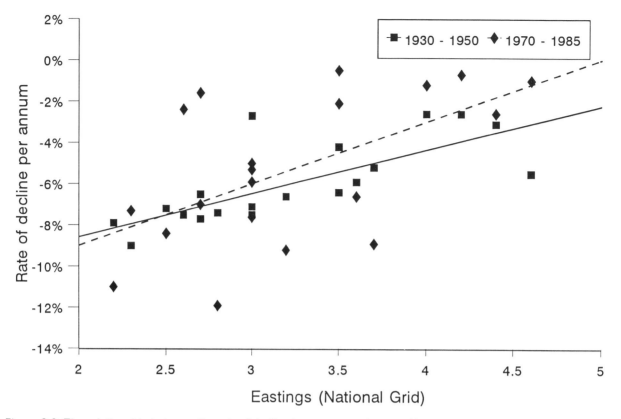

Figure 3.9. The relationship between the rate of decline in grouse numbers and longitude; the decline was greater on the west side of the country during both periods.

*Overall decline 1930 – 1980:* Overall the rate of decline was greatest in the north west of the country; 49% of the variation in the rate of decline between regions can be accounted for from the geographical location of the region, ie the latitude and longitude grid references of the region[a].

*War time decline 1930 – 1950:* The rate of decline between 1930 and 1950 varied between 3% and 9% per annum and was faster on the west side of the country[b].

*Post war recovery 1950-1970:* All regions showed a post-war recovery, varying between 1% and 6% per annum. The rate of this recovery was not associated with the rate of decline between 1930 and 1950[c]; in other words, areas with a high rate of decline between 1930 and 1950 did not show a large rate of recovery.

*Mid seventies decline 1970 – 1985:* All regions showed a fall in bag records between 1970 and 1985 varying from –0.5% per annum in parts of northern England to –11.9% per annum in Scotland. The rate of this decline was positively associated with the rate of decline during the war years (1930-1950), such that areas that had declined at a fast rate in the war years also tended to decline at a fast rate in the late seventies[d]. This period of decline tended to be greater in the west, as was found during the war time decline.

### 3.9. Summary

Numbers of grouse shot varied both with time and between locations. Generally, bag records fell into four periods of shooting with high bags before and after the First World War. Between 1930 and 1950 numbers of grouse shot fell, but they subsequently showed some recovery until the mid 1970s when they declined again. The rate of decline tended to be most in the north and west of the country and those areas that declined the greatest between 1930 and 1950 also showed the greatest decrease between 1970 and 1988.

### 3.10. Notes:

a. Rate of decline was negatively correlated with northings and positively correlated with eastings; in a step-up multiple regression these two variables accounted for 49% of the variation in regional rates of decline.

b. The rate of decline decreased with eastings ($r^2$=0.556, $N$=20, $b$=0.211, $P$=0.00016).

c. There was no association between regions in the rate of decline between 1930-1950 and the subsequent recovery 1950-1970 ($P$>0.10, $N$=20).

d. There was a positive correlation between the decline in 1930-1950 and 1970-1985 ($r$ = 0.525, $P$<0.02, $N$=20).

### 3.11. References

1. Hudson, P.J. (1986). *Red Grouse. The Biology and Management of a Wild Gamebird.* Game Conservancy, Fordingbridge, Hants.

2. Barnes, R.W. (1987). Long term declines of red grouse in Scotland. *Journal of Applied Ecology,* **24**, 735-741.

# CHAPTER 4

# VARIATION IN GROUSE YIELDS BETWEEN ESTATES: ANALYSIS OF BAGS IN RELATION TO ENVIRONMENTAL FEATURES

**Numbers of grouse shot varied between estates. Average grouse bag increased with June temperature, heather productivity and the employment of keepers to control predation by foxes and crows.**

## 4.1 Introduction

Why is it that an average Scottish estate yields fewer grouse per unit area than an average English grouse moor? Could a Scottish moor, with the same inputs as an English grouse moor, produce similar numbers of grouse? Such questions are frequently asked by grouse moor managers. A simple way of examining them is to analyse the variation in bag records between estates and determine how much of this variation can be accounted for by associated environmental features. The drawback with such studies is that they only reveal the factors associated with bag records, they cannot demonstrate the factors which actually caused these differences.

A study in 1966 used a similar approach and examined the bag records from 26 estates in north-east Scotland. This survey found that richness of underlying base rich rocks (and presumably soils) and heather management accounted for 67% of the variation between estates in the numbers of red grouse shot[1] and suggested that within north-east Scotland, base rock and heather burning could be major factors influencing grouse production. To determine whether this relationship holds true for grouse moors in general, this chapter extends this analysis to grouse bags collected from estates throughout Britain. Furthermore, by using a larger sample of estates, the analysis allows us to examine more variables associated with grouse management.

## 4.2 Grouse bag records

The examination of grouse bags presented in Chapter 3 found four periods of grouse shooting: The first two periods were essentially similar, but punctuated by the

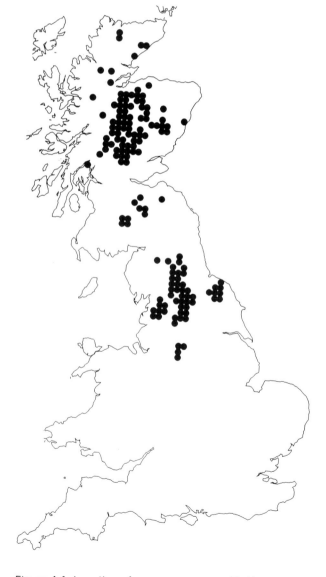

Figure 4.1. Location of grouse moors used in the analysis of variations in numbers shot.

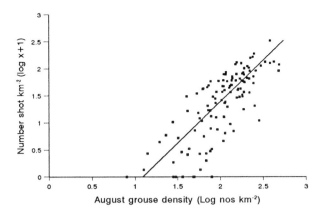

Figure 4.2. The relationship between density of grouse in August and the number of grouse shot per square kilometre in the following shooting season. In general, grouse bags reflect the density of grouse in August.

First World War, while in the last two periods there were differences in density and trends in the population. To represent the periods of different densities, we examine the variation in numbers of grouse shot during each of the decades: 1930s, 1960s and 1980s.

Details of bag records were obtained from a total of 532 estates in Scotland, England and Wales. Not all this information could be used in the analysis because the whole range of environmental features examined was not available for every moor. Some of the variables used also required a visit to the estate. After the moors with insufficient data were excluded a total of 147 estates were used in the analysis. Even with this reduced sample size, bag records were not available for all these estates in each of the three decades examined. Nevertheless, the distribution of the 147 estates (Figure 4.1) provides a representative cross-section of the grouse moors in Britain.

### 4.3 Grouse bags and density

To determine whether grouse bags in the sample reflected the density of grouse on the ground, count and bag data were examined from 287 instances where grouse were counted in August and the number of grouse shot from the whole estate was recorded in the subsequent shooting season. Overall, there was a strong relationship between numbers of grouse present and number shot per square kilometre (Figure 4.2), suggesting that grouse bags reflected grouse density.

### 4.4 Environmental features examined

A large range of environmental features could influence grouse density and subsequent bag; the following were examined in the analysis:

*(i) Base richness:* As with previous studies[1], soil fertility (and presumably its influence on heather quality) was estimated from an index of base richness, calculated from maps of solid geology and ranked from poor (rank 1) to high (rank 5) as:

1. acid igneous and quartzite
2. sandstone
3. intermediate igneous rocks, mudstone and siltstone
4. calcareous schists and mixed sequence stone bands
5. limestone, basic and ultrabasic igneous rocks.

Once these rankings were fixed, the mixed schists and fine grained pelite were considered intermediate between ranks 2 and 3, so were given the score of 2.5. Each estate used in the analysis was drawn onto a solid geology map and the index of base richness estimated from the relative area of each rock type underlying each estate.

*(ii) Altitude:* The altitude of each estate was taken as the average of the highest and lowest parts of the grouse moor from a 1:50,000 Ordnance Survey map.

*(iii) Area of moor:* The area of heather moorland was obtained from the questionnaire survey or estimated from a map of the estate.

*(iv) June temperature:* Average daily June temperature was included as a measure of the availability of invertebrates to grouse chicks during the period of maximum chick growth. During the first two to three weeks of life, chicks feed on insects but are unable to control their body temperature well and so must return to their mother at regular intervals to be brooded. When the temperature is low, the chicks must be brooded frequently and time available for foraging of insects is reduced. Accurate estimates of food availability could not be obtained, so this provides only a coarse measurement of time available for feeding.

*(v) Days of snow cover:* Snow cover may influence vulnerability of grouse to predators during winter months and the availability of food. Average number of days of snow cover was determined from maps supplied by the Meteorological Office.

### 4.5 Biological features examined

A number of biological features from each estate were also included in the analysis:

*(i) Wetness:* Average number of wet days (where rainfall exceeded 1 mm.) was included as a measure of

wetness of the ground. This is generally considered a better measure of ecological wetness than total rainfall[2] since it reflects the duration of wetness, while high rainfall can represent both short periods of heavy rainfall or long periods of low rainfall. In areas with an excess of 170 wet days there is consistently an excess of water (difference between precipitation and evapotranspiration) resulting in the development of peat and the production of blanket bog on flat ground[3,4]. Both the average number of wet days (obtained from Meteorological Office) and the classification of the estate as either a bog (mire) or freely drained heather moorland were included in the analysis.

*(ii) Heather productivity index:* Average estimates of heather growth would require detailed measurements of heather plants over a number of years and were quite clearly not possible within the limitations of this study. Nevertheless, detailed studies in northeast Scotland have found that year to year variation in the production of heather shoots are closely associated with temperature and rainfall between mid-April and August[5]. Assuming such a relationship describes heather productivity in general, an average index of heather productivity can be obtained using temperature and rainfall data[a].

In their study of red deer performance, Albon & Clutton-Brock[6] used the same index and proposed that this index would tend to reflect the quality of heather feed available to moorland herbivores.*(iii) Growing season:* The growing season of grass is generally taken as the point at which the average daily temperature increases above 6°C (43°F). Variations between areas depend chiefly on altitude. Studies on grass have evaluated the relationship between length of growing season and average air temperature and altitude[b]. Growing season was included as a separate variable in the analysis but was correlated with average heather productivity.

*(iv) Heather mosaic ranking:* Obtaining a quantifiable measurement of the extent and size of heather burning patterns was not possible in an extensive study of this nature. Instead a subjective assessment was made on a ranked scale from 1 to 5 where 1 indicated a mosaic pattern of few or large fires and 5 represented a mosaic pattern of many small fires and a varied age structure in the heather. Estates were visited and classified in each of these ranked levels. Since heather mosaic ranking could only be determined within the past five years, this variable could only be included in the analysis of bag records for the 1980 decade.

*(v) Keeper density:* Practical aspects of moor management are undertaken by keepers with the fundamental

tasks of burning heather and controlling predatory foxes and crows. The employment of keepers is the major cost of grouse management (Chapter 2) and hence it follows that the greater the density of keepers employed on the estate, the greater the management inputs. Previous analysis[7] had shown that when more keepers were present fewer foxes were killed, implying that keeper density was a good measure of the level of predator control.

Keeper density was not associated with the heather mosaic ranking (iv above). In other words, good patterns of heather burning were not necessarily present on estates which employed many keepers. The reason for this was probably that the number of fires and pattern of burning was influenced by the number of additional personnel employed for the task and the availability of suitable weather conditions for burning. On small estates with a single-handed keeper there is a need to employ additional help for safety and practical reasons while larger estates with many keepers tend to use estate keepers to work together at heather burning rather than employing additional help.

*(vi) Louping ill:* Louping ill is a disease of sheep and grouse caused by a flavivirus transmitted between hosts by the sheep tick. Previous studies[8,9] found that infected grouse chicks can suffer 80% mortality (see Section 8). The presence of louping ill was determined through the questionnaire survey, through consultations with shepherds and veterinary officers, and on some moors after the collection of blood serum samples. The presence and absence of ticks and the presence or absence of louping ill were included in the analysis.

*(vii) Sheep management:* Sheep grazing intensity can influence the extent of heather moorland and may act to reduce suitable cover and in some instances availability of food for grouse. Ewe density was taken as the density of ewes present on the hill during the summer months and determined through the questionnaire survey. In addition to this, the presence of sheep in winter and the occurrence of winter feeding were also included (see Section 9).

*(viii) Presence of other herbivores:* Presence or absence of other herbivores including red deer stags, red deer hinds, roe deer and blue hares was recorded in the analysis by an examination of game books and direct recording during estate visits.

*(ix) Adjacent land use practices:* Unlike managers of grouse moors, forestry managers consider deer and hares as pests because they damage trees, whereas predators such as foxes are considered favourably

since they may help to reduce the hare numbers. Since these activities tend to conflict with the activities of grouse moor managers, the presence of forestry plantations exceeding 5km² (approximately 1250 acres) was included in the analysis and determined through the examination of O.S. maps, correspondence and visits to estates.

## 4.6 Analysis of bags and features recorded

The multiple regression analysis conducted showed that between 54% and 70% of the variation in bag records could be accounted for through the variables examined (Table 4.1).

The average number of grouse shot within estates in each of the three decades increased with June temperature and heather productivity. These results imply that areas favourable for heather growth and with a warm June, and consequently a long period of foraging time for chicks, tend to have increased grouse density and shoot more grouse. Once again note that such a causal relationship is not shown but only indicated by this analysis. Both of these variables are a function of weather conditions and consequently the location of the grouse moor in the British Isles.

The relationship between average bag, heather productivity and June temperature was not consistent between each of the three decades, showing no common underlying relationship throughout these three periods[c]. In the 1960s and 1980s, bag records increased with keeper density (predator control) and when this variable was included and comparisons were made between the two decades, no significant difference[d] was found. This implies that the main factors influencing grouse were essentially similar in the 1960s and 1980s. When the data from each decade were included in an overall analysis, then once again heather productivity, keeper density and June temperature were the three variables accounting for most of the variation observed.

Keeper density was not incorporated as an important variable in the 1930s and this is interesting to examine in more detail. One possible explanation is that in the 1930s, predators were reduced to such low densities that the employment of additional keepers did not increase the level of predator control. Instead of keeper density, the size of the estate was important, with large estates shooting fewer grouse per square kilometre than small estates. However, size of estate and keeper density were correlated during the 1930s[e], with larger

**Table 4.1** Ranked order of significant variables accounting for variation in average number of grouse shot per square kilometre between estates during three periods of grouse shooting.

| Variable | 1990 | 1960 | 1980 | All Decades |
|---|---|---|---|---|
| June Temp. | 3 + | 1 + | 1 + | 1 + |
| Heather Productivity | 2 + | 2 + | 4 + | 3 + |
| Keepers | NS | 3 + | 2 + | 2 + |
| Heather Mosaic | zero | zero | 3 + | zero |
| Estate size | 1 − | NS | NS | NS |
| Altitude | NS | NS | 5 − | NS |
| Base Richness | NS | NS | 6 + | 5 + |
| Wet days | NS | NS | NS | 4 + |
| Variation Explained | 65% | 54% | 70% | 55% |

Key: Numbers refer to relative importance of variables i.e. 1 = most important variable, NS = not significant, zero = variable could not be included in analysis. The positive and negative symbols under each ranked level indicate the direction of the relationship; a ' + ' indicates an increase in bag size with an increase in the variable and a '·' a reduction in bag size with an increase in the variable.

estates employing fewer keepers per square kilometre. Either way the evidence is that predation is an important factor influencing the size of grouse populations.

Base richness, or the quality of the underlying rock, has generally been considered an important variable influencing productivity and numbers of grouse shot[10]. In the first two decades this was not a significant variable, but entered the analysis as a minor variable in the 1980s and in the overall comparison of all decades. The relatively low importance of underlying rock in this wide-ranging analysis could be due to base richness being associated with other variables such as June temperature. It is generally true that the limestone moors in the Pennines are warmer areas than the base-poor and cooler moors in northern Scotland. Nevertheless, most of the estates in northern England – some of the most productive in the British isles – are based on poor quality millstone grit.

Heather burning, assessed as the heather mosaic ranking, was an important variable in the 1980s and may well have been important in each of the previous decades, although no such assessment could be made for these earlier periods. The earlier analysis conducted in north-east Scotland[1] found heather burning to be important, so it seems reasonable to suppose that this is an important aspect of grouse management.

### 4.7. Implications for management

Essentially four variables are associated with the average number of grouse shot from an estate. Two relate directly to management inputs and to the traditional ways of managing a moor through heather burning and predator control. Keeper density is considered to be an indirect measurement of predator control and suggests that predator control is an important factor influencing numbers of grouse shot. Heather mosaic ranking was a measure of the burning practice conducted on the hill and suggests that burning also improves grouse numbers, although this variable could only be examined in the most recent decade.

Two environmental features also contributed to the variation in grouse bag and reflect both the location of the grouse moor and the availability and perhaps quality of food available to the grouse. June temperature was incorporated in the analysis as a measure of the time available for feeding by young chicks when they are still dependent on the hen. Overall it came out as the most important variable. This could be because a warm June provides long periods for chicks to feed, but June temperature is also associated with the general location of the moor and could influence a number of other aspects of grouse biology.

The measurement of heather productivity is based on a calculation of temperature and rainfall, two factors which change with the geographical location of the estate. Greater levels of heather productivity reflect both longer growing periods and drier summers, which will tend to improve heather growth, availability and overall quality of the shoots. While weather variables cannot be altered directly, it may be possible to manage the heather in a way to maximise the availability of good quality heather through judicious grazing systems and a selective burning programme.

### 4.8 Summary

The average numbers of grouse shot per square kilometre from 147 estates were analysed for three decades (1930s, 1960s and 1980s) and compared with a wide range of biological and environmental variables. Overall, three variables were of paramount significance and grouse density increased with each: (i) June temperature (ii) heather productivity, an index of the average conditions for heather growth and (iii) keeper density, a measure of the degree of predator control and not the pattern of heather burning. The relationships between grouse density and these variables were similar in the 1960s and the 1980s, implying that similar factors were operating in both decades. Quality of underlying rock explained only a small amount of variation in the number of grouse shot during the 1980s and was a relatively insignificant factor in the analysis.

### 4.9. Notes

a. Heather productivity, measured as the annual production of shoots (H), was estimated from mean daily temperature in degrees centigrade between April and August (T) and rainfall in millimetres during the same period (R):

$$H = 29.3\,T - 0.168R - 56.0.$$

b. Growing season (G) was estimated from the relationship between air temperature in degrees centigrade and corrected for altitude (Ta) and altitude in metres (A) derived by Smith[6]:

$$G = 29Ta - 0.15A - 17$$

c. Analysis of covariance $F = 14.856$, df $= 6375$, $P < 0.001$

d. Analysis of covariance, $F = 1.95$, d.f. $= 4250$, $P > 0.05$)

e. Correlation between keeper density and size of estate in 1930s, $r = 0.578$, d.f. $= 76$, $P < 0.001$.

### 4.10. References

1. Picozzi, N. (1966). Grouse management in relation to the management and geology of heather moors. *Journal of Applied Ecology* **5**, 483-488.

2. Ratcliffe, D. A. (1968). An ecological account of Atlantic Bryophytes in the British isles. *New Phytologist,* **67**, 365-439.

3. Stroud, D.A., Reid, T.M., Pienkowski, M.W. & Lindsay, R.A. (1987). *Birds, bogs and forestry.* Nature Conservancy Council Peterborough.

4. Hudson, P.J. (1992). Herbivore management on ombrogenous mires and dry dwarf shrub heaths. In: *Peatland ecosystems and man – an impact assessment.* (Ed by O. Bragg, H. Ingram & R.A. Lindsay) pp 336-341. Blackwell Scientific Publications, Oxford.

5. Miller, G.R. (1979). Quantity and quality of the annual production of shoots and flowers by *Calluna vulgaris* in north-east Scotland. *Journal of Ecology* **67**, 109-129.

6. Albon, S.D. & Clutton Brock, T.H. (1988). Climate and the population dynamics of red deer in Scotland. In: *Ecological change in the uplands* (Ed by M.B. Usher & D.B.A. Thompson), pp 93-107. Blackwell Scientific Publications, Oxford.

7. Hudson, P.J. (1986). *The Red Grouse: the Biology and Management of a Wild Gamebird.* The Game Conservancy Trust, Fordingbridge.

8. Reid, H.W, Duncan, J.S., Phillips, J.D.P., Moss, R. and Watson, A. (1978). Studies on louping ill virus (Flavivirus group) in wild red grouse *(Lagopus lagopus scoticus). Journal of Hygiene,* **81**, 321-329.

9. Hudson, P.J. & Dobson, A.P. (1991). Control of parasites in natural populations: nematodes and virus infections of red grouse. In: *Bird Population Studies* (Ed Perrins, C.M., G. Hirons & Lebreton). Oxford University Press.

10. Watson, A. & Miller, G.R. (1976). *Grouse management.* The Game Conservancy, Fordingbridge.

# CHAPTER 5

# CHANGES IN ABUNDANCE OF FOXES, CROWS AND STOATS ON GROUSE MOORS

**While numbers of grouse have decreased, the number of foxes and crows killed on estates has increased. The increase in the fox population over the past 25 years has been associated with the overall fall in numbers of keepers and recovery of the rabbit population after myxomatosis. Crow numbers have increased with afforestation, probably because plantations provide abundant places to nest and a safe refuge. Numbers of stoats killed by keepers fluctuated with grouse numbers.**

## 5.1 Introduction

Numbers of red grouse shot on managed grouse moors in Britain show a general pattern with four periods of abundance and an overall decline. While all estates keep details of numbers of grouse shot, a number also maintain records on the number of predators killed by keepers including fox, carrion/hooded crow and stoat. In Chapter 4, a comparison between estates in the number of grouse shot showed that the number of keepers employed was an important variable associated with the size of the bag, probably because keepers actively reduce numbers of predatory foxes and crows. To examine the relationship between predators and grouse in more detail we now examine changes in the abundance of some of the predatory species, in particular the fox, crow and stoat, three important predators of grouse that are regularly trapped and shot on grouse moors.

## 5.2 Methods

Information on the number of predators killed on moorland estates was obtained during the three surveys conducted for grouse bag records (reported in Chapter 3). These records can be expressed in two ways, either as the number killed per unit area of moorland or as the number killed per keeper. Neither method provides an accurate estimate of predation pressure. Numbers expressed per unit area of moorland are not representative since none of the predatory species are specialists that live exclusively on moorland and keepers frequently leave the moorland area to kill or trap these predators on neighbouring ground. Neither is number killed per keeper a good reflection of predation pressure since an estate which employs several keepers may kill more predators per unit area than an estate with few keepers even though the number killed per keeper would be fewer.

Other biases may also exist; the data are based on the number of predators killed by keepers and as such do not provide an accurate estimate of predator population size and indeed could provide an inaccurate measure of it between areas. For example, it is quite possible for a keeper not employed actively in grouse moor management to kill as many foxes as an active grouse moor keeper although the density of foxes on the two areas may be very different. Such differences are unlikely to occur through time since management activities are more constant within an estate than between estates, so an increase in numbers of foxes killed within an estate is usually a true reflection of an increase in the number of foxes. For the fox at least, there is some evidence that numbers killed do reflect true changes in the size of the population[1].

32

The employment of keepers, and their role in the control of foxes and crows, is important in producing a good yield of grouse (Chapter 4). *Game Conservancy*

Heather burning is important in maintaining the habitat for grouse and other moorland birds (Chapters 4 and 6). *Game Conservancy*

Crows take grouse eggs. In Scotland, numbers of crows killed by keepers are increasing exponentially at nearly 5% per annum (Chapter 5).

Grouse are killed by a range of predators; this cock was taken by a stoat. More stoats are killed in years of good grouse yield (Chapter 5).

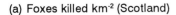

(a) Foxes killed km⁻² (Scotland)

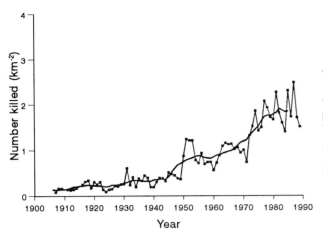

(b) Foxes killed per keeper (Scotland)

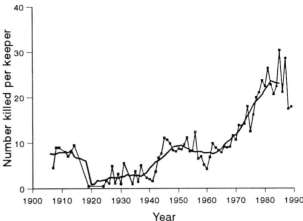

Figure 5.1. Relative number of foxes killed on Scottish grouse moors. Number killed per unit area (a) and number killed per keeper (b) both show a steady increase in the fox population with a three to four fold increase in the past 40 years. Points show annual figures and the thicker line is the 10 year running average given as the general trend line.

(a) Foxes killed km⁻² (England)

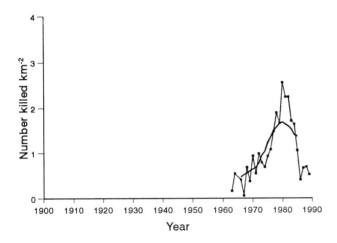

(b) Foxes killed per keeper (England)

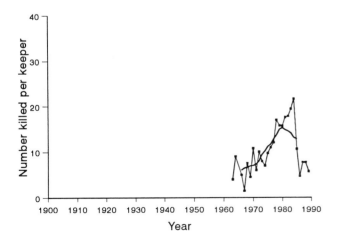

Figure 5.2. Relative number of foxes killed on English grouse moors. While the run of English data is not as long as the Scottish data the recent increase in fox numbers was at a similar rate. Scottish keepers have killed consistently more foxes than English keepers and more per unit area.

## 5.3. Fox: numbers killed on grouse moors

Numbers of foxes killed per unit area on managed Scottish grouse moors have increased since 1950 four-fold, while numbers killed per keeper have increased three-fold (Figure 5.1). Prior to the last war numbers killed remained relatively stable. There is not a sufficiently good run of data on foxes killed on English grouse moors to examine any differences in pattern between the two areas, although the rate of increase in number of foxes killed since 1960 is similar to that observed in Scotland (Figure 5.2). The cause of the recent fall in foxes killed in England is not clear and further data are required to test whether this fall is indeed real. In both Scotland and England the number of foxes killed per square kilometre increased to approximately two foxes per km². Scottish keepers kill consistently more foxes than English keepers[a] probably because there are fewer keepers per unit area; on average a Scottish keeper kills 23 foxes per annum while an English keeper kills 13 foxes per annum.

The increase in fox numbers varied between regions, both southern and eastern Scotland showed a dramatic rise in numbers of foxes killed since the early to mid seventies, coinciding with the beginning of the grouse decline in those areas. In western Scotland, comparable numbers of foxes were killed per keeper but because fewer keepers were employed, the number shot per unit area was relatively low (Figure 5.3). Many of these western areas are not managed for grouse; keepers are frequently employed in stalking and other duties, and so fox control is undertaken at a much lower level.

In southern and eastern Scotland a total of six estates

33

# A. Number of Foxes Killed km²

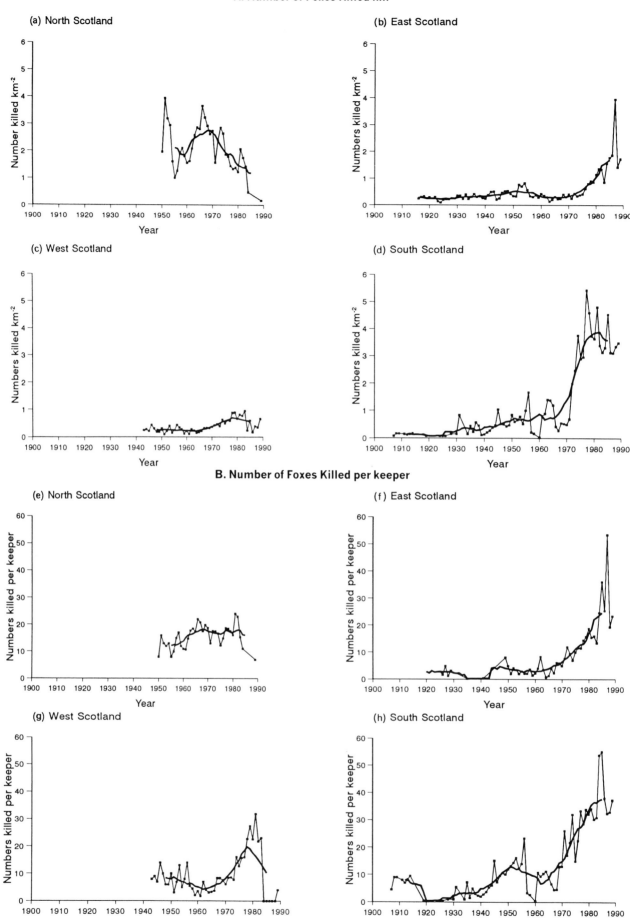

Figure 5.3. Regional variation in the relative number of foxes killed in Scotland. The main areas for grouse moors in southern and eastern Scotland show a rapid increase in the number of foxes killed over the past 25 years. Changes in numbers killed in western and northern Scotland may not reflect true changes in the population since many of these areas are principally deer forests where fox control is not considered an important part of estate management.

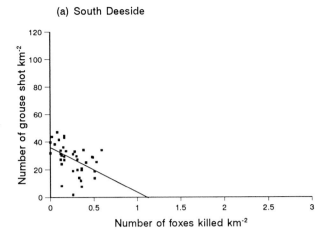

(a) South Deeside

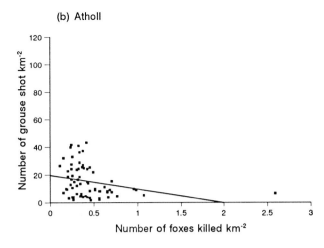

(b) Atholl

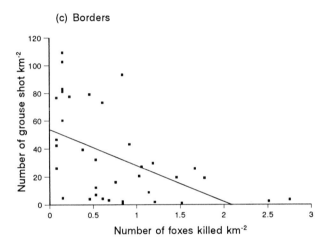

(c) Borders

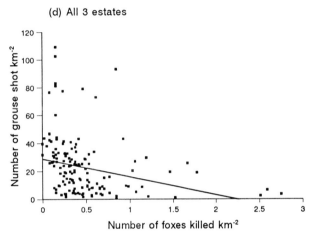

(d) All 3 estates

Figure 5.4. Numbers of grouse shot on three estates were related to fox numbers, with fewer grouse shot in years when many foxes are killed. The relationship from these estates does not differ.

had sufficient runs of data to examine the relationship between numbers of grouse and foxes killed. Three of the six data sets showed a negative association between fox and grouse numbers implying that in years when there were few foxes, grouse numbers were high (Figure 5.4). Such data do not demonstrate a causal relationship since it is quite possible that some other factor influences both fox and grouse abundance. Nevertheless the data are consistent with the general hypothesis that predation is an important factor influencing the abundance of grouse.

One way of examining whether the relationship between foxes and grouse is one of cause and effect is to conduct a controlled experiment where one area has no fox control and a second comparable area has fox control. Such an experiment has not been conducted in a rigorous scientific manner, although there are a number of cases where grouse bags have increased dramatically following the implementation of fox and crow control. One good example was on two moors in northern England, both of approximately 4500 acres

on opposite sides of a Dale where the bag records fluctuated in parallel until on one of the moors the level of fox control decreased following an illness of the keeper (Figure 5.5). Fox control decreased sharply on the moor with the sick keeper and remained so low that on the 12th August in one year more foxes than grouse were killed in the first drive. Numbers remained low until the sick keeper was replaced with an active keeper who removed the foxes. These results are consistent with The Game Conservancy's Salisbury Plain Project where predator numbers were controlled in a strictly experimental manner[4].

Number of foxes killed per unit area increased with the density of keepers employed on an estate, suggesting predator control was better in areas with more keepers (Figure 5.6). Most of these data arise from Scottish estates; within English estates the opposite relationship was found[5] because well-managed estates had effectively removed most of the foxes already, so few foxes were killed.

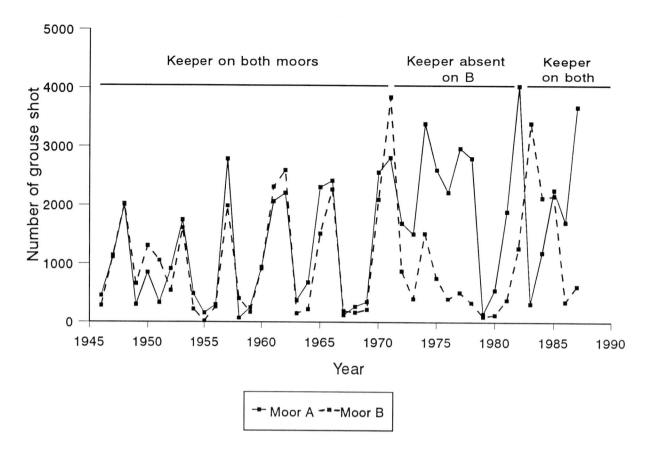

Figure 5.5. Effects of reduced predator control on size of grouse bag. The absence of active predator control on Moor B resulted in a fall in the size of the grouse bag, this subsequently recovered when a keeper was reinstated.

Overall, the impression from this analysis is that since the number of foxes killed on grouse moors has increased so has the total population of foxes; this will have intensified predation pressure on grouse. Additional information on fox populations has been gathered by Hewson & Kolb[2,3] in a series of papers which examine the number of foxes killed in each of the The Forestry Commission Conservancies. Between 1961 and 1978, the total number of foxes killed in the four Forestry Commission Conservancies has increased (Figure 5.7, Table 5.1). These records are comparable within Conservancies, although it is not clear how the number of rangers involved in fox control or the area over which this occurred may have varied during this time interval. Each of the four Conservancies coincided roughly with the four regions used in our own

**Table 5.1:** Change in numbers of foxes killed between 1961 and 1978 from Forestry Commission Conservancies and managed grouse moors. Figures show the proportional numbers of foxes killed (i.e. 2 shows a doubling in the numbers killed and 1 no change) calculated from the regression line fitted from 1961 to 1978.

| Region | Forestry Commission | Grouse Moors | |
|---|---|---|---|
| | | Foxes/km² | Foxes/keeper |
| Eastern Scotland | 2.16 | 13.76 | 5.15 |
| Southern Scotland | 1.31 | 2.00 | 2.42 |
| Western Scotland | 1.86 | 4.04 | 5.67 |
| Northern Scotland | 3.83 | 0.71 | 1.01 |

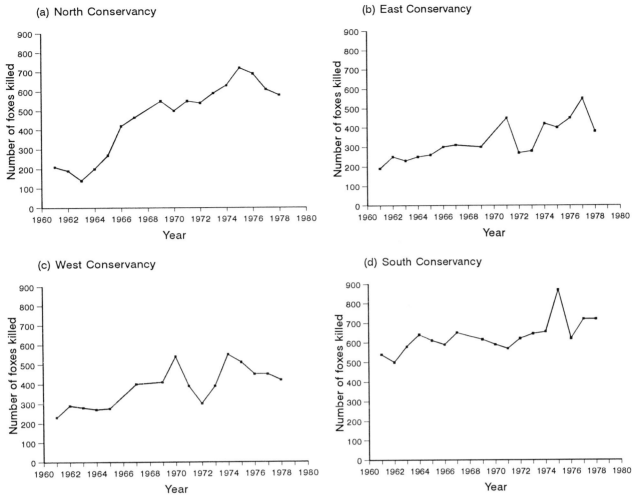

Figure 5.7. Total numbers of foxes killed in Forestry Commission Conservancies confirm that the Scottish fox population has been increasing. (Data extracted from references 2 & 3).

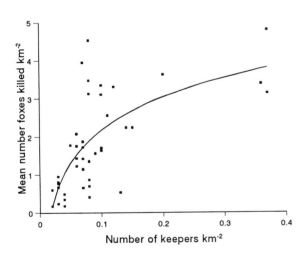

Figure 5.6. Average number of foxes killed during the 1980s in relation to density of keepers. Overall, more foxes are killed on estates employing more keepers. (Best fit logarithmic regression curve.)

analysis, and so provides an independent measurement of changes in fox numbers. The proportional increase in western, eastern and northern Scotland was larger on grouse moors than in Conservancies irrespective of whether foxes per keeper or foxes per unit area were examined (Table 5.1). In northern Scotland, the Forestry Commission data showed an increase in fox numbers but grouse moors found no increase. This is probably because predator control on estates has been reduced but it could equally imply increased activities by the Commission to control foxes.

The data from both the Forestry Commission and grouse moors confirm there has been an increase in the size of the Scottish fox population which, coupled with the decrease in numbers of red grouse, will have increased predation pressure on grouse stocks over the past 20 years. The next step is to ask why fox numbers have increased? The increase could be a result of reduced control practices and/or a change in the availability of food for foxes.

Whereas there has been a general and continuing reduction in the number of keepers employed in grouse management (Chapter 2, Figure 2.8), there has been no sudden reduction which could have been large enough to account for the rapid increase in fox numbers. During part of the 1970s and 1980s as

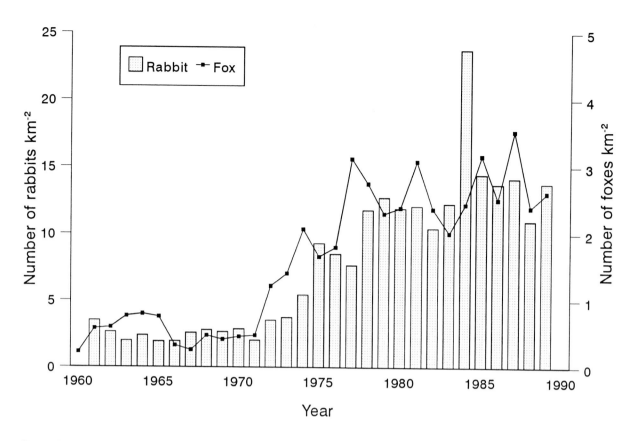

Figure 5.8. The increase in number of foxes killed on grouse moors in eastern and southern Scotland in relation to number of rabbits killed on a selection of estates throughout the same area (source of rabbit data: National Game Census). The close association between fox numbers and rabbit numbers suggests that the increase in foxes may have been influenced by an increase in the availability of rabbits and led to increased predation pressure on grouse.

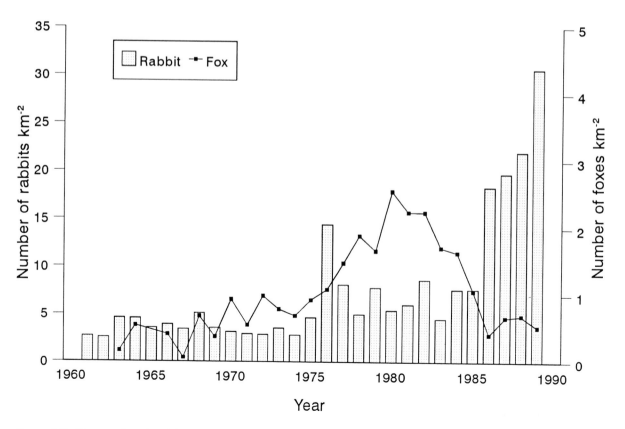

Figure 5.9. Changes in upland fox and rabbit numbers in northern England. Unlike Figure 5.8, fox numbers did not continue to increase after 1980, perhaps because of differences in fox control pressure in the two areas.

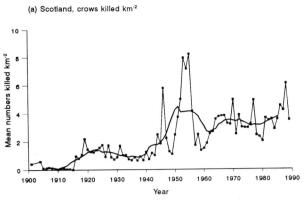

(a) Scotland, crows killed km⁻²

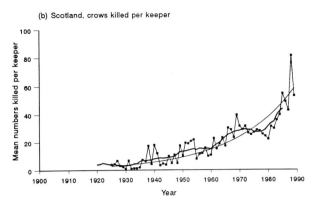

(b) Scotland, crows killed per keeper

Figure 5.10. Relative numbers of crows killed in Scotland. Both number killed per square kilometre and number killed per keeper have increased. The number killed per keeper has increased exponentially at nearly 5% per annum (thin line curved in (b)).

grouse numbers fell, a number of estates sold land to alternative land use practices, usually for commercial forestry. As a consequence the total number of keepers within an area will have fallen and may have resulted in increased numbers of foxes. The total number of keepers employed in Scotland (extracted from the National Population Census) confirms there has been a steady decline in keepers, but no dramatic fall at this time (Chapter 2, Figure 2.8).

Foxes are generalists and will eat a wide range of food including carrion, game and other species of wildlife. Numbers of most moorland birds and blue hares have shown a decline during this period and overall there has been a reduction in the biomass of food available for foxes on the hill. Numbers of sheep in most parts of Scotland have remained relatively stable (see Section 10) although the availability of sheep carrion may have

increased as subsidies have encouraged quantity rather than quality in sheep flocks. There has been an increase in number of red deer (Section 10) and no doubt an increase in carrion from dead deer which may provide food during winter months. Nevertheless in southern Scotland the increase in fox numbers will not have been affected by this carrion since deer are absent from this part.

The most obvious change in available food for foxes has been the increase in the number of rabbits following the recovery of the population after the 1956 outbreak of myxomatosis. The recovery of rabbits (as measured by numbers shot on both upland and lowland estates) has shown a five-fold increase and coincides well with the increase in fox numbers during the same period[b] (Figure 5.8). This increase in foxes probably arose because keeper numbers were

(a) England, crows killed km⁻²

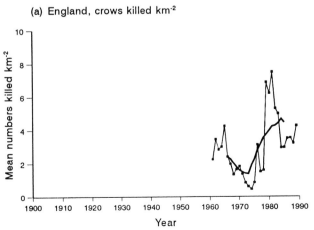

(b) England, crows killed per keeper

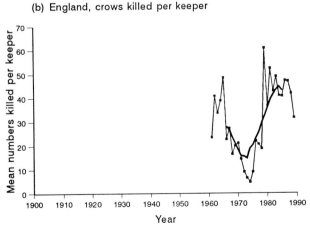

Figure 5.12. Relative numbers of crows killed in England. While numbers killed have fluctuated these do not differ significantly from the Scottish data for the same period.

## A. Number of Crows Killed km⁻²

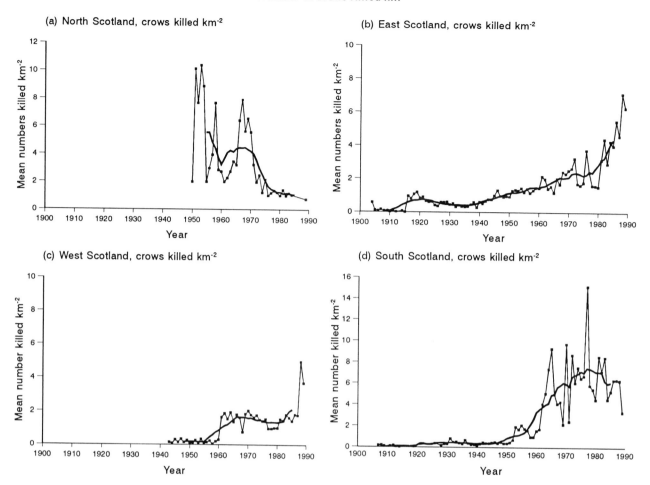

Figure 5.11. Regional variation in the relative number of crows killed in Scotland. The data for southern Scotland excludes the results from one estate which was killing in excess of 500 crows per annum after the last war and greatly influenced the figures.   (A, above; B, right)

insufficient to control them and the rabbit population provided sufficient food to sustain high numbers of foxes. Interestingly, in England fox numbers did not increase even though rabbit numbers did (Figure 5.9). This was probably because there were sufficient keepers in England to control the foxes irrespective of the increase in rabbits. Prior to myxamotosis there were also more keepers in Scotland - probably sufficient to control the foxes.

### 5.4. Crow: numbers killed on grouse moors

The number of crows killed on grouse moors has shown a steady increase in Scotland, an increase that appears to have started before the last war (Figure 5.10). The numbers killed per keeper shows an exponential increase of 4.7% per annum. This steady increase has been the result of a high number of crows killed in southern Scotland coupled with a recent increase in eastern Scotland (Figure 5.11). In England similar numbers of crows are killed although insufficient data exists for a complete analysis of changes in numbers killed over time (Figure 5.12).

The data for southern Scotland show a remarkable increase in crow numbers since the last war. As with foxes, this increase could be the result of an increase in food availability, in particular the availability of sheep carrion during the winter months. In the uplands, one of the limiting features to the size of the breeding crow population is likely to be the presence of suitable trees for nesting. The increase in the number of crows killed in both the main grouse shooting areas of south and east Scotland has been associated with the increase in the extent of forestry (Figure 5.13). A similar relationship was found for west Scotland but a negative relationship for northern Scotland[c].

As with the interaction between fox and grouse, there have been no controlled experiments to investigate the interaction of crows and grouse. To understand the effects of crows would require the selection of sites where fox predation was equal and probably best if it were absent. Foxes are absent on a number of west coast islands and there have been a number of interesting differences in levels of crow control and size of grouse bag. On one island estate, crow control was

## B. Number of Crows Killed Per Keeper

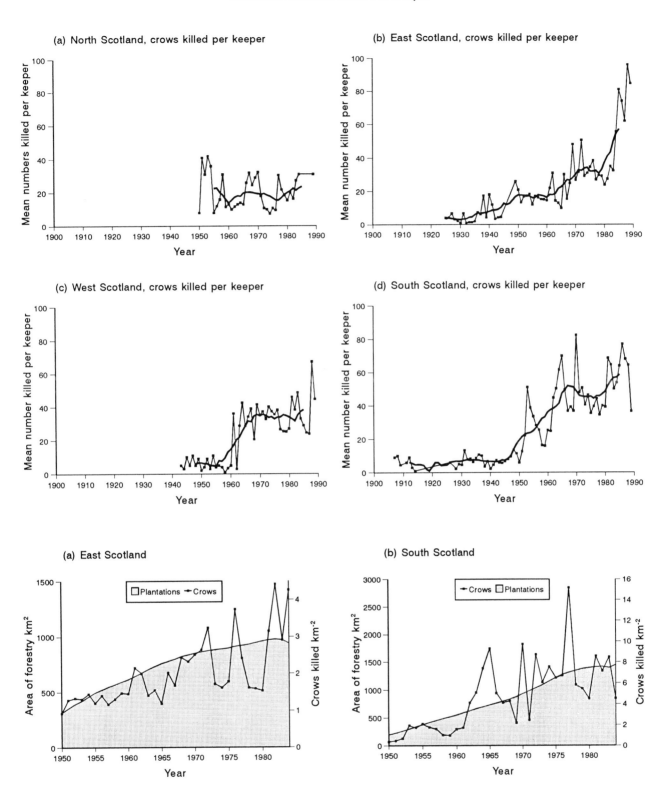

Figure 5.13: The increase in the number of crows killed on grouse moors has increased with the extent of afforestation in both eastern and southern Scotland[c].

initiated at a high level in 1981 and grouse bags rapidly increased (Figure 5.14). Subsequently there was a change in management and the intensity of crow control was reduced in 1987, after which grouse numbers fell. This does not appear to be a coincidence because in the same year a nearby estate started crow control, which has since led to an increase in grouse bags.

### 5.5. Stoat: numbers killed on grouse moors

Numbers of stoats killed on grouse moors have fluctuated but show no clear pattern of any recent increase or decrease (Figure 5.15). Generally grouse keepers killed fewer stoats during the 1980s than were killed in the 1920s and 1930s; this is probably because stoats

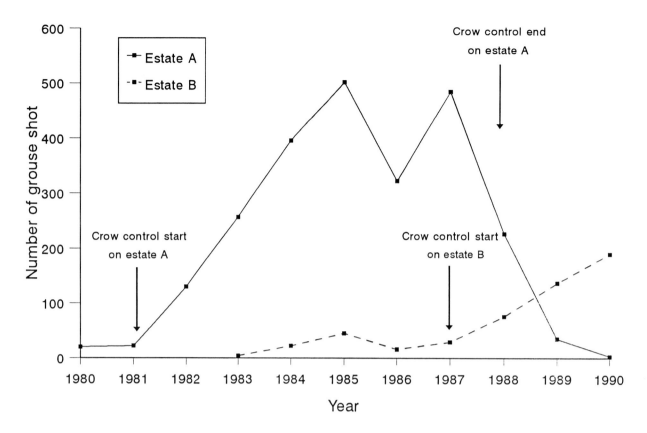

Figure 5.14. Numbers of grouse shot in relation to periods of crow control on two island estates where foxes were absent. Grouse numbers increased during periods of crow control.

are considered a predator of secondary importance and may be only intensively trapped when fox and crow numbers are well controlled. Furthermore, with more keepers employed in the 1920s and 1930s and without four-wheel-drive vehicles much of the grouse keepers' time was spent walking the hill when shooting and trapping stoats would have been a matter of course.

Despite the differences in keepering techniques, it is interesting to note that there is a positive association between the number of grouse shot in Scotland and the number of stoats killed on Scottish grouse moors[d]. This would imply that abundance of stoats on the hill may be influenced by the abundance of grouse. Other explanations are possible, for example in good grouse

years keepers may have reduced fox and crow numbers and may then concentrate their efforts on the stoats. If this were the case then we would expect an increase in the number of weasels also trapped on grouse moors and a good association between the two species. Such an association does not exist[d], indicating that changes in numbers of stoats may quite simply be influenced by the abundance of grouse. Another factor influencing stoat numbers may be the availability of rabbits as an alternative feed, numbers of which fell following the outbreak of myxomatosis in 1956.

There was no consistent difference in the number of stoats killed by keepers in England and Scotland (Figures 5.15, 5.16): More weasels were killed per square kilometre in Scotland than in England (Figure 5.17)

## 5.6 Wildcat: numbers killed on grouse moors

Wildcats were killed by keepers on managed grouse moors until they became protected in 1988. For completeness these data are presented in Figure 5.17.

### 5.7 Management implications

In the case of foxes, the increase in abundance was closely associated with the recovery of rabbits after myxomatosis in Scotland but not in England. This would imply (but we stress does not prove) that the

## Scotland, stoats killed per keeper

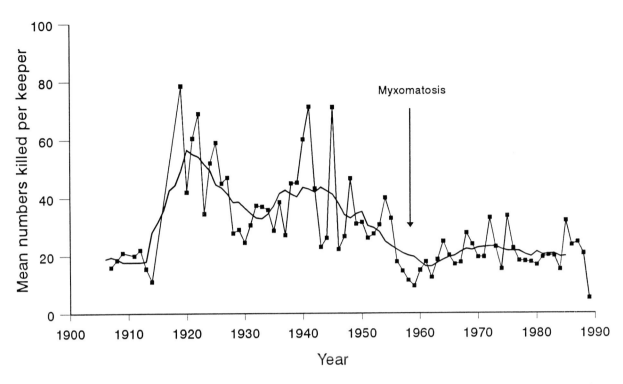

Figure 5.15. Relative numbers of stoats killed in Scotland. Variations in numbers were correlated with average grouse bags.

Figure 5.16. Relative numbers of stoats killed in England.

increase in foxes was due to insufficient keepers in Scotland being able to control the foxes and so numbers increased with the abundant rabbit population. While rabbit and fox numbers have become associated, this was not the case prior to myxomatosis when rabbits were abundant but foxes were scarce. This difference

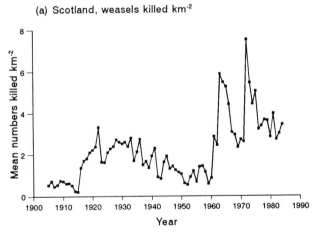

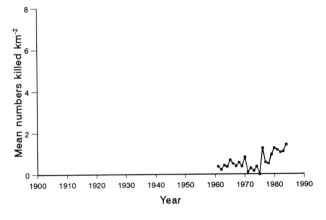

Figure 5.17. Relative number of weasels killed in both Scotland and England; surprisingly few were recorded by English estates and there is no correlation with number of stoats killed.

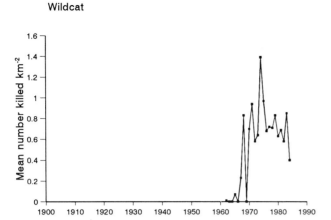

**Wildcat**

Figure 5.18. Relative numbers of wildcats killed on Scottish estates. Wildcats were protected in 1988.

could be related to the much higher keeper density in Scotland at that time, which effectively controlled the fox population irrespective of the rabbit population. With fewer keepers and an increase in the food available for foxes, keepers are now unable to keep on top of the fox problem.

The increase in crow numbers was associated with the increase in afforestation and it is suggested that forestry provided both a safe haven for nesting crows and abundant nesting sites. Knowing the location of suitable nest sites and implementing crow control through effective use of Larsen and cage traps, coupled with shooting, may well help to control crows locally.

Changes in stoat numbers are related to the abundance of grouse on the hill. This could be a result of a numeric response by stoats to the grouse, so increased trapping lines may be needed with an increasing grouse population to reduce the effects of stoats.

### 5.8 Summary

Numbers of foxes and crows killed by keepers on grouse moors have increased over the past 60 years, indicating an increase in predation pressure on grouse populations. Numbers of foxes killed on grouse moors in eastern and southern Scotland have increased five-fold over the past 20 years, an increase that has been associated with the recovery of rabbits after myxomatosis, probably because there were insufficient keepers to control them. The general increase in fox numbers was also recorded in data collected from Forestry Commission Conservancies.

Crow numbers have increased: the number killed by Scottish keepers increasing exponentially at nearly 5% per annum. This increase has been associated with increased afforestation which may provide both a safe haven for crows and an abundance of suitable nest sites. Stoat numbers have fluctuated in parallel with the abundance of grouse but probably not with intensity of trapping since there was no association between numbers of stoats and weasels killed on grouse moors.

## 5.9 Notes

a. Scottish keepers consistently killed more foxes per unit area than English keepers; Wilcoxon Matched Pairs sign test by year T = 41, z = 3.42, P>0.001. Scottish keepers killed more foxes per individual keeper; Wilcoxson Matched Pairs sign test by year T = 3, z = -4.38, P>.001.

b. Number of foxes killed on grouse moors in eastern and southern Scotland increased with number of rabbits killed, r=0.829, P>0.001, d.f. = 27.

c. Increase in crows killed was correlated with area of forestry in southern Scotland: r=0.70, P>0.001, eastern Scotland: r=0.65, P>0.001, western Scotland: r=0.59, P>0.001, but not northern Scotland: r=0.61, P>0.001.

d. No association was found between number of stoats and number of weasels killed per square kilometre in Scotland, r=0.1843, d.f. = 78, P<0.10.

## 5.10 References

1. Kolb H. H. & Hewson R. (1980). A study of fox populations in Scotland from 1971 to 1976. *Journal of Applied Ecology* **17**: 7-19.

2. Hewson R. & Kolb H.H. (1973). Changes in the numbers and distribution of foxes (*Vulpes vulpes*) killed in Scotland from 1948-1970. *Journal of Zoology,* London: **171**: 345-365.

3. Hewson, R. (1984). Changes in the numbers of foxes (*Vulpes vulpes*) in Scotland. *Journal of Zoology* **204**, 561-569.

4. Tapper, S.C., Brockless, M. & Potts, G.R. (1991). The effect of predation control on grey partridges. *Transactions of the 20th Congress of the International Union of Game Biologists. Gôdôllô, Hungary.*

5. Hudson, P.J. (1986). *Red Grouse, The Biology and Management of a Wild Gamebird.* Game Conservancy Trust, Fordingbridge.

# CHAPTER 6

# CHANGES IN ABUNDANCE OF OTHER MOORLAND ANIMALS: UPLAND BIRDS AND BLUE HARES

**Frequency of golden plover sightings were geater in well keepered areas with high grouse bags, whereas hen harrier and peregrine sightings showed no such relationships. Meadow pipits and blue hares were more abundant on areas with high grouse bags.**

## 6.1 Introduction

Heather moorland is a habitat of both national and international significance which maintains an important assemblage of upland birds. Two factors have played a role in producing and maintaining this habitat. First, the climatic conditions in northern Britain are characterised by having warm wet summers which encourage heather growth. Second, the tradition of grouse moor management - heather burning and a balanced grazing pressure - maintains the heather, principally as a habitat for grouse but also as a winter food source for sheep and deer.

A number of upland bird species have a large proportion of their population within northern Britain, principally because of the traditional land use practices which - unlike parts of Europe - have maintained the heather and prevented the spread of commercial afforestation. Since these species are considered of international importance many of them are given protection under Schedule 1 of the Wildlife and Countryside Act 1981 or under Annexe 1 of the European Community's Directive on Bird Conservation. Eight moorland species have special protection under Annexe 1 and most of these have a large proportion of their European Community population within Britain (Table 6.1). Table 6.1 tends to over-emphasise the importance of Britain within Europe since the figures are only for the European Community and do not include either Norway or Sweden, countries that carry a high proportion of the European upland bird community such as merlin, golden plover and dunlin.

Certain aspects of grouse moor management, such as burning and care for the heather moorland habitat and the control of predatory foxes and crows, are likely to influence the abundance of other moorland birds. This chapter examines bird communities in the uplands and records relative abundances of a number of species, which may benefit directly or indirectly from red grouse management.

Table 6.1 Moorland nesting birds provided with special protection under Annexe 1 of the European Community's Directive on the Conservation of Wild Birds. Source: [1,2] and others.

| Species | Population size (Pairs) | % EC Population | Trend |
|---|---|---|---|
| Golden Eagle | 510 | 25% | Stable |
| Hen Harrier | 550 | 24% | Increasing |
| Peregrine | 850 | 26% | Increasing |
| Merlin | 600 | 95% | Stable |
| Golden Plover | 27 000 | 96% | Decreasing |
| Greenshank | 950 | 100% | Decreasing |
| Dunlin | 10 000 | 90% | Decreasing |
| Short Eared Owl | 1000 | 80% | Stable |

## 6.2 Methods

As a matter of course, the grouse research team record the presence of other moorland birds when visiting both intensive and extensive study areas. No conscious effort was made to search out specific species but when a bird was seen during routine field work it was noted. At the end of each period of field work the relative presence of each moorland species was then recorded on a ranked scale from 1 (not seen) through to 5 (abundant and continuously present), as defined in Table 6.2.

Table 6.2 Rank scales of observations on moorland bird species.

| Ranked level of observation | Definition |
| --- | --- |
| 1 | Species not recorded |
| 2 | Presence recorded but only once |
| 3 | Presence recorded several times |
| 4 | Present most of the time |
| 5 | Present almost continuously while worker in the field |

*Note that the presence is ranked and relates more to frequency of observation rather than actual abundance. Hence, a golden eagle seen continuously during field work would be marked as rank 5 even though only a single individual was seen whereas a party of golden plovers passing through the study area would be ranked as 3. This approach does have certain limitations because the ranked level is totally subjective and is not necessarily comparable between species (i.e. a golden eagle rank of 5 is very different numerically from a meadow pipit ranked 5) but does provide some estimate of relative presence without involving intensive counts.*

The relative abundance of bird species is presented in one of two ways. First, as the proportion of visits during the summer when the species was recorded or, second, as the proportion of visits to a specific moor where the relative presence of the bird was ranked as 3 or more and hence considered at high density.

## 6.3 Structure of upland bird communities in relation to heather moors

A wide range of factors can influence whether a bird species is present in an area, including biological, environmental and anthropogenic (man-induced) factors. All these can vary regionally as environmental conditions, soil fertility and habitat structure change. Rainfall increases the further north and westwards one travels in Britain while temperature decreases with both latitude and altitude so that fewer bird species are found in the north west than the south east of Britain. For woodland bird species this is striking; 50 breeding species in south eastern England, yet only 25 in north western Scotland.

This general pattern does not extend to the uplands, where out of a total of 48 breeding upland species the richest area is found in the central Scottish Highlands (41 species), compared to 38 in Wales and 39 in northern England[3]. Overall, there is no clear trend in species richness and soil fertility, probably for two reasons. First, many of the upland birds feed on insects and other arthropods and the total biomass (dry weight) of these is not related to soil fertility; areas of blanket bog produce more insects than areas of freely drained moorland, even though blanket bog is of lower fertility[4]. Second, the moorland areas are structurally simple and the presence of a structurally complex habitat with more suitable nesting sites will increase species richness.

The presence of cliffs provides a whole range of new nest sites utilized by species such as peregrines and rock doves. Structural complexity can also influence the density of species. Meadow pipits nest at the interface of blanket bog and mineral rich grasslands alongside river beds. While feeding their first broods the pipits exploit the abundant crane flies produced in late May from the blanket bog and for their second brood when the blanket bog is unproductive they take the insects produced from the grassland areas[5]. Burning heather moorland can also increase structural complexity of the habitat providing more areas for golden plovers and red grouse. Generally, the upland bird communities fall into two types, the structurally complex habitats which include crags, old buildings and woodlands, and the structurally simple including heather, blanket bog, conifers and grasslands. There is more affinity within these groups simply because the introduction of a complex site allows more nest site opportunities (Figure 6.1).

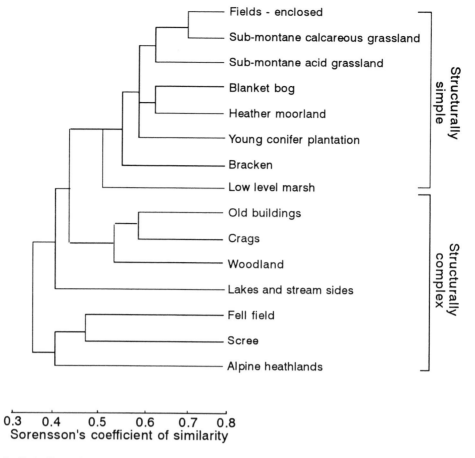

Figure 6.1. Similarity in the upland bird community. The structurally complex habitats tend to feature one group of birds and the structurally simple another. The degree of similarity was calculated from Sorensson's index; the greater the value the greater the similarity in the bird communities, so a value of 1 would show an identical bird fauna. (Data extracted from reference[6]).

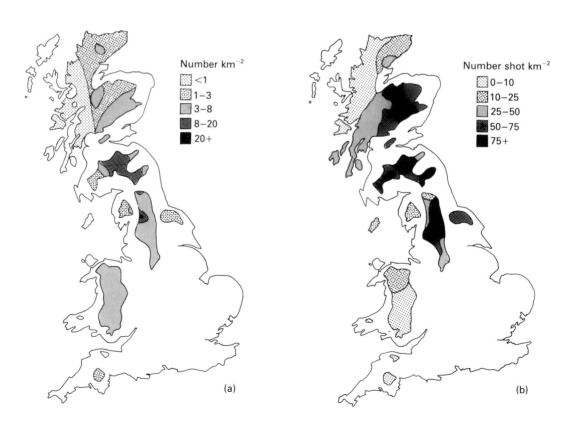

Figure 6.2. Breeding densities of golden plovers (a) (source: Ratcliffe[7]) and red grouse shot km$^{-2}$ (b). Densities of both species tend to be lower in the north and west and there is a weak positive association between the two species[3].

Golden plovers are characteristic birds of the uplands and their distribution and abundance is closely linked with that of red grouse (Chapter 6).

Blue hare numbers fluctuate with red grouse numbers on estates where foxes are controlled (Chapter 6).

Common sandpiper. The presence of upland birds on an area of moorland depends on the availability of suitable habitats. Streams, lochs and crags increase the diversity of bird species present (Chapter 6). *The Earl Peel*

Heather should be burnt in small fires to produce a mosaic of different aged heather stands (Chapter 4).

## (a) Keeper density

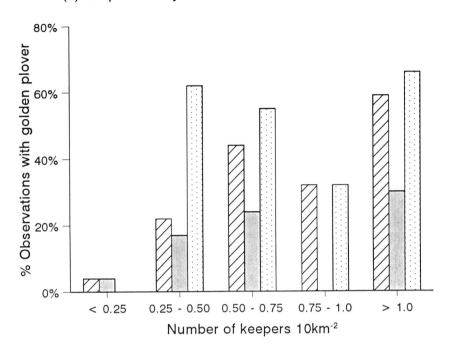

## (b) Grouse density

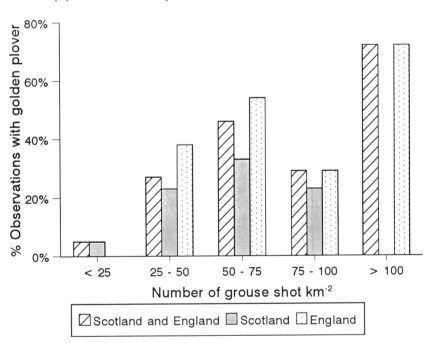

Figure 6.3. Relative presence of golden plovers (percentage of observations when golden plovers recorded) increased with both (a) density of keepers employed on the estate and (b) average grouse bag.

## 6.4 Golden plovers on grouse moors

Golden plovers, like red grouse, are one of the typical moorland birds and clearly benefit from the effects of grouse moor management. Golden plovers selectively nest on areas of short vegetation and consequently benefit from the burning programme initiated for grouse, while avoiding areas with tall rank heather or thick grassland (eg. *Molinia*).

The distribution and abundance of golden plovers was recorded in a national survey during the 1960s and 1970s[7]. The abundance of plovers varied greatly from 1 to 16 pairs per km[2] but rarely exceeds 8 pairs per km[2]. There is an association between areas of high plover density and those shooting many grouse[a] (Figure 6.2). As Ratcliffe noted, the density of golden plovers was also correlated with soil fertility, with some of the highest densities on the base rich limestone areas. Nevertheless, soil fertility alone does not provide a complete explanation since Breadalbane, a base rich area, carried relatively few plovers and the Moorfoots carried a greater density than a comparable area of Dumfriesshire.

As ground nesting birds, golden plovers are susceptible to predation and control of predators undertaken by keepers is likely to be beneficial. For example, high predation on the nests of golden plover was recorded at Kerloch when part of the hill was planted and keepering activities were reduced[8]. Within our study areas, there is a direct association between the proportion of visits to the hill when golden plovers are recorded, and the density of keepers - a measure of predator control[a] (Figure 6.3). There is also a direct association with grouse density[1].

Two further points on golden plovers should be noted. First, the golden plover population has fallen and this decline coincided with the decline in red grouse, so both may be associated with similar factors. Second, there may be an interesting three way relationship between plovers, grouse and blue hares where abundance in all three species is correlated with the abundance of foxes.

## 6.5 Hen harriers on grouse moors

Hen harriers are a characteristic bird of heather moorland and heathland. They were once found throughout much of Britain. The distribution of harriers was dramatically reduced by the turn of the century, when harriers were restricted to just Orkney and the Outer Hebrides. During the First World War, harriers became re-established in northern Scotland but this population was then eliminated (probably by persecution, although parts of north-west Scotland do not provide a good habitat for harriers). After the Second World War, the increase in forestry plantations provided a protected habitat and the birds slowly spread through east Sutherland southwards into Moray, Inverness-shire, Perthshire, Stirlingshire and also through south-west Scotland as far south as Lancashire and northern Wales. In 1950, harriers became re-established in Ireland.

Harriers breed well in young plantations, particularly when they have access to open unplanted ground to hunt. However, such areas do not sustain a population for long and generally harriers leave plantations when the trees are about 10 years of age. Numbers of hen harriers on Orkney were once high, although they have since fallen as agricultural improvements have reclaimed moorland, removing suitable nesting sites and reducing the availability of voles. As ground nesting birds, we may well expect predation by foxes

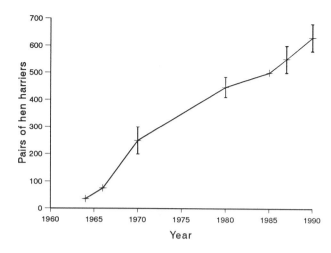

Figure 6.4. Estimated population size of hen harriers according to a series of population estimates, (mostly by BTO and RSPB).

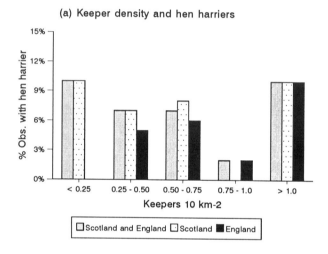

Figure 6.5. Relative presence of hen harriers in relation to grouse density and density of keepers employed. These observations are based only on recordings during routine field work and do not include periods of harrier observation. No relationship was found with either[b], although there was a tendency for harriers to be seen less often on areas with high numbers of grouse.

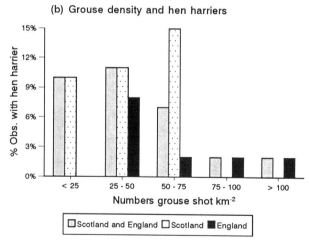

to influence the abundance of harriers. Many of the island populations of harriers have done well and most of these did not have foxes present, while on Skye - where foxes are present - harriers are relatively scarce (Table 6.3). Other factors will also influence the abundance of harriers on these islands, such as the occurrence of prey species and the level of protection the harriers receive. The harriers on the Isle of Man are interesting; numbers have increased over the past 20 years and there is now a good breeding population, but foxes were illegally introduced into the island several years ago and this could lead to increased predation and a reduction in the population.

**Table 6.3.** Hen harriers were relatively abundant on main islands around Scotland where foxes are absent. Foxes are absent from all except Skye where harriers are relatively scarce. Foxes have recently been introduced onto the Isle of Man.

| Island | Hen Harriers Relative Abundance | Foxes Present |
|---|---|---|
| Skye | Scarce | Yes |
| Orkney | Abundant | No |
| Harris & Lewis | Scarce | No |
| Uists | Abundant | No |
| Mull | Scarce | No |
| Islay | Abundant | No |
| Jura | Scarce | No |
| Arran | Abundant | No |
| Isle of Man | Abundant | No (but now present) |

While predation and prey availability are factors influencing the abundance of harriers, there can be little doubt that the patchy distribution of harriers on grouse moors is the result of direct persecution by some keepers. In places, persecution may also be preventing colonization of other areas where keepers would not kill harriers. With increased protection it seems likely that numbers may become re-established in other areas.

Overall, the population of hen harriers in Britain has increased steadily over the past 30 years (Figure 6.4). This increase has been steady and not an exponential increase as expected, probably because harriers have decreased in some local areas. Some of these losses will have been the result of forestry plantations reaching maturation and the loss of suitable nesting sites. Increased predation by the dramatically rising fox population (Chapter 5) may also have played a significant part, as will agricultural improvements and the loss of suitable nesting habitat through overgrazing. How important persecution has been is difficult to assess, although increased awareness by the general public and campaigns to prevent persecution have

clearly had an effect on many estates. It seems unlikely that any recent fall in harrier numbers has been caused by persecution alone. Indeed in Ireland, the harrier population continues to decrease where persecution is unlikely to be a significant factor, while fox predation and agricultural changes could be more important. Estimating harrier nesting densities is not simple and it is possible that numbers have been over-estimated, particularly if observers record the number of displaying pairs rather than the number of nesting females.

During routine field work (excluding data on specific observations on harriers) there was a tendency for a fall in the frequency of harriers observed with increasing grouse density recorded[b] (Figure 6.5), the opposite of the expected if harriers were responding to high grouse numbers. However, the observations at the greatest density grouse populations were all made in northern England where harriers are almost totally absent. If persecution alone was the factor determining relative abundance then one could argue that sightings should fall with keeper density; such a relationship is not apparent[b] (Figure 6.5). On the other hand, if well-keepered grouse moors are more attractive (less foxes, more prey, etc) then we may expect an increase with keeper density and this was not found either.

While these data do not refute the fact that persecution continues on some grouse moors, they indicate that the density of keepers employed is not the sole factor influencing harrier density. Possibly some keepers have a detrimental effect on local populations whereas others have a beneficial effect on harriers by providing increased prey availability and reducing the effects of fox predation. Nevertheless, in the absence of persecution, the distribution and abundance of harriers would certainly be greater. The interesting question is: 'In the absence of the benefits of grouse moor keepering what would the hen harrier population be?'.

### 6.6 Peregrines on grouse moors

Peregrines are not restricted totally to the uplands or specifically to grouse moors and they can be found nesting in cities, along sea cliffs and in other mountainous regions where heather and grouse are absent. Even within the uplands the peregrine may be rare or absent from areas where there are no crags or other suitable nesting sites. While the British peregrine population suffered considerably from the effects of the persistent organo-chlorine pesticides, the current population has shown a remarkable recovery after the dieldrin based compounds were removed from the market (Figure 6.6(a)), and in some areas breeding density is now higher than previously recorded (Figure 6.6(b)). While the overall picture of peregrine density

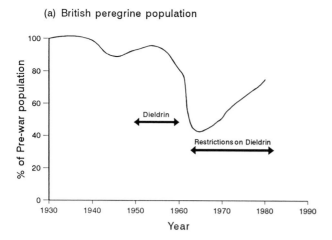

(a) British peregrine population

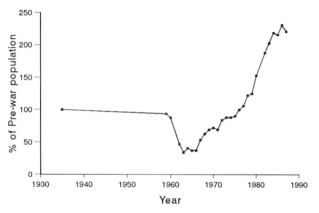

(b) Peregrine population: NW England

Figure 6.6. Recovery of the British peregrine population after the ban on DDT and dieldrin (1963-1966)(a). In some areas, including N.W. England (b) the density is now believed to be higher than previously recorded (After Ratcliffe[9]).

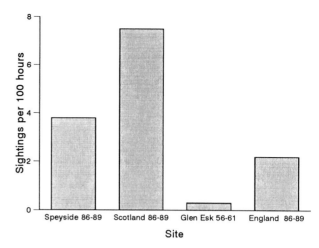

Figure 6.7. Frequency of sightings of peregrine during routine fieldwork from different studies. Glen Esk data from Jenkins et. al.[10].

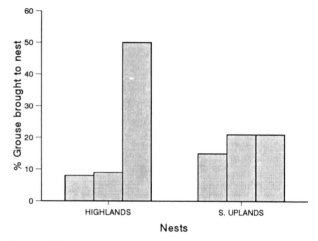

Figure 6.8. Diet of peregrines recorded at six nests, three in the Highlands and three in the Southern Uplands. (After Ratcliffe[9])

shows an increase in the national population at the time of the grouse decline it should be noted that the peregrines in the Highlands of Scotland did not suffer badly from the effects of the organo-chlorine pesticides, even though the frequency of our observations was greater than those recorded in Glen Esk between 1957 and 1961 (Figure 6.7).

Currently, peregrine populations are at a high level with most known nest sites occupied; within parts of Tayside there is currently one pair to every 60 km² (15 000 acres)[11]. Breeding densities of peregrines vary according to the presence of suitable nesting areas and further north in Strathspey where there are more nesting crags available density is closer to one pair to 40 km² (10 000 acres). In 1991 a national survey of peregrine numbers was conducted but this more detailed information on abundance and distribution was not available at the time of writing. The previous survey in Scotland in 1981 indicated that there were 409 breeding pairs living in 643 territories. A subsequent survey in 1989 covered a smaller area and

recorded 398 pairs living in 473 territories but indicated there has been an increase in occupancy from 64% to 84%. Even so, there are variations between areas and even in the eastern Highlands numbers may have fallen slightly. Further declines have been reported from western Scotland, but this is thought to be due to a decrease in the availability of suitable food species, including grouse, influenced by changes in land use away from the more traditional sporting estates and towards afforestation and reduced levels of farming and estate management. In southwest Scotland there may be a decline associated with the removal of adult birds and interference at the nesting sites[11].

Variations between areas are determined principally by the availability of suitable nesting sites and food. In some areas, peregrines have been persecuted relentlessly for years but the population has extraordinary persistence and pairs removed from nesting sites are often rapidly replaced, sometimes within a day or two. Protection of peregrines at nesting sites has resulted in

## (a) Keeper density

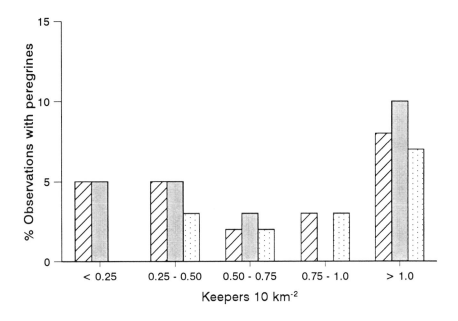

Keepers 10 km$^{-2}$

## (b) Grouse density

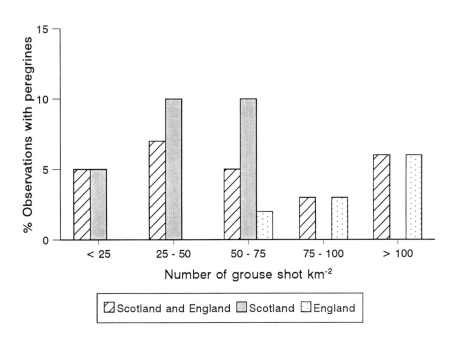

Number of grouse shot km$^{-2}$

Scotland and England   Scotland   England

Figure 6.9. There is no clear relationship between the frequency of peregrine sightings and either keeper density(a) or average grouse bag(b).

a decrease in the extent of nest robbing by egg collectors and persecution by keepers and pigeon fanciers.

The diet of peregrines is principally birds, caught on the wing. In cities and areas near pigeon flight lines feral or racing pigeons usually form a major part of the diet. In areas of heather moorland red grouse are a major constituent of the diet (Figure 6.8). Peregrines are frequently present on grouse moors and a careful search of the sky can often locate a peregrine 'waiting

on'. As with harriers, there is a difference between English and Scottish grouse moors in the frequency of observation (Figure 6.9). Overall, peregrines were observed less frequently on English moors although in England there was an increase in the frequency of sightings with the average grouse bag, suggesting peregrines were more active on areas where grouse are abundant. Differences between England and Scotland reflect the greater abundance of suitable nesting sites in Scotland. Similarly, there is no overall trend of an

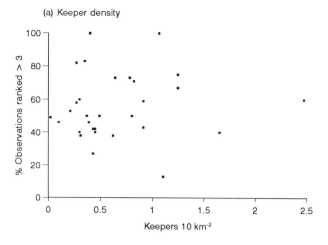

(a) Keeper density

% Observations ranked > 3

Keepers 10 km⁻²

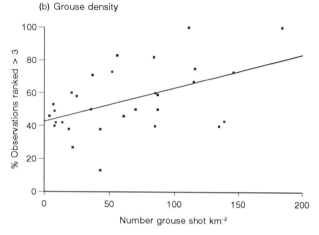

(b) Grouse density

% Observations ranked > 3

Number grouse shot km⁻²

Figure 6.10. Relative abundance of meadow pipits increased with average numbers of grouse shot. Each point represents one estate and relative frequency is the proportion of visits to the estate during summer when meadow pipit abundance was ranked greater than three[d]

fluenced by the availability of suitable insects and other invertebrates.

Meadow pipits were present on all moorland areas, so variations in density between individual grouse moors were determined as the proportion of visits where density was ranked as three or greater. Overall, there was an increase in the ranked density of meadow pipits with density of grouse shot, but not with keeper density (Figure 6.10). This implies that there may be a common factor influencing both grouse and meadow pipits, not related to keeper density and hence predator control. Burning pattern may be important since both pipits and grouse tend to be found alongside the edge of fires and both species may be influenced by the abundance and availability of insects and other arthropods.

### 6.8 Association between grouse and blue hares

Information on the number of blue hares killed on moorland estates was obtained during the three surveys of grouse bags described in Chapter 3.

The relationship between the abundance of blue hares and red grouse was investigated through an examination of the bag records from a number of estates in Scotland. A total of 37 moors provided details of both numbers of blue hares and red grouse shot each year for more than 30 years. Of these, 22 estates (59%) showed a positive association with more hares shot on estates with more grouse.

Further experimental work would be needed to examine the association between grouse and hares but it is interesting to compare the differences between estates showing no association and those showing a positive association. Estates without any association between grouse and hares did not have more ticks, or more louping ill, nor were there differences in underlying rock quality, heather productivity or length of growing season (Table 6.4). However, estates without a positive association did tend to shoot more foxes per square kilometre than those with a positive association. This would suggest that foxes may be influenc-

increasing frequency of peregrine observations with keeper density although there is a tendency for such an association within both England and Scotland[c].

### 6.7 Meadow pipits on grouse moors

Meadow pipits are the most abundant bird species in summer on moorland and, like most moorland birds they nest on the ground where they are vulnerable to predators such as the fox, stoat and weasel. While there appear to be abundant nesting sites for meadow pipits, variations in nesting density may be in-

**Table 6.4.** A comparison of factors associated with estates which have grouse and have hare bag records correlated and those which do not.

| | Blue Hare & Grouse | | |
| --- | --- | --- | --- |
| | No Association | Association | Significance |
| Foxes Killed | 0.75km⁻² | 0.37km⁻² | P = 0.03 |
| Ticks | 42% | 35% | NS |
| Louping Ill | 18% | 29% | NS |
| Heather Productivity | 206.8 ± 11.05 | 223.4 ± 3.69 | NS |
| Growing Season | 154.2 ± 8.59 | 166.6 ± 6.54 | NS |
| Soil Grade | 1.88 ± 0.16 | 2.61 ± 0.23 | NS |

ing the relationship; when foxes are well controlled then variables that influence productivity (e.g. food or weather) may influence abundance in both grouse and hares, but when foxes are present they may interact with this relationship by reducing survival or productivity in one or both species.

## 6.9 Summary

The relative abundance of several upland bird species was examined in relation to grouse bag and keeper density. Golden plover density was greater on areas with a high grouse bag and areas with many keepers implying that grouse management may benefit golden plovers. Numbers of hen harriers have been increasing in Britain. Fox control may benefit ground nesting harriers although other factors including persecution and the loss of habitat have influenced harrier abundance and distribution. Overall, fewer harriers were seen on high density grouse moors although these observations were made in northern England where harriers were effectively absent. In England, sightings of peregrines were associated with the numbers of grouse shot but sightings were greater in Scotland where there are more suitable nesting sites. Meadow pipits were more abundant on areas with more grouse but not associated with keeper density. Bag records from 37 estates showed there was a positive correlation between grouse and blue hares on 59% of these estates and those estates without such an association shot significantly more foxes.

## 6.11 References

1. Ratcliffe, D. (1990). *Bird Life of Mountain and Upland.* Cambridge University Press.

2. Stroud, D.A., Reid, T.M., Pienkowski, M.W. & Lindsay, R.A. (1987). *Birds Bogs and Forestry: the peatlands of Caithness and Sutherland.* NCC, Peterborough.

3. Hudson, P.J. (1988). Spatial variations, patterns and management options in upland bird communities. In: *Ecological change in the uplands* (Ed M. B. Usher & D.B.A. Thumps). Blackwells Scientific Publications, Oxford, pp 381-397.

4. Coulson, J.C. (1988). The structure and importance of invertebrate communities on peatlands and moorlands, and effects of environmental and management changes. In: *Ecological change in the uplands* (Ed M. B. Usher & D.B.A. Thompson). Blackwells Scientific Publications, Oxford, pp 365-380.

5. Coulson, J.C. & Whittaker, J.B. (1978). The ecology of moorland animals. *Production ecology of British Moors and Mountain Grasslands* Ed. O.T.. Heal & T.V.. Perkiness, pp 52-93. Springer Verlag, Berlin.

6. Ratcliffe, D.A. (1977) Uplands and birds - an outline. *Bird Study* **24**, 140-158.

7. Ratcliffe, D.A. (1976) Observations on the breeding biology of the golden plover in Great Britain. *Bird Study* **7**, 81-93.

8. Parr, R. (1989). *Demographic effects of nest predation on Golden Plovers and other waders.* NCC Chief Scientists Directorate commissioned research report no 1026.

9. Ratcliffe, D.A. (1980). *The Peregrine Falcon.* T & A D Poyser, Calton.

10. Jenkins, D. Watson, A. & Miller, G.R. (1964). Predation and red grouse populations. *Journal of Applied Ecology,* **1**, 183-195.

11. P.K. Stirling-Aird. Personal communication.

## 6.10 Notes

a. Golden plover sightings increased with keeper density; Spearman rank correlation $rs = 0.9$, $P > 0.05$: Golden plover increased with grouse density; Spearman rank correlation $rs = 0.9$, $P > 0.05$.

b. Hen harrier presence was not associated with keeper density; Spearman rank correlation $rs = -0.38$, $P < 0.05$; or with grouse bag density; Spearman rank correlation $rs = 0.725$, $0.10 > P < 0.05$.

c. Peregrine presence was not associated with keeper density; Spearman rank correlation $rs = 0.175$, $P < 0.05$ or with grouse bag density; Spearman rank correlation $rs = 0.625$, $P > 0.05$. In English data peregrines were more frequently seen on areas with high grouse bag density; Spearman rank correlation $rs = 1.0$, $P > 0.05$

d. Frequency of meadow pipit observations recorded as three or greater (i.e. relatively abundant) increased with the density of grouse shot: $r = 0.50$, $P > 0.001$, d.f. = 28.

# CHAPTER 7

# THE FALL IN GROUSE NUMBERS 1975-1983

**Changes in the average grouse bag were associated with July weather conditions prior to and during the decline in grouse numbers, although during the decline fox numbers increased and were associated with low grouse bags. Weather variables that influenced grouse directly or indirectly may have initiated the decline but it is suggested that the effects of increased fox predation exacerbated the decline.**

## 7.1 Introduction

Numbers of red grouse harvested in Scotland have shown a general long term downward trend which accelerated rapidly between 1975 and 1983 (Figure 7.1a). Without detailed knowledge and historical records of the inimical factors that could influence grouse numbers it is not possible to build a complete picture of what may have happened. Nevertheless, from our comparative analysis we have some indication that the rise in the fox population, changes in heather productivity and weather variables could be involved.

This chapter examines quantitatively the factors associated with the decline, particularly in the eastern Highlands. Qualitative descriptions have been made in the sporting press and have included descriptions of the browning of heather in severe winters and outbreaks of trichostrongylosis.

## 7.2 Methods

The data presented in this analysis concentrate on bag records from Angus and South Deeside from 1965 to 1989 where detailed data on annual numbers of foxes killed and weather variables are available.

The variables considered in this analysis include the following:

*(i) Numbers of foxes killed:* The average number of foxes killed per square kilometre of moorland ground in the eastern Highlands.

*(ii) Heather productivity index:* The same index used in the comparative analysis in Chapter 4. Annual heather growth is estimated for each year according to the temperature and rainfall between mid-April and August.

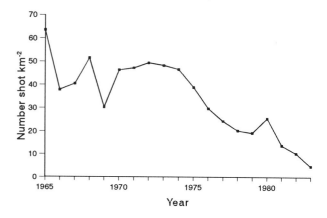

**(a) Grouse shot in Eastern Scotland**

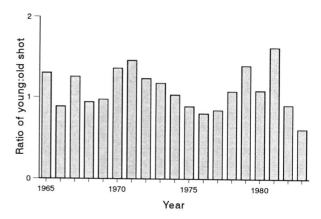

**(b) Breeding production**

7.1. Change in numbers of grouse shot in eastern Scotland (a) and breeding production (b), estimated as the average ratio of young to old shot from 4 estates.

*(iii) Growing season:* Duration of growing season estimated as the number of days on which the average daily temperature increased above 6°C, corrected for altitude.

56

*(iv) Previous years bag:* To include the possibility that density dependent factors could be important in the change in numbers of red grouse, the number of grouse shot in the previous year was included.

*(v) Weather variables:*
For each month previous to the shooting season the following weather variables were included:

a. Monthly total potential evapotranspiration (mm). This is a measure of the atmospheric potential to take up moisture from grassland through the combined effects of evaporation and transpiration.

b. Monthly total actual evapotranspiration (mm).
c. End of month soil moisture deficit (mm). This is calculated from a model of soil moisture extraction and replacement from information on rainfall and evapotranspiration.

d. Monthly total effective precipitation (mm).

e. Monthly total rainfall (mm).

f. Monthly total sunshine (hours).

g. Monthly mean air temperature (degrees Centigrade). Half the sum of daily maximum and minimum temperatures.

h. Monthly mean vapour pressure (mb).

i. Monthly mean wind speed (miles per day).

While the analysis of these variables may indicate which were associated with changes in the grouse bag it should be emphasised that such associations cannot show what actually caused the change in numbers.

## 7.3 Factors associated with change in grouse numbers

Multiple regression analyses was used to identify which combination of variables accounted for average bag records during two periods:

(i) The pre-decline years between 1965 and 1975
(ii) The decline years between 1975 and 1983

*Pre-decline years:*
Between 1965 and 1975 two weather variables were associated with the average bag of grouse in eastern Scotland (Table 7.1). These were July temperature and July soil moisture deficit, both having a negative as-sociation such that low bag records were associated with warm, dry Julys. These two variables accounted for 80% of the variation in average annual bag at this time. July has been identified as a significant month in our analyses in Section 7 where the rate of summer infection with the strongyle worm was greater when the July temperature was high.

*Decline years*
During the years of decline, 1975 to 1983, both July temperature and dryness (as potential evaporation) were again important although during this period the relationship with temperature was positive, with greater bags in years with warm Julys. During this period, the number of foxes killed in the previous year was also identified as an important variable such that average bags were lower in years following high numbers of foxes being killed (Table 7.1). Overall, these three variables accounted for 97% of the variation in the grouse bag during this time period.

Table 7.1 Summary of the variables accounting for variation in the average bag of grouse shot in eastern Scotland for periods between 1965 and 1989 (S.M.D. = soil moisture deficit, P.E. = potential evapotranspiration). Symbols indicate direction of relationship, + = positive, − = negative, 0 = no relationship.

| | PERIOD | |
| --- | --- | --- |
| | 65-75 | 75-83 |
| July S.M.D. | — | 0 |
| July Temp | — | + |
| July P.E. | 0 | — |
| Foxes killed in previous year | 0 | — |
| Variation Explained | 80% | 97% |

## 7.4 Discussion

July temperature and dryness were revealed as important variables associated with average grouse bag during both the years of pre-decline and the decline itself. The biological significance of the weather variables on grouse are not clear although patterns of infection with the trichostrongyle worm are associated with July weather conditions. One complication is that prior to the decline, bag records were lower in years with warm Julys but during the decline bags were higher during years of warm Julys. The reason for this difference is not apparent from this analysis although one explanation is that there is a trade-off in survival and July temperature depending on relative grouse density. When density is high, infection rate of the trichostrongyle worm is greater and may reduce survival but when density is relatively low, infection rate will be less important and warm Julys have a beneficial effect. In Chapter 3, average bag was associated with June temperature in a comparison between moors and further examination of these results show that a similar relationship is found for July temperature.

Irrespective of the effects of July weather, numbers of foxes killed during the previous year were important to the relationship, such that fewer grouse were shot following years when many foxes were killed. A similar relationship was found between bag records and grouse shot km$^{-2}$ on three estates in Scotland (Chapter 5, Figure 5.4) suggesting that fox predation is an important variable influencing the decline in grouse numbers. It seems likely and biologically plausible that this increase in fox numbers may have had a significant influence on the decline of grouse.

Discussions with keepers and others involved with grouse production refer to harsh weather conditions in the years just at the time grouse numbers started to decline. Drying easterly winds were observed which caused severe heather browning so there was little heather available for the hens and breeding production was consequently poor. These descriptive weather conditions may well have influenced grouse breeding production and initiated the decline in grouse. The data on breeding production (Figure 7.1b) shows a falling breeding production between 1971 and 1975 with years of poor breeding between 1974 and 1977. Nevertheless breeding production subsequently increased after 1977 and was relatively high in two of the following five years, yet the grouse population continued to fall. What seems likely is that these severe weather conditions initiated the decline but increasing fox numbers and predation acted to continue the decline and kept grouse densities low.

## 7.5 Summary

July weather conditions were associated with annual average grouse bag prior to and during the period of decline. However, prior to the decline, July temperature was greater during years of low grouse bags, while during the decline July temperature was greater during years of high grouse bags. July temperature is associated with infection rate in high density populations but may have a beneficial effect when densities are low. During the period of decline the grouse bags were lower in years following many foxes being killed. Observations at the time indicate that drying weather conditions caused severe heather browning and initiated the decline. The increasing fox predation may have exacerbated the decline.

# DEMOGRAPHY AND ANNUAL CHANGES IN GROUSE POPULATIONS

# CHAPTER 8

# YEAR TO YEAR VARIATIONS
# IN GROUSE LOSSES

**Analysis of data from 30 grouse populations shows that year to year changes in numbers of red grouse were invariably influenced by the pattern of winter loss.**

## 8.1 Introduction

Red grouse populations are influenced by a wide range of factors including predators, parasites and food quality. Some of these factors were examined in Chapter 4 when an extensive survey was made of average bag size in relation to environmental factors and aspects of management. This section looks in more detail at specific study populations where detailed information has been collected on breeding production and losses from the population. This chapter identifies the important periods of loss that cause year to year changes in grouse numbers while the next chapter examines which factors are associated with these year to year changes.

## 8.2 Methods: intensive study areas and key factor analysis

Basic population data were collected from 10 study areas (Figure 8.1). Study areas established before 1984 were 0.8km² (200 acres) in area but all subsequent study areas were 1.0km². Trained pointing dogs were used to conduct total counts of each area in April to estimate breeding density and again in July, when chicks were seven weeks of age, as an estimate of breeding production. In May of each year, grouse nests were found using the pointing dogs and clutch size and the subsequent number of chicks hatched were recorded.

Population data can be analysed in a number of different ways depending on the type of questions being asked. Key-factor analysis can answer the question 'Which period of mortality determines annual changes in numbers?' This technique estimates a series of losses from the population and then compares each loss with the total loss from the population. The loss that accounts for most of the variation in the total loss essentially determines the year to year changes in the total loss and hence changes in the size of the popula-

tion. The period of loss that accounts for this year to year variation is known as the key-factor. The requirement for such an analysis is to have at least five consecutive years of detailed population data. From the count data, shooting information, clutch size and hatching data we can identify five periods of loss:

*(i) Shooting losses ($k_0$)*
Shooting mortality was estimated from the total number shot from the estate and corrected for size of study area

*(ii) Over-winter loss ($k_1$)*
Over-winter losses included both mortality on the study area and the net change through immigration and emigration between October and April.

*(iii) Failure to lay a full clutch ($k_2$)*
Maximum clutch size in grouse was taken as 12 and the failure to lay a full clutch taken as the reduction to the average clutch size recorded for each year

*(iv) Egg mortality ($k_3$)*
Egg mortality included failure to hatch and included both total and partial mortality from the clutch

*(v) Chick mortality ($k_4$)*
Estimated from hatching to seven weeks of age.
Each loss was expressed as the difference in numbers before and after the period of loss; as is usual with this type of analysis, the numbers were transformed into logarithms so that each period of loss was determined as:

$$k_i = Log_{10}(N_i) - Log_{10}(N_{i+1})$$

where $k_i$ is the mortality or loss, and $N_i$ and $N_i + 1$ are the number of individuals entering and the number surviving the ith period of loss.

Figure 8.1. Location of study areas; intensive study areas are shown by a large dot and extensive study areas with a small dot.

Note that some losses are identified as mortality (e.g. egg mortality) when we know that the only cause of loss from the population was caused by actual death. Other periods we must call a 'period of loss' because it is possible that some of the individuals had moved from the study area and were not actually dead.

Overall loss was the sum of each of the periods of loss $(K_{TOT} = k_0 + k_1 + k_2 + k_3 + k_4)$. Combined harvesting and winter losses $(k_0 + k_1)$ are shown as $k_{01}$ and breeding losses $(k_2 + k_3 + k_4)$ as $k_{234}$.

Key factors were identified for each population as the single factor that contributed most to the variation in

$K_{TOT}$ by plotting each period of loss $(k_i)$ against total loss. The key factor that accounted for most of the variation in total loss and produced a slope closest to a one to one slope (regression coefficient) was taken as the key-factor.

### 8.3 Extensive population data

Population data were collected from a further 20 sites (Figure 8.1) of either 0.8km² or 1.00 km². For the analysis, the size of the study area was of little significance since the size of all study areas remained constant throughout the study. In comparisons between losses and density, density was corrected to birds km⁻².

Details of clutch size and hatching success were not available from the extensive study areas so overall breeding losses were estimated and shown as $k_{234}$.

### 8.4 Key factor identification

Key factor analysis of the population data from the 10 intensive studies identified winter loss $(k_1)$ as the key factor in six populations. Failure to lay a full clutch $(k_2)$ was the key factor in one population; there was no apparent key factor in the remaining three.

Harvesting mortality $(k_0)$ was estimated from the number of birds shot from the whole estate on which each study area is based and as such is not a true reflection of the actual mortality from the study area. To avoid possible inaccurate separation of both harvesting mortality $(k_0)$ and consequent winter loss the two losses were combined as overall winter loss $(k_{01})$. In this way overall winter loss was the key factor in 7 of the 10 intensive population studies.

Considering both the 10 intensive and 20 extensive population studies, overall winter loss $(k_{01})$ was the key factor in 19 of the 30 populations, while in a further two populations, winter loss was almost significant $(0.1 < P < 0.05)$ and may well be identified as the key factor with additional data. In the remaining nine populations, breeding loss $(k_{234})$ was the key factor in seven and a further one was not quite significant at the 5% level $(P = 0.052)$.

### 8.5 Discussion

In general terms, winter loss (October to April inclusive) was the key factor influencing year to year changes in grouse numbers from study areas throughout most of the British distribution of red grouse. However, the importance of winter loss as a key factor may vary both spatially and temporally.

Neighbouring study areas, often within 1km of each other can exhibit different key factors even though the populations are effectively contiguous. Similarly, the importance of key factors can change with time, for example early analysis of population data from study areas in Glen Esk identified winter loss as the key factor although when more recent data from the same study area were included in the analysis the key factor changed from winter to breeding loss.

This apparent change in the significance of losses from one time period to another or between neighbouring populations could reflect real changes in the biological factors driving population changes or simply be the result of the same factors acting on both winter and summer losses. Detailed analysis of the population data from the intensive study at Gunnerside demonstrated strong associations between all losses, indicating that a common factor may influence both winter and breeding losses (see Chapter 27).

### 8.6 Summary

Key factor analysis was conducted on population data from 10 intensive study areas and 20 extensive study areas. Winter loss was the key factor explaining most of the variation in annual loss in seven of the 10 intensive sites. In an analysis of all 30 sites winter loss was the key factor in 19 and breeding losses in seven study areas.

# CHAPTER 9

# FACTORS ASSOCIATED WITH BREEDING AND WINTER LOSSES

**Year to year changes in winter losses and breeding losses were associated with the level of parasite burden in old grouse in populations where louping ill was absent. Variations between populations were due to differences in breeding production and in particular the effects of louping ill.**

## 9.1 Introduction

Winter loss was identified as the key factor influencing the year to year changes in grouse numbers in 63% of the grouse populations studied in Chapter 8. This chapter first examines the size of these annual losses and the factors associated with these losses and second examines variations in mean density of grouse between estates.

## 9.2 Factors influencing grouse populations:

A number of inimical factors are known to influence grouse populations and whenever possible, details were collected on these.

*(i) Louping ill:* (See Chapter 4.5(vi))

*(ii) Trichostrongyle worms:* Mean intensity of worms in adult red grouse was determined through the collection of gut samples from grouse shot in August and September. Methods used for extracting worms are described in Section 7.

*(iii) Heather Mosaic Ranking:* (See Chapter 4.5(v))

*(iv) Keeper density:* (See Chapter 4.5(v))

*(v) Base Richness:* (See Chapter 4.4(i))

*(vi) Heather productivity:* (See Chapter 4.5 (ii))

*(vii) Growing season:* (See Chapter 4.5(iii))

*(viii) Meteorological data:* Two meteorological variables which may have biological significance were also considered. First, mean number of wet days at each study area, where a wet day is a period of 24 hours within

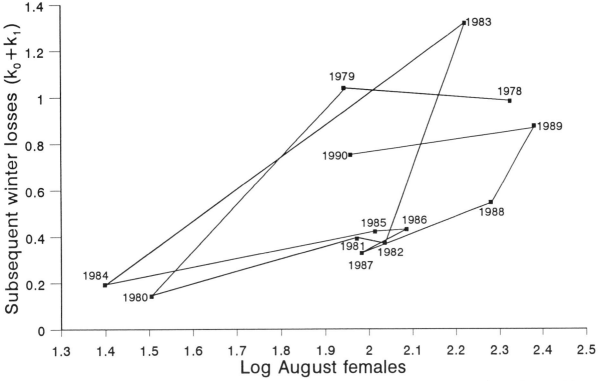

Figure 9.1. Delayed density dependence in winter losses of red grouse from the main study area at Gunnerside, illustrated from a plot of winter losses against density of females in autumn and showing the characteristic circular pattern.

which there is precipitation of at least 1mm. Areas with an excess of 170 wet days have a consistent excess of precipitation over evapotranspiration resulting in peat development and the production of blanket bog on flat ground. Second, mean daily June temperature was included as a measure of the availability of invertebrates to chicks during the period of maximum chick growth as identified in Chapter 4.

## 9.3 Annual changes in winter losses:

In 55 cases, information was available on both annual winter loss and intensity of trichostrongyle worm infection within the breeding population of grouse. Overall winter loss increased with the parasite burdens of the grouse[a] although this only accounted 9.5% of the variation in winter loss.

Annual heather productivity was not associated with subsequent winter loss on the main study areas.

On Gunnerside, North Yorkshire, where we have detailed population data for 10 years, plotting each successive winter's loss $(k_{01})$ against previous density (Log$_{10}$ female density in August) revealed an anticlockwise progression (Figure 9.1). Such a relationship is indicative of a density dependent mechanism acting with a time delay (delayed density dependence). In other words the winter loss is dependent on the density of grouse at an earlier time. To identify at which time density was important, regression analyses were used with winter losses plotted against female breeding density and previous autumn female density. A statistically significant relationship was found with the density of breeding females but not the autumn

density of females one year before. Similar analysis on all 30 populations studied found that a total of 12 (40%) also showed a significant association with female breeding density prior to the loss.

The proportion of populations showing significant delayed density dependence increases as those with shorter time series are excluded (Figure 9.2).

## 9.4. Annual changes in breeding losses $(k_{234})$:

Breeding losses were density dependent in only one of 30 populations and inversely density dependent in a further two. No evidence of delayed density dependent breeding losses was identified.

Annual breeding losses were not correlated with mean levels of infection in red grouse but when data from moors suffering from louping ill were removed from the analysis annual breeding losses were positively correlated with intensity of infection. Grouse populations with louping ill present suffered significantly greater breeding losses than populations without louping ill[b].

In the 10 intensive study areas where failure to lay a full clutch $(k_2)$, egg loss $(k_3)$ and chick loss $(k_4)$ were recorded, failure to lay a full clutch was density dependent at two study areas. Egg loss was density dependent at one site and chick loss at another.

Annual breeding loss was not associated with heather productivity on any study area.

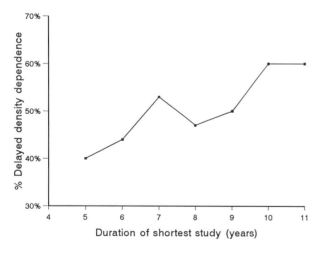

Figure 9.2. The increase in the detection of delayed density dependence in red grouse population studied in relation to duration of study: There was an increase in delayed density dependence as shorter studies were shed from the analysis.

Six day old grouse chick. An over-riding factor reducing chick survival is the disease louping ill (Chapters 9 and 33). *The Earl Peel*

Average grouse density is greater in populations with good chick survival (Chapter 9). *The Earl Peel*

When grouse numbers are high, mortality of grouse through shooting is not an important factor influencing year to year changes in numbers (Chapter 8). *The Earl Peel*

The decline in Scottish grouse numbers in the late seventies was associated with poor weather conditions and increased predation by foxes (Chapter 7). *The Earl Peel*

## 9.5 Variations in mean density between study areas

Previous analysis within this chapter has examined year to year differences in losses from grouse populations and the factors associated with these losses. We now examine differences between populations in the average density of female grouse to determine which types of mortality may be important and the factors associated with these losses.

Within the 10 intensive study areas variations in mean female density, both in autumn and when breeding, were influenced by chick loss ($k_4$) and failure to lay a full clutch, ($k_2$). Expanding this analysis to all 30 study areas, breeding losses ($k_{234}$) contributed significantly to variations in both autumn and spring female density. Hence differences in density between areas are influenced by breeding losses, although the key factor analysis (Chapter 8) revealed that differences in density between years were due to winter loss.

In an analysis of winter loss ($k_{01}$), only average intensity of infection with the trichostrongyle worm was a significant factor associated with winter loss[a] between populations. Keeper density, base richness, heather mosaic ranking, number of snow days, mean daily temperature in April, growing season, heather productivity and the number of wet days made no significant contribution.

The only significant factor associated with breeding losses ($k_{234}$) was the presence or absence of louping ill.

## 9.6 Shooting losses

Shooting losses increased with density of grouse (Figure 9.3) although the variance at high density was high. Overall, shooting was compensated for through reduced winter loss (Figure 9.4).

## 9.7 Discussion

In general, the results from this extensive analysis of population data would confirm that the trichostrongyle worm (*Trichostrongylus tenuis*) was a significant factor associated with population losses.

Breeding losses were greater in grouse populations infected with the viral infection louping ill. Young grouse infected with louping ill can suffer an 80% mortality, although overall losses tend to be in the region of 50% (see Section 8). Winter losses from these populations are low, probably through increased immigration during late summer into infected areas, which sustains the population. When the population data sets from areas known to be infected with louping

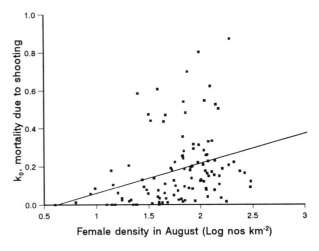

Figure 9.3. Relationship between harvesting mortality and density of grouse: While the losses are density dependent there is high variation at high densities.

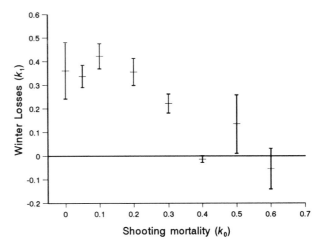

Figure 9.4. Compensation of shooting mortality with reduced winter losses, shown as the relationship between winter losses and shooting losses. Note in some instances winter losses appear negative; this must be the result of immigration of individuals into the study area after harvesting.

ill were removed from the analysis, breeding losses were associated with levels of trichostrongyle worm infection. Experimental manipulations have shown that the parasitic trichostrongyle worm is a significant factor increasing breeding losses in grouse (Chapter 27).

In this extensive analysis of grouse population data it would seem reasonable to suppose that delayed density dependent winter losses (the rate of loss increasing with density but acting after a period - hence delayed) are the key factor causing changes in grouse numbers. Infections with the parasitic trichostrongyle worm are probably the main regulator. The variation in the importance of winter and breeding losses and the spatial variation in association between these losses appears confusing, although the importance of a single factor influencing both losses could explain some of this apparent variation. While this analysis indicates the trichostrongyle worm may be the most ubiquitous of the regulating factors on managed grouse moors it is also apparent that the viral infection louping ill could over-ride these factors. It is likely that other factors, such as predation, could have a further major part to play and indeed interact with the other factors and influence the dynamics of red grouse.

## 9.8 Summary

Variations in winter loss were associated with the level of parasite burden in old grouse. Delayed density dependence was found on one of the main study areas where winter losses were greater following years of high female breeding density. The likelihood of identifying this delayed density dependence increased with the duration of the study. Breeding losses were higher in populations with louping ill but when these populations were removed from the analysis, breeding losses were associated with the levels of the trichostrongyle worm infection.

Variations between mean population density of female grouse both in spring and autumn were determined by breeding losses and were lower in areas with louping ill. Variations in winter loss between estates were associated with the average level of infection with the nematode parasite.

## 9.9 Notes

a. Winter loss increased with parasite burdens; ($r=0.307$, $P>0.05$ $N=53$).

b. Breeding losses were significantly greater in populations with louping ill (t test, $t=4.73$, $P>0.001$, $N=30$)

c. Breeding losses were not correlated with mean levels of infection in red grouse ($r=0.0.77$, $N=55$, $P<0.10$) but when data from moors suffering from louping ill were removed, annual breeding losses were positively correlated with intensity of infection ($r=0.313$, $N=47$, $P>0.05$).

d. Winter loss increased with average intensity of infection with the strongyle worm[2] ($b=0.234$, $P=.0002$, $r^2=0.466$)

## 9.10 References

1. Picozzi, N. (1966). Grouse management in relation to the management and geology of heather moors. *Journal of Applied Ecology*, 5, 483-488.

2. Miller, G.R. (1979). Quantity and quality of the annual production of shoots and flowers by *Calluna vulgaris* in north-east Scotland. *Journal of Ecology*, **67**, 109-129.

3. Smith, L.P. (1976). *The Agricultural climate of England and Wales. MAFF Technical Bulletin 35.* HMSO, London.

4. Watson, A. (1971). Key factor analysis, density dependence and population limitation in red grouse. *Dynamics of Populations* (Ed. by P.J. den Boer & G.R. Gradwell), pp 548-564. Centre for Agriculture Publishing & Documentation, Wageningen.

5. Hudson, P.J., Newborn, D. & Dobson, A.P. (1992). Regulation and stability of a free-living host-parasite system: *T. tenuis* in red grouse. I Monitoring and population reduction experiments. *Journal of Animal Ecology*, **61**,477-486.

# POPULATION BIOLOGY OF LOW DENSITY GROUSE POPULATIONS

# CHAPTER 10

# THE PROBLEM OF WHAT CAUSES WINTER LOSSES

**Are changes in grouse density due to the intrinsic effects of the bird's own behaviour or are they due to extrinsic factors such as predation and parasitism? This is a question of fundamental importance to grouse management.**

## 10.1 Introduction

Discovering a dead hen grouse on the hill in winter that has obviously been killed by a fox does not necessarily mean that the grouse population will be one less in the following spring. Other factors may have influenced the condition or status of the grouse and predetermined its fate. For example, the hen grouse may not have held a territory, had no prospective mate and was consequently unlikely to enter the breeding population in the following spring. Her death may result in another bird living; for example if she were territorial then it may be possible that another bird, that was previously non-territorial and thus doomed to die, will replace her and subsequently breed. In such a case, the actual breeding population remains constant even though the individuals within the population change.

We need to define the circumstances in which losses to predation result in a decrease and in which circumstances these losses are compensated for through population processes. In the case of red grouse we can consider, at the extreme, two competing and alternative hypotheses for explaining changes in numbers.

*First hypothesis*: that the social behaviour of the birds in autumn pre-determines the breeding density of grouse and any non-territorial birds are considered a doomed surplus which will fail to breed unless an accident befalls a territorial individual and the non-territorial grouse can then replace the lost bird.

*Second hypothesis*: in the absence of predation, accident or disease, the number of grouse remaining at the end of the shooting season will remain constant at a limit determined by local resources (food or nesting sites) and subsequently breed in the following spring. Any mortality that befalls a grouse during the intervening period will result in one less bird in the following spring.

These are the extremes of the two mechanisms that could generate changes in the breeding population of red grouse. By themselves, both seem incongruous since in the absence of predation a population may be regulated by individuals dispersing to other areas to breed. Similarly it seems incongruous to suppose that the bird's own behaviour in autumn would determine the following spring population irrespective of the mortality rate that may occur between autumn and spring. Which mechanism or combination of mechanisms operate? When grouse move away from an area, are the birds that leave pushed out as 'doomed surplus' or do they disperse of their own accord in an attempt to improve their own conditions? Which mechanism may operate has repercussions for management. How important is predator control and the removal of parasites in improving the number of grouse? If social behaviour determines density then keepering during winter months and other activities are not necessary since the bird's themselves effectively determine density.

In this chapter we consider both hypotheses in more detail. In later chapters we examine the evidence from the low density populations of Scotland to determine which, if any, is the more likely.

## 10.2 Spacing behaviour hypothesis

The spacing behaviour hypothesis states that as a result of the behaviour of the more dominant individuals, subordinate individuals fail to breed subsequently. In red grouse, the system proposed is that the density of breeding birds is determined in autumn by the number of territorial birds. Non-territorial birds are effectively excluded because winter mortality falls mostly on the non-territorial individuals (Figure 10.1a) or because some of the territorial individuals die and are replaced by non- territorial individuals (Figure 10.1b). Either way the number of territorial individuals determines the spring population and the number of territories established is always less than the potential number of recruits.

Spacing behaviour is also believed to operate in other situations[1] when spacing behaviour could limit numbers in autumn but spring numbers are lower than the number of territorial birds in autumn (Figure 10.2). This could occur because additional mortality has fallen on territorial birds. One explanation for this is that

spacing behaviour changes during the winter months so a bird that was territorial in autumn becomes non-territorial in winter and thus reduces further the potential size of the breeding population. Alternatively, it could be because predation causes additional mortality. The argument put forward[1] is that spacing behaviour is limiting in autumn and may act in combination with predation, so that both become limiting. We consider that such a system cannot be proven because it is practically impossible to test a hypothesis which effectively states that spacing behaviour will operate under all circumstances.

Within the framework of this Report we use the simple definitions shown diagrammatically in Figure 10.1. In this respect, if spring numbers of breeding birds are

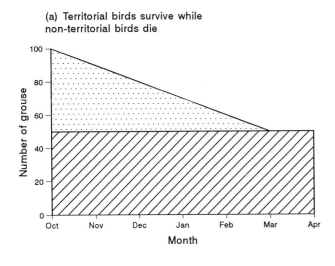

(a) Territorial birds survive while non-territorial birds die

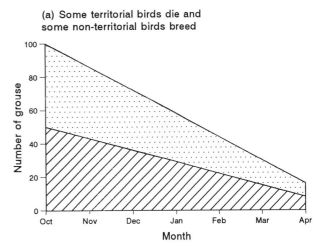

(a) Some territorial birds die and some non-territorial birds breed

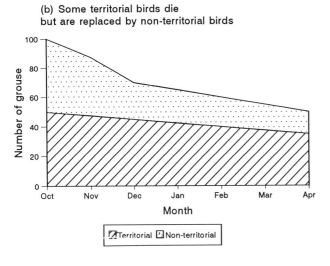

(b) Some territorial birds die but are replaced by non-territorial birds

Territorial  Non-territorial

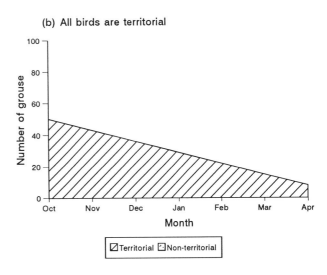

(b) All birds are territorial

Territorial  Non-territorial

Figure 10.1. Schematic representation of the spacing behaviour hypothesis. Autumn population contains both territorial and non-territorial birds, spring density is determined by the number of territorial birds in autumn. (a) All non-territorial birds die during winter while all territorial birds survive. (b) Some of the territorial birds die but are replaced by non-territorial birds so spring density is determined by number of birds in autumn.

Figure 10.2. Schematic representation of two systems in which spacing behaviour may be influencing spring density but is not limiting. The autumn population contains territorial birds but a proportion of these are lost and not totally replaced by non-territorial birds. (a) Both territorial birds and non-territorial birds die. (b) All birds are territorial and some die. Note that for spacing behaviour to influence spring density the number of territorial birds must be equal or lower than the number of autumn territorial birds.

greater than the number of territorial birds identified in autumn, then spacing behaviour is not determining density. If numbers in spring are less than territorial birds in autumn, then spacing behaviour is unlikely to be having a major effect in limiting the population, although this should be considered in combination with the seasonal pattern of mortality.

If we could find differences in the survival of territorial and non-territorial individuals within the population, this would support the spacing behaviour hypothesis and suggest that the mechanism of spacing behaviour could be limiting density. On the other hand, if the birds are using up all the resources available or leave sufficient space for a territorial pair to establish a territory and subsequently breed, then spacing behaviour is not limiting density.

### 10.3 Extrinsic factors hypothesis

Essentially, the second hypothesis states that losses to the population caused by extrinsic factors such as predation, parasitism, starvation and accidental collisions with fences are an additive mortality that will effectively reduce the size of the population in the subsequent spring. Whereas any losses to the territorial birds in the spacing behaviour mechanism are compensated for by an increase in the survival rate of the remaining birds; in this system any compensation would come about through the movement of birds from other areas. In this respect, density in spring can be less or greater than the autumn territorial density; if it is the same then care should be taken to determine that spacing behaviour is not operating.

The major prediction from this hypothesis is that reductions in extrinsic causes of mortality such as predation and parasitism will result in an increase in the grouse population in the following spring. Similarly, increases in breeding production will result in an overall increase in the size of the subsequent breeding population, although this will also be influenced by overall breeding density and the movement of birds from areas of high density to areas of low density. Note that in this case territorial behaviour may not limit density unless resources such as food or nesting sites were themselves limiting.

This hypothesis could be refuted if losses to extrinsic factors have no relationship with actual changes in the population. A reduction in losses through predator control or parasite removal would have no effect on the population. Other features of these hypotheses are discussed in later chapters.

### 10.4 Summary

Two possible mechanisms that could influence changes in grouse numbers are described. Firstly that year to year changes are caused by changes in the social behaviour of the grouse and secondly that year to year changes are caused by extrinsic factors, in particular the effects of predation and disease.

If spacing behaviour operates, then part of the population does not breed as a consequence of the territorial behaviour of more dominant individuals. In red grouse, territorial behaviour may determine the number of grouse that subsequently survive and breed in the following spring. However, spacing behaviour could only be limiting populations if numbers in spring are not greater than numbers of territorial birds in autumn. If predation and parasitism cause changes in numbers, then reducing the levels of parasites or reducing the predaion rate should result in an increase in the grouse population.

### 10.5 References

1. Watson, A. & Moss, R. (1990). Spacing behaviour and winter loss in red grouse. In: *Red grouse population processes.* Eds A.N. Lance and J.H. Lawton. BES and RSPB. pp 35-52.

# CHAPTER 11

# PATTERNS OF RED GROUSE MORTALITY

**Predation was the major cause of death of full grown grouse although the relative importance of predator species and other causes of death varied between areas and during the year. Higher levels of mortality occurred in autumn and spring and mortality was invariably higher in Scotland than England. Predators did not take the weaker individuals from low density populations.**

## 11.1 Introduction

One advantage of studying birds as large as red grouse is that it is often possible to find corpses and in many instances record the cause of death. Obtaining such information provides knowledge of the factors that ultimately caused death but does not necessarily reveal the factors that predisposed the individual to that death. As an example, consider an individual grouse suffering from a heavy burden of parasites; such infection may well weaken the grouse and thus make it vulnerable to predation. When the corpse is retrieved, predation is determined as the ultimate cause of death, but the parasites made the grouse weak in the first instance and the parasites should be considered the predisposing cause of death.

This chapter examines the ultimate causes of mortality of grouse collected from a number of study areas and explores the condition of the grouse to determine whether predators selectively killed the weaker grouse from the population. Such a finding has important consequences for understanding the role of predators in influencing grouse populations. If predators take only weak individuals which are going to die anyway they are unlikely to be having any effect on the population, whereas predators taking healthy birds that were potential breeders may be having a significant effect on population size and subsequent bag levels.

## 11.2 Essential methods

Corpses of dead red grouse were retrieved from Scottish and English populations. Details were collected from every corpse found during routine field work on grouse moors throughout the country. Such information provided an overall description of causes of death and variations between regions. Standardised searches were also conducted on a total of 13 one kilometre square study areas (six in Scotland and seven in northern England, Figure 11.1) in the same week of each month to provide details of monthly and seasonal patterns of mortality.

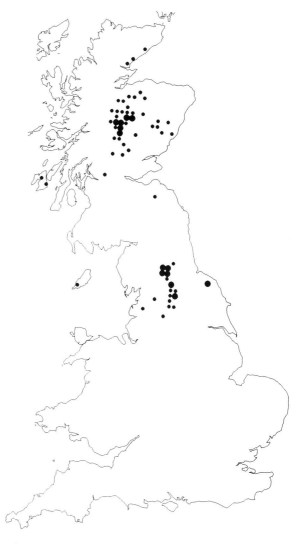

Figure 11.1. Location of 13 main study areas where corpses were collected from one square kilometre sites each month (large dots) and the location of 49 other grouse moors from which corpses were also collected (small dots).

Detailed information on factors associated with the death of each grouse was collected when the body was located on the hill and further information was gathered from subsequent analysis conducted in the laboratory. Details included information on age (determined usually from feathers), sex and, where possible weight of chest muscles. The cause of death was classified as either associated with predation, collision with a fence or other obstacle, or simply 'found dead'. Grouse placed in the found dead category were further classified as being killed by parasites if they appeared emaciated and carried high worm burdens. Some birds were simply classified 'found dead' when no obvious cause of death could be determined.

Those that appeared to be predator kills were classified further (wherever possible) as either a kill by a mammal or a raptor, with the accuracy ranked on a subjective scale from 1 to 5 (Table 11.1). Further classification to level of predator species that killed the grouse was also made when possible and once again the accuracy of this ranked on the 1-5 scale. Other information was collected, including the type and height of vegetation and notes on how the prey had been eaten (e.g. head present, breastbone notched etc).

**Table 11.1** Accuracy rankings used to determine first the type of predator (Mammal or Raptor) and second the species of predator.

| Rank Scale | Observation |
| --- | --- |
| 1 | Predator inferred as a possible predator type |
| 2 | Predator type probable from characteristics of kill |
| 3 | Likely predator determined from way grouse killed or from signs left by predator |
| 4 | Predator type inferred as most probable because of way grouse killed and other signs (e.g. mutes, scats and foot marks) all confirm one predator) |
| 5 | Certain of predator since predator seen to kill |

In the laboratory, analysis was conducted on all corpses that provided sufficient material in reasonable condition. Measurements were taken of various bones, organs and muscles. If all or part of the chest muscles were intact, then both the main muscle used for downward movement of wings in flight (pectoralis major) and the smaller muscle used for raising wings in flight (supracoracoideus) were removed, weighed, dried to constant weight and weighed again. The size of these muscles can provide an accurate measure of the condition of the grouse. Where possible worm counts were

undertaken in the remaining guts and the sex of the bird confirmed from an examination of the gonads.

## 11.3 Corpse examination – a true reflection of mortality?

Examination of corpses recovered from the study areas provides only an indication of the predators and patterns of mortality recorded. Care must be taken in interpreting these data, since they may not reflect true patterns of mortality. For example, raptor kills may be over-represented because raptors tend to pluck the grouse and leave piles of feathers, while a grouse dying from parasites may hide under the heather and not be located. Furthermore, some predators may remove prey from the study areas, particularly when feeding young, while other predators may eat prey at the point where they made the kill.

Tests were undertaken to assess for bias in the methods used for the collection of corpses. A comparison was made between corpses found and the mortality of radio-tagged grouse, where cause of death could be determined for most individuals. The radio-tagged individuals allowed the cause of death to be determined even when the individual did not die on the study area. For example, one radio-tagged grouse was poached from the study area and subsequently recovered from the poacher's house 13 km (8 miles) away. Such a comparative study determined whether the recovery of corpses on site reflected the true patterns of mortality in the population.

The cause of death was determined for a total of 49 radio-tagged grouse whose movements and fate were followed in upper Speyside. All birds used in experiments, birds whose radios were removed before death and birds dying within one month of being fitted with a transmitter were excluded from this analysis. Overall, there were no differences between the cause of death of these radio-tagged grouse and the birds collected from the main study areas in the same area (Figure 11.2[1]).

## 11.4 Regional differences in cause of death

In addition to the corpses retrieved from the 13 main study areas, corpses were also collected from 49 other study areas and grouse moors (Figure 11.1). In total, the remains of 1383 grouse were examined, all collected over five years between January 1986 and January 1991.

Grouse corpses collected in England were more likely to have died from parasites and less likely to have died through a violent death (in collision with fence lines or overhead power cables) than corpses collected in

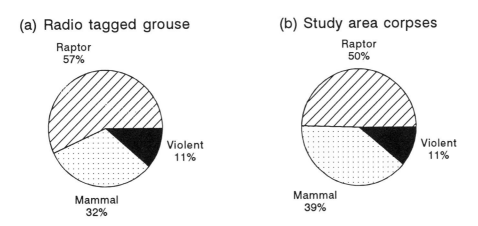

Figure 11.2. The cause of death of 49 radio-tagged grouse compared with the death of 472 corpses collected from the main study areas. There was no difference between the two[a] suggesting that corpses examined were representative of the cause of death in the population studied.

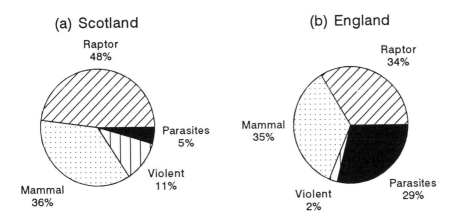

Figure 11.3. Cause of death of grouse corpses collected from study areas in England and Scotland. Predators were more important in Scotland and parasites more important in England[b].

Scotland (Figure 11.3[b]). The higher number of corpses found dead through the effects of parasites in England was probably just a consequence of the higher densities and prevalence of the parasites in England. The high proportion of deaths in Scotland associated with violent causes reflects the greater lengths of wire fences passing across areas of Scottish moorland (deer and stock fences) compared to areas of English moorland where there is little need for deer fences. Grouse on Scottish study areas may also move about more or disperse further.

Peregrines were the principal species of raptor that killed grouse in both England and Scotland. A higher proportion of Scottish grouse were killed by hen harriers and a smaller proportion by short-eared owls (Figure 11.4[c]). This difference was not surprising since harriers were absent from most of northern England while short-eared owls were generally more abundant. Amongst the mammalian predators, foxes were by far and away the most important predators in Scotland,

with relatively few grouse killed by wild-cats or stoats on our study areas. In England, proportionately more grouse were killed by stoats (Figure 11.4[c]). This could be because stoats were more numerous and at higher densities in areas with many grouse (as found in Chapter 5). However, other data (Section 2) suggest that foxes were quite simply less numerous in England so that stoats appear relatively more important.

A more detailed examination of the Scottish data shows that grouse from West Scotland were more likely to have died through raptor predation and violent causes of death, and less likely to have died from mammalian predation, than were grouse in East Scotland (Figure 11.5[c]). From the figures of raptor predation, there was no regional difference in the proportion of kills associated with the various raptor species[e].

Within the whole of Scotland, there was sufficient information from five regions to examine variation between these regions. There were a higher propor-

73

# (a) Raptor predators

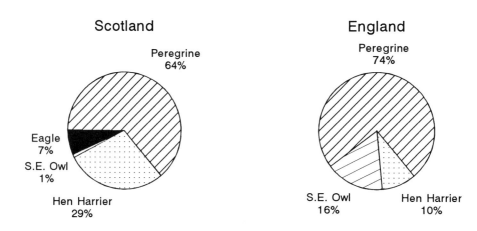

### Scotland

Peregrine
64%

Eagle
7%

S.E. Owl
1%

Hen Harrier
29%

### England

Peregrine
74%

S.E. Owl
16%

Hen Harrier
10%

# (b) Mammal predators

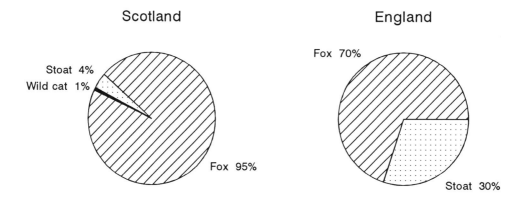

### Scotland

Stoat 4%
Wild cat 1%

Fox 95%

### England

Fox 70%

Stoat 30%

Figure 11.4. Relative importance of raptor species and mammalian predators in Scotland and England. Peregrines were the most important raptor species, although in Scotland more hen harrier kills and fewer short-eared owl kills were recorded. Foxes were the most important mammalian predator and this was significantly greater in Scotland.

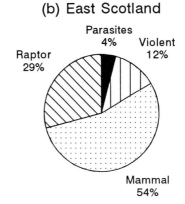

**(a) West Scotland**

Raptor 50%
Parasites 5%
Violent 17%
Mammal 28%

**(b) East Scotland**

Parasites 4%
Violent 12%
Raptor 29%
Mammal 54%

Figure 11.5. Relative importance of cause of death between East and West Scotland. Raptors were relatively more important in West Scotland[d].

tion of mammal kills in Angus and Monadhliath and a higher proportion of violent deaths in Cairngorm (Figure 11.6[f]).

## 11.5 Age and sex related differences in cause of mortality

In both Scotland and England, there were no differences in the cause of mortality between male and female grouse (Figure 11.7[g]). However, in Scotland, immature grouse were more likely to be found killed by violent causes of mortality than mature grouse (Figure 11.8[h]). This could be because immature grouse moved around more during the winter months (Chapter 14) and consequently were more likely to collide with fences and overhead power cables. Mature grouse were not only more sedentary (Chapter 16) but may also be more aware of the dangers within their home range than the inexperienced immature grouse. No such difference was found in the corpses in England presumably because few English grouse were killed by violent accidents.

## 11.6 Seasonal changes in recovery and cause of death

The general pattern of mortality on both Scottish and English study areas is for reduced rates of mortality in the summer between June and August with increased losses during autumn and early spring. There were, however, differences between England and Scotland, with England recording a higher proportion of kills during May and Scotland a higher proportion in the last few months of the year (Figure 11.9[i]). Such differences were associated with the higher number of deaths caused by parasitism on the English study areas.

Overall, the annual patterns of mortality reflected the greater losses during winter and spring and the over-

all importance of winter loss (October – April) as a major factor influencing changes in grouse numbers (Section 3). This is made clearer when the mortality recorded is translated into monthly rates of corpse recovery (Figure 11.10). Not only did the percentage of the population found as corpses increase in autumn and again in spring, but in every month the rate of corpse finding was greater in Scotland than England. In some months, 10 times as many grouse were found dead per live grouse on Scottish than on English study areas.

The relative importance of predators changed during the year. Mammals (mostly foxes) tended to be relatively less important in winter months. The proportion of kills by peregrines remained relatively stable throughout most of the year (Figure 11.11[j]).

## 11.7. Do predators select grouse in poor condition?

Other work (Chapter 31) has shown that parasites tend to weaken grouse and these individuals are more likely to fall victim to a predator. This is hardly surprising since the parasites can weaken grouse to a level where the birds are incapable of sustained flight and become vulnerable to predation; even dogs were capable of catching these heavily infected individuals. However, parasites were not prevalent in low density populations. The very nature of low density populations generally means that parasites are not prevalent and thus unlikely to weaken the grouse. The question we wish to ask is whether, in these low density populations, the predators selectively kill the weaker individuals from the population.

One problem in determining this is knowing the condition of the grouse when the predator made the kill. If the predator left sufficient remains this could be deter-

## (a) Monadhliath

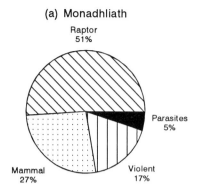

Raptor
51%

Parasites
5%

Violent
17%

Mammal
27%

## (b) Moray

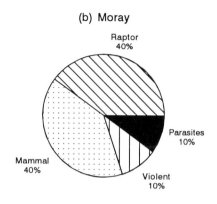

Raptor
40%

Parasites
10%

Violent
10%

Mammal
40%

## (c) Cairngorm

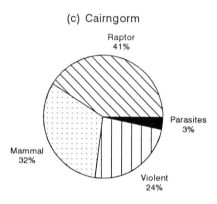

Raptor
41%

Parasites
3%

Violent
24%

Mammal
32%

## (d) Angus

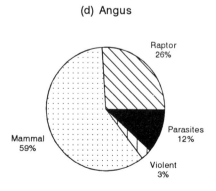

Raptor
26%

Parasites
12%

Violent
3%

Mammal
59%

## (e) Tayside

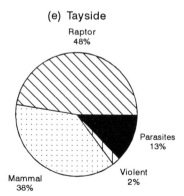

Raptor
48%

Parasites
13%

Violent
2%

Mammal
38%

Figure 11.6. Cause of death in five regions of Scotland.

## (a) Scottish Study Areas

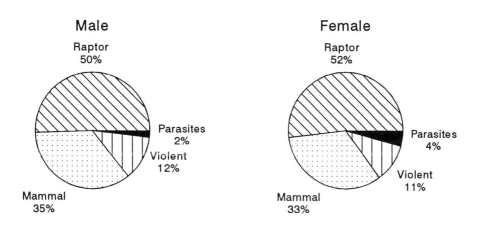

## (b) English Study Areas

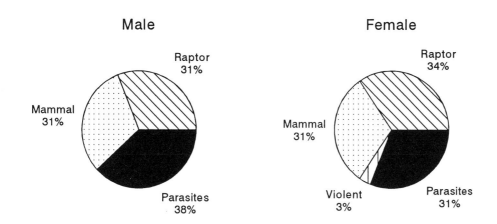

Figure 11.7. The cause of death of male and female grouse in both England and Scotland, identified through an examination of corpses. There was no statistical difference in the cause of death between males and females in either Scottish or English study areas[g].

## (a) Scottish Study Areas

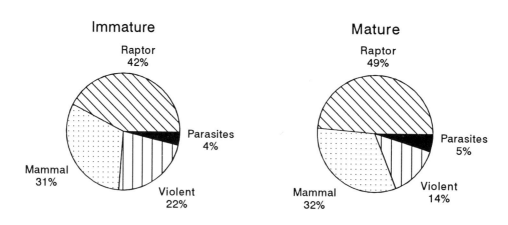

## (b) English Study Areas

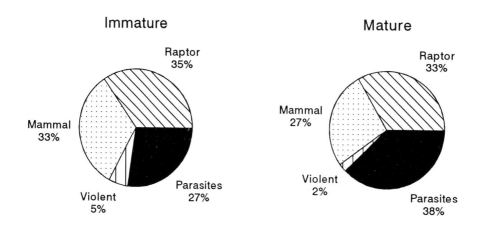

Figure 11.8. Cause of death of immature and mature grouse from English and Scottish study areas. In Scotland, immature grouse were more likely to be killed by violent causes of death, such as deer fences, perhaps because they are less sendentary than mature birds[h].

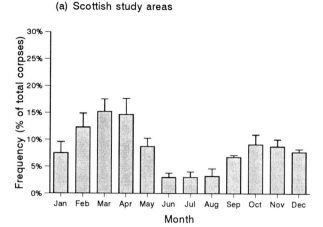

(a) Scottish study areas

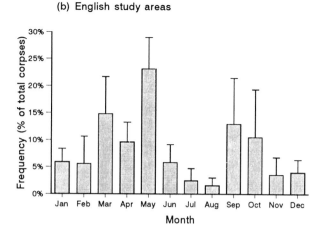

(b) English study areas

Figure 11.9. Pattern of annual mortality expressed as the average percentage of total annual corpses (five years data) recovered in each month from Scottish and English study areas. While there is a general pattern for more corpses to be recovered during the winter and spring months, there were more Scottish birds killed in winter months. The vertical bars are standard error bars and provides an estimate of the error in the estimate of the mean (average).

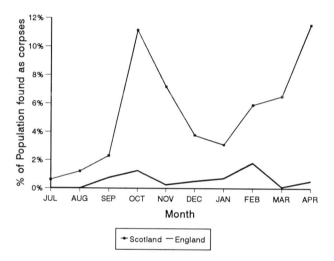

Figure 11.10. Rates of monthly mortality estimated as the percentage of birds found as corpses on the study areas. Figures are an average for five years. Higher rates of mortality were recorded in the autumn and spring and Scottish study areas appeared to suffer a greater mortality. Note that no data exists for the months of May and June; this is because counts cannot be conducted during these months when birds are incubating or have young broods.

killed by predators showed no differences between individuals killed by raptors and mammalian predators or between individuals shot and found dead (Figure 11.13[m]). These results suggest that predators were not selectively killing individuals in poor condition.

## 11.8 Management implications

From this analysis, the importance of foxes as main predators of grouse and the relatively high level of mortality during autumn and early summer is clear. If such mortality influences the grouse population, then fox control must be undertaken throughout the year rather than leaving most fox control until late spring.

mined from the size of the chest muscles because healthy grouse tend to have bigger chest muscles than weak individuals.

Muscle measurements were taken from both female and male grouse but had to be treated separately since females were smaller than males. For a total of 46 males, there were no statistical differences in either the size of the pectoralis muscle or the supracoracoideus muscle of birds that were killed by predators, violent causes or simply found dead (Figure 11.12[k]). Neither were there differences in the size of muscles collected from 29 female grouse that had died from different causes (Figure 11.12[l]). More detailed analysis on males

## (a) Mammal and raptor kills

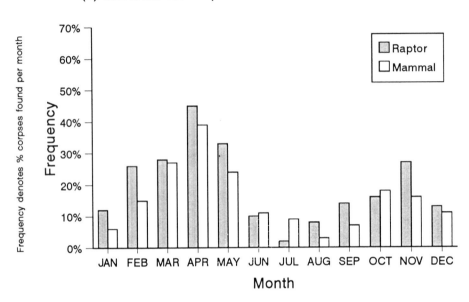

## (b) Predator species

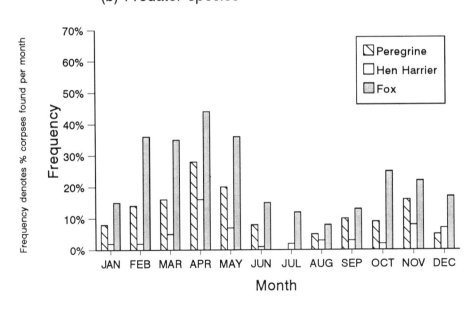

Figure 11.11. Month by month changes in the relative importance of mammalian and raptor species on the number of adult grouse found as corpses on the study area.

Clutch size in grouse varies according to female condition and parasite burdens: average clutch size is about 9 eggs (Chapters 8 and 27).

The net loss of grouse over the winter months is the key factor influencing year to year changes in grouse numbers (Chapter 8). *The Earl Peel*

Grouse killed by a peregrine with head missing and chest muscles partly eaten. Peregrines did not select the weaker or non-territorial individuals from low density grouse populations (Chapter 11).

Grouse after being struck by a peregrine. The proportion of grouse taken by peregrines was greater at low density (Chapter 12).

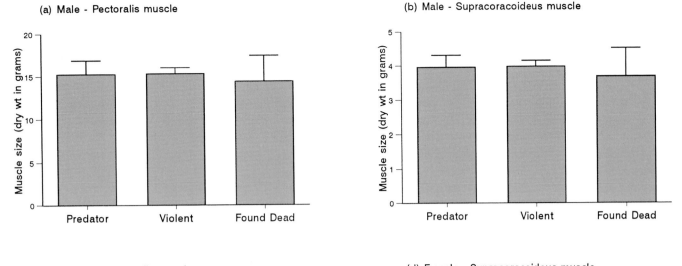

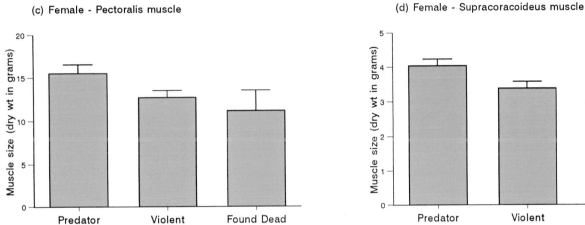

Figure 11.12. Chest muscle weights, a reflection of birds condition, of grouse killed by different causes. Those killed by predators did not have significantly smaller muscles than grouse dying from other causes suggesting that predators did not selectively kill the weak individuals.

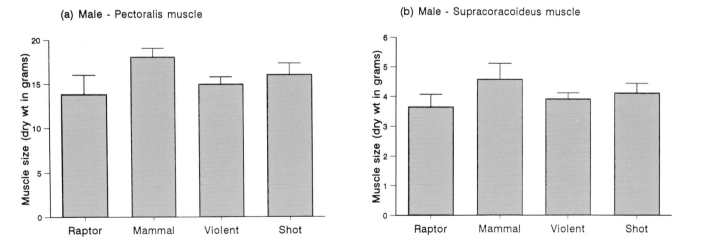

Figure 11.13. Muscles weights of male grouse killed by raptors and mammals: these were not significantly smaller than grouse dying from other causes suggesting neither type of predator were selectively killing the weaker individuals.

## 11.9 Summary

Grouse corpses were collected from study areas throughout England and Scotland. Most grouse had died from predation although in England grouse were more likely to die of parasites and less likely to die from violent causes such as collisions with fences. Foxes were the principal mammal predators although stoats appeared relatively more important in England, probably because there were fewer foxes. Peregrines were the principal raptor species that killed grouse, with relatively more grouse killed by hen harriers and fewer by short-eared owls in Scotland. Within Scotland, foxes appeared to be more important in eastern Scotland, in particular in the Angus and Tayside areas. Young grouse were more likely to die from violent causes of death than mature grouse, probably because they moved more and were not familiar with new areas. The annual pattern of mortality was for higher losses during the winter, although the pattern was different in England, probably because mortality from parasites tended to occur in late spring. Mortality rates were greater in Scotland than England and tended to peak in autumn and spring. From an examination of the flight muscles of grouse, predators did not selectively kill grouse in poor condition.

## 11.10 Notes

a. There was no difference between the cause of death of radio-tagged grouse and grouse collected from the main study area, chi-squared $X^2 = 1.02$ $P = 0.60$ d.f. $= 2$.

b. Cause of death of corpses collected from England and Scotland were significantly different, $X^2 = 111.4$, d.f. $= 3$, $P = 4.5_* 10^{-7}$.

c. There were differences between the relative importance of raptor species between England and Scotland (excluding eagles since these are absent in England), $X^2 = 55.12$, d.f. $= 2$, $P = 1.36_* 10^{-12}$. There were also differences in relative importance of mammalian predators as determined from grouse corpse analysis (excluding wildcats) chi-squared, $X^2 = 39.9$, d.f. $= 1$, $P = 3.4_* 10^{-10}$.

d. Raptors were a more important cause of death in West Scotland and mammals in East Scotland, $X^2 = 84.96$, d.f. $= 3$, $P = 4.49_* 10^{-5}$,

e. No difference was found in the relative proportion killed by different raptor species; $X^2 = 0.86$, d.f. $= 2$, $P = 0.65$

f. There were significant differences between five regions of Scotland and the cause of death, $X^2 = 97.28$, d.f. $= 12$, $P = 1.30_* 10^{-13}$.

g. There were no differences between male and female grouse in Scotland; chi-squared, $X^2 = 3.74$, d.f. $= 3$, $P = 0.291$: or England; chi-squared, $X^2 = 0.29$, d.f. $= 3$, $P = 0.86$.

h. There were differences between immature and mature grouse in Scotland; chi-squared, $X^2 = 9.87$, d.f. $= 3$, $P = 0.02$: England; chi-squared, $X^2 = 1.81$, d.f. $= 3$, $P = 0.61$.

i. There were seasonal variation in kills between England and Scotland, chi-squared; $X^2 = 38.67$, d.f. $= 11$, $P = 5.98_* 10^{-5}$.

j. There were month to month differences in type of predator, chi-squared, $X^2 = 50.4$, d.f. $= 22$, $P = 5.23_* 10^{-4}$

k. Muscle weights of males were not different with respect to cause of death: Pectoralis muscle ANOVA $F = .0627$, d.f.. $= 2,43$, $P = 0.94$; Supracoracoideus muscle $F = 0.107$, d.f. $= 2,43$ $P = 0.90$.

l. Female muscle weights did not vary with cause of mortality: Pectoralis muscle ANOVA $F = 1.377$, d.f.. $= 2,26$, $P = 0.21$; Supracoracoideus muscle $F = 1.27$, d.f. $= 2,26$ $P = 0.30$.

m. No difference was found in muscle weights between males killed by raptors and those killed by mammalian predators: pectoralis, $t = 1.30$, d.f. $= 7$, $P = 0.12$; supracoracoideus, $t = 1.30$, d.f. $= 7$, $P = 0.12$. No difference in muscle weights between males killed by violent causes and those shot: pectoralis, $t = 0.70$, d.f. $= 32$, $P = 0.25$; supracoracoideus, $t = 0.53$, d.f. $= 32$, $P = 0.30$.

# CHAPTER 12

# MORTALITY AND LOSSES AT LOW GROUSE DENSITY

**Count data coupled with corpse analysis show the importance of winter losses to low density grouse populations. Unrecorded losses (probably dispersal) accounted for year to year changes in winter loss, with predation as the major cause of mortality. Unrecorded losses increased with grouse density but mortality through predation decreased with density.**

## 12.1 Introduction

The analysis of grouse corpses collected from the Scottish study areas showed that predation was the principal cause of death. However, this analysis concentrated solely on the birds found dead and did not show the relative importance of these deaths to the total loss of grouse from the population. The final number of individuals remaining on the study area was influenced not only by the known deaths but also by the unrecorded deaths and the net loss of individuals dispersing outside the study area. To examine the relative importance of the known losses and the unrecorded losses, this chapter takes the analysis further by examining the year to year changes in the losses from the Badenoch study areas.

## 12.2 Methods and analysis

This analysis is based on the information gained through the regular counts and corpse searches conducted on six, one kilometre square study areas in Badenoch from 1985 to 1991. These data were analysed using key factor analysis, which effectively looks at the mortality and losses from the grouse population at various stages during the course of the year and then determines which period of loss is associated with the total annual losses from the population. The period of loss (mortality plus net emigration from study area) that explains most of the variation in the year to year changes in total loss is known as the 'key factor' and can be considered the period of loss that causes year to year changes in abundance. This is not necessarily the largest loss but simply the one that varies consistently with year to year changes in total loss. A more detailed description of this method is presented in Chapters 8 and 30.

Five periods of loss were considered:
(i) *Shooting mortality*
(ii) *Winter losses*: from the end of shooting through to the breeding of the birds (October – April) and including mortality and dispersal of birds from the study area.
(iii) *Failure to lay a full clutch*: the clutch size of the birds and how much smaller the clutch was than the maximum clutch size, taken here as 12 eggs per female.
(iv) *Egg mortality*: includes both total losses of eggs and partial losses because eggs failed to hatch.
(v) *Chick losses*: death of chicks from hatching to seven weeks of age.

Note that once again some of these periods are known as periods of mortality when we know that the reduction in the number of animals present is through death, while other periods must be known as 'loss', because the period could include both a reduction in numbers through mortality and through movement from the study area.

The analysis presented in Section 4 included the data from the main Badenoch study areas; some is highlighted again here but this chapter contains a more detailed analysis of winter losses.

## 12.3 Key factors in Badenoch study areas

The analysis of the data for the low density grouse areas can be considered at three levels; first at the level of the six one kilometre square study sites, second at the level of the moor (which is three moorland areas of two square kilometres) and third at the level of the region, where we combine all study areas and consider one large study area of six square kilometres. This analysis concentrates on the level of losses first at the moor level and then at the region level.

At the moor level, winter losses were the key factor that influenced year to year changes in the total losses from Drumochter and Ralia but not at Crubenmore. At Crubenmore, both chick losses and winter losses were of some importance but further data would be needed to assess which was the single most important factor (Table 12.1).

## 12.4. Factors associated with winter loss

Winter loss was the key factor influencing year to year changes in numbers of red grouse on the low density study areas in Badenoch. The next step was to examine this period of loss in more detail. From corpse searches on the main study areas, we have information on the number of deaths known to be due to predation – both by raptors and mammalian predators – so we can examine whether these could account for or were associated with the year to year changes in winter loss. Once again, we use the key factor analysis method but this time concentrate on just the period of winter loss and examine the relative importance of mammalian predation, raptor predation, total predation and the unknown losses. The sex of many of the corpses collected was recorded so we can examine this variation for each sex and the population as a whole.

On both Crubenmore and Ralia, the unknown losses were of prime importance in influencing year to year changes in the winter loss. On Drumochter no one variable was statistically associated with the winter losses, although the combined predation by raptors

and mammals was the variable most closely associated with total losses (Table 12.2).

## 12.5 Patterns of loss in relation to grouse density

In the cases of predation overall, and predation by foxes and peregrines, the proportion of grouse taken from the population was greater at low grouse densities and this was similar for both male and female grouse (Figure 12.1[a], 12.2[b]). In ecological terms, this is known as inverse density dependence and it can have some interesting consequences for the population. In effect it will produce a 'predation trap' whereby grouse at low density could be held at low density by high levels of predation. Once conditions allow the population to increase then the population can escape the predation trap.

The unknown losses were density dependent (Figure 12.1[a], 12.2[b]). Some of these unknown losses could be caused by predation but they may also be due to dispersal away from the study areas. At low density, there was immigration into the study areas. Since these unknown losses increase with density, the general impression was of birds moving away from high density areas into areas of low density where they were killed by predators. This density dependent dispersal would tend to stabilise and regulate red grouse numbers.

Table 12.1 Key losses from Badenoch study areas, winter loss was the key factor at both Drumochter and Ralia while no factors were statistically significant at Crubenmore. The amount of variation in the total loss explained by variation in the key factor (estimated from multiple regression analysis) is presented along with the slope and statistical significance of the relationship. The closer the slope of the relationship to 1 the closer the variables are to explaining the year to year total variation.

| Study Area | Key Factor | Variation Explained | Slope and Significance | |
| --- | --- | --- | --- | --- |
| **Moor Level:** | | | | |
| Crubenmore | Winter Loss | 38% | 0.8 | NS |
| | Chick loss | 71% | 0.9 | NS |
| Drumochter | Winter Loss | 90% | 0.9 | ** |
| Ralia | Winter Loss | 83% | 1.0 | * |
| All three | Winter Loss | 61% | 1.0 | NS |

Significance levels, NS = not statistically significant, stars below show significance with * < 5% probability ** < 2% probabitlity

Table 12.2 Causes of winter loss from Badenoch study areas; overall the unrecorded losses (dispersal) were most important at both Crubenmore and Ralia while no factors were statistically significant at Drumochter. The amount of variation in the winter loss explained by variation in each cause of loss is presented and the statistical significance of the relationship.

| Study Area | Key Factor | Variation explained | Significance |
|---|---|---|---|
| **Moor level** | | | |
| Crubenmore | | | |
| Males | Unrecorded | 86% | * |
| Females | Unrecorded | 85% | * |
| All birds | (Unrecorded) | 77% | NS |
| Druchmochter | | | |
| Males | (Total predation) | 37% | NS |
| Females | (Total predation) | 61% | NS |
| All birds | (Total predation) | 32% | NS |
| Ralia | | | |
| Males | Unrecorded | 98% | ** |
| Females | Unrecorded | 99% | ** |
| All birds | Unrecorded | 99% | ** |

Significance levels, NS = not statistically significant, stars below show significance
with * < 5% probability ** < 2% probabitlity

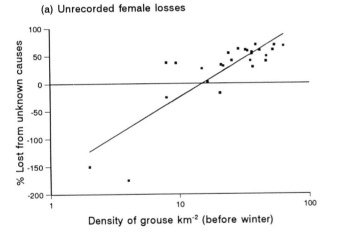

(a) Unrecorded female losses

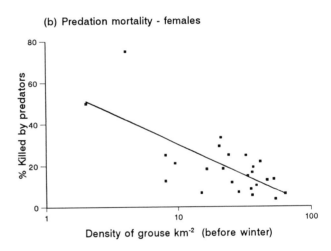

(b) Predation mortality - females

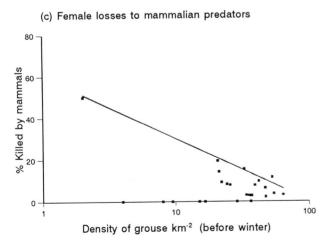

(c) Female losses to mammalian predators

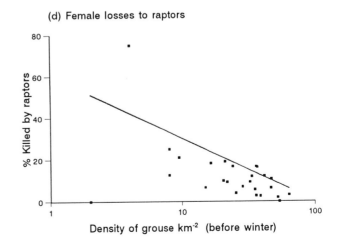

(d) Female losses to raptors

Figure 12.1. Female winter mortality and losses from the grouse population in relation to initial grouse density. For both raptor and mammalian predators the predation rate decreased with an increase in grouse density while unknown losses tended to increase.

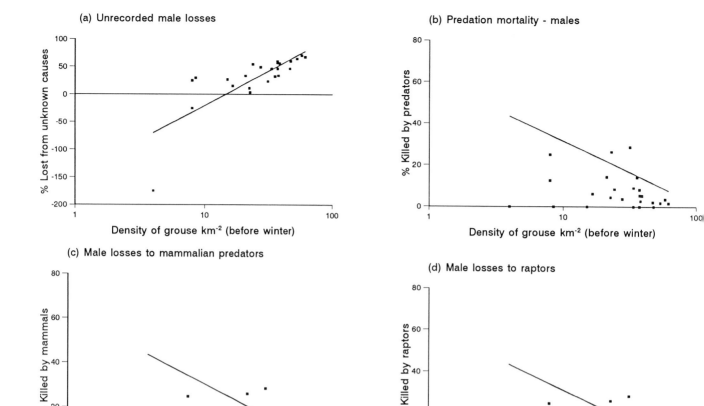

Figure 12.2. Male winter mortality and losses from the grouse population in relation to initial grouse density. As for females, both the raptor and mammalian predation rates decreased with an increase in grouse density, while unrecorded losses (dispersal) tended to increase.

## 12.6 Are they pushed or do they go willingly?

Unrecorded losses, most of which must occur through dispersal, are having an important impact on the low density populations studied in Badenoch. The next stages were to determine whether most of these losses were really occurring through dispersal, and then to determine whether the birds that moved away from the good areas went because the birds in their natal areas excluded them or whether they went of their own accord. The final and important exercise was to decide whether, if predation was absent, the birds would have survived and bred.

## 12.7 Summary

On the low density Badenoch study areas, winter losses were the key factor influencing year to year changes in abundance on two of the three study moors. Winter losses were caused by a combination of raptor, mammalian predation and unrecorded losses. Changes in winter losses were caused by changes in unknown losses from year to year rather than by year to year changes in the level of predation on the study areas. Rates of predation decreased as the density of grouse increased, while dispersal rates increased with densities of grouse. The interaction between these two variables will be assessed later.

## 12.8 Notes

a. The relationships between female mortality and losses versus density: unrecorded losses $r=0.84$, $P<0.001$, d.f.= 24; Predation $r=-0.68$, $P<0.001$, t.v.. = 24; Mammal kills $r=-0.44$, $P<0.05$, d.f.=24; Raptor kills $r=-0.48$, $P<0.02$, d.f.=24.

b. The relationships between male mortality and losses versus density: unknown losses $r=0.84$, $P<0.001$, d.f.=23; Predation $r=-0.57$, $P<0.01$, d.f.=23; Mammal kills $r=-0.17$, $P=$ NS, d.f.=23; Raptor kills $r=0.54$, $P<0.02$, d.f=23.

# CHANGES IN THE SEX RATIO OF GROUSE POPULATIONS

**Populations of breeding grouse generally had more cocks than hens. This bias was greater when grouse densities were low and occurred due to proportionately greater loss of females during the winter months.**

## 13.1 Introduction

In general terms, the male to female sex ratio of most monogamous bird species is equal, with similar numbers of males and females in the breeding population. Variations from this are of interest since the absence of one sex may limit the number of breeding pairs or result in polygamous behaviour where one individual may have two mates. Although detailed studies of sex ratio at hatching have not been undertaken for red grouse, the overwhelming evidence from most bird species is that sex ratio at hatching is equal[1]. Nevertheless, variations in sex ratio after hatching are frequently recorded as a consequence of differential survival or dispersal between the two sexes at some stage during their life.

## 13.2 Methods

The numbers of males and females within the population were counted in summer and spring on study areas. In spring, sex ratio was determined by identifying the sex of every bird flushed on the study area; in summer, sexes of adult birds were identified but the sex ratio of young birds was taken as 1:1.

The sex ratio within a population can be presented as straight sex ratio (number of males divided by number of females) or percentage of males within the population. Such methods incorporate a number of inherent biases and data need to be corrected for statistical reasons and to allow a fair comparison. In this study, sex ratios are presented as percentage males but corrected using an arcsine transformation so that actual figures are not percentages but degrees which range from 0 degrees to 90 degrees with equal sex ratio at 45 degrees.

## 13.3 Changes in sex ratio with density

Overall, the sex ratio of grouse in spring favoured males. From a total 407 counts, 64% had more males, 21% females and 15% were of equal sex ratio[a]. In July, with both young and mature birds combined, the sex ratio favoured females. From a total of 447 July counts, 38% had more males, 48% females and the remaining 13% were of equal sex ratio[b].

From the spring count data, there was an overall tendency for the proportion of males in the population to be greater at low density than high density (Figure 13.1[c]). This relationship held even when counts which included less than 30 individuals were excluded from the analysis[c] (most of which were from low density areas).

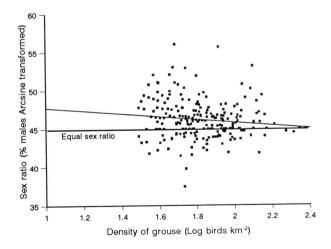

13.1 Sex ratio in relation to density showing a preponderance of males at low density. Sex ratio is shown as percentages, transformed to arcsines where 45 degrees represents an equal ratio of males and females.

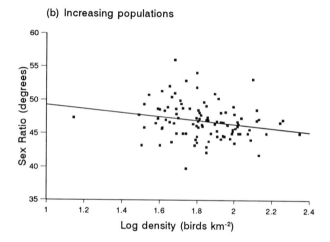

**(a) Declining populations**

*Sex Ratio (degrees)* vs *Log spring density (birds km⁻²)*

**(b) Increasing populations**

*Sex Ratio (degrees)* vs *Log density (birds km⁻²)*

13.2 Changes in sex ratio in relation to density of grouse in increasing and decreasing populations. There is no significant difference between the two figures, implying that sex ratio is a function of density rather than pattern of change in the grouse population.

During a detailed population study of grouse at Kerloch[2], a change in sex ratio was observed during two population fluctuations in which the sex ratio favoured males predominantly during the period of

decline but not when the population increased. To determine whether such a relationship occurred in other grouse populations, sex ratios in the spring breeding populations were compared in populations which were increasing and in those that were decreasing. In both cases there was a decrease in sex ratio with density, with a greater proportion of males at low density and a more equal sex ratio at high density. There was no difference between increasing and decreasing populations[d].

### 13.4 Cause of sex ratio change due to winter loss

Changes in sex ratio were determined from series of population data from spring to summer and also from summer to following spring. Between autumn and spring, 41% of the data sets became male biased while only 10% became female biased[e]. Between spring and summer, the opposite was the case and 42% of populations reverted from an adult male bias to an adult female bias whereas only 10% changed from female to male biased populations[e]. Hence, the sex ratio bias observed in the spring is the result of loss of birds during the winter months rather than a consequence of summer loss carried over to the following spring.

### 13.5 Summary

The male biased sex ratio observed in breeding grouse populations was a function of grouse density, with low density grouse populations containing proportionately more males in the population. There was no difference in this pattern when sex ratios of increasing and decreasing populations were examined and a biased sex ratio was the result of the loss of females during the winter months (April-October). This could be the result of differential survival or dispersal of these females. During the summer months populations reverted from a male bias to a female biased population.

### 13.6 Notes

a. Sex ratio favoured males during the breeding season, binomial test, $z = 19.6$, $P < 0.0001$.

b. Sex ratio favoured females in summer, binomial test $z = 19.6$, $P < 0.0001$

c. There was a decrease in sex ratio with density, $r = 0.268$, $P < 0.001$, d.f. $= 410$. Excluding counts with less than 30 individuals this is still significant, $r = 0.2$, $P < 0.002$, d.f. $= 285$.

d. There was a decrease in sex ratio with density in both declining and increasing populations. Declining populations $r = 0.238$, $P < 0.01$, slope $= \cdot 2.99$; increasing population $r = 0.272$, $P < 0.002$, slope $= \cdot 2.92$.

e. Change from autumn to spring shows a change in favour of males, McNemar Significance of change $X^2 = 26.8$, $P < 0.001$, and in summer in favour of females, $X^2 = 45.84$, $P < 0.001$.

### 13.7 References:

1. Clutton Brock, T.H. (1986) Sex ratio variation in birds. *Ibis* **128**: 317-329.

2. Watson, A., Moss, R., Rothery, P. & Parr, R. 1984. Demographic causes and predictive models of population fluctuations in red grouse. *Journal of Animal Ecology* **53**, 639-662.

# CHAPTER 14

# DISPERSAL PATTERNS OF YOUNG GROUSE FROM LOW DENSITY POPULATIONS

**Immature grouse dispersed from their natal area during autumn and early winter, females travelled further than males. Survival and subsequent breeding success were not different between dispersing and non-dispersing individuals.**

## 14.1 Introduction

Winter losses were an important factor influencing year to year changes in numbers of red grouse from the low density study areas in Badenoch. However, we could not find a sufficient number of corpses to account for these winter losses nor were changes in the number of corpses found associated with changes in the total winter losses. One explanation is that unrecorded losses could be caused partly or even wholly by the dispersal of birds away from the study area. This component of population studies is frequently difficult to assess, since when an individual disappears from the study area it is never clear whether the bird has moved to another area, or has died and simply not been recorded.

Observations on low density populations showed that in some years birds moved into the low density areas, so at least part of these unrecorded losses were caused by dispersal of some kind. This chapter examines the pattern of dispersal in immature grouse from the area in which they were caught as chicks to their final breeding site (natal dispersal). The aim is to determine how important dispersal was in this unrecorded loss and whether the individuals that dispersed bred successfully or were excluded from the breeding population.

In Chapter 13, we recorded the presence of a biased sex ratio in favour of cocks in most low density populations. This could have arisen for a number of reasons depending on patterns of dispersal, survival and relative density of hens. All this should become clearer by the examination of individual radio-tagged grouse.

## 14.2 Methods

Most intensive studies on the dispersal of immature grouse were undertaken on the main study areas at Drumochter and Ralia. Immature grouse were located in early July using trained pointers. The broods were then flushed and individuals carefully watched until they landed and ran to cover. These individuals were rapidly relocated using the dogs and were subsequently caught in a large net. Each grouse was fitted with a neck-mounted radio collar produced by Biotrak Ltd. Grouse were then tracked throughout the following winter on foot using a three-element hand-held yagi antenna and a Televilt receiver. All were followed to their death and corpses recovered to confirm sex and if possible the cause of death.

The location of individuals was determined once a week during the 1988/1989 and 1990/1991 winters and twice a week during the 1989/1990 winter. Each location is referred to as a radio fix. Radio-tagged birds were not usually disturbed during radio-tracking although we did flush birds at regular intervals to determine sex and whether the bird was paired. Each location was plotted on a 1:1250 Ordnance Survey map in the field, the grid reference was taken and later transferred to master maps back in the laboratory. Mortality of male and female grouse was determined during the winter months by calculating weekly survival rates[1] using accepted methods[2].

During the three winters, 53 immature grouse were radio-tracked from their natal areas, 26 were identified as males and 17 as females. The lower proportion identified as females was probably not because of differences in the sex ratio within the population but because males were more likely to be positively identified by their call. Possibly, the 10 unidentified individuals were females.

## 14.3 Methods used in the estimation of home range

By regularly recording the location of individual grouse, it is possible to estimate the area utilised by an individual during its normal activities. This is known usually as the home range. Within this study we are interested in the home range of grouse, in particular immature birds, from July through to subsequent nesting. The area of the home range need not be the same as the area of the territory because during winter months the home range for a young male might include locations of the individual within the father's territory, movement from the father's territory and then locations within the young male's own territory.

The simplest method of estimating home range is to join the outer radio fixes together and measure the area encompassed (simple minimum convex polygon) but such a method is greatly influenced by the occasional long distance movement of individuals, hence it incorporates areas never used by the individual. Furthermore, this technique fails to take into account the relative use of the home range, so that one radio fix, a long distance from the centre of the home range, would greatly increase the area of the home range and be more important than 30 radio fixes in the centre. To avoid such problems, a number of more sophisticated probability techniques have been developed[2,3], two of which were used in this study: the harmonic mean method and the cluster analysis. Both were calculated using the computer programme RANGES (ITE Furzebrooke).

The harmonic mean method has the advantages of providing an accurate calculation of the centres of activity and estimating contours of range use (known as isopleths). Hence this method allows not only an estimate of the size of the home range but also produces a contour map of range use and thus determines the size of the home range for, say, 25%, 50% and 95% of range use. The second technique, known as cluster analysis, determines whether the radio-fixes are in groups or clusters and thus can be used to estimate the number of core areas an individual utilises and so determine if some individuals are concentrating on a single area or moving between two or three core areas. The advantage over the harmonic mean method is that clusters are treated independently and not pulled together with contours covering areas not regularly used.

The size of the home range will be influenced not only by biological samples but also by the number of radio fixes recorded. The more radio-fixes, the more accurate the home range estimate will be, and there will be a minimum number of radio-fixes needed to determine home range size. The harmonic mean method was used to estimate home range size (at the 95% use contour) with an increasing number of radio fixes. This method was used for both male and female grouse

separately by plotting home range area against number of radio fixes. Home range size increased with the number of radio-fixes but reached a constant size when the number of radio fixes was between 20 to 30 fixes. For this reason, the area of home range could only be estimated for individuals for which more than 20 fixes had been obtained.

## 14.4 Core areas and number of core areas

Grouse, like many animals, do not use their home range in a uniform manner but tend to concentrate their activities in preferred areas. These, referred to as core areas, often provide a more accurate measure of the ground utilized. One method of identifying the core area is to plot the contours of range use against the calculated size of the home range. If one part of the total home range is used uniformly as a core area, this area will remain relatively constant with increasing contours of home range use. Once the animal starts making long distance forays away from the core area then the home range size will increase. The size of the home range in both male and female grouse remains relatively constant up to the 85% contour, above which there is an obvious increase in the size of the home range (Figure 14.1). Hence, the 85% contour was used as an estimate of the core area of the home range.

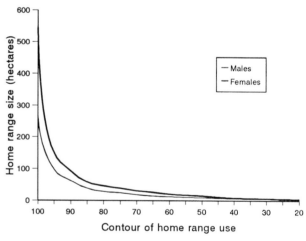

14.1. Change in size of home range with decreasing contours of range use. When range use exceeds the 85% contour the size of the home range increases in both male and female grouse, indicating that the 85% contour is equivalent to the size of the core home range.

Core areas of females were larger than those of males for the 85% isopleth and this difference was statistically significant from the 85% down to the 50% isopleth[a]. This suggests that females have more core ranges and hence move from one area to the next, whereas males are relatively sedentary. For home range sizes at the 95% value, there was no significant difference between females and males[b]. This lack of difference at the higher

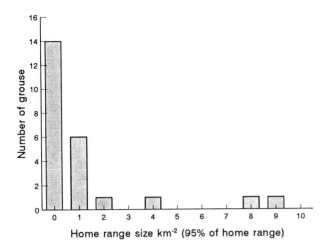

14.2. Home range size of male grouse on Drumochter. Most males have a home range of less than 1km² although a few individuals have ranges in excess of 4km².

values was a consequence of large variation between individual males rather than females. Some males undertook long distance forays with home ranges exceeding 100 hectares (250 acres) and one individual had a home range over 500 hectares (1250 acres). Two others were highly sedentary and had home ranges of less than 10 hectares (25 acres) (Figure 14.2ᶜ).

Females had a greater number of nuclei within their home range than males at the values of 95% and 100% of home range size but were not different at lower values (Figure 14.3). This conforms with the previous conclusion that males are relatively sedentary and that females may tend to disperse from one area and become established in a second area.

## 14.5 Patterns of movement

The natal dispersal distance (distance from place of birth to first breeding location) was less than 1km for all males

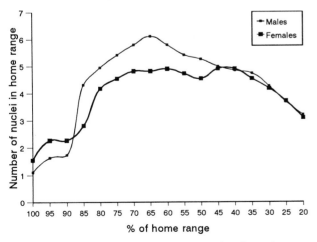

14.3. Number of nuclei in home ranges of male and female grouse. At the low levels of home range the males appear to have more nuclei than females, but this is not statistically significant; at 95% and 100% of home range size, females do have more nuclei than males.

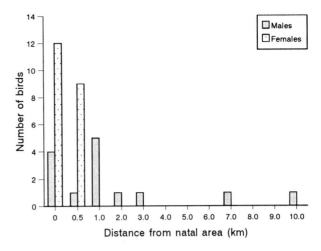

14.4. Distance moved by male and female grouse from their natal area to the point of breeding. Males are highly sedentary, not moving more than one kilometre while females will move more than 10km.

but was greater for females. One female bred more than 10 kilometres (6 miles) from the point of capture (Figure 14.4).

Much movement occurred between the beginning of August and December (Figure 14.5), particularly for the females which tended to move greater distances. After December, the average distance from the natal area remained relatively constant as females tended to remain at what became their new breeding ground.

Table 14.1. Survival of male and female immature grouse on Drumochter. There are no differences in survival although females move further than males.

| | Females | Males | Significance |
|---|---|---|---|
| **Weekly Survival Rates:** | | | |
| Mean | 0.9829 | 0.9840 | NS |
| Standard deviation | ±0.0449 | ±0.0333 | |
| Sample size | 45 | 45 | |
| **Interfix Distance (Log $_{10}$):** | | | |
| Mean | 281.6 | 586.90 | 0.004 |
| Standard deviation | .0.29 | .0.14 | * |
| Sample size | 17 | 8 | – |

## 14.6 Costs of dispersing

From the pattern of grouse dispersal, it is clear that females moved more than males and that by the beginning of December most dispersal had taken place. Deciding which individuals can be considered to be dispersing birds and which are not will ultimately rely on some kind of arbitrary decision. A number of different definitions can be used, we consider three:

1. A dispersing grouse is an individual that has moved more than 500 metres from its natal area by 1 December. Using this definition, there was no difference in the survival of dispersing and non-dispersing individuals

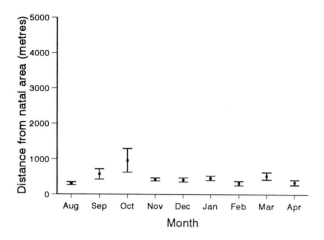

### (a) Immature male movement

### (b) Immature female movement

14.5. Monthly distance moved from natal area of male and female grouse (mean ± 1 standard error shown). Note that females move further than males and that most movement is complete by the beginning of December.

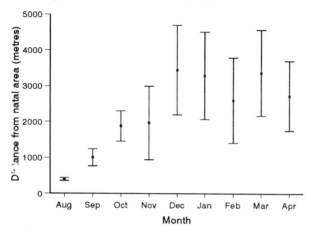

(Table 14.2). Even if we just consider the males, then there was still no significant difference in survival.

Table 14.2. Survival of dispersing and non-dispersing grouse according to a series of different definitions Figure shown means ± 1 standard error.

| Dispersal | Weekly survival rate | Annual survival rate |
|---|---|---|
| All birds by 1 Dec | | |
| <500m | 98.2% ± 0.1% | 38.9% |
| >500m | 98.3% ± 0.1% | 41.0% |
| Males only by Dec 1 | | |
| <500m | 98.4% ± 0.1% | 43.2% |
| >500m | 98.6% ± 0.1% | 48.0% |
| All birds by 1 Dec | | |
| <1km | 98.2% ± 0.1% | 38.9% |
| >1km | 98.6% ± 0.1% | 48.0% |
| All birds at all times after 1 Sept | | |
| <1km | 97.8% ± 0.1% | 31.4% |
| >1km | 97.7% ± 0.1% | 29.8% |

2. A dispersing grouse is an individual that has moved more than one kilometre from its natal area by 1 December. Using this definition there was still no significant difference in the birds' survival rate (Table 14.2).

3. A dispersing grouse is an individual that has moved more than one kilometre from its natal area at any time after 1 September. Once again there is no significant difference (Table 14.2).

We found that dispersal did not tend to increase the mortality of individuals.

There could be advantages or disadvantages to dispersing. Obtaining details of breeding success from all the birds that subsequently bred was not simple, since by the following summer the batteries on the radio transmitters were reaching the end of their normal life. Of the birds whose radios did continue (both cocks and hens) there was no significant difference in breeding success between those birds that dispersed more than 1 km and those that moved less than 1 km from their natal breeding area (Table 14.3). In terms of subsequent breeding success there were no short term benefits of dispersing.

Table 14.3 Brood sizes of dispersing and sedentary grouse

| | Moved <1 km | Moved <1 km |
|---|---|---|
| Brood size | 4.37 ± 1.21 | 5.25 ± 0.48 |
| Sample size | 8 | 4 |

### 14.7 Mortality of female and male grouse

There were no significant differences in the weekly survival rates of male and female grouse on the Drumochter study areas (Table 14.4)[d].

Table 14.4 Overall survival of male and female immature grouse from Drumochter and Ralia study areas combined.

| | Male | Female |
|---|---|---|
| Weekly survival | 0.975 ± 0.001 | 0.972 ± 0.001 |
| Annual survival | 26.8% | 22.8 |

The corpses of radio-tracked immature birds did not provide sufficient data for a rigorous analysis of the cause of death, although all died from either predation or collision with fences. On the main study area, corpses were collected and the cause of death determined as either due to mammalian predators, raptors or other causes (e.g. fence strike). In a comparison where both corpse age and sex could be identified, there was no significant difference between the cause of death of young males and females or between old and young grouse (see Chapter 11).

### (a) Radio tagged grouse

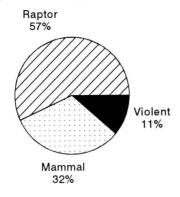

Raptor
57%

Violent
11%

Mammal
32%

### (b) Study area corpses

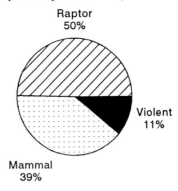

Raptor
50%

Violent
11%

Mammal
39%

14.6. Cause of death in radio-tagged immature grouse and birds found dead on Drumochter study area.

## 14.8 Differences between Ralia and Drumochter

From the preliminary analysis of the data from Drumochter, it is apparent that males had smaller home ranges than females and tended to move less. Within the Badenoch area, the two populations were an interesting contrast because Drumochter was at a relatively high density and according to the analysis of the corpse data presented in Chapter 12 should show greater dispersal than Ralia.

Analysis of the radio-tracking data showed that amongst the immature birds, females on Ralia moved significantly less than females on Drumochter[e], although there were insufficient data from these study areas to analyse for male movement and survival (Table 14.5)

Table 14.5 Differences in the survival and dispersal of grouse from Drumochter and Ralia. NS = not significant.

|  | Drumochter High Density | Ralia Low Density | Significance |
|---|---|---|---|
| **Survival** |  |  |  |
| Weekly survival | 97.4% | 98.1% | NS |
| Annual survival | 25.4% | 36.9% |  |
| **Female Dispersal** |  |  |  |
| Distance (metres) | 2929 | 814 | P<0.05 |
| Percentage <1km | 0% | 84% | P<0.01 |
| N | 6 | 19 |  |

## 14.9 Losses from study areas

From a total of 45 radio-tagged individuals on the Drumochter study area, 58% moved 500 metres or more from their natal area to die or breed. This represents a coarse measure of the individuals which left the study area and compares with the average winter 'unrecorded loss' from the Drumochter study area of 51.4%. The study of the radio-tagged grouse suggests that most of the unrecorded losses were due to dispersal of birds.

## 14.10 Synthesis

Immature female grouse dispersed from their natal areas and the distance moved and proportion of individuals undertaking this dispersal increased with density. A similar movement may occur in males but at a lower rate. Dispersing individuals did not incur a higher mortality rate or a lower breeding rate. Females probably spaced themselves out, moving from high density areas to low density areas, which may reduce the chances of density dependent losses during the nesting season. We know from the analysis of data from high density grouse moors in England (Section 7) that breeding production was dependent on density (the delayed density dependent effects of parasites). Under natural conditions with no form of predator control during the breeding season, predation rates of both crows and foxes would increase with grouse density. Studies in Ireland where there are low management inputs have found evidence that nesting success was density dependent[4] as in partridges[5] and other gamebirds.

Males were relatively sedentary during the winter and spring months and consequently may appear to set breeding density, although females are invariably the limiting sex (Chapter 13) so that actual breeding density is determined by the proportion of females that settle. The proportion of females present is density dependent.

## 14.11 Summary

Female grouse had larger home ranges, tended to move further and to have more centres of activity than males, although from this initial work the movement did not influence survival or breeding production. No females in the high density population moved less than 1km from their natal area, whereas all the females in the low density population moved less than 1km. Overall, losses detected by radio-tracking studies account for the losses from the population, suggesting that the unknown losses were principally due to dispersal away from the study areas. Females may be dispersing to avoid density dependent predation losses during the breeding season.

## 14.12 Notes

a. Differences between home range size of males and females tested using t test at each increment of 5% home range size; t test, $P<0.05$.

b. Home range size of males and females was not significantly different at the 95% contour larger for females; t test $t=1.066$, $P=0.15$.

c. At the 95% isopleth the coefficient of variation in males $=0.68$ and in females $=0.48$.

d. There was no significant difference in the survival rate of male and female immature grouse on Drumochter, Wilcoxson matched pair sign test $T=123$, $N=23$, $N.S.$

e. Female grouse on Ralia tended to move less than females on Drumochter; Mann Whitney $U=10$, $P<0.05$.

## 14.13 References

1. Trent, T.T. & Rongstad, O.J. (1974). Home range and survival of cottontail rabbits in southwestern Wisconsin. *Journal of Wildlife Management* **38**, 459-472.

2. Kenward R. E. (1987). *Wildlife Radio Tagging: Equipment, Field techniques and data analysis.* Academic Press, London.

3. Harries, S., Cresswell, W.J., Forde, P.G., Trewhella, W.J., Wollard, T. & Ray, S. (1990). Home range analysis using radio-tracking data – a review of problems and techniques particularly as applied to the study of mammals. *Mammal Review,* **20**, 97-123.

4. Bergerud, A.T. & Gratson, M.W. (1988). *Adaptive strategies and Population ecology of Northern grouse.* University of Minnesota Press, Minnesota. An analysis of data collected by Watson, A. & P.J. O'Hare 1979 *Journal of Applied Ecology* **16**: 433-452.

5. Potts, G.R. (1986). *The Partridge, pesticides, predation and conservation.* Collins, London.

# CHAPTER 15

# WHY DOES WINTER PREDATION NOT INCREASE WITH GROUSE DENSITY?

**Predators took fewer grouse at high density during winter months. This could be because at high density grouse form into packs and may be more difficult to attack.**

## 15.1 Introduction

Predators usually respond to changes in their prey density by taking a greater proportion of the prey as the prey density increases. This may come about through one or a combination of two mechanisms: first an increasing proportion in the diet of each individual predator and second an increase in the number of predators. The red grouse studied in Badenoch did not show this expected density dependent predation, indeed they took proportionately fewer grouse as the density of grouse increased. This inverse density dependent relationship is intriguing and has interesting repercussions for the dynamics of the grouse population. This chapter discusses this relationship and the mechanisms that could generate it.

## 15.2 Inverse density dependence and changes in predator numbers

The proportional decrease in the number of grouse taken by predators was probably because the predators were taking the same number of grouse irrespective of grouse density. Examination of the relationships shown in Figure 12.1 for the proportion of females taken by predators indicated that the predators consistently took 2.1 female grouse km$^{-2}$, 64% of which were taken by raptors (mostly peregrines) and the remaining 36% by mammals (mostly foxes). A similar rate of loss was seen for the males in Figure 12.2 although the raptors took proportionately more.

The response by the foxes to this change in density may not be surprising when one considers that foxes are heavily controlled on grouse moors. Keepers are trying hard during the winter months to reduce the effects of predation by foxes on grouse and are continually reducing numbers. Any increase in the fox

population is likely to result in an increase in numbers killed by the keepers.

The predation by peregrines, the main raptor predator during the winter months is more interesting. In this case, peregrines may not take more grouse with increasing grouse density because there is no numerical increase by the predators to an increase in grouse density. This seems likely since peregrines are highly territorial and defend their territories during the winter months and against other peregrines that may attempt to establish a territory. This is supported by the evidence presented in Chapter 6 where we found no clear increase in peregrine sightings with grouse density (Figure 6.9). In moorland areas with sufficient food present, peregrine numbers may well be limited by the availability of suitable nesting habitat.

## 15.3 Inverse density dependence and grouse distribution

A further explanation why the predators consistently take the same number of grouse per square kilometre during the winter months may be that the predators do not find it easier to locate and catch at high, as opposed to low, densities. This could be because a specialist predator like the peregrine spends much of its time and energy in chasing, catching and consuming the grouse and not in locating it. Furthermore, if the grouse form into groups or packs at higher density, then the peregrine needs to locate a suitable group to attack and trying to select and catch a single bird from a pack may be more difficult than chasing a single bird.

The packing behaviour of grouse was recorded on each of the six main study areas in Badenoch by counting the number of groups of different sizes during monthly grouse counts. The pattern of dispersion or degree of packing was best measured as the variance-to-mean ratio. The statistical variance in the size of the grouse groups recorded was divided by the average or mean group size; when the variance was larger than the mean the grouse were aggregated; when the variance was the same as the mean the grouse were distributed at random and when less than the mean, the grouse were regularly distributed.

From the grouse counts conducted during the winter months the variance-to-mean ratio for most of the counts was less than one, indicating a regular distribution of grouse in groups – quite simply because the grouse were distributed regularly in pairs on territories. Even so, in three of the four main winter months (November, December and February) the variance-to-mean ratio increased with grouse density, demonstrating that grouse tended to be more aggregated at high densities (Figure 15.1).

While there will be more birds available for the peregrine to attack at high densities and peregrines could find it easier to locate a group of grouse, this increased aggregation could well reduce the hunting success of peregrines. Indeed the increased packing at high densities may be an adaptation by the grouse to avoiding predation by peregrines.

## 15.3 Summary

Proportionately fewer, but numerically similar numbers of grouse were caught by mammalian (foxes) and raptor (peregrine) predators at high grouse densities. For foxes this may simply be because fox numbers are controlled. Two possible mechanisms for the absence of any increase in predation by peregrines are discussed. First, peregrines are highly territorial and appear to be limited by the availability of suitable nesting habitat in moorland areas, so territorial peregrines may prevent any increase in peregrine numbers. Second, at high densities the grouse become more packed so even though peregrines may find it easier to locate grouse, they may find it harder to kill the grouse.

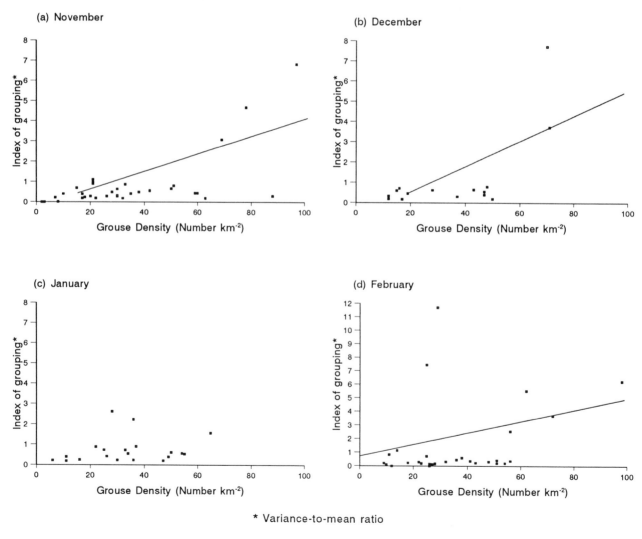

* Variance-to-mean ratio

Figure 15.1. In three of four winter months grouse were more aggregated (as measured by the variance-to-mean ratio) at high grouse densities. This may well reduce the hunting success of peregrines and account in part for the lower proportion of grouse taken by peregrines at high density.

Fox predation on grouse has probably increased in recent years in Scotland as rabbit numbers have recovered after myxomatosis and keeper numbers declined (Chapters 2, 5 and 11). *Game Conservancy*

Grouse frequently form into a pack during the winter months and this packing behaviour may reduce the ability of predators to catch grouse (Chapter 15). *The Earl Peel*

The development of suitable catching techniques for controlling crow numbers has meant that egg losses appear relatively unimportant to changes in grouse numbers. Even so, the results from a natural experiment show clearly the importance of crow control (Chapter 5).

# CHAPTER 16

# DISPERSAL AND HOME RANGE OF ADULT GROUSE DURING WINTER

**While immature females had larger home ranges than immature males, this difference was not found in adult birds. Overall there was no difference between adult males and females in either home range size or survival rate.**

## 16.1 Introduction

The pattern of dispersal in immature birds has been described in Chapter 14. The birds tended to move during late autumn, with immature females moving more than males. This chapter compares information on adult grouse with that on immature grouse to assess whether the survival and home range of adults (defined as birds that are more than a year old) differed from the same features in the immature birds.

## 16.2 Methods

Both adult and immature grouse were caught during autumn by dazzling them at night with a strong quartz halogen lamp. Birds were sexed and aged according to shape of their outer wing feathers and the presence or absence of toe nail scars. Individuals were then fitted with neck mounted radio-transmitters and located weekly during the winter months. The basic techniques are described in more detail in Chapter 14. In this experiment, all birds known to be alive after 1 September were included in the analysis of survival rates.

As with the immature birds, weekly survival rates were estimated and compared between sexes and age cohorts. Home range size was determined for each individual where more than 10 locations had been made using the harmonic mean method.

## 16.3 Survival of adult grouse

There was no statistical difference[a] between the survival of adult and immature birds over winter (Table 16.1).

## 16.4 Home range size of adults and immatures

Mean home range size of adult females did not differ between study areas[b] so data from both Ralia

Table 16.1 Survival of adult and immature red grouse over winter months. Figures show mean weekly and annual survival rates expressed as percentages, together with the standard error.

|  | Weekly Mean | Annual Survival |
|---|---|---|
| Adults | 98.9% ± 0.4% | 65.3% |
| Immature | 98.6% ± 0.3% | 48.0% |

and Drumochter were combined. Unlike the immature grouse, there was no difference between the home range size of adult male and female grouse during winter[c] (Table 16.2). Furthermore there were no differences between the home range size of adult males and immature males or for adult females and immature females.

Table 16.2 Mean home range size (hectares) of adult and immature birds after September 1st.

|  | Males | Females | Sig |
|---|---|---|---|
| *Adults:* |  |  |  |
| Drumochter | 23.5 (2) | 60.6 (4) | NS |
| Ralia | 34.4 (2) | 55.1 (5) | NS |
| Both | 29.0 (4) | 57.5 (9) | NS |
| *Immatures:* |  |  |  |
| Drumochter | 62.9 | 161.5 (17) | P<0.02 |
| Ralia | 76.8 | 55.9 (10) | NS |

## 16.4 Management implications

Many of the early texts on grouse management claim old cocks take larger territories than immature cocks and as a consequence urge the selective killing of old cocks to increase grouse density. This analysis found no evidence of any such difference in the home range size of adult and immature grouse and does not confirm this as a suitable reason for selectively killing old cocks.

There may be alternative reasons for killing old birds, for example, older birds were found to carry significantly greater worm burdens than young birds and could form a significant source of an increase in disease. In such cases selective killing of old birds could be considered beneficial to the population.

## 16.5 Summary

There was no difference between the winter survival of adult and immature grouse. Adult grouse have smaller winter home ranges than immature grouse and unlike immature grouse the adult males and females have similar home range sizes.

## 16.7 Notes

a. Weekly survival rates of adult and immature grouse were not significantly different, Wilcoxon Matched Pairs sign test by week, $T = 60$, NS

b. There was no difference between female home range size on Ralia and Drumochter, Mann Whitney Test, $U = 6$, $P = $ N.S.

c. There was no difference between home range size of male and female grouse, Mann Whitney Test, $U = 28$, $P = $ N.S.

# SOCIAL BEHAVIOUR OF GROUSE

# CHAPTER 17

# ANNUAL CHANGES IN THE TERRITORIAL BEHAVIOUR OF RED GROUSE

**Annual changes in the territorial behaviour of grouse are described. Peaks in territorial behaviour occurred in autumn and spring and were associated with the establishment of territories.**

## 17.1 Introduction

The red grouse is a territorial species. The males actively defend their territories against other males and will chase and fight intruding individuals. In March and April, these activities can lead to prolonged chases between rivals and ultimately to severe fights during which beaks, wings and feet are all used to inflict injuries on adversaries. Usually such fights are nothing more than a skirmish, but on some occasions they can escalate and result in serious injuries to the protagonists.

Chases and fights are clearly active aggression against territorial intruders, but male defence also includes a number of passive displays which effectively inform other birds that a cock is in residence on his territory and which also serve to attract females. Perhaps the best known form of display is the characteristic song flight of the grouse, during which the cock grouse flies steeply from the ground and calls with a series of loud barking 'aa' calls, followed by a descent with rapidly beating wings, head, wings and tail extended and a slowing 'ka ka ka ka' call[1]. In some instances, song flights will set off a chain reaction, with neighbouring cocks responding to the calls of successive males. A second, but less obvious threat display is produced by a standing cock when he stretches out his neck and produces a rattling 'ko-ko-ko-krr', known as the ground call[1].

Hens also produce a number of calls. Perhaps the most distinct is a rattling ground call, similar to the cock ground call but given at a higher pitch and often for longer. We call this the hen call, it seems to be a type of low key aggression towards other hens.

As with many bird species, territorial activity and song in red grouse are greatest in the morning, with a peak soon after dawn. However, unlike many species, the red grouse dawn chorus continues throughout much of the year. Changes in the calling of the grouse during the year tend to reflect changes in the intensity of spacing behaviour. This is described in detail in this chapter on the basis of a series of dawn watches conducted each week on study areas in Scotland and England.

## 17.2 Methods

The annual fluctuation in territorial behaviour of red grouse was recorded during a series of weekly dawn watches. Dawn watches were conducted from February 1989 through to April 1990 both at the Crubenmore study area in Scotland and the Gunnerside study area in northern England. A central location on the hill was chosen and records taken from a vehicle, driven to the location before dawn. The number of song flights and ground calls were recorded during each five minute period from just prior to dawn until no calls were heard for a period of five minutes.

During each dawn chorus, ranked measurements were made of weather variables on an intensity scale from 1 (none) to 5 (high intensity). These included temperature, rain, snow cover, wind speed and visibility.

## 17.3 Daily pattern of dawn chorus

The general pattern of dawn chorus was for an increase in the frequency of song flights per five minutes to reach a peak of activity within the first hour, before falling and finishing after a period of between 30

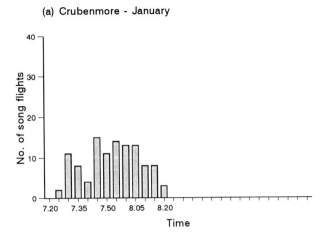

(a) Crubenmore - January

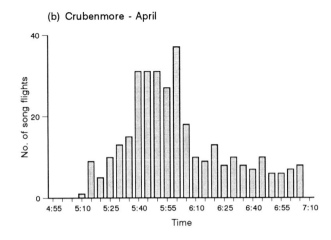

(b) Crubenmore - April

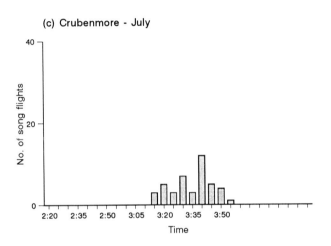

(c) Crubenmore - July

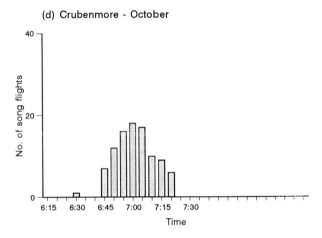

(d) Crubenmore - October

Figure 17.1. Changes in the frequency of song flight calls at dawn from the Crubenmore study area. Frequency of calls increased soon after first light and reached a peak before subsequently falling although the intensity and duration of these calls varied with time of year. Observations commence when time starts on axis.

minutes and 2 hours 30 minutes (Figure 17.1). The intensity of these song flights and the duration of the calling period changed during the year, although the basic pattern remained the same.

Frequency of male ground calls also showed a general daily pattern of activity, with a rise to a peak and a subsequent decrease (Figure 17.2), although this pattern was less distinct.

The pattern of hen calling also showed a general increase in frequency and a subsequent decline (Figure 17.3).

**17.4 Monthly changes in frequency of song flights**

The frequency of song flights varied monthly when this was measured as (i) the duration of the dawn chorus from the peak to the end of the period, (ii) the number of song flights from peak to end and (iii) the number of calls during the peak five minutes. Frequency for all three of the parameters reached a high level in spring and again in early autumn (Figure 17.4).

There was a decrease in the number of song flights during the summer months after nesting although the calling rate was still high during May, a period when most hens have mated and started incubation. Only by June, when chicks had hatched, did the rate decrease and the defence of the territory lessen. This was probably because adults did not want to draw attention to their brood. Observations on nesting hens indicated that hens that left the nest in May attracted males from neighbouring territories and their own males continued to chase intruding birds. The increased calling rate started again in September, coinciding with brood break up and the re-establishment of territories by older males. This rate of calling remained high until late December. The lower level in midwinter was probably associated with periods of snow cover when birds were no longer territorial.

Variations in song flights between months were examined in relation to weather conditions. Frequency of song flights was lower during months with strong wind at Crubenmore but not at Gunnerside (Table 17.1). This decrease with wind speed may result from

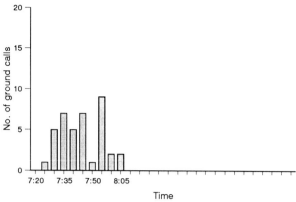

(a) Gunnerside - January

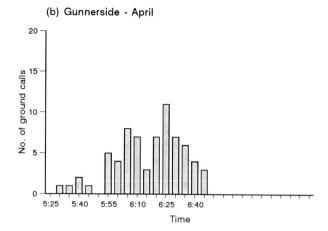

(b) Gunnerside - April

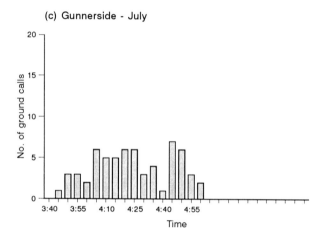

(c) Gunnerside - July

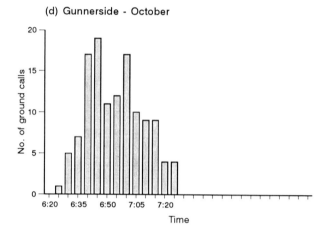

(d) Gunnerside - October

Figure 17.2. Changes in the frequency of ground calls at dawn from the Gunnerside study area. As with song flights there is a tendency for a peak of activity soon after dawn but with differences between months.

wind interference with the bird's ability to perform song flights, but could also influence observers ability to hear and record song flights. Even so, in one instance when the wind speed increased greatly during a period of observation it was apparent that the birds immediately ceased displaying, suggesting that wind was having a direct effect on the bird's behaviour.

Table 17.1 Significant correlations between monthly song flight behaviour and weather variables.

|  | Temp | Rain | Snow | Wind | Visibility |
|---|---|---|---|---|---|
| **Crubenmore:** | | | | | |
| Peak song flights | + | 0 | 0 | − | 0 |
| Peak song ±5 minutes | 0 | 0 | 0 | − | 0 |
| Peak to end song | 0 | 0 | 0 | − | 0 |
| **Gunnerside:** | | | | | |
| Peak song flights | 0 | 0 | 0 | 0 | 0 |
| Peak song ±5 minutes | 0 | 0 | 0 | 0 | 0 |
| Peak to end song | 0 | 0 | 0 | 0 | 0 |

− = $P<0.05$ statistically significant negative association
+ = $P<0.05$ statistically significant positive association
0 = No relationship

Variations between months could also be associated with changes in day-length and hormone production. The frequency of song flights recorded was associated with the monthly change in day-length at the Gunnerside study area, but not at Crubenmore (Table 17.2).

Table 17.2 Associations between monthly song flight behaviour and changes in day-length

|  | Crubenmore | Gunnerside |
|---|---|---|
| Peak song flights | 0 | * |
| Peak song ±5 minutes | 0 | ** |
| Peak to end song | 0 | * |

.* = $P<0.05$ ** = $P<0.01$ ; statistically significant associations all showing an increase in song flights with an increase in daylength. 0 = No association

### 17.5 Monthly changes in ground calls

Ground calls showed a seasonal change with an increase in the frequency of calls in early autumn and another increase in early spring (Figure 17.5). There are some interesting differences between the two study areas with a greater calling rate on Gunnerside compared to Crubenmore, and this rate remained relatively high throughout the winter months. This difference in calling behaviour may be related to density since Gunnerside carried a greater density of grouse than Crubenmore in both 1988 (54 pairs versus 13 pairs per km²) and 1989 (32 pairs versus 18 pairs). At high densities, conflicts between grouse are more likely to occur and the birds may use the passive ground calls to avoid serious conflicts.

## 17.6 Monthly changes in hen calls

Hen calls also showed an annual change in frequency at both sites with high levels during autumn and spring (Figure 17.6). As with male ground calls, the frequency of these calls appeared greater at Gunnerside despite the lower rate of song flights. This may

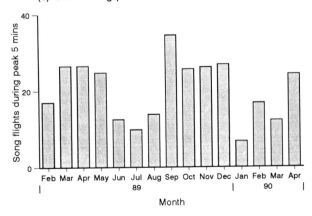

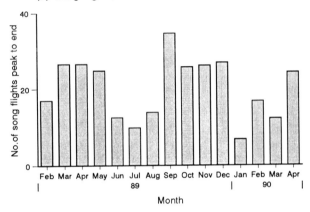

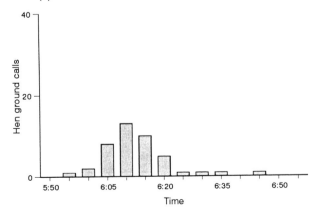

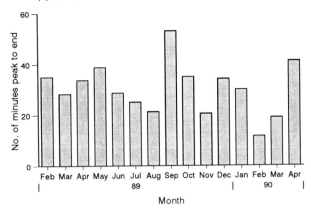

(a) Dawn chorus duration, Crubenmore

(b) Song flights, Crubenmore

(c) Calls during peak 5 mins, Crubenmore

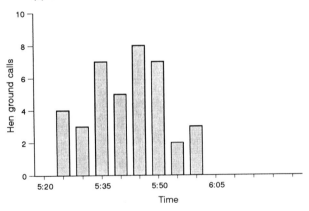

(a) Crubenmore - March 1989

(b) Gunnerside - March 1990

Figure 17.3. Changes in the frequency of hen ground calls from both Gunnerside and Crubenmore. The general pattern is once again for a peak soon after dawn.

Figure 17.4. Annual changes in the frequency of song flights at Crubenmore. Duration, number of calls and peak number of calls per five minutes all show the general pattern of greater intensity in autumn and again in spring.

103

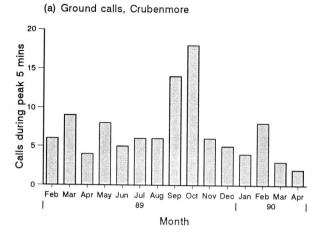

(a) Ground calls, Crubenmore

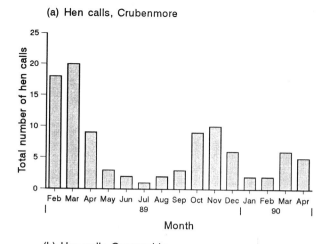

(a) Hen calls, Crubenmore

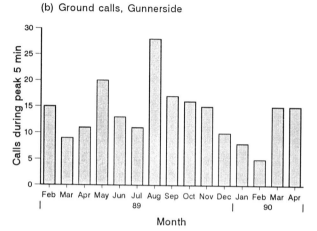

(b) Ground calls, Gunnerside

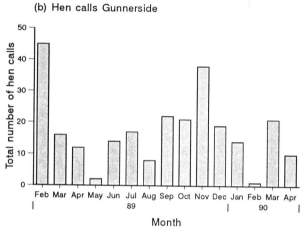

(b) Hen calls Gunnerside

Figure 17.5. Annual changes in the frequency of ground calls by red grouse at Gunnerside and Crubenmore.

Figure 17.6. Annual changes in the frequency of calls by hens at Gunnerside and Crubenmore.

indicate higher levels of female aggression associated with the higher density.

## 17.7 Discussion

This analysis provides a quantitative description of annual changes in the intensity of territorial behaviour of red grouse. The results conform with the previous descriptions of grouse establishing territories in autumn followed by a period of less active defence during the winter and then an increase associated with the re-establishment of territories in spring. The high levels of activity in autumn indicate the importance of autumn as a time for establishing territories.

An interesting contrast between the two study areas is that the Gunnerside population was declining from a high density whereas the Crubenmore population density was increasing. In this respect it is interesting to note that song flights were less in the Gunnerside

population when compared with frequency of hen calls and ground calls. If spacing behaviour were an important factor influencing density and causing a fall in density we would expect to see greater levels in the decreasing population. The initial evidence does not support the hypothesis that spacing behaviour was causing such changes in density but further work is needed to test this rigorously.

## 17.8 Summary

Dawn chorus showed a peak of activity soon after first light and a subsequent fall in the frequency of calls. The duration and intensity of calling varied throughout the year and tended to be greatest in autumn and spring, associated with the establishment of territories. Relative numbers of song flights were infrequent on a high density declining population compared with ground calls and frequency of female calls.

## 17.9. References

1. Watson, A. & Jenkins, D. (1964). Notes on the behaviour of the red grouse. *British Birds*, **57**, 137-170.

# CHAPTER 18

# SOCIAL STATUS AND SURVIVAL

**Previous studies in north-east Scotland found that territorial status conferred a great advantage to survival and that only grouse with winter territories subsequently bred. In studies of grouse at low density, no such system was found to operate and there was no clear advantage to individuals defending autumn territories.**

## 18.1 Introduction

Territorial defence and the consequences of this behaviour for changes in bird numbers are an interesting but at times a difficult subject to comprehend. In the 1960s, the pioneering ornithologist David Lack proposed that territorial defence in bird species was a mechanism for spacing individuals[1] in relation to their resources. At low densities, individuals would space themselves out across a resource such as food or nesting sites even though none of these was limiting the density of the population. With an increase in the population, the resources would be divided but the birds would still be spaced out through the actions of territorial defence and this would continue until territory size corresponded to the minimum quantity of food or other resource required by a territorial pair. In such a system, the food or other resource is limiting the density of the birds and the territorial behaviour is the mechanism through which the resource is divided.

Another early influential research worker, Dennis Chitty[2], pointed out that such conditions are not necessary and the birds spacing behaviour could limit density at a level before food or other resources were limiting. Instead of resources being important, territory size could be influenced by the level of aggression of territorial birds. In some instances, when aggressive birds were intolerant of their neighbours and established large territories, breeding density was low. At other times, grouse would become more tolerant and less aggressive and allow a higher breeding density of birds on the ground. In such instances the behaviour of the birds determines breeding density.

Observations on red grouse in north-east Scotland[3] by the then Nature Conservancy (now Institute of Terrestrial Ecology) showed that after the period of high territorial activity, grouse could be identified as either territorial or non-territorial. Territorial status at this stage determined the subsequent survival of

grouse, with between 99% and 100% of territorial grouse surviving while only between 2% and 6% of non-territorial grouse survived[3]. These observations provide strong support for the hypothesis that territorial behaviour in autumn can limit density of grouse by excluding the non-territorial individuals. The non-territorial individuals became known as the 'doomed surplus' because these birds were destined to die and would only have an opportunity to breed if a territorial bird was shot or accidently died. For red grouse, such a mechanism must also have to account for the large scale changes in grouse density that have been recorded, so that extensive and large scale decreases in grouse density (often as much as 90% over one or two years) were brought about by large changes in the tolerance and aggression of the territorial birds. The next stage in these studies has been to evaluate what determines the large change in spacing behaviour which could lead to such massive changes and even the local extinction of grouse on some study areas.

Such work has important implications for game management, since if aggression and tolerance are related to intrinsic changes within the birds themselves, then management activities such as winter predator control may have little or no effect upon grouse breeding density and so the size of the harvest. If this were the case, grouse managers could concentrate on heather burning and the reduction of crows and foxes during the breeding season and make grouse keeping a part time vocation. Furthermore, if the decline in grouse density (Section 2) during the mid seventies and the subsequent low breeding density was a consequence of changes in spacing behaviour, then subsequent recovery might not be influenced by increased management inputs.

## 18.2 Methods

Red grouse were caught in late summer and early autumn and fitted with radio-transmitters. These birds were then followed regularly, at least once a week until the birds either bred or died.

Territorial status was determined between mid-October and late December using definitions determined in the work conducted in north-east Scotland[3]. Females which remained in the same area and were regularly seen paired with males were considered 'territorial'. Three definitions of the term 'regularly paired' have been used:

*Definition A*: Female paired during November

*Definition B*: Female paired for 25% or more of observations from mid-October (week 42) until the end of December (week 52).

*Definition C*: Female paired for 50% or more of observations from mid-October (week 42) until the end of December (week 52).

Non-territorial males are not paired, but a cock can hold a territory without attracting a mate so territorial males were defined as being paired and/or regularly recorded on a territory within each of these three time periods.

### 18.3. Territorial status and survival

Combining both sexes of grouse, there was no difference between the survival of territorial and non-territorial individuals, and this result was clearly very different from the previous studies of grouse in north-east Scotland (Table 18.1).

Table 18.1. Weekly and annual survival rates of territorial and non-territorial red grouse of both sexes between mid-October and 1 April.

| | Territorial | Non-territorial |
|---|---|---|
| **Weekly survival rates:** | | |
| Speyside 1986-1991 Definition A | 98.8% | 98.6% |
| Speyside 1986-1991 Definition B | 99.2% | 97.9% |
| Speyside 1986-1991 Definition C | 99.2% | 98.2% |
| **Annual survival rates:** | | |
| Speyside (C) 1986-1991 | 65.6% | 38.9% |
| Glen-Esk[3] 1957-1963 | 98.6% | 0.2% |
| Kerloch[3] 1961-1967 | 100% | 0.6% |

### 18.4. Territorial status and survival of females

There was no difference between the survival of territorial and non-territorial females using definitions A and B, although definition C (females paired for 50% or more of observations) showed that territorial females had a higher survival rate than non-territorial females (Table 18.2).

Table 18.2 Weekly survival rates of female territorial and non-territorial birds, according to three definitions. Figures are average weekly survival plus/minus standard error.

| | Territorial | Non-territorial | Significance |
|---|---|---|---|
| Definition A | 98.6%±0.5% | 99.15±0.5% | NS |
| Definition B | 99.2%±0.3% | 97.9%±0.8% | NS |
| Definition C | 99.3%±0.3% | 98.0%±0.7% | P<0.05 |

NS = no statistically significant difference

The difference between the territorial and non-territorial females provided some support for the suggestion that paired birds in autumn are more likely to survive than unpaired birds, although the difference in survival between these two groups was not as large as the difference recorded in studies in north-east Scotland.

### 18.5 Territorial status and survival of males

Territorial males did not have a greater survival rate than non-territorial males in any of the three definitions (Table 18.3).

Table 18.3 Weekly survival rate of territorial and non-territorial males during winter. Figures are average weekly survival plus or minus standard error, (a measure of the error in the estimate).

| | Territorial | Non-territorial | Significance |
|---|---|---|---|
| Definition A | 98.7%±0.4% | 97.9%±1.2% | NS |
| Definition B | 98.7%±0.4% | 97.9%±1.2% | NS |
| Definition C | 98.6%±0.4% | 98.4%±0.9% | NS |

NS = no statistically significant difference

### 18.6. Cause of death and territorial status

The cause of death where known was determined for territorial and non-territorial individuals to determine whether birds of different social status were more prone to one type of predator or another. Overall there was no difference for either sex or for both sexes combined (Table 18.4)

Table 18.4 Cause of death of territorial and non-territorial birds.

| | Territorial | Non-territorial | Significance |
|---|---|---|---|
| **Females** | | | |
| Mammals | 3 | 3 | |
| Raptors | – | 3 | |
| Other | 3 | 4 | NS |
| **Males** | | | |
| Mammals | 3 | – | |
| Raptors | 5 | 1 | |
| Other | 2 | 2 | NS |
| **Both sexes** | | | |
| Mammals | 6 | 3 | |
| Raptors | 5 | 4 | |
| Other | 5 | 6 | NS |

## 18.7 Breeding and territorial status

There was no difference between the breeding production of territorial and non-territorial birds for either sex or when both sexes were considered together (Table 18.5).

Table 18.5 Breeding production measured as average number of young per hen and territorial status of grouse determined in autumn (definition C). Numbers in brackets indicate sample size.

| | Territorial | Non-territorial | Significance |
|---|---|---|---|
| Females Young/hen | 5.75 (4) | 3.67 (3) | NS |
| Males Young/hen | 3.50 (4) | 7.50 (2) | NS |
| Both sexes Young/hen | 4.62 (8) | 5.20 (5) | NS |

NS = not statistically different, differences determined using t test.

## 18.8 Discussion on status and survival

Territorial status did not influence the survival of male grouse nor generally of females, although one of the three definitions found a significant result. Either way these results contrast with the earlier findings in north-east Scotland (Table 18.1) where territorial status more or less guaranteed survival. Clearly the system recorded in north-east Scotland was not operating within these populations. There are several possible explanations that could explain the difference between these findings and those of previous studies.

First, the system could be essentially the same as recorded in previous studies, whereby the grouse population divide into territorial and non-territorial individuals in autumn but differ in that territorial birds are now more vulnerable to predation. This difference could occur since predation pressure has increased (predator numbers up and grouse numbers down, Section 2) and there has been a change in the pattern of grouse mortality, with more deaths attributable to peregrines and hen harriers. However the overall mortality of grouse is no different, so this seems unlikely.

Second, the advantages and disadvantages of defending a winter territory may vary in different situations. The benefits of maintaining and defending a winter territory are clear if the territorial bird has a strong likelihood of surviving, retaining it mate and breeding in the following year. However, this will depend on the availability of females; when females are sparse, a more profitable strategy for the cocks may be to assess the availability of females in other areas. In such cases the cocks may face two alternative strategies. First, stay on a territory and hope to attract a mate; staying in an area they know well may provide advantages against certain predators but may increase risk to others. Second, do not invest energy into territory defence but move around and assess areas where breeding success was previously good, with high chances of establishing a territory and breeding. Such a strategy may involve more risk but it will provide better advantages if it works.

Third, mortality occurs not only during the periods of territorial defence but also during mid-winter when territorial behaviour is reduced and grouse are frequently in packs and not on their territories. Once again, breeding may be determined by ownership of a territory, but survival is independent of territorial status.

These three alternative scenarios are not the sole explanations and clearly all three may be operating together. The interesting feature is that in the original system described in north-east Scotland, there was complete compensation to any effects of predation. That is, when a territorial grouse was killed it was replaced by a non-territorial individual that would otherwise have died. Hence, predation would have no effect on the final size of the population. In the system described during this study there would be no such compensation and at least part of the losses would result in a fall in the overall breeding population, and hence predation has at least some part to play in determining density.

## 18.9 Summary

Overall, territorial status did not confer a survival advantage to grouse although one of the three definitions of territorial status revealed a higher survival for territorial females. This difference was not as large as found in previous studies, which had recorded guaranteed survival of territorial birds and almost certain death in non-territorial individuals. Cause of death and breeding production did not vary with territorial status, although additional information would be instructive.

## 18.10 References

1. Lack, D. (1966). *Population studies of birds.* Clarendon Press, Oxford.

2. Chitty, D. (1967). The natural selection of self-regulatory behaviour in animal populations. *Proceedings of the Ecological Society of Australia,* **2**, 51-78.

3. Watson, A. (1985). Social class, socially induced loss, recruitment and breeding of red grouse. *Oecologia* Berlin, **67**, 493-498.

# CHAPTER 19

# SPACING BEHAVIOUR EXPERIMENTS

**In the low density populations in Badenoch, the predictions of the spacing behaviour hypothesis were not satisfied. More birds bred in spring than had been territorial birds in autumn. Not all available habitat was occupied, although experiments showed that such ground was suitable. There were practically no surplus birds in autumn or spring.**

## 19.1 Introduction

The essential element of the spacing behaviour hypothesis is that part of the population does not breed as a result of the behaviour of the more dominant individuals. Three conditions[1] need to be demonstrated to show that spacing behaviour is limiting numbers in such a way:

(i) The presence of a non-breeding proportion of the population
(ii) Non breeders are capable of breeding
(iii) Other resources such as food or nest sites are not limiting.

In the past, biologists have tested the first two of these conditions using removal experiments. Territorial birds have been removed from their territories and observations conducted to see if they are subsequently replaced by the non-territorial 'doomed surplus' birds. Such experiments have, however, a number of problems. First, the origin of the replacement birds must be determined; the replacements could be neighbours expanding their territories, or birds that have yet to settle and would have bred anyway even if territorial birds had not been removed. Second, the experiments cannot determine the eventual fate of the replacement birds, because some of these birds might have bred elsewhere. Third, removal experiments should be conducted when non-territorial birds are available to act as replacements and not after all non-territorial birds have died or moved elsewhere.

Of the conditions listed above, number (iii), to demonstrate that other resources are not limiting, is extremely difficult to satisfy. A limiting resource is one which is in short supply and if additional quantities of this resource are added, the breeding density of grouse increases. For example if food is limiting, addition of food would result in more breeding pairs, if nest sites were limiting the provision of suitable areas of nesting habitat should increase numbers; or if females are limiting the addition of more females would increase the population. If none of these or other resources are limiting, then spacing behaviour itself could be limiting density but testing all possible limiting resources is difficult, if not impossible.

We have already seen (Section 4) that the sex ratio in the breeding population invariably favours males, so it seems likely that females may be the first resource that is likely to limit the density of breeding pairs. This chapter examines the importance of spacing behaviour within the low density populations in central Scotland by a series of observations and experiments.

## 19.2 Territorial birds in autumn and following spring

The evidence that spacing behaviour is important rests on three lines of evidence. One of these is critical to testing the importance of spacing behaviour[2]. The population of grouse in spring should never exceed the number of territorial grouse in the previous autumn.

To examine this, we conducted a total of 20 counts in late October on our main study areas in Scotland and determined the social status of the grouse. Paired hens were assumed to be territorial and so too were paired cocks together with single cocks that showed territorial behaviour.

In 18 out of 20 cases the number of territorial hens in spring was greater than the number in autumn, demonstrating that hen social status did not determine numbers in the subsequent spring. From the same data set, there were more territorial males in spring than autumn in 12 of the 20 cases, suggesting that spacing behaviour was not determining their density.

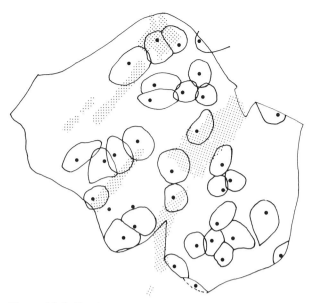

Figure 19.1. Territory mapping on a low density population in Badenoch in 1988 showing the extent of the territories mapped in spring together with the location of broods found in the subsequent breeding season. Hatched areas indicate wet, marshy ground, considered relatively suitable for grouse. The important point to note is that not all suitable habitat is used and some of these areas were utilised in subsequent years.

## 19.3 Occupation of suitable habitat

Territorial behaviour could only limit density when the birds occupy all suitable space, or at least do not leave sufficient space for other birds to establish a territory and subsequently breed. Furthermore, if vacant areas were used in one year but not in others this would imply that at least part of the vacant area was suitable for nesting and that territorial behaviour was not limiting density.

The distribution of grouse territories was mapped over an area of 9.7km$^2$ of the Ralia study area in two successive years. In both years grouse did not occupy all the heather dominant vegetation (Figure 19.1). In 1988, 62% of the heather dominant vegetation was not occupied. According to the spacing in the rest of the study, an estimated 60 pairs of grouse could have used this vacant area. In 1989, 73% of the heather moorland was not occupied and, with the greater crowding recorded in that year, could have held 142 extra pairs . Comparison between years of the distribution of breeding birds shows that vacant areas in one year were used in other years: a total of seven pairs used areas in 1989 that were not utilised in 1988 and 12 territories used in 1988 were not used in 1989.

There was sufficient space within the study areas for other birds to utilise and breed, suggesting that if losses during the previous winter had been lower, the breeding population would have been higher.

## 19.4 Grouse density experiments: trap and transfer

To determine whether territorial behaviour was limiting density and to see whether the number of breeding birds could be increased on the study area, grouse were introduced onto an area of moorland in spring (Figure 19.2). If territorial behaviour was limiting density then none of the introduced birds would be able to establish territories and subsequently breed.

In the springs of two years, grouse were caught and transported more than 30km  and introduced into a second population within two hours of capture. A number of the females caught were radio-tagged, while males and other females were tagged with short wing streamers. The experiment was conducted soon after territories on the experimental areas had been re-established in spring, following snow thaw. The experiment was repeated four times; introductions were made twice into the low density populations in Badenoch with five pairs km$^{-2}$, once into a medium density population also in Badenoch with 15 pairs km$^{-2}$, and once into a high density population in northern England with 50 pairs km$^{-2}$. The grouse introduced into the medium density population were caught from a medium density population so levels of aggression would be similar or lower than levels expected on the site where the birds were introduced. The introductions into a high density population were also taken from a high density population where aggression should have been low.

In each of the four experiments, about 25% of the introduced birds were subsequently found breeding – at least to incubation – all within 5km of the point of release (Table 19.1). A total of six birds settled within

TRAP AND TRANSFER EXPERIMENT

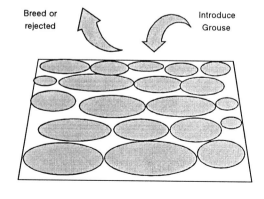

Figure 19.2. A summary of trap and transfer experiment where grouse were introduced into an area and their subsequent breeding or loss monitored.

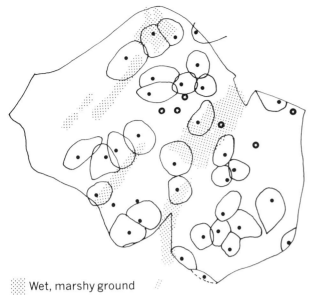

:::: Wet, marshy ground

**o** Nest site of released grouse.

Figure 19.3. Location of breeding grouse after the trap and transfer experiment showed where released grouse subsequently bred in relation to other territories. We can conclude from this experiment that spacing behaviour was not limiting density and some of the extra birds had space to breed.

the 9.7km² area which was mapped: five in heather moorland which was otherwise vacant. The remaining bird settled on the edge of heather moorland where some of the habitat was not heather (Figure 19.3). In the low density population, a total of seven grouse had been radio tagged and monitored since the previous autumn and none of these moved or were displaced following the introductions.

These experiments indicate that spacing behaviour did not prevent introduced birds from establishing a territory and breeding and that space left after the winter loss was suitable enough for other birds to breed within.

Table 19.1. Results from the trap and transfer experiment showing that at least 24% of released birds subsequently bred.

| Density | Number Released | Number Breeding | Percent Breeding |
|---|---|---|---|
| Low | 36 | 9 | 25% |
| Low | 44 | 10 | 23% |
| Medium | 7 | 2 | 29% |
| High | 12 | 3 | 25% |
| Total | 99 | 24 | 24% |

### 19.5 Grouse density experiments: removal and release

To identify the possible presence of surplus, non-territorial females within the study populations a series

of removal and release experiments were conducted (Figure 19.4). These were designed first to repeat the classic removal experiments and second to determine whether surplus females were available in the population. To test the fate of removed and replacement birds, the removed females were subsequently released. If replacements occurred, the replacements would either be non-territorial birds or territorial birds coming from another location. Releasing the removed bird once more would result in: (i) The released bird regaining her original mate, in which case the replacement bird might become non-territorial and subsequently die. (ii) The released bird not regaining her original mate, in which case she would have become non-territorial and should not have subsequently bred. (iii) One of the birds moving to another territory and subsequently breeding.

Territorial females were removed from their territories in spring and again in autumn and kept in cages on the hill for six days or until replaced by other females. Both released and replaced females were fitted with a radio tag and subsequently followed to determine whether the birds bred. If territorial behaviour was limiting, the non-territorial female in each group should have died if the territorial female had not been removed.

CATCH AND RELEASE EXPERIMENT

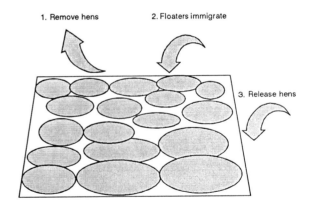

Figure 19.4. Experimental procedure for the catch and release experiment outlined in the text.

The first of these experiments was conducted during the spring of 1989. Six females were removed from their territories when grouse re-established their winter territories after the snow melt. During a period of six days, none of the territorial females were replaced (Table 19.2). In the absence of non-territorial females, the original territorial females were released and all of them subsequently bred, four with their original cocks. In autumn of 1989 the experiment was repeated on the same area, 12 of the females were caught but only one was replaced. Five of the released birds subsequently survived the winter and bred. The experiment was repeated again in spring 1990 when nine were caught, none were replaced and eight were known to subsequently breed.

Table 19.2 Results from the female removal and release experiment.

| Period | No. caught | No. replaced | No caught that bred |
|---|---|---|---|
| Spring 89 | 6 | 0 | 6 |
| Autumn 89 | 12 | 1 | 5 |
| Spring 90 | 9 | 0 | 8 |

These experiments show that there were no surplus birds in either spring or autumn that could have replaced the territorial individuals and as a consequence suggest that spacing behaviour did not limit numbers.

## 19.6 Discussion

The experimental and observational evidence indicates that spacing behaviour did not limit grouse breeding density in these low density populations in Badenoch. Numbers of territorial birds in autumn did not determine the number of territorial birds in the following spring. Mapping of the territories showed that not all suitable habitat was utilised and suggested there was sufficient space for additional birds to breed. Experiments subsequently showed that there was room for additional birds to breed and removed birds were not replaced in either spring or autumn.

This evidence demonstrates that spacing behaviour did not limit density within these populations and that if winter losses had been less, then breeding density would have been greater. In light of the factors associated with the death of the grouse it seems reasonable to suppose that reduced losses to predation would result in an increase in the population.

## 19.7 Summary.

This chapter examines whether spacing behaviour is limiting density on the low density Badenoch study areas. Numbers of territorial birds in spring were frequently greater than the number in autumn showing that spacing behaviour was limiting density. Grouse did not occupy all suitable habitat and some territories used in one year were not used in other years. Introduction experiments showed grouse were able to use these areas and moved into areas not already occupied. Removal experiments showed that there were no surplus hens in autumn or spring.

## 19.8 References

1. Watson, A. & Moss, R. (1970). Dominance, spacing behaviour and aggression in relation to population limitation in vertebrates. In: *Animal populations in relation to their food resources*, Ed. A. Watson, pp 167-220. Blackwell Scientific Publications.

2. Watson, A. & Moss, R. (1990). Spacing behaviour and winter loss in red grouse. *Red grouse population processes* Eds A. Lance & J. Lawton, pp 35-52.

Young hen red grouse disperse further from their natal area than do cocks (Chapter 14). *The Earl Peel*

Groups of hens may disperse early in the season, resulting in a high proportion of cocks on the hill and a male biased sex ratio in the bag (Chapters 13 and 14). *The Earl Peel*

Hen grouse with brood located by a pointer. Hen distraction displays varied greatly between years and areas and this variation was associated with predation pressure (Chapter 20).

The social status of grouse in the autumn did not determine their subsequent fate (Chapter 18). *The Earl Peel*

# CHAPTER 20

# DISTRACTION DISPLAYS OF RED GROUSE

**Red grouse perform a 'broken wing' distraction display to lure predators away from their offspring. The proportion of birds performing this display varies greatly from year to year and place to place. Much of this variation is associated with differences in predation pressure and the risk of losing young.**

## 20.1 Introduction

Red grouse actively defend their brood by performing a 'broken wing' distraction display during which the adult feigns injury and attempts to draw a predator away from the offspring. The behaviour places the parent at some risk of being caught but studies in Norway[1] found that adults performing the display have larger broods. Casual observations have, not surprisingly, shown that the behaviour succeeds in fooling some predators. However, there is also evidence that some predators, such as foxes, may use the display as a signal that a hen has chicks and then search intensively for the chicks[2].

The proportion of grouse performing the distraction display varies greatly between years and places. Although the cause of this variation is not apparent, four explanations (hypotheses) have been proposed:

(i) Variation in distraction displays is the result of differences in the risk of predation on the brood with an increase in distraction display with chick vulnerability.
(ii) Frequency of distraction displays relates to the risk of predation to the parent, with a fall in display intensity as the vulnerability of the parent increases.
(iii) Distraction display is a function of parent condition such that parents in good condition are more likely to perform a distraction display than birds in poor condition.
(iv) Distraction displays depend on the investment the parents have made in their brood and how much effort would be needed to replace the brood to the same stage of breeding.

This study presents detailed information on the factors associated with the variation in distraction displays performed by red grouse between years and areas, and tests a number of predictions from the hypotheses proposed. Although the hypotheses cannot be considered mutually exclusive, the results indicate that the frequency of distraction displays was associated with changes in the risk of predation and not the condition of the parents or the costs of investment to the parent.

## 20.2 Methods

Distraction displays were recorded in response to brood disturbance by pointing dogs. The dogs located and flushed the parents and then found the chicks which were counted, aged according to size and tagged with small individually numbered tags. Brood size was taken as the number of chicks found by the dogs.

The presence of male and female birds was recorded and the intensity of display noted. This was ranked on a subjective scale depending on the risk of capture to the displaying bird from 1 (minimum risk) to 5 (maximum risk) (Table 20.1). The categories 2 and 3 were considered a low risk form of the display while categories 4 and 5 were considered high risk.

Table 20.1 Ranked levels of distraction displays performed by red grouse during brood disturbance

| Ranked Response | Behaviour of grouse |
|---|---|
| **No Display:** | |
| 1. | Parents flushed and left with the minimum of risk. |
| **Low Risk Display:** | |
| 2. | Parent ran for a short distance before flying away. |
| 3. | Parent performed a slight distraction display feigning injury with wings open. |
| **High Risk Display:** | |
| 4. | Parent performed an active distraction display feigning injury and circling the observer and dog. |
| 5. | Parent performed an active distraction display feigning injury, running towards the observer or dog with close or actual physical contact between the dog and parent. |

Observations were obtained each year between 1982 and 1988 on Gunnerside Estate, Swaledale, North Yorkshire. Comparative data were gathered in 1985 from several grouse populations in England and Scotland to obtain measures of spatial variation in the distraction display.

Mean body weight of adult birds shot in August, two months after observations, was used as an index of condition. Condition of grouse is influenced by the size of the worm burden, so body condition was experimentally improved by catching female grouse in spring and treating them with an anthelmintic which reduced the parasite burden and improved their condition. Females were tagged and the intensity of their distraction displays was recorded and compared with untreated females.

### 20.3 Variation in distraction displays

Red grouse have been recorded performing distraction displays to mammalian predators but not to avian predators (Table 20.2).

Table 20.2. Distraction display response of red grouse with broods to predators. Distraction displays are performed against mammalian predators and rarely against avian species.

|  | Typical Response of Grouse | | |
| Predator | None | Low | High |
| --- | --- | --- | --- |
| **Mammals:** | | | |
| Fox | | | + |
| Dog | | | + |
| Pine marten | | | + |
| Man | | + | |
| | | | |
| **Birds:** | | | |
| Buzzard | + | | |
| Golden Eagle | + | | |
| Hen harrier | + | | |
| Merlin | + | | |
| Peregrine | + | | |
| Short eared owl | + | | |
| Crow | + | | |
| Raven | + | | |

The proportion of grouse exhibiting distraction displays (high + low risk) on the main study area varied greatly between years[a] (Figure 20. 1.). They also varied between different regions within the same year[b], with a higher frequency of display in Scotland than England (Figure 20.2).

Grouse that performed distraction displays produced larger broods[c] (Figure 20.3).

**(a) Females**

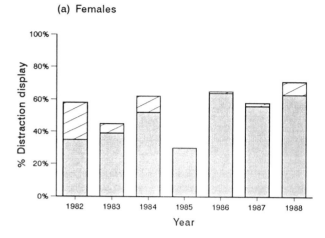

**(b) Males**

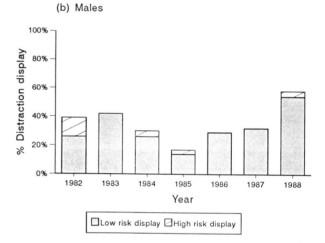

Figure 20.1. Changes in the frequency of distraction displays performed by (a) female and (b) male grouse on the main study area. There are large scale differences in the frequency of these displays between years. Females performed a greater intensity of distraction display than males.

### 20.4. Risk of predation on brood (Hypothesis (i))

This first hypothesis proposes that parents will perform distraction displays in response to the risks of brood predation. If this were true then we can make several predictions about the frequency of distraction display which should increase with the vulnerability of offspring to predators and hence with (1) increased predation pressure, (2) size of brood – the more chicks the more likely a predator is going to notice one, (3) reduced cover where chicks are more vulnerable in open areas and (4) when parents are brooding their chicks and the chicks are vulnerable when the bird is disturbed. Each of these predictions was examined:

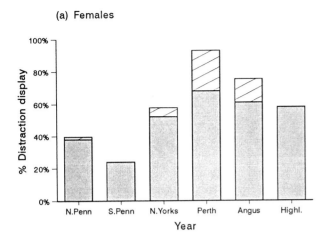

(a) Females

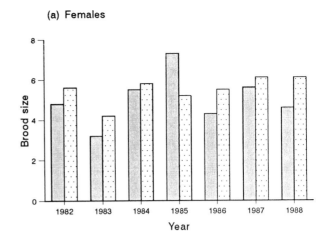

(a) Females

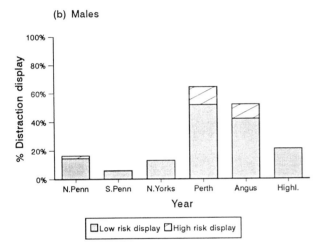

(b) Males

Low risk display ☐ High risk display

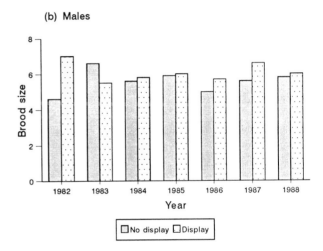

(b) Males

☐ No display ☐ Display

Figure 20.2. Changes in the frequency of distraction displays between regions recorded from several grouse populations in 1985 for (a) females and (b) males.

Figure 20.3. Brood size compared between grouse performing and not performing displays for (a) females and (b) males. Overall, birds performing displays had larger broods at seven days of age than birds that did not display.

*1. Distraction displays should increase with predation pressure:*

Foxes are known to be significant predators of grouse and distraction displays are only performed in front of mammalian predators. The number of fox litters removed by keepers per square kilometre in spring was taken as a measure of predation pressure. The frequency of high risk distraction displays increased with the number of fox litters found for both female (Figure 20.4) and male grouse[d] but there was no association between fox litters and the frequency of low risk displays[d].

Similar information on fox litters was not available for all areas studied, and although there was information on the number of foxes killed, this probably provides a coarser measure of predation pressure. In the comparison between areas, the frequency of high

risk distraction displays performed by grouse did increase with the number of foxes killed per 10 square kilometres for females, but was not statistically significant for males (Figure 20.5).

*2. Distraction displays should increase with brood size:*

The frequency of distraction displays was associated with brood size for both females and males but not with either brood age or clutch size (Table 20.3). Closer inspection of differences in distraction display revealed that only the frequency of low risk display was associated with brood size.

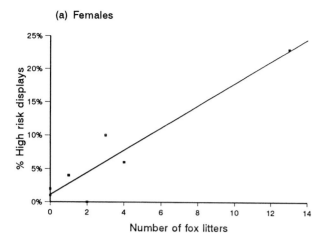

(a) Females

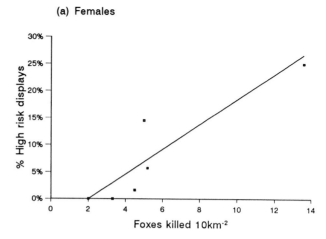

(a) Females

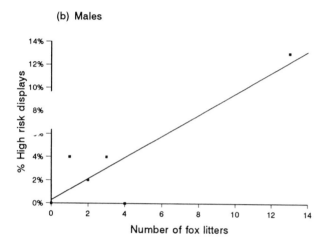

(b) Males

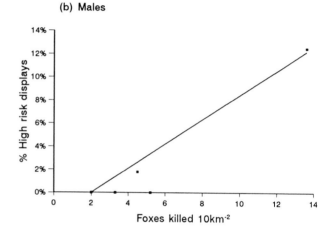

(b) Males

Figure 20.4. Frequency of high risk distraction display between years on the main study area increased with predation pressure where this was measured as number of fox litters killed by keepers.

Figure 20.5. Frequency of high risk distraction display increased with predation pressure between study areas in 1985 where predation pressure was measured as the number of foxes killed 10 km⁻².

Table 20.3. Relationship between frequency of distraction displays and breeding variables, showing where there was a statistically significant increase in proportion of distraction displays with brood size. No relationship is indicated by NS (not significant).

| Display | Brood Size | Brood Age | Clutch size |
|---|---|---|---|
| **Female:** | | | |
| Low Risk | Increase** | NS | NS |
| High Risk | NS | NS | NS |
| Both | Increase** | NS | NS |
| **Male:** | | | |
| Low Risk | Increase*** | NS | NS |
| High Risk | NS | NS | NS |
| Both | Increase** | NS | NS |

** = $P<0.001$; *** = $P<0.001$

*3. Distraction displays should be greater when the brood is in poor cover:*

Males produced more intense distraction displays when disturbed in areas of low vegetation height:

Females were also more likely to perform distraction displays when vegetation height was low but this was not quite statistically significant[f].

*4. Distraction displays should be greater when the parent is disturbed during brooding:*

There was no difference in the frequency of distraction displays performed by females disturbed when brooding compared to hens not brooding[g].

### 20.5 Risk of predation to parent (Hypothesis (ii))

In this hypothesis, parents will perform distraction displays while the risk of predation to themselves is relatively low. This hypothesis predicts that individuals are more likely to perform displays when (1) mates are present and (2) when their mates perform distraction displays: Both of these situations dilute the risk of predation on the individual when the mate is present or performs.

*1. Widowed birds should perform distraction displays less frequently:*

Hen grouse without mates were less likely to perform both high and low risk distraction displays than hens with mates present[h]. In 18 incidents where males were found alone with a brood, none performed a high risk distraction display, but the frequency of both displays was not different from paired males.

*2. The intensity of distraction displays should be correlated within a pair:*

In a total of 1216 cases where both males and females were present, the intensity of the female display was greater in 1132 cases (93.1%)[i] and the intensity of the male distraction display increased with the intensity of female display. Similarly on the main study area, the proportion of males performing high risk displays was greater in years when more females performed high risk displays although neither the frequency of low risk displays or total displays were correlated between years[j]. Furthermore, in comparisons between areas the frequency of both displays was correlated between males and females[j].

## 20.6 Distraction displays and condition of parent (Hypothesis (iii))

This hypothesis states that the condition of the parent bird influences the frequency of distraction displays. In this respect predictions will include an increase in distraction display with (1) body weight between years and (2) experimentally improved body condition.

*1. The frequency of distraction display will increase with body weight:*

No correlation was found between the frequency of high and low risk displays and body weight in either females or males between years (Table 20.4). There

was a decrease in the frequency of displays performed by females and average body weight, but this was opposite to the predicted direction.

Table 20.4. Relationships between distraction displays and body weight of females and males.

|  | Females | Males |
| --- | --- | --- |
| Low Risk | NS | NS |
| High RIsk | NS | NS |
| Both | Decrease* | NS |

\* = $P < 0.05$

*2. Distraction displays should be greater in grouse with improved body condition:*

In 1988, distraction displays were recorded from 28 females with reduced worm burdens: 18 (64%) performed distraction displays but this was not significantly greater than the 73% (N = 88) of untreated hens that performed distraction displays[k].

## 20.7 Distraction displays and costs to parent of losing a brood (Hypothesis (iv))

This hypothesis states that the intensity of distraction display should increase with the level of parental investment. Predictions include an increase in distraction display with (1) age of brood and (2) clutch size.

*1. Distraction displays should increase with age of brood:*

No correlation was found between the age of the brood and the proportion of distraction displays performed by either the hen or the cock (Table 20.3). Chicks are capable of flight by the time their wing length exceeds 75mm; 52% of broods of 14 days old fly when disturbed. As such, there is a decrease in offspring vulnerability after 14 days of age; however, there is no change in the intensity of distraction displays of either hens or cocks[l]. Furthermore, the effect of brood age and distraction display could be masked if the male leaves the hen and brood after a certain age; however, there was no relationship between the age of brood (to 20 days) and the presence or absence of the cock.

*2. Distraction displays should increase with clutch size:*

In birds with young that leave the nest soon after hatching, much of the adults' breeding investment is channelled into egg production, since young are not directly fed and the energey costs of caring for a small brood cannot be expected to be smaller than for a large brood. Hence we may expect an increase in distraction displays with clutch size rather than brood size. Nevertheless, no significant correlation was found

between the frequency of displays and clutch size (Table 20.3).

## 20.8 Discussion on variations in distraction display

Variations in distraction display were generally associated with the risk of predation on offspring (Hypothesis (i)) and parents (Hypothesis (ii)). While this study did not produce conclusive evidence, there are reasonable grounds to refute the hypothesis (iii) that the body condition of the parent influences the intensity of distraction displays. Further support for this comes from a study on willow ptarmigan in Norway[1] that found no association between the frequency of distraction displays and body weight. However, the frequency of distraction displays was not associated with overall breeding success in either this study or the Norwegian one, although there was an association in a study conducted in Glen Esk, Angus[3]. This would imply that predation was not a significant factor influencing brood size in our study and other factors were ultimately important in influencing breeding success. This is not surprising since fox numbers are reduced in spring and other evidence has demonstrated that parasitism was an important factor reducing breeding success on our main study area.

No evidence was found to support the hypothesis (iv) that the intensity of distraction display should increase with the cost of replacing a brood and consequently the level of parental investment. However, red grouse rarely produce a second clutch if the first is lost during the last few days of incubation or if the whole brood is lost. In this respect we could only expect the frequency of distraction display to be related to parental investment if this investment reduced the chances of the parents surviving and breeding successfully in the following year. There is no evidence for this in red grouse.

One criticism of this and other studies of brood defence is the use of dogs as fox substitutes. Nevertheless, this criticism is not significant to this study since the object was to discover why there was large scale variation in the intensity of distraction display between years and areas.

A further criticism is that predation pressure is taken as the density of foxes removed by keepers from the estate in April when hen grouse are about to commence incubation, so when the chicks have hatched the predation pressure has effectively been removed. While this criticism is valid, the data provide an interesting examination of the possible mechanisms used by grouse to evaluate predation pressure and this is discussed in the following section.

## 20.9 The adaptive value of variation in distraction displays

Red grouse have a life expectancy of less than three years and the loss of a brood to predators will greatly reduce lifetime reproductive success. While brood defence places the parent at some risk of capture from the predator, the costs of not performing a distraction display and losing the brood appear relatively high. In this respect we might expect short-lived birds to perform high levels of brood defence in each year and not the large variation recorded in this study. However, this would not be the case if the relative benefits of performing a distraction display vary from one occasion to the next.

Dr Sonerud has taken observations on fox feeding behaviour when the fox disturbed both a black grouse and a capercaillie and noted that when each female performed a distraction display, the fox appeared to use the display as a stimulus for search, and subsequently found and caught chicks[2]. Modelling these observations through game theory has demonstrated that a female grouse should perform a distraction display only to a naive or 'dumb' fox and should not perform to an experienced or 'smart' fox. There is evidence to suppose that years of high fox density usually follow years of successful breeding in foxes when the population will consist of a high proportion of young and naive individuals. Thus, in years of high fox density we should expect females to perform relatively more distraction displays. This prediction is supported by the results of this study.

This explanation does beg the question: how do females monitor predation pressure? An interesting finding that emerged from this study is that the intensity of the females' distraction display is associated with a measure of fox breeding density before incubation commenced. This implies that female grouse may monitor predation pressure prior to incubation and respond accordingly.

This study has provided evidence to support the hypothesis that the intensity of distraction display is influenced by the risk of predation to the offspring and refuted the hypothesis that the body condition of the parent was a significant factor. The adaptive value of the high variation provides support for the 'dumb fox hypothesis'.

## 20.10 Summary

Red grouse perform distraction displays when disturbed by mammalian predators and the frequency and intensity of these displays varies greatly, both between areas and years. Four different explanations for this variation were examined. First that the increase in distraction displays was a consequence of the risk of brood predation. This was suppported by an increase in distraction displays with predation pressure, brood size and poor cover. Second that distraction displays reduced the risk of predation on the parent. This was supported by a lower frequency of display by females without mates and the similarity in the levels of dis-play between members of a pair. Third, distraction displays were not a reflection of body condition since females with reduced worm burdens do not perform more. Fourth, the freqency of distraction displays was not related to the energetic costs of replacing the brood since there was no association between the displays and either clutch size or brood age. Generally distraction displays tend to be greater in areas with high predation pressure.

## 20.11 Notes

a. Differences in distraction displays between years; females: $X^2 = 29.6$, $P<0.001$, d.f=6; males: $X^2 = 30.5$, $P<0.001$, d.f. =6.

b. Differences between areas; females: $X^2 = 73.04$, $P<0.001$, d.f. = 5; males: $X^2 = 77.8$, $P<0.001$, d.f. = 5).

c. Overall both females and males that performed distraction displays tended to have larger broods (combined $P$ from t test within each year; Females: $P<0.05$; Males: $P<0.01$).

d. Frequency of high risk distraction displays between years was positively correlated with the number of fox litters for both female ($r=0.95$, $P<0.01$) and male grouse ($r=0.89$, $P<0.01$). There was no association between fox litters and the frequency of low risk displays (females $r= 00.60$, NS; males $r= -0.19$, NS).

e. In the between area comparison, the frequency of high risk distraction displays did increase with the number of foxes killed per square kilometre ($r= 0.98$, $P<0.01$), but the frequency of high risk distraction displays performed by males was not significant at the 5% level ($r=0.79$, $P<0.1$).

f. Distraction displays were negatively correlated with vegetation height for males ($r= -0.14$, $P<0.05$, $N= 191$), but were not significant at the 5% level for females ($r= -0.12$, $P<0.1$, $N=222$).

g. There was no difference in the frequency of distraction displays performed by females disturbed when brooding compared to hens not brooding ($X^2 =0.01$, $P=0.92$).

h. Widowed grouse were less likely to perform both high and low risk distraction displays than hens with mates present ($X^2 = 11.6$; $P<0.001$), but there was no difference for males ($X^2 =0.42$; $P=0.52$).

i The intensity of the female display was greater than males in 1132 cases; Wilcoxson Matched Pairs test, $V =413656$, $Z =9.02$, $P<0.001$. Female and male distraction displays correlated, $r=0.508$, $P<0.001$, $N=1216$.

j. Between years on study areas male and female frequency correlated, $r=0.91$, $P<0.01$. Males and females positively correlated between areas (low risk: $r=0.84$, $P<0.05$; high risk: $r=0.85$, $P<0.05$).

k. No difference in proportion of hens performing distraction display when treated or not treated, $X^2 = 0.43$, $P=0.51$.

l. There is no change in the intensity of distraction displays of either hens ($X^2 = 1.5$, $P=0.47$) or cocks ($X^2 = 3.1$, $P=0.21$) after 14 days of age.

## 20.12 References

1. Pedersen, H.C. & Steen, J.B. (1985). Parent care and chick production in a fluctuating population of willow ptarmigan. *Ornis Scandinavica*, **16**, 27--276.

2. Sonerud, G.A. (1988). To distract display or not: grouse hens and foxes. *Oikos*, **51**, 233-237.

3. Jenkins, D., Watson, A. & Miller, G.R. (1963). Population studies on red grouse, *Lagopus lagopus scoticus* (Lath.), in north-east Scotland. *Journal Animal Ecology*, **32**, 153-161.

# HEN HARRIER PREDATION AND DISTURBANCE OF GROUSE

# CHAPTER 21

# THE IMPACT OF HEN HARRIERS ON RED GROUSE BREEDING SUCCESS

**Hen harriers are known to be predators of grouse chicks. In this chapter Steve Redpath examines how many chicks harriers take and how this number varies with grouse density.**

## 21.1 Introduction

Hen harriers frequently take chicks of red grouse during the summer months[1]. During a study[2] of the prey items brought to harrier nests conducted on a high density grouse moor, harriers removed an estimated 7.4% of the grouse from an area of 96 km[2]. Whilst this provided a measure of losses at one grouse density, a clearer understanding of the dynamics of predation by harriers can be obtained by examining how losses from the grouse population vary with the density of grouse. This is important if we are to understand the relationship between harriers and grouse.

This study examined the effect of harrier predation on the breeding success of red grouse; first, by measuring chick losses from grouse populations and, second, by recording the diet of harriers.

## 21.2 Methods and study areas

Extensive studies were conducted on six pairs of managed grouse moors in 1987 and on eight pairs in 1988. On each moor, grouse brood size was estimated as the number of young per female (including females with no chicks) at the end of July. Broods were located and flushed using pointing dogs, as described in Chapter 8. Counts were generally done during a single day for each site, to prevent recounting of broods. Each pair of moors was approximately 15 km apart; one of the pair had breeding harriers, whereas on the other (the control) harriers did not breed.

Intensive studies were conducted on one pair of moors in Speyside during 1986-87 (AH, with harriers; AC, control) and a second pair in Perthshire during 1988 (BH and BC). On these moors, mean grouse brood size was estimated in early June, when chicks were approximately 10 days old, and therefore after most deaths caused by factors other than predation[3]. A second brood estimate was taken six weeks later and was used to assess overall chick loss.

Harriers establish breeding home ranges in April, commence laying in late April or early May and initiate incubation before completing the clutch. Incubation is about 30 days, so most harrier eggs hatch in early June. At this time grouse chicks are about one week old. The harriers feed their young at the nest for five weeks[1,2].

The two study areas were selected as being representative of the local moorland and could be observed from good vantage points. Study area A was 4 km[2] and B was 6 km[2]. The sites were hunted by three pairs of harriers in 1986, two pairs in 1987 and between three and five pairs in 1988. Gamekeepers were active on both study and control areas, where they removed other predators of grouse, in particular foxes, stoats and crows.

Harrier nests on the intensive study moors were found by watching the moor for displaying birds in April and for the classic food passes where the male supplies food for the female by passing it to her in the air during May[1].

Hunting harriers were observed as they flew over the study sites and each strike at prey was recorded, although usually only the larger prey (grouse and hares) could be identified. These observations provided an independent estimate of chick losses over the six-week period to compare with losses estimated from counts of grouse broods and from the food brought to the nest. Observations were conducted throughout the six week period and data for male and female harriers were pooled. Chick losses to harriers were calculated using the following equation:

$$\text{Chicks taken Km}^{-2} = H*R/SA \quad (1)$$

Where: H = available hunting time: 631-hours, based on 15 hours per day for six weeks
R = rate at which grouse chicks were caught: number seen taken from study area per hour
SA = study area (km²).

This relationship assumes that all successful attacks on grouse chicks during the observation period were seen. This was unlikely because two of the twenty-six interactions observed in 1988 were noticed only after hearing the attacked grouse call. Presumably some interactions could have occurred unseen. However, as the amount of hunting observed per hour was small (3.1 minutes per hour, based on 578 observations in spring and summer) and one observation of a hunting bird followed directly from another only four times in three years, the number of unobserved interactions is likely to have been small.

For comparison with data from hunting observations a second estimate of harrier diet was obtained from nest watches in 1988. Hides were placed 20-30m from three harrier nests and moved over a one-week period to 5-7m from each nest. At this distance most prey (85%) could be identified. Both nest and hunting observations were carried out over the same period.

The changes in harrier diet due to variation in grouse density were examined by comparing data from this study with those from other similar surveys. The density of adult grouse was measured in July by walking with a trained dog over 1km². In two studies, density was not measured, but grouse numbers were estimated. Both of these were from low density grouse populations on moorland not managed for red grouse.

### 21.3 Extensive studies

Counts on paired moors in July (Figure 21.1) showed that moors with harriers consistently produced smaller broods than moors without breeding harriers[a] although the brood sizes were only significantly greater within three of the fourteen pairs. Overall, areas with harriers produced on average 17% fewer grouse chicks. There was little difference[b] in the density of grouse on the moors (moors with harriers carried 10.9 females km⁻²; moors without harriers carried 12.6 females km⁻²).

One pair of moors, where there was no apparent difference in keepering activity between the years, was monitored for three years. During this time the number of harriers changed from three resident pairs in 1986, to only being partly hunted by an adjacent pair in 1988. The control area had no harriers in 1986 and 1987 but was on the edge of the range of one pair in 1988. Grouse brood size was lower than the control moor in 1986 and 1987 but not in 1988 when harrier densities were similar (Figure 21.2). This finding was consistent with the idea that the density of harriers was the cause of the difference in chick survival between the paired moors.

### 21.4 Intensive studies: grouse counts

Mean brood size in June, when grouse chicks were one week old, was not different between the intensive study areas with and without harriers, but by July the average brood size was lower on the area with harriers (AH) than on the control (AC) (Table 21.1:).

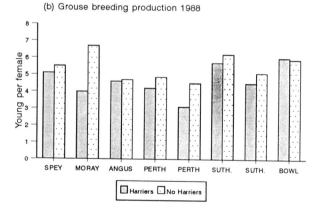

Figure 21.1 Numbers of young grouse per female counted on paired moors in July 1987 and 1988. Grouse moors with harriers present consistently produced fewer grouse.

In 1988, grouse on the control moor BC were infected by the parasitic worm which reduced breeding success and on part of this moor some of the grouse were treated with an anthelmintic drug to kill the parasites. There was no evidence of an outbreak occurring on BH. In June, brood sizes on treated and untreated areas of BC were not different from BH. However, in July, brood size was larger on the treated area than on BH but not on the untreated.

Table 21.1. Comparison of mean grouse brood sizes in relation to presence and absence of harriers on the intensive study areas with harriers present (AH + BH) and the control areas without harriers (AC + BC) in June and July 1986-88. Data are presented as grouped means ± 1 Standard Error. In 1988, the control moor data are divided into two: A = treated for parasites, B = untreated (see text).

| | Harriers | | No Harriers | | |
|---|---|---|---|---|---|
| | Moor AH Mean Brood | N | Moor AC Mean Brood | N | P |
| 1986 June | 4.75 | 12 | 5.32 | 28 | NS |
| July | 4.-8 | 26 | 5.65 | 91 | ** |
| 1987 June | 5.78 | 28 | 5.81 | 26 | NS |
| July | 4.26 | 65 | 5.87 | 106 | ** |
| | Moor BH | | Moor BC | | |
| June | 4.80 | A | 6.0 | 10 | NS |
| | | B | 4.20 | 15 | NS |
| 1988 July | 3.99 +−.29 | A | 5.62 | 21 | ** |
| | | B | 3.30 | 23 | NS |

## 21.5 Intensive studies: hunting observations

Harriers were not strongly territorial, except close to the nest, and hunting ranges overlapped considerably. In 1988, five separate males were regularly seen hunting less than 1km from the nest of a neighbour, without the resident birds responding.

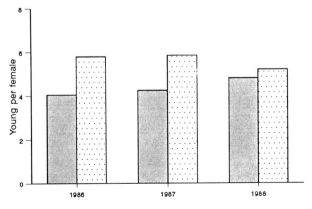

Figure 21.2 Grouse breeding success measured as number of young per hen over a three year period with varying numbers of harriers. In 1986 three harriers bred on area 1 and none on area 2; in 1987 two on area 1 and none on area 2 and in 1988 one on both areas 1 and 2.

Observations of hunting individuals were conducted throughout the six weeks after the harrier chicks hatched and they were seen to take up to ten grouse chicks from the main study areas (Table 21.2). Estimates, derived from observed changes in brood size, of the expected number of grouse chicks taken by harriers during the observation period indicated that predation by harriers could account for practically all the losses of grouse chicks. During the three years of this study, predation by harriers accounted for 91% of grouse chick losses in the six-week period.

## 21.6 Intensive studies: prey taken to harrier nests

During the hide observations conducted in 1988, 299 items of prey were identified (Figure 21.3), of which 32% were red grouse chicks. The proportions of the four main prey categories (grouse, pipits, small mammals and hares) differed between nests[e], with nest B receiving more than twice as many grouse chicks as either nest A or C.

The diet of harriers observed hunting did not differ from the relative proportion of prey items brought to the nest, suggesting that harriers did not selectively carry certain prey types[f] back to the nest. Nest watches recorded that 32% of the items in the diet were grouse chicks (299 prey items). Hunting observations recorded that 40% of the items taken were grouse chicks (27 prey items caught). Since no significant difference was found, hunting observations conducted during 1986 and 1987 could be used to estimate the percentage of grouse in the diet.

Table 21.2. Observation time and loss of grouse chicks from intensive study areas AH (1986 + 1987) and BH (1988). The estimates of grouse chick loss km$^{-2}$ are derived from the equation in 21.4.

| | Moor AH | | Moor BH |
|---|---|---|---|
| | 1986 | 1987 | 1988 |
| Size of study area (ha) | 600 | 600 | 400 |
| Hours observation after grouse hatch | 139.45 | 114.50 | 137.40 |
| Number of harrier pairs per hunting area | 3 | 2 | 503 |
| Number of grouse chicks present in June | 57 | 139 | 278 |
| Number of grouse chicks seen taken from study area | 3 | 4 | 10 |
| Expected losses from change in brood size km$^{-2}$ | 1.70 | 6.60 | 10.20 |
| Estimated number of grouse chicks lost in six weeks km$^{-2}$ | 2.30 | 3.70 | 11.50 |

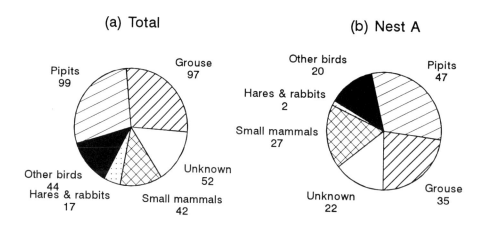

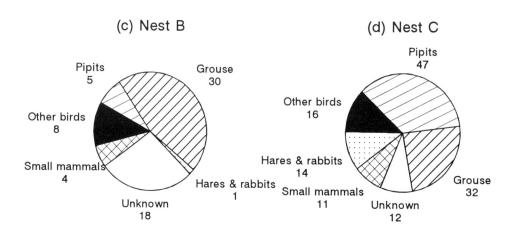

Figure 21.3 Numbers of prey items identified at three harrier nests from hides placed 5-10 metres from nest on Moor B in 1988. Grouse and pipits formed the bulk of the harrier diet at all three nests but this did vary between nests.

### 21.7 Effect of grouse density on harrier diet

Data from the three years of this study and those from other studies were collated to examine harrier diet in relation to grouse density. There was a rapid increase in the proportion of grouse in the diet of harriers with an increase in grouse density, reaching an upper limit of 30-35% of the diet at a grouse density of approximately 10 females km$^{-2}$ (Figure 21.4).

Harriers brought prey items to the nest at the rate of 0.6 to 0.82 items per hour (Table 21.4). Grouse density accounted for 66% of the variation in prey delivery rate between nests but two other factors also played a part. First, the number of harrier chicks in the nest[8] and, second, the proportion of hares and rabbits in the diet[8].

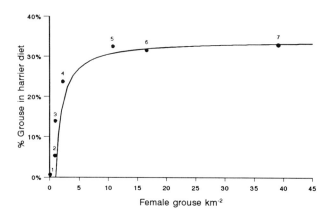

Figure 21.4 Change in the diet of grouse with grouse density as reconstructed from a series of studies; 1 = unpublished data from Linfoot, 2 = reference[3], 3, 4 and 6 = this study, 5 = reference[6], and 7 = reference[2].(See Appendix at end of this chapter).

Table 21.4. Feeding rates and percentage prey types (GR = grouse chicks; SM = small mammals; LAGS = hares + rabbits and hares; PASS = pipits) in harrier diet.

| Ref | No. of chicks | Items h$^{-1}$ | %GR | %SM | %LAGS | %PASS |
|---|---|---|---|---|---|---|
| 3 | 4 | 0.44 | – | 4 | 13 | 56 |
| | 2 | 0.32 | – | 7 | 29 | 50 |
| | 3 | 0.42 | – | ? | ? | ? |
| | 2 | 0.36 | – | ? | ? | ? |
| 4 | 4 | 0.80 | – | 37 | 10 | 37 |
| 1 | 4·5 | 1.12 | 29 | 1 | 10 | 53 |
| | 4 | 1.04 | 32 | 1 | 5 | 54 |
| | 3 | 0.78 | 27 | 5 | 5 | 61 |
| 2 | 1.5 | 0.47 | 15 | 0 | 0 | 67 |
| | – | 0.23* | 35 | 3 | 0 | 46 |
| | – | 0.21 | – | 5 | 18 | 53 |
| 5 | 2 | 0.82 | 29 | 21 | 1 | 47 |
| 6 | 2 | 0.59 | 62 | 8 | 2 | 21 |
| | 3 | 0.60 | 26 | 9 | 12 | 50 |

* Items chick$^{-1}$ h$^{-1}$.

From these relationships it is possible to derive the number of chicks taken per pair of harriers in the six-week period between counts. The association between harrier diet and grouse density indicates that the highest proportion of chicks taken during the first six weeks of life will be taken from moors where grouse are at low to medium densities (Figure 21.5). Within this relationship, grouse brood size is set at five young per hen and considered for three densities of harriers: 0.01 pairs km$^{-2}$ (1 pair to 25 000 acres), 0.05 pairs km$^{-2}$ (1 pair to 5000 acres, similar to the density on RH) and 0.1 pairs km$^{-2}$ (1 pair to 2500 acres, the density on BH). Chicks losses are high when the density of grouse is less than 10 females km$^{-2}$.

This relationship can be tested by comparing the calculated rate of loss in Figure 21.4 with the observations from the nests shown in Table 21.2. From the grouse density and harrier density, the estimated harrier predation for the six-week period in each case lay within 6% of observed losses, suggesting that Figure 21.4 is a true reflection of harrier diet in relation to grouse density (Table 21.5).

Table 21.5. Comparison of grouse chick losses observed (from hunting observations) on study areas and estimated, knowing harrier density (pairs km$^{-2}$), grouse density (females km$^{-2}$) and the number of grouse chicks available.

| Year | Number of grouse chicks (km–2) | Harrier density | Grouse density | Estimated losses(%) | Observed losses(%) |
|---|---|---|---|---|---|
| 1986 | 9.5 | 0.05 | 2.0 | 26 | 24 |
| 1987 | 23.2 | 0.04 | 4.0 | 14 | 16 |
| 1988 | 69.5 | 0.12 | 14.5 | 22 | 16 |
| 1947* | 131.2 | 0.07 | 41.0 | 10 | 12 |

*Estimated from Picozzi[1].

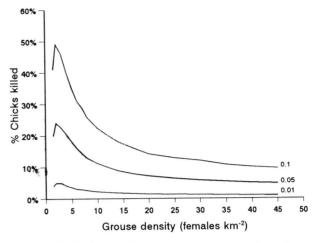

Figure 21.5 Relationship between grouse density and percentage of grouse chicks taken from the population by harriers in six weeks. This figure is derived from Figure 21.4 and the delivery rate equation. Initial grouse brood size is set at five chicks per hen and three densities of harriers are shown: 0.01 km$^{-2}$ (1 harrier nest per 25 000 acres), 0.05 (1 harrier nest per 5000 acres) and 0.1 (1 harrier nest per 2500 acres).

## 21.8 Discussion on harrier predation

Grouse moors with breeding hen harriers consistently produced fewer young grouse per female than moors without harriers. This may be the result of predation by harriers or may reflect differences in overall management, with harriers breeding in areas where grouse production was low as a consequence of other factors. The inference that harriers were the cause of many of these losses was supported by data from one pair of moors, where grouse breeding success varied with harrier density. Overall, the data suggested that chick losses due to predation by harriers were in addition to other losses, at least until the end of July. This was further supported by intensive observational studies.

Intensive studies indicated that harriers removed up to a minimum of 24% of the grouse chick population during the six-week period. However, harriers presumably continue to eat grouse beyond this time. Observations on radio-tagged harriers showed that harriers tended to stay within their home range for 21 days after fledging[7]. We also recorded harriers hunting within the study area up until August. Predation therefore continued after the period recorded here and if they continue to take grouse chicks at the same rate this could lead to chick losses 30% greater than were recorded.

Bird prey items formed the bulk of the harrier diet (80%) during the breeding season. In 1988, red grouse chicks formed a minimum of 32% of the diet (by number) of nesting harriers, although there were considerable differences between nests. Harrier diet was examined from both nest and hunting observations and whilst nest watches may provide an over-estimate of larger prey, no difference was found during this study in the proportion of grouse recorded. One difficulty with estimating diet from hunting observations is that sample sizes tend to be small and only large prey can be easily identified.

Harrier diet was associated with changes in grouse density, the shape of this association indicating that grouse chicks are a preferred prey item of harriers, and disproportionately more are taken at low grouse density. In other words, harriers will have greatest effect on grouse breeding success at low grouse densities.

Whilst the relationships presented in this study suggest how harrier predation responds to grouse availability, at any one density the number of grouse chicks killed will also depend upon the densities of both harriers and alternative prey species. A number of birds of prey are known to show a numerical response to their preferred prey species and will increase breeding density as prey items become available. This was recorded for harriers in Wisconsin, America where the number of harriers increased with an increase in the voles taken by the harriers[8]. Harriers show no strong territorial behaviour so it seems likely that in the absence of persecution, their numbers would increase with prey density. In this respect Figure 21.5 shows the minimum impact of harriers on grouse and it is possible that the impact of harriers at higher densities would be much greater.

At any one density, alternative prey availability may vary considerably and this could influence predation intensities on grouse, through both the functional (proportion of grouse chicks taken against density of grouse) and numerical (increase in harriers with grouse density) responses. For example, if alternative prey reduced harrier predation on grouse, then improving the habitat for these prey species may present an acceptable form of management on moors where harriers breed. However, whilst improving alternative prey densities may reduce grouse losses to individual harriers, it may also increase harrier numbers (through a numerical response), culminating in an overall increase of chick losses. Such a response has been recorded in the impact of goshawks feeding on pheasants in Sweden[9]. As rabbit numbers increased (the alternative prey), more goshawks were attracted into the area, resulting in greater pheasant losses.

In this study, the association between harrier predation and grouse density was determined from populations on separate areas and it is possible that low density grouse populations suffered high predation levels, due to differences in habitat quality. Although there were no obvious differences in cover between areas, moor AH had fewer insect-rich bog flushes, known to be attractive to grouse broods. Broods may therefore have spent more time searching for food, making them more vulnerable to predation. However, brood size was high on AH at 10 days old, indicating that there was no shortage of insect food on the moor.

### 21.9 Summary

Extensive studies of grouse breeding success found that moors with harriers present produced on average 17% fewer young grouse. On one moor, the losses of grouse chicks varied between years and were greater when harriers were present, indicating the harriers were a direct cause of this loss. Observations of hen harrier hunting over three years showed that 91% of observed chick losses could be accounted for through harrier predation. Observations at three harrier nests recorded 299 items; 32% were grouse chicks although this varied between nests. When the data from this study were collated with other data, the relationship between grouse density and the proportion of grouse in the harrier diet indicated that grouse populations at low density are most vulnerable to high chick losses.

## 21.10 Notes:

a. Breeding success of grouse was consistently lower on moors with harriers present; 1987 T = 0, $P = 0.05$; 1988 T = 1, $P = 0.02$, Wilcoxon Matched Pair Test, two-tailed.

b. Moors with harriers did not carry significantly fewer females, $t = 26$, $P > 0.1$, Wilcoxon two-tailed.

c. Intensive study area with harriers carried significantly smaller grouse broods than the area without harriers, 1986 $t = 2.62$; $P < 0.01$: 1987 $t = 3.09$; $P < 0.01$.

d. Brood size was greater on the control area that had been treated with the anthelmintic: $t = 2.59$; $P < 0.01$ but was not larger on the untreated control area with an infection of strongyle worm than on the area with harriers, BH, $t = 0.74$; N.S.

e. Prey items varied between nests $X^2 = 44.0$, $P < 0.001$.

f. 66% of the variation in prey delivery rate between nests could be accounted for through density of grouse: $Y = 0.45 + 0.013X$; $N = 11$, $r = 0.81$, $P = 0.002$.

g. Prey delivery rate (Y) was also influenced by the number of chicks in the nest (relationship = $Y = 0.18 + 0.16X$; $N = 12$, $r = 0.61$, $P < 0.05$) and proportion of rabbits and hares in the diet (relationship = $Y = 0.86 - 0.15X$; $r = 0.71$; $P < 0.05$; $N = 12$).

## 21.11 References

1. Watson, D. (1977). *The Hen Harrier*. Poyser Press, Berkhamsted.

2. Picozzi, N. (1978). Dispersion, breeding and prey of the hen harrier *(Circus cyaneus)* in Glen Dye, Kincardineshire. *Ibis* **120**, 489-509.

3. Picozzi, N. (1980). Food, growth, survival and sex ration of nesting hen harriers *(Circus cyaneus)* in Orkney. *Ornis Scandinavica,* **11**, 1-12.

4. Balfour E. & MacDonald, M.A. (1970). Food and feeding behaviour of the hen harrier in Orkney. *Scottish Birds,* **6**, 157-166.

5. Schipper, W.J.A. (1973). A comparison of prey selection in sympatric harriers, *Circus,* in Western Europe. *Le Gerfaut* **63**, 17-120

6. Redpath, S.M. (1989). *The effect of hen harriers and other predators on red grouse populations in Scotland.* Ph.D. thesis, University of Leeds.

7. Beske, A.E. (1981). Local and migratory movements of radio-tagged harriers. *Raptor Research,* **16**, 39-53.

8. Hamerstrom, F. (1979). Effect of prey on predators: voles and harriers. *Auk* **96**, 370-374

9. Kenward, R.E. (1986). Problems of goshawk predation on pigeons and other game. *The 18th Symposium of the International Ornithologists Congress.* Pp. 666-678.

## Appendix

Unpublished data used in Figure 4 of prey items observed from hides at harrier nests by Linfoot, Unpubl. (1) and Redpath 1989 (2). Linfoot data from 1980-87 at eight nests combined, and Redpath from 1988 at one nest.

| Prey Items | Study 1 | Study 2 |
|---|---|---|
| Red Grouse chicks | 1 | 8 |
| Meadow Pipit | 22 | 6 |
| Skylark | 5 | 0 |
| Other pipits | 24 | 4 |
| Precocial chicks | 5 | 1 |
| Small mammals | 3 | 3 |
| Hares | 9 | 4 |
| Total prey | 69 | 26 |

# CHAPTER 22

# HEN HARRIER HUNTING BEHAVIOUR

**The hunting behaviour of hen harriers will vary according to a range of factors including the abundance of other prey species and habitat structure. In this chapter Steve Redpath examines the hunting behaviour of harriers.**

## 22.1 Introduction

Lions on the African plains, sharks in the ocean and harriers on the grouse moor must decide how to allocate their hunting time, which prey to take, where to hunt and which areas to concentrate in. This chapter describes the hunting behaviour of hen harriers, in relation to the density and distribution of their main prey species on two grouse moors. Harriers are a good subject for this type of work as they hunt low over open habitats and are easy to observe for relatively long periods. The abundance and distribution of prey species can be examined and harrier diet measured through observations of hunting birds.

## 22.2 Methods

Observations were conducted on the two study areas described in Chapter 21. On each moor the vegetation was mapped and classified into seven distinguishable types:

(i) mature or building heather > 0.1m high (MH);
(ii) pioneer or young heather < 0.1m high (YH);
(iii) heather/bog myrtle mix (BOG);

(iv) bog flush; mix of heather and sphagnum (BF);
(v) rushes (MARSH);
(vi) burnt heather (BURN);
(vii) distinct edges approximately 2m either side of a boundary (EDGE).

Edges could only be determined along distinct boundaries between young heather or burnt patches and other habitats.

Habitat compositions were different on the two moors[a] (Figure 22.1). Moor A had an area of marsh and a substantial amount of heather/bog, myrtle bog mix. Moor B had neither of these habitats, but had bog flush and more pure stand heather.

The distribution and relative abundance of different prey species were estimated as the number flushed during transects with a dog in early June. Pipit and hare counts only produced relative densities, whereas grouse densities were more accurate as dogs were searching specifically for broods. Small mammal densities were estimated with 100 to 150 break back traps, set 10 metres apart for 10 nights in spring and baited with peanut butter. Abundance is given as the

### (a) Moor A

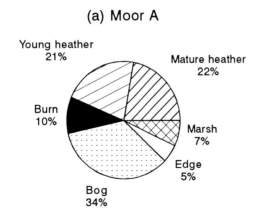

### (b) Moor B

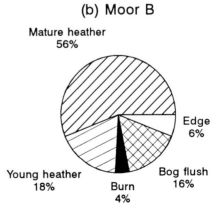

Figure 22.1 Relative proportions of various habitat types on moor A and moor B. Moor A had no bog flush while moor B had no bog or marsh.

Hen harrier hunting; harriers hunted selectively in the habitats preferred by grouse and meadow pipits (Chapter 22). *Peter Moore*

Hen harrier carrying a red grouse chick back to the nest site: 45% of their strikes on red grouse were successful (Chapter 22). *Peter Moore*

Male harrier delivering food to the nest site. Overall 35% of items brought to the nest were grouse chicks (Chapter 21). *Peter Moore*

Young meadow pipits, blue hares and grouse chicks comprised the majority of the diet of hen harriers (Chapter 21).

Female harrier at the nest site with her brood. The harrier population in Britain has increased in recent years although there are still large areas of suitable habitat not yet colonised (Chapters 6, 21, 22 and 23).

During the shooting season grouse may form into packs and the tendency to do this was greater on a moor with harriers present (Chapter 23). *The Earl Peel*

number caught per 100 trap nights. These figures for prey species represent apparent abundance, although the findings are comparable between the two areas.

Hunting harriers were observed in spring and summer, from vantage points in the study areas and the number and success of strikes at prey was recorded. From 1986 to 1988, 578 hours were spent watching the moor for hunting harriers, during which 18 hours of hunting observation were obtained. These observations indicated when prey were caught, but apart from grouse chicks and hares it was impossible to distinguish between prey types. Once grouse chicks had hatched, observations of hunting birds were used to assess the proportions of prey in the diet.

In 1987 moor A was divided into 24 squares of 25 hectares, covering an area of 6km², using wooden posts. In each of these squares, the area of different habitats, the numbers of prey species and the amount of harrier hunting time was recorded. Individual harriers were watched as they flew into view and their movements dictated into a continually running tape recorder until they were no longer visible from the vantage point. The amount of time spent hunting (defined as flight <10m above ground) was recorded, along with the type of habitat over which they hunted. Observations were ignored if it became apparent that the birds were not hunting (eg. carrying food or nest material, or involved in courtship).

The distribution of grouse broods and pipits in relation to habitat type was determined from the number flushed from each habitat on both moors. Leverets less than three weeks old (i.e. small enough to be taken

by harriers) were rarely observed during transects and their habitat use could not be ascertained. However, young leverets are not weaned until about four weeks old, and stay in or near the forms which are usually situated in mature heather.

Habitat selection by both harriers and prey was determined using Ivlers Preference Index[1]:

$$P = \frac{H_1/H_2 - A_1/A_2}{H_1/H_2 + A_1/A_2}$$

Where P is the preference index, $H_1$ is the number of observations in habitat 1, $H_2$ is the total number of observations, $A_1$ is the area of habitat 1 and $A_2$ is the total area. P values range from $-1$ (maximum avoidance) to $+1$ (maximum preference), with 0 indicating no selection. The time spent by harriers in each habitat type was recorded.

For each harrier-grouse interaction observed, the number of strikes at the grouse brood as well as the duration of interaction and defence behaviour of the adult grouse was recorded. Defence behaviour was recorded as JUMPS, where the adults flew directly at the harrier, and CHASES, where grouse pursued harriers for more than 10m from a brood. Whether or not a harrier returned to a brood was recorded during hunting observations and indirectly from hides near three nests on moor B in 1988. Nest data provided inter-prey times between successive grouse chicks brought to the nests, which were compared to the times between grouse chicks and other prey. Runs of identified prey items were not long enough to test whether or not prey were brought to the nest at random.

### 22.3 Prey densities and diet

Pipit densities were similar on the two study areas whilst densities of grouse and hares were higher on moor B (Table 22.1). When harrier diets on moors A and B were compared, there was an increase in the proportion of large prey (grouse and hares) at greater harrier densities[b]. Correspondingly, the proportion in the diet of small prey (pipits and small mammals) decreased from A to B in spite of pipit densities remaining unchanged and an increase in small mammals[c]. Thus grouse and hares appeared to be preferred prey, whilst pipits and small mammals were alternative prey.

### 22.4 Harrier hunting and habitat selection

Harrier hunting time was associated with pipit density in the 24 squares on moor A, but not to grouse chick number[d]. Both harrier hunting and pipit density were

Table 22.1. Relative densities of prey species and estimated body mass in June on moors A and B and their percentage as harrier prey (by number). Grouse, pipits and hare densities are given as the number km$^{-2}$ and small mammals as the number caught per 100 trap nights in spring.

| | MOOR A 1986 | | | | MOOR B 1988 | |
| | Density | % | | | Density | % |
|---|---|---|---|---|---|---|
| Red grouse chicks (180g) | 9.5 | 16% | 23 | 25% | 69.5 | 41% |
| Pipits (20g) | 141 | } 84% | 151 | } 75% | 132 | } 52% |
| Small mammals (25g) | (.001) | | (.60) | | (2.0) | |
| Hares (250g) | 3 | 0% | 3 | 0% | 3 | 7% |

negatively correlated with the amount of YH in the squares (Table 22.2). Harrier hunting was correlated positively with the amount of MH and negatively with the amount of EDGE. The number of grouse chicks was positively correlated with YH and both the number of chicks and grouse brood size was correlated with the amount of EDGE in each square.

Pipits selected the edge habitat on both moors, but otherwise showed differences in habitat preferences between moors (Figure 22.2). Grouse broods also selected the EDGE habitat on moor A and avoided the BURN and MARSH. On moor B they avoided the mature heather (MH) and young heather (YH) and selected the bog flush (BF) habitat, not present on A. These differences possibly resulted from grouse and pipits having a priority order of vegetation preference dependent on cover and insect availability.

Harriers spent more time hunting in the habitats preferred by their avian prey, notably the EDGE on both moors and the bog flush (BF) on moor B. Selection values for harriers hunting the habitats were correlated with values for pipit[s] on moor A but not for grouse. On moor B, habitat use by harriers was correlated with grouse but not pipits[g]. Grouse density was higher on moor B than A, whilst passerine density was approximately the same on both moors (Table 22.1). Grouse and pipits were not correlated on either moor.

## 22.5 Harrier hunting and grouse brood defence

During intensive observations, 187 strikes at prey were recorded, of which 45% were successful (Table 22.3). Apart from one prey robbed from a short eared owl, all prey items were caught on the ground.

Table 22.2. Correlation matrix, showing the association between habitat types, prey availability and harrier hunting behaviour recorded within the 24 squares, each of 25ha studied on moor A. Habitat types as in Figure 22.1. (MARSH only occurred in three squares and was therefore excluded from the analysis), GR = No. grouse chicks, PIP = No. pipits, HNT = amount of harrier hunting time (secs) and YNG = No. of young grouse per brood. Minus sign = negative relationships.

| | MH | BOG | BRN | YH | EDG | GR | PIP | HNT | YNG |
|---|---|---|---|---|---|---|---|---|---|
| BOG | NS | | | | | | | | |
| BURN | NS | NS | | | | | | | |
| YH | NS | NS | | | | | | | |
| EDGE | NS | NS | * | * | | | | | |
| GROUSE | NS | NS | NS | * | * | | | | |
| PIPIT | NS | NS | NS | −* | NS | | | | |
| HUNT | * | NS | NS | −* | −* | NS | * | | |
| YNG | NS | NS | NS | NS | * | NS | NS | * | |

Table 22.3. Observations of hen harriers during the spring and summer 1986-88 on grouse moorland.

| | MOOR A | | MOOR B | |
| | 1986 | 1987 | 1988 | Totals |
|---|---|---|---|---|
| Observation time (hrs) | 200 | 241 | 137 | 578 |
| Observation on Harriers | 10.6 | 9.4 | 9.4 | 29.4 |
| Observation on Hunting Harriers | 7.9 | 5.4 | 4.7 | 18.0 |
| Observation on Hunting Harriers after Grouse hatch | 6.3 | 2.9 | 4.7 | 13.9 |
| Total number of strikes | 59 | 78 | 51 | 188 |
| No. strikes successful | 26 | 31 | 29 | 86 |
| % strikes successful | 44% | 40% | 57% | 46% |

Interactions between harriers and grouse broods were observed 41 times and lasted between two and 597 seconds (Table 22.4). During 10 of these, the harrier left without striking, in 11 the harrier left after one or more unsuccessful strikes, and in 20 the harrier captured a chick. Harrier hunting behaviour differed between moor A and B in that harriers spent longer inter-

acting with grouse on moor A[e] and the length of time before a harrier left a grouse brood without capturing a chick (i.e. the 'give-up' time) was longer on the low density moor A[e]. Data from all three years suggested that the rate at which harriers encountered grouse and the percentage of successful strikes increased with increasing grouse density, whereas the number of strikes per interaction declined as grouse density increased (Table 22.4).

On six occasions grouse broods were observed as a harrier approached. Both interactions occurred in the EDGE habitat and both times the male grouse pressed himself to the ground whilst the female gathered

Table 22.4. Duration (in seconds) and outcome of harrier-grouse interactions observed over three years on moor A and B.

| | MOOR A | | MOOR B |
| | 1986 | 1987 | 1988 |
|---|---|---|---|
| No. interactions | 6 | 6 | 29 |
| Av. time(s) | 90 | 129 | 25 |
| No. strikes | 9 | 9 | 15 |
| Successful strikes | 4 | 4 | 12 |
| % successful interactions | 67% | 67% | 41% |
| % successful strikes | 44% | 67% | 80% |
| Strikes per interaction | 1.5 | 1.0 | 0.5 |
| Interactions per hour | 0.9 | 2.1 | 6.2 |

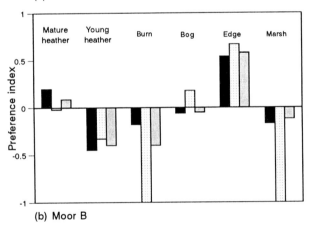

(a) Moor A

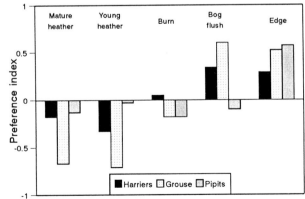

(b) Moor B

Figure 22.2. Preference index values (P) for hen harriers, grouse broods and pipits on the six main habitat types on moor A (1986/87) and moor B (1988). Selection values range from +1 (selection) to –1 (avoidance).

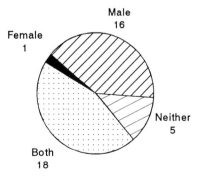

Figure 22.3. Active defence by adult grouse in response to attacks of harriers on broods. Males responded more than females and harrier success rate was greater when adults did not respond.

131

the chicks and moved to the cover of the mature heather. Once the harrier was overhead the adult grouse resorted to active defence. Male grouse actively defended chicks in most of the interactions and more than females (Figure 22.3). When no active defence was observed interactions were brief (2-10s) and in five of the six occasions resulted in the capture of a grouse chick. Grouse occasionally made contact with the harriers and once knocked a female harrier from the air after she had caught a chick. Grouse chicks were not seen to take active measures to avoid capture. Adult grouse were not attacked by harriers during the period when chicks were present and were never seen to desert chicks and fly away on the approach of a harrier.

When the adult grouse jumped at a harrier this appeared to prevent the harrier from striking a grouse chick. After such an interaction, the harrier would fly 10-20m, turn, come back and repeat the attempt. Of the 16 interactions that occurred in the EDGE habitat, only one was successful in the mature heather side of the edge, whilst five were successful in the burn or young heather, suggesting chicks may be more vulnerable where cover is poor. However, as attacks took place on both sides of the EDGE concurrently it was not possible to calculate success rate in poor and good cover. There was no obvious relationship between cover and predation levels in other habitats (Figure 22.4).

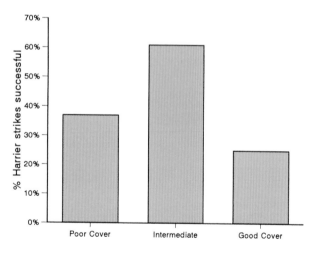

Figure 22.4 Percentage of successful harrier-grouse interactions in different types of cover.

Observations continued for at least one hour after 19 of the 20 successful strikes at grouse. In only one of these (on moor B) did the harrier return within an hour and relocate the brood (though it did not capture a chick). Six times on moor B a male was observed killing a grouse chick, carrying the chick back to the nest

and then immediately flying off in the opposite direction to hunt. After three (37%) of the successful strikes (on moor A), harriers were seen to return to the interaction site after more than one hour, but within the same day.

Observations during 1988 showed the order with which male harriers brought prey to the nest (Table 22.5). There were no apparent runs of grouse chicks and no differences in the times between captures after grouse chicks had been caught and captures after other prey had been caught. In other words, once a chick had been captured there was no indication that harriers returned immediately to the brood to catch another one.

Table 22.5. Runs of identified prey items brought back to harrier nests by males on moor B in 1988, where N = 8 or more items. G = grouse chick, H = hares, Pi = pipits, SM = small mammal, P = Passerine.

| DATE | PREY ITEMS |
|------|-----------|
| 13/6 | G · Pi · Pi · P · Pi · P · G · P · H · G |
| 19/6 | Pi · Pi · SM · Pi · Pi · Pi · P · Pi |
| 22/6 | Pi · Pi · · Pi · · Pi · · Pi · P · G · ? · G · Pi · G · G |
| 23/6 | P · P · Pi · G · P · Pi · Pi · Pi · Pi · G · Pi |
| 7/7 | H · G · P · P · Pi · H · SN · P |
| 9/7 | P · Pi · Pi · P · Pi · P · Pi · H · P |

**22.6 Discussion**

Harriers selected habitats for hunting according to the density of large prey. When and where large prey were scarce, harriers concentrated on the patches with the highest abundance of pipits, but when and where grouse were common, harriers concentrated on patches with the highest abundance of grouse. This resulted in a higher percentage of grouse in the diet as grouse density increased (see also Chapter 30).

On moor A, both pipits and grouse selected the EDGE habitat. Harriers, which appeared to hunt for pipits at low grouse density, hunted the EDGE and therefore located more grouse broods opportunistically. In other words, grouse may have been more prone to predation because they preferred the same habitat as pipits.

Harriers did hunt areas where avian prey (i.e. their main food) were scarce, possibly to continue to monitor these poorer patches. As prey abundance and habitat use vary seasonally, harriers may profit from monitoring prey availability in other patches. Alternatively, it is possible that harriers were not actually hunting these patches at all, but merely travelling between good patches and taking prey from poor patches opportunistically.

Increases in the density of prey not only altered habitat selection, but also influenced the amount of time harriers were prepared to search for grouse chicks. Where grouse were scarce, harriers attacked broods for longer, presumably because the probability of quickly locating another prey item was low. Where large prey were more abundant, harrier attacks on grouse broods were shorter. This resulted in a higher percentage of successful strikes, but a lower percentage of successful encounters as grouse density increased.

Grouse chicks relied on cryptic colouring combined with motionless behaviour to avert detection by predators. Once located by harriers, adult grouse actively defended their young. Adult grouse were not killed, presumably because they were too large to be carried back to the nest. This allowed grouse to protect their young and to attempt to prevent harriers from killing a chick until it became more profitable for the harriers to hunt elsewhere.

The observations of grouse taking their young to cover suggest that the success of harriers in catching grouse chicks may depend on the ability of adult grouse to detect an approaching harrier and warn their young to seek cover. Predation levels were not obviously related to cover, but the number of broods not located by harriers in various habitats is unknown. It seems likely, however, that other factors such as the number of chicks in a grouse brood may also be important in determining the outcome of harrier-grouse interactions.

Once a harrier had captured a grouse chick it was never seen to return to the brood and successfully capture another. Prey brought to the nest also gave no indication that harriers successfully exhibited a win-stay strategy to grouse. Whether or not such a strategy was unviable because of increased grouse brood movements after an attack or some other factor such as increased vigilance is not unknown.

## 22.7 Notes

a. There were differences in the vegetation structure of the two study area A and B: Kolmogorov-Smirnov two-sample test: $X^2 = 22.7$, T.V.. = 2, $P<0.001$.

b. An increase in grouse and hares in the diet of harriers as density increased between moor A & B: $X^2 = 5.2$, $P<0.05$.

c. Items of small prey decreased between moor A and B $X^2 = 6.5$, $P = 0.01$.

d. Harrier hunting time was associated with pipit density $r = 0.41$, $P<0.05$ but not density of grouse chicks $r=-0.33$, $P=0.12$.

e. Interaction time was longer on the low density moor A than high density moor B; Mann-Whitney $z = 2.97$, $P<0.01$, and longer before leaving a brood A $= 219 \pm 98$s, B $= 15 \pm 4$s, U $= 1$, $P<0.001$.

f. Harriers did not appear to bring runs of grouse chicks, T $= 1.13$, d.f. $= 48$, $P>0.1$, log-transformed data.

g. Harrier hunting was correlated with pipits on moor A $r=0.95$, N $=6$, $P<0.05$, not grouse $r=0.71$, $N=6$, NS. On moor B harriers were correlated with grouse $r=0.98$, $N=5$, $P<0.05$, not pipits $r=0.42$, $N=5$, NS.

## 22.8 References

1. Ivlev, V.S. (1961) *Experimental ecology of the feeding of fishes* Yale University Press. New Haven.

2. Picozzi, N. (1978). Dispersion, breeding and prey in the hen harrier *(Circus cyaneus)* in Orkney. *Ornis Scandinavica* **11**: 1-12.

# CHAPTER 23

# DISTURBANCE OF GROUSE BY HEN HARRIERS DURING THE SHOOTING SEASON

**Harriers are known to disturb grouse during the shooting season and consequently influence the daily bag. Observations indicated that grouse moors regularly disturbed by harriers were more likely to pack early in the season and effectively reduce the potential bag by 45%. Daily bags were reduced by 60% probably due to other aspects of disturbance.**

## 23.1 Introduction

While harriers kill grouse they also cause a certain amount of disturbance to the grouse during the shooting season when organised let days can be disrupted by the presence of harriers. Behaviour of grouse changes when harriers are present; the birds can no longer be driven by the line of beaters but fly in all directions, often forming into large packs. Some individuals fly to a high altitude. If the grouse moor is one where harriers have bred and have been present for some time then the grouse often appear 'spooked' and driving the grouse over the guns can become difficult, since the birds fail to respond to the beaters but react in a way to avoid harrier predation. On the other hand, if the harrier is simply an itinerant individual passing across the hill then it may clear part of the hill or even drive grouse from one moor on to the next.

Quantifying the disturbance that harriers make on a driving day is not easy. Harriers may pass through a drive before the drive has started and the effects may vary according to which way the harrier flew, the grouse flight lines on the hill and the history of harrier disturbance. This chapter examines differences in the packing behaviour of grouse on two comparable moors and estimates the effects of packing on the bag.

## 23.2 Methods

The behaviour of grouse was recorded on two grouse moors in northern England, one where harriers were well established and there were known to be at least eight successful breeding female harriers on or close by

the grouse moor; and another in the central Pennines where harriers were not present but the density of breeding grouse was comparable (Table 23.1). During July, grouse were counted on both moors and the number of grouse in different group sizes was recorded. Each moor was then visited on two days during the early part of the shooting season and the size of the grouse packs driven over the butts was recorded during each drive.

Table 23.1 Details on study areas and grouse population used in a comparison of the effects of hen harriers on the packing behaviour of grouse.

|  | Harriers Present | Harriers Absent |
| --- | --- | --- |
| Area of grouse moor driven | 14 km² | 14 km² |
| Breeding female harriers | 8 | 0 |
| Females grouse km⁻² | 27 | 18 |
| Young grouse no km⁻² | 138 | 116 |

During part of our earlier work on grouse[1] the pack size and the success of guns at killing grouse from packs of various sizes was recorded. These data were collected on shooting days from a number of grouse moors and were considered to represent the average efficiency of guns at killing grouse. These data were used here to compare how successful the average grouse team would be at shooting grouse on the two study areas and the effective reduction in grouse bag.

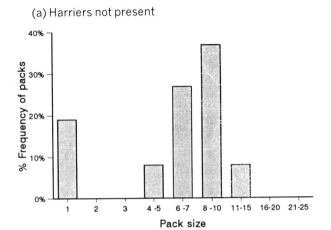

(a) Harriers not present

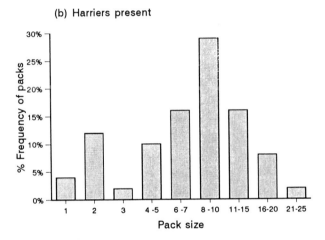

(b) Harriers present

Figure 23.1 Frequency distribution of grouse pack size on two moors counted in mid-July, one with harriers present, the other without harriers. The moor with harriers present had more grouse in packs with more than 11 birds present[a].

### 23.3 Pack sizes during July

On the moor with harriers present, a number of broods had formed into small packs by the middle of July: 47% ($N = 370$) were in groups of 11 or more birds and there was one group of more than 20 birds (Figure 23.1). On the comparable area without harriers, pack sizes were much lower[a]. Only 14% ($N = 224$) of the grouse were in groups of 11 or more and none of these had more than 15 birds (Figure 23.1). Grouse become more grouped when harriers are present.

### 23.4 Pack size during August

During August, pack size of grouse passing through the line of guns was different on the two study moors. On the grouse moor with harriers present, 68% ($N = 1303$) of the individual grouse were in packs

of 11 or more birds and 17 groups of more than 25 individuals were recorded, one with more than 50 individuals (Figure 23.2). Fewer grouse were in large packs on the moor with harriers absent[b]; 32% ($N = 651$) were in packs of more than 11 individuals and only one group of more than 25 individuals was recorded. These observations imply that grouse were more likely to form into packs when harriers were present, although we should like to stress this is not demonstrated clearly since other factors will vary between estates.

### 23.5 Pack size, shooting success, harriers and bag

The proportion of grouse killed on a shooting day depends on the shooting ability of the sportsmen, the packs that fly over the guns and the flight behaviour of the grouse. The average grouse gun will kill 60% of the singletons that pass over the line of guns but

(a) Harriers present

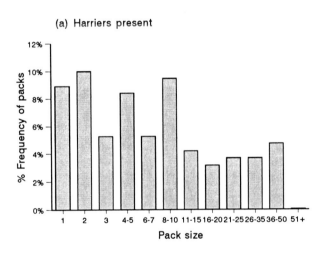

(b) Harriers not present

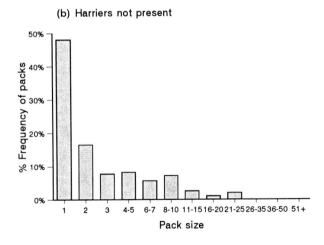

Figure 23.2 Frequency distribution of grouse pack size passing over guns on shooting days in mid-August, one with harriers present the other without harriers. Grouse on the moor with harriers were in larger packs[b].

135

the proportion of individuals shot falls dramatically as pack size increases (Figure 23.3), not because the packs confuse the guns but because the grouse pack passes the butts too fast for the guns to fire enough shots[2].

The effects of the harrier disturbance on the bag can be estimated from information on the observed pack size (Figure 23.2) and the shooting success (Figure 23.3). According to the pack sizes observed, 21.5% of the grouse over the guns should have been shot on the moor without harriers and only 11.8% of the grouse on the moor with harriers[c]. In other words the daily potential bag was reduced by 45% through the possible effects of harrier disturbance on pack size of grouse alone.

To examine the relative importance of this, the daily bag records from the two study areas were examined in more detail. The moor with harriers present shot on average 86 grouse per day, 60% fewer than the moor without harriers, which shot an average of 218 grouse per day. This figure is larger than the 45% expected from the effects of group size alone and may be a consequence of other disturbance factors.

The total bag on the two estates was not that different, although the estate without harriers present shot only five days (bag = 1088 grouse), while the estate with harriers shot a total of 12 days (bag = 1033 grouse).

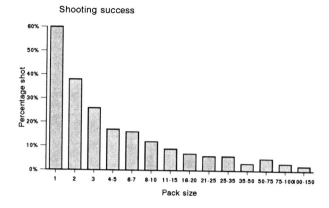

Figure 23.3 Frequency distribution of packs and relative success rate of killing grouse from different pack sizes. Grouse in small groups are more likely to be shot than grouse in large packs.

### 23.6 Summary

The packing behaviour of grouse was compared on two similar moors, one with harriers present and one without harriers. In July, on the moor with harriers present, 47% of grouse were in packs of more than 11 while on the comparable moor only 14% were in packs of more than 11. By August the proportion in packs had increased to 68% on the moor with harriers and 32% on the moor without harriers. The increased aggregation of grouse reduced the daily bag size although the annual bag was not reduced since the moor with harriers shot more days.

### 23.7 Notes

a. During July, grouse on the moor with harriers present were in larger packs than moors without harriers, $X^2 = 67.6$, $P < 0.001$.

b. During August, grouse on the moor with harriers present were in larger packs, $X^2 = 243.0$, $P < 0.001$.

c. Success rate at shooting grouse was reduced significantly through the presence of harriers and their effect on pack size, $X^2 = 31.11$, $P < 0.001$.

### 23.8 References

1. Hudson, P.J.(1986) *The Red grouse: Biology and Management of a Wild Gamebird*. Game Conservancy Trust, Fordingbridge, Hants.

2. Hudson, P.J. (1985) Harvesting red grouse in the North of England. In: *Game Harvest Management*. Ed. Beasom and Robinson, pp319-326.

# POPULATION BIOLOGY OF CYCLIC POPULATIONS: THE EFFECT OF THE TRICHOSTRONGYLE WORM

# CHAPTER 24

# POPULATION CYCLES IN RED GROUSE

**The majority of managed grouse moors produced bag records that exhibited cyclic fluctuations in numbers, the period of these cycles increased the further north and west the population was located.**

### 24.1 Introduction.

A wide range of animal populations exhibit regular fluctuations in numbers known as population cycles. For example, the numbers of Canadian Lynx trapped for the Hudson Bay Trading Company show 10 year cycles with more than a 600 fold fluctuation in numbers. Vole populations show four year population cycles with a 100 fold fluctuation in numbers, but this pattern is not universal since some populations may show cycles while others do not. Several species of grouse also show cyclic fluctuations; red grouse bag records exhibit cyclic fluctuations and the regularity and period of these cycles may vary throughout the British Isles.

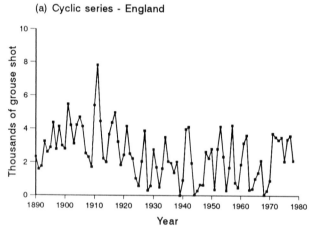

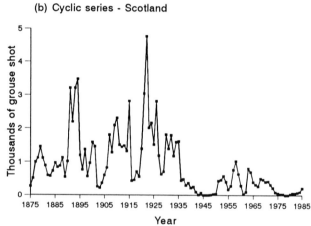

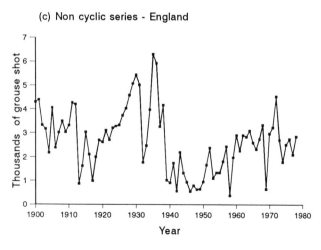

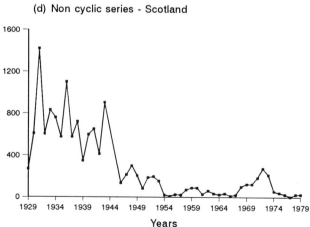

Figure 24.1 Cyclic and non-cyclic bag records from English and Scottish grouse moors.

Describing and ultimately understanding the cyclic fluctuations in grouse numbers is of importance to the managers of grouse populations. Periodic crashes in grouse numbers result in the loss of revenue and cash flow for estates and the factors which reduce density to low levels may also lead to reduced levels of investment and management, causing further problems for the grouse population. Within this chapter, the variations in the cyclic behaviour of grouse bag data are described.

## 24.2 Methods: Analysing population cycles in bag records

Extensive and long term bag records were obtained during two surveys. Records from 63 estates in England were collected during 1979 and from 110 estates in Scotland during 1983. The pattern of fluctuations and trends in the series differed between England and Scotland (Figure 24.1).

Many of the bag series showed a long term, downward trend in numbers caused by loss of habitat or other factors which were not relevant to the study of short-term fluctuations. These trends were discounted from the series by averaging the series several times, producing a smoothed trend line and then subtracting the actual bags from the smoothed line to provide a corrected series[1]. Some of the series had no details for the war years but since these points were less than 3% of the series, the missing figures were simply interpolated.

Once the trends were removed from the series, the presence of statistically significant cycles could be determined. While we have used a number of techniques to identify the nature of these cyclic patterns, the analysis used here was based on serial correlations whereby the numbers shot in one year were correlated with numbers shot in the following year and then with each subsequent year.

The correlation coefficients, which describe the strength of the association between numbers shot in one year and with each subsequent year (years 1,2,3,4 hence) are brought together graphically in a correlogram and the significance of these correlations determined. For a series that shows cyclic fluctuations of four years, significant positive correlations occur at the points relating to the full cycle period of 4,8,12,16 years and negative correlations at intervals of 2,6,10,14 years.

## 24.3 Cyclic and non-cyclic grouse populations

The majority of the bag record series examined (58%

in England and 77% in Scotland) produced significant coefficients consistent with the premise that the populations were producing cyclic changes in numbers. Many of the series showed a significant positive correlation between numbers shot in one year and numbers shot in the subsequent year (Figure 24.2). Those exhibiting cyclic fluctuations showed a statistically significant negative correlation consistent with half the cycle period, but few showed subsequent positive coefficients coinciding with a full cycle period. In other words a series with a cycle period of four years would consistently fall to low numbers two years after a year of high numbers but would not consistently show high numbers again at year four. The cycles were heavily damped in what is classified as

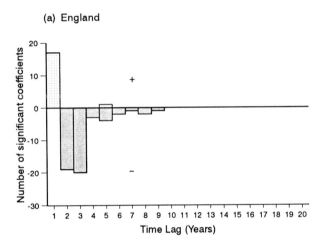

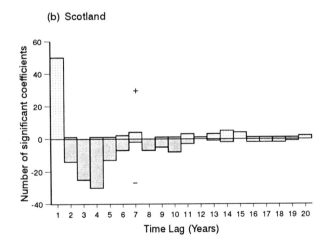

Figure 24.2 The number of statistically significant positive and negative correlation coefficients from (a) English and (b) Scottish grouse populations. In both areas, populations show significant positive coefficients corresponding to a time lag of one year and negative coefficients corresponding to half the cycle period. Few show positive coefficients corresponding to the full cycle period.

'phase forgetting quasi-cycles' as distinct from a truly cyclic series, known as 'phase remembering quasi-cycles'[2]. Such terms are accurate but cumbersome to use, so further reference to 'cycles' will imply phase forgetting quasi cycles. The tendency to produce damped cycles was similar in both Scotland and England (Figure 24.2).

In England, the majority of grouse moors exhibited cycles of 4-5 years in length whereas in Scotland the cycle period was longer and the majority were between 4-8 years in length (Figure 24.3). The duration of cycles tends to increase the further north and west in the British Isles the grouse populations is situated (Figure 24.4).

A number of factors tend to influence whether a series of data is classified as cyclic or non-cyclic (Figure 24.5). The proportion of series exhibiting significant cycles increases with the duration of the series but makes no large affect until the series is longer than 80 years (Figure 24.5a). The tendency to produce significant cycles is more sensitive to the area of moorland, with a sharp increase in the proportion of series exhibiting significant cycles when the moor exceeds 15km[2] (3700 acres) in size (Figure 24.5b). Ignoring the series from areas of less than 15km[2], and comparing altitude, July temperature and days of rainfall, we find that cyclic moors tend to be wetter and significantly colder in July than non cyclic moors (Table 24.1).

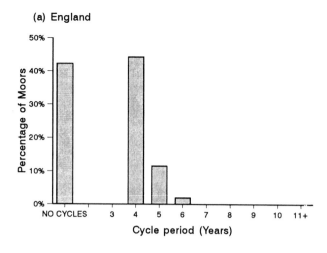

**(a) England**

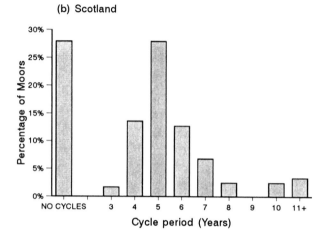

**(b) Scotland**

Figure 24.3 Cycle period of (a) English and (b) Scottish grouse moors. Scottish moors tend to produce cycles of a longer duration.

Table 24.1 Factors associated with the tendency for populations to be cyclic or non-cyclic. Cyclic populations tend to be located in areas with cooler Julys and drier areas than non-cyclic populations.

| Factor | Cyclic Population | Non-Cyclic Population | Significance |
|---|---|---|---|
| Number | 134 | 41 | |
| Altitude (metres) | 373.8 (±9.4) | 366.3 (±17.7) | NS |
| July temp (°C) | 14.15 (±0.05) | 14.57 (±0.12) | P<0.001 |
| Days of rainfall | 158.4 (±1.18) | 153.3 (±3.43) | P<0.05 |

## 24.4 Cause of population cycles

Studies of population cycles in animal species have led to detailed discussion and experimentation on the cause of the fluctuations. Generally, cycles are believed to be caused by a density dependent regulatory effect acting with a time delay[3]. Simple computer programmes can be constructed to show that if the proportional loss from a population increases with density this will tend to stabilise numbers but when such effects act with a time delay there is a tendency for the numbers to cycle. The problem is to identify the density dependent factor, demonstrate it's effect and show it acts with a time delay sufficient to generate population cycles.

In red grouse there are a number of factors that could act in a density dependent manner to cause these fluctuations:

(i) Predation
(ii) Food quantity & quality
(iii) Shooting pressure
(iv) Parasitism
(v) Dispersal
(vi) Spacing behaviour

(1) *Predation:*

If an increase in the grouse population resulted in

Figure 24.4. Geographical variation in the cycle period of grouse populations, determined from bag record data.

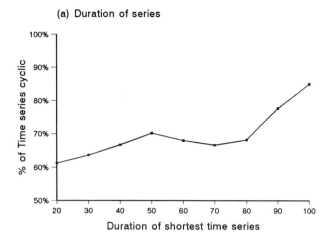

**(a) Duration of series**

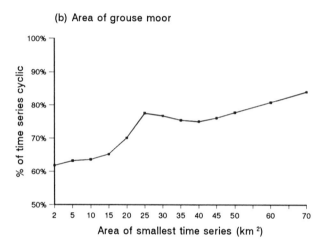

**(b) Area of grouse moor**

Figure 24.5. Two factors that influence the probability of a bag record series being identified as cyclic, (a) the duration of the series and (b) the area of grouse moor. Grouse moors above 15 km² tend to produce bag records more likely to show cycles.

more predators and greater levels of predation in the following year then such actions could act to generate population cycles. However, predation is unlikely to be the cause of the fluctuations in red grouse since predators and the effects of predation are severely curtailed on grouse moors exhibiting cyclic fluctuations. Furthermore, the analysis of population data and the collection of dead grouse during a decline show that most die from disease and not predation.

### (ii) *Food quantity & quality:*

If an increase in grouse density reduces either the quantity or the quality of food taken by birds in the subsequent year, then this could result in a time delayed feed back through survival or breeding production sufficient to cause population cycles. This could operate through the behaviour of the grouse if grouse territory size was determined by either of these factors. These

relationships seem unlikely since grouse only eat about 2% of the green heather available[4]. Furthermore, fertilising experiments designed to increase nitrogen and phosphorous levels failed to stop a population falling on the fertilised area and numbers even fell to a level where there were no more birds present.

### (iii) *Shooting pressure:*

Shooting pressure can be a major cause of annual mortality on a grouse population and on many of the cyclic populations when numbers are increasing this may be the largest single cause of mortality. Nevertheless it is quite apparent from the data available that shooting pressure alone could not be causing the cycles since a lower proportion of grouse tend to be shot at high and low densities than at medium densities. This is because at high densities grouse tend to pack, the birds become difficult to drive and insufficient shooting days can be arranged without the grouse becoming 'butt shy'. Furthermore, some shot populations are not cyclic while there is evidence that some unshot populations are cyclic.

### (iv) *Parasitism*

The idea that parasitism causes the population cycles in red grouse is not new. At the end of the nineteenth century, research workers suggested a number of parasites which could cause the severe mortality and periodic crashes seen in grouse numbers. This was supported by the recovery of large numbers of corpses from birds that had died during a population crash that were heavily infected with the caecal nematode *Trichostrongylus tenuis*. A clear presentation of this work was provided by Edward Wilson in 'The Grouse in Health and in Disease', edited by Lord Lovat and published in 1911[5]. Although population cycles had not been recognised at that time, Wilson suggested that crashes in the grouse population were caused by the direct effects of the parasite on the survival of the grouse. However further detailed studies conducted in Glen Esk[6] between 1956-1961 found that insufficient numbers of grouse died from the parasite to account for these falls in numbers.

In a detailed modelling of parasite host systems, Professors Anderson & May[7,8] demonstrated that three aspects of a parasite system (such as the grouse-*T. tenuis* system) would destabilize host numbers and could generate population cycles:

(i) A reduction in the breeding production of the grouse by the parasite
(ii) A random distribution of parasites throughout the grouse population.

(iii) A time delay in the parasite life cycle.

Each of these will tend to destabilize grouse numbers and could result in population cycles, although the overall effect depends on the tension between these three variables and other aspects of the system which may act to stabilize numbers, such as parasite-induced mortality. The interesting point to note is that the effects of the parasite on grouse breeding production will tend to destabilise numbers and could lead to population cycles, whereas the effects on grouse survival will not cause cycles but tend to stabilize numbers. Previous workers had only considered the effects on grouse survival, not breeding. In this respect a population of grouse could show parasite-induced population crashes without producing large numbers of dead birds, but simply through poor breeding success.

## (v) *Dispersal*

Dispersal is one mechanism that does not actually result in grouse dying on the site but it still acts as a loss from the population being monitored. If the net rate of dispersal was greater following years of high density and was sufficiently large, then population cycles could be generated. However, note that this must be net dispersal from the study population. If a number of neighbouring populations were all decreasing at the same time, the total loss of birds would be large and the birds would have to go somewhere or die. The intensive radio-tracking studies and the counts conducted on our study areas suggest that dispersal does occur but the analysis presented in Chapter 12 shows this to be density dependent and that no sign of a year's time delay was found. As such, dispersal would tend to stabilize rather than destabilize grouse numbers. Contrary to this, studies at Kerloch grouse moor between 1969 and 1977 found low levels of dispersal during a period of population increase and high levels during a population decline.

## (vi) *Spacing behaviour*

Studies in north East Scotland provide evidence that grouse densities can be limited by the territorial behaviour of the grouse. This is generally accepted as a mechanism of limiting population size and one which tends to stabilize numbers rather than causing population cycles. As such it is difficult to believe that spacing behaviour alone could act to cause some populations to fall to such low densities that they can be considered to be locally extinct as recorded in north east Scotland[9]. Nevertheless, if the territorial behaviour of the grouse is determined in a delayed density dependent manner then population cycles could be generated.

A number of hypotheses for this have been investigated by research workers at the Institute of Terrestrial Ecology[10,11]. A genetic hypothesis was considered whereby there was a selective advantage to the more dominant aggressive individuals at high density. These take large territories and exclude the more passive individuals and would cause the population to fall; at low density there would then be a selective advantage for more tolerant individuals which may breed faster, so the population would increase. Through detailed laboratory and field experiments this hypothesis was investigated after a population cycle but the results were the opposite to those predicted by the hypothesis. Aggressiveness of the birds should have increased before the decline but in fact it only increased after the population had started to decline.

More recently, another hypothesis has been proposed, based on differential dispersal of related and non-related individuals. If genetic relatedness among neighbours changes with population density and cocks are highly tolerant of kin (brothers) and intolerant of unrelated neighbours, then it has been shown through mathematical models that population cycles could be generated. We know that cocks do establish territories adjoining their kin (Chapter 14) and there is limited evidence for differential behaviour between related and unrelated neighbours. However the magnitude of these differences must be large and other aspects of the model carefully chosen to produce cycles. At the current time there is little evidence to support this fascinating hypothesis and experimental work is required.

## *Conclusion*

The factor or combination of factors that cause population cycles in red grouse must act in a delayed density dependent manner and while there are a wide range of factors that could act, only two appear strong contenders, parasitism and spacing behaviour. Even the latter seems unlikely to be a sole factor although it may well interact with parasitism to cause and explain the variations observed.

## 24.5 Summary

The majority of grouse moors produce bag records which exhibit statistically significant population cycles, strictly speaking these are known as 'phase forgetting quasi-cycles'. The period of cycles was 4-5 years in England and 4-8 years in Scotland. The tendency for a series to produce cycles increased with the duration of the series and the size of the grouse moor. Ignoring short durations and records from small moors the cyclic populations were located in wet areas with cool Julys.

Six factors which could cause population cycles were considered, namely: predation; food quantity and quality, shooting pressure, parasitism, dispersal and spacing behaviour. The inimnical factor that causes these cycles must increase with grouse density and act with a suitable time delay. Of the factors considered only parasitism and spacing behaviour could operate to cause these cycles.

## 24.6 References:

1. Potts, G.R., Tapper, S.C. & Hudson, P.J. (1984). Population fluctuations in red grouse: analysis of bag records and a simulation model. *Journal of Animal Ecology,* **53**, 21-36.

2. Nisbett, R.M. and Gurney, W.S.C. (1952). *Modelling fluctuating populations.* John Wiley & Sons, Chichester.

3. May, R.M. 1981. *Theoretical Ecology, Principles and Applications.* Blackwell Scientific Publications, Oxford.

4. Savory, C.J. (1978). Food consumption of red grouse in relation to the age and productivity of heather, *Journal of Animal Ecology,* **47**, 269-282.

5. Lovat, Lord (1911). *The Grouse in health and in disease,* Smith & Elder, London.

6. Jenkins, D., Watson, A. and Miller, G.R. (1953). Population studies on red grouse *Lagopus lagopus scoticus* (Lath.) in north-east Scotland. *Journal of Animal Ecology,* **32**, 317-376.

7. Anderson, R.M. and May, R.M. (1978). Regulation and stability of nest-parasite population interactions. I Regulatory processes. *Journal of Animal Ecology,* **47**, 219-249.

8. May, R.M. & Anderson, R.M. (1978). Regulation and stability of host-parasite interactions. II Destabilising processes. *Journal of Animal Ecology,* **47**, 249-268

9. Watson, A., Moss, R. & Parr, R. (1984). Effects of food enrichment on numbers and spacing behaviour of red grouse. *Journal of Animal Ecology,* **53**, 663-678.

10. Moss, R. & Watson, A. (1985). Adaptive value of spacing behaviour in population cycles of red grouse and other animals. *Symposium of the British Ecological Society.* **25**, 275-294.

11. Moss, R. & Watson, A. (1991). Population cycles and hen selection in red grouse *Lagopus lagopus scoticus. Ibis,* **133**, 113-120.

Electronmicrograph of adult strongyle worms burrowing into the gut wall of a grouse. The parasites cause internal bleeding and reduce the condition of the bird (Chapter 25).

A caecal dropping of a red grouse containing the eggs of the strongyle worm. Warm humid conditions are necessary for development and survival of the free living stages (Chapter 25).

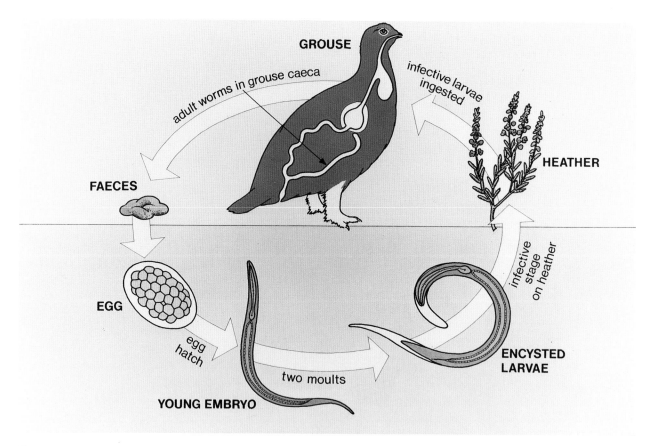

Figure 25.1. The life cycle of *Trichostrongylus tenuis*, a nematode parasite of red grouse. Two features of the life cycle are important. First, any increase in the number of worms inside a bird results from direct infection. Second, this is a direct life cycle with no intermediate hosts, so rates of infection will increase with the density of the grouse (Chapter 25).

The parasitic strongyle worms can reduce the condition, breeding success and survival of hen red grouse (Chapter 27).

# THE LIFE CYCLE OF THE TRICHOSTRONGYLE WORM:
## *TRICHOSTRONGYLUS TENUIS*

**The pattern of parasite distribution within the grouse population and delays in the development of certain stages may act to influence changes in grouse numbers. These features and the life cycle of the parasite are described.**

### 25.1 Introduction

Bag records from grouse populations show cyclic fluctuations in numbers and the discussion in the last chapter led us to suppose that the parasitic trichostrongyle worm may be an important driving force in causing these cycles. Three conditions were considered which could generate the population cycles:

(i) A random distribution of parasites within the grouse population
(ii) Time delays in the parasite's life cycle
(iii) Parasite induced reduction in grouse breeding.

This chapter describes aspects of the life cycle of the parasite and in particular examines the first two of these conditions.

### 25.2 Summary life cycle

Adult *T. tenuis* inhabit the relatively large caeca of red

grouse (70 cm). Their eggs pass from the host in the bird's caecal faeces (Figure 25.1. See facing page), these being the brown glutinous droppings which contrast with the more typical fibrous droppings. Within the eggs, the worm embryos develop when the temperature exceeds 5°C and the subsequent survival through two larval stages to the infective larvae is dependent on temperature, providing the moisture is adequate[1,2,3]. Under optimal conditions, development from egg to the third stage infective larva is seven days, although eggs may remain unhatched for several months. The third stage infective larvae migrate from the caecal faeces to the growing tips of heather, and grouse become infected when they feed.

Once inside the grouse the larvae normally develop to adult worms within 10 to 14 days. However, this may not be immediate; some larvae can moult their outer sheath and cease development in an arrested stage. Arrested larvae are usually found only during the winter months although the period of this arrestment and the factors initiating an infective larva to arrest are not clearly known.

Two important points within the life cycle of nematodes like the trichostrongyle worm are:

(i) All parasites found within the grouse have been ingested by the bird, numbers cannot increase within the bird.

(ii) The parasite life cycle is a direct life cycle without any intermediate hosts and although the parasite has been recorded in other gamebirds such as partridges, this is essentially a simple 'one host one parasite' system.

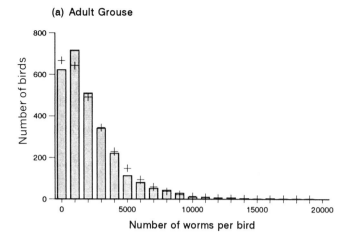

**(a) Adult Grouse**

**(b) Immature Grouse**

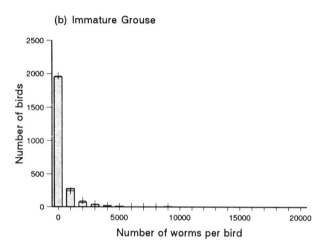

Figure 25.2. Frequency distribution of trichostrongyle worm in (a) old grouse and (b) immature grouse. Bars show numbers observed in each worm category and points the predictions of the negative binomial distribution. Overall, parasites show an aggregated distribution with a few grouse carrying a proportionately high number of worms.

## 25.3 Parasite distribution within the grouse population

While we have conducted extensive work on the numbers of parasites in red grouse from a wide range of populations throughout northern England and Scotland, this study concentrates on the intensive studies conducted at one site, Gunnerside in North Yorkshire. At this site we have obtained detailed information on the grouse and worm populations for 11 years.

Gut samples were collected from young and old grouse on shooting days in August and September and the number of worms per bird estimated through a technique of washing. The total number of worms per bird was estimated by flushing the caeca with water, collecting the contents over a 210 micrometer gauze, diluting into 300ml of water and subsampling three times in 10mls. Average intensity of worms per bird is expressed as the geometric mean ($Log_{10} x + 1$) worms per bird.

All adult grouse inspected (2739 birds) and 99.2% (2723 birds) of immature grouse were infected with the parasite. The 21 uninfected birds were all less than two months old.

The overall pattern of worm distribution throughout the population of old grouse was aggregated (Figure 25.2) with a number of grouse carrying a higher proportion of the worm population than expected by chance (statistically the variance was greater than the mean). No significant difference was found between the distribution of parasites in adult male and female grouse[a].

The pattern of nematode distribution in the adult grouse population varied between years. This can be described in a number of ways but the simplest is to consider the ratio of the two statistics that describe the pattern of distribution, the variance (the spread) and the mean (the true average). A random distribution has a variance to mean ratio (variance divided by mean) of one, ratios greater than one are aggregated and when lower than one they show a regular distribution. Within this study the variance to mean ratio varied in different years between 0.81 and 2.50 (10 year mean = 1.854, Standard Error = 0.219) and was less than one in two of the 10 years (Figure 25.3).

While the overall distribution was aggregated, it should be noted that in comparison with other parasite distributions the degree of aggregation is relatively

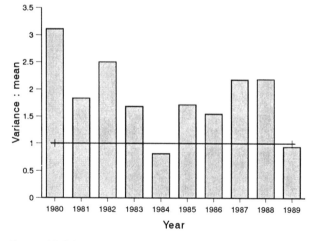

Figure 25.3 Changes in the pattern of distribution of worms in grouse over 10 years, as measured by the variance to mean ratio. When the variance to mean ratio equals one then the distribution is random, while ratios greater than one indicate an aggregated distribution. Although the overall distribution is generally aggregated, for a parasite system this is a relatively low level of aggregation.

low; most parasite systems have a much higher level of aggregation. This is partly a consequence of high prevalence and intensity of infection and partly because there is little resistance by the birds to the infection.

## 25.4 Adult worm mortality

Estimating the survival of adult worms is not simple unless captive grouse with artificial infections are used, but grouse kept in captivity tend to develop guts with smaller caeca than wild birds[6]. Captive grouse experiments[4] have demonstrated a decline in egg production by worms over 72 weeks following artificial infection. Maximum egg production was reached within six weeks of infection and then fell exponentially (a constant proportional rate).

If egg production per worm was constant, the decline in egg production would indicate a worm survival of 34% per annum. Later experiments[5] also recorded a decrease in egg production with age of infection in captive grouse, but found that egg production decreased with age so our assessment of adult worm survival would be an underestimate. However, they also found differences in the rate of egg production between captive and wild grouse, thus making extrapolation between captive and wild birds difficult.

## 25.5 Worm egg production

Egg concentrations in caecal content were estimated from 422 grouse shot during August and September. From one of the two caeca, worm eggs were sampled by collecting approximately 1g of caecal contents from the proximal end, this being the material most likely to be defaecated next. Eggs were counted using the McMaster egg counting technique. Intensity of worm infection was determined from the second caeca and egg concentration expressed as eggs worm$^{-1}$ g$^{-1}$ caecal contents.

Concentration of eggs in caecal contents was 6.05 eggs worm$^{-1}$ g$^{-1}$ (standard error = */ 1.109) for the 422 individuals sampled. There is evidence of a slight fall in egg production with intensity of worm infection in old grouse but this is addressed in more detail in Chapter 29.

The quantity of caecal faeces produced per day was determined by weighing faeces collected from night roosts and averaged 18.84 g bird$^{-1}$ (S.E. = 1.06, N = 52). Additional caecal faeces were rarely found away from night roost sites. Overall worm fecundity can be calculated from the rate of egg production and the average quantity of caecal faeces produced as

$4*10^4$ eggs worm$^{-1}$ y$^{-1}$. Counts of eggs inside the worms[5] found female fecundity to be 356 eggs per female worm per day, with a sex ratio of 1.35 males/female this gives a comparable figure of $5.5*10^4$ eggs worm$^{-1}$ y$^{-1}$.

## 25.6 Periods of infection and time delays in development

Intensity of infection in young grouse was determined in each year by collecting samples during the shooting season. In 1982 samples were collected from young birds every two weeks from early July to mid December. Serial sampling of grouse (Figure 25.4) indicates that there are two periods of recruitment into the worm population; the first in late summer, the second in late winter.

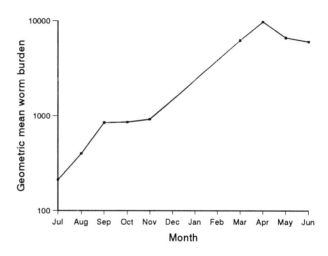

Figure 25.4. Mean worm burdens in grouse killed from the summer of 1982 through to the summer of 1983, showing two periods of infection: one during spring and a second during the winter. Note no samples were collected in December, January and February.

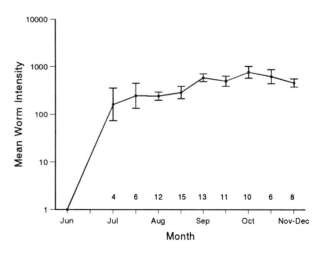

Figure 25.5. Worm uptake by young grouse during the summer of 1982, points show mean ± 1 Standard error.

147

To determine whether environmental conditions influenced year to year differences in the recruitment rate of parasites, details of daily rainfall for Gunnerside village (SD 951983; 3 km from the study area) and minimum and maximum temperature for Malham Tarn (SD 895672; 33 km from the study area) were obtained through The Meteorological Office at Newcastle Weather Centre.

*Summer recruitment:* The uptake of worms during the summer (Figure 25.5) is associated with the availability of infective larvae recovered from heather. Summer recruitment was defined as the average (geometric mean) number of worms in immature grouse ($W_i$) shot during September.

The size of the summer infection increased with minimum July temperature[b] but not with rainfall or either maximum or minimum temperature in any other month. Variations between year were also positively correlated[c] with density of grouse (adults and immatures) in the July of the previous year, and with intensity of parasite infection in adult grouse[d]. Further analysis of these variables (through partial correlation[e]) suggest that density in the previous year was more closely associated with level of summer infection when the effects of parasite intensity in adults and July minimum temperature were removed, although this relationship relies on a single outlying point (Figure 25.6).

In summary the changes in the summer infection between years is influenced by the density of grouse in the preceding July.

*Winter recruitment:* Serial sampling of grouse reveals an increase in intensity of infection in late winter (Figure 25.4), when infective larvae cannot be recovered from

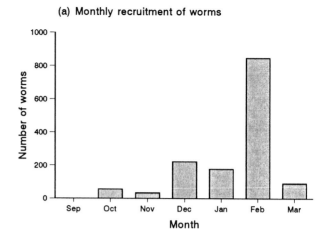

**(a) Monthly recruitment of worms**

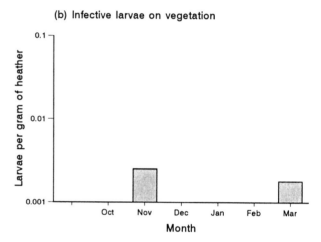

**(b) Infective larvae on vegetation**

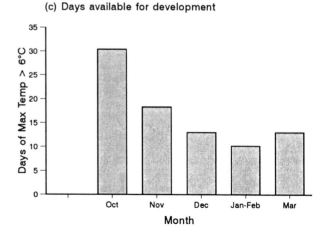

**(c) Days available for development**

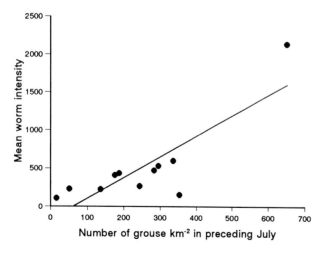

Figure 25.6. Uptake of worms during the summer was correlated with the density of grouse in July, more than one year earlier.

Figure 25.7. Winter recruitment of parasites occurs (a) during late winter when (b) few infective larvae are recovered from the vegetation and (c) there are few days when temperature is above 6°C and worms can develop.

vegetation (Figure 25.7). The most likely explanation for this recruitment is that larvae which infected hosts during the autumn enter a period of arrestment or hypobiosis[7], a period of temporary delay from development which is resumed during the following February or March.

The net winter recruitment ($R_w$) could not be assessed directly but was estimated indirectly from consecutive worm counts of adult and immature grouse. This was the difference between mean worm burdens in adult grouse in autumn of year $t+1$ ($W_{a(t+1)}$) and mean worm burdens in all grouse in autumn of year $t$ ($W_t$) and the level of summer infection measured in immature grouse in year $t+1$ ($W_{i(t+1)}$):

$$R_w = W_{a(t+1)} - W_{i(t+1)} - W_{(t)}$$

This assumes that infection rate in adult and immature grouse is similar, a reasonable assumption since there appears to be little resistance to infection (Chapter 26).

In all but one year, levels of winter recruitment were greater than summer recruitment. Year to year variations in winter recruitment were not associated with weather conditions nor previous levels of infection, but were correlated with density of grouse in the previous July[f] (Figure 25.8) although this relationship is dependent on one outlier.

### 25.7 Discussion and management options

While this chapter presents a range of results on the life cycle of the trichostrongyle worm, two of the conditions raised in the introduction which could cause cycles were examined in particular:
(i) the distribution of parasites within the grouse population
(ii) time delays in the development of the parasite within the life cycle.

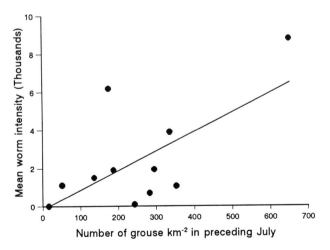

Figure 25.8. Uptake of worms during the winter was correlated with the density of grouse in the preceding July.

While the overall distribution of parasites was aggregated and not a random distribution, the extent of the aggregation was low and in the majority of years (Figure 25.3) close to random. Unlike this distribution, the majority of other parasite distributions are highly aggregated. This low degree of aggregation will tend to cause numbers to cycle.

The second factor considered was time delays in the development of the parasites life cycle which, in combination with the direct effects on the grouse, could generate population cycles. Parasite infection rates were correlated with the preceding density of grouse in July and thus showed delayed density dependent infection rates. The actual mechanism of delay within the system may simply be through slow development times at low temperature but it may also act through arrested larval development.

### 25.8 Management implications

The relationship between July density and subsequent levels of infection allows a prediction of future population changes and should be used to trigger management techniques. Essentially, high July densities lead to increased infection levels in the subsequent years, so control techniques such as medicated grit and direct dosing should be applied to rising populations.

### 25.9 Summary

The overall pattern of worm distribution within the grouse population was aggregated, with a minority of grouse carrying the majority of the worms. Nevertheless the level of this aggregation varied between years and compared to other parasite systems was low. Worm survival was estimated at about 34% per annum and egg production at 40 000 eggs per worm per year.

There are two periods of recruitment into the worm population. Summer recruitment is a direct consequence of ingesting infective larvae; it increases when July temperature is high but more importantly when the grouse density was high in the July of the previous year. Winter recruitment may occur through direct infection but also when larvae enter a period of arrested development. The extent of this winter recruitment is also related to grouse density in the preceding July. The low degree of aggregation coupled with the delay in development will tend to destabilize grouse numbers and will influence the tendency for grouse populations to cycle in relation to the direct effects of the parasite on grouse survival and breeding.

## 25.10 Notes

a. No difference between the distribution of parasites in adult male and female grouse; Contingency test, with classes of 1000 worms and classes greater than 9000 worms combined: $X^2 = 7.18$, d.f. $= 9$, $P > 0.05$.

b. Size of the summer infection increased with minimum July temperature: $r = 0.83$, $N = 10$, $P < 0.01$

c. Summer infection correlated with density of grouse (adults and immatures) in the July of the previous year: $r = 0.844$, $N = 10$, $P < 0.01$.

d. Summer infection associated with intensity of parasite infection in adult grouse $r = 0.828$, $N = 10$, $P < .01$.

e. Partial correlation with density, $r = 0.78$, $P < 0.02$; parasites in adult grouse $r = 0.68$, $P > 0.5$; July minimum temperature $r = 0.70$, $P < 0.05$.

f. Winter recruitment was not associated with weather conditions nor previous levels of infection, but was correlated with density of grouse in the previous July: $r = 0.751$, $N = 10$, $P < 0.01$

## 25.11 References

1. Hudson, P.J. (1986). *The Red Grouse. Biology and Management of a Wild Gamebird.* Game Conservancy Trust, Fordingbridge.

2. Watson, H. (1988). The ecology and pathophysiology of *Tricholstrongylus tenuis.* Unpublished PhD Thesis, University of Leeds.

3. Shaw, J.L., Moss, R & Pike, A.W. (1989). Development and survival of the free-living stages of *Trichostrongylus tenuis,* a caecal parasite of red grouse *(Lagopus lagopus scoticus). Parasitology,* **99**, 253-258.

4. Wilson, G.R. (1979). The effects of the caecal threadworm *Trichostrongls tenuis* on red grouse. Unpublished PhD thesis, University of Aberdeen.

5. Shaw, J.L. & Moss, R. (1989). The role of parasite fecundity and longevity in the success of *Trichostrongylus tenuis* in low density red grouse poulations. *Parasitology,* **99**, 253-258.

6. Moss, R. (1972). Effects of captivity on gut lengths of red grouse. *Journal of Wildlife Management,* **36**, 99-104.

7. Shaw, J.L. (1988). Arrested development of *Trichostrongylus tenuis* as third stage larvae in red grouse. *Research in Veterinary Science,* **45**, 256-258.

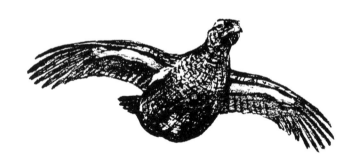

# CHAPTER 26

# WORM EGG PRODUCTION AND RESISTANCE TO PARASITE INFECTION

**Grouse carry remarkably high burdens of worms and the birds appear to exhibit little resistance to the parasite.**

## 26.1 Introduction

Parasitic worms are highly fecund[1]; in many species the females may produce thousands of viable eggs each year. However, rates of egg production in many parasite systems are highly variable and this variation severely compromises the use of faecal egg counts to estimate worm burdens. High variation in egg production could be influenced by a number of factors although two features are believed to be of prime importance:

(i) density dependent competition between worms for resources resulting in the suppression of egg production, i.e. a reduction in egg production by worms with the size of the worm burden.

(ii) density dependent response of the host (immunological or non-specific) to the infection, i.e. increased resistance to the parasite burden by the grouse.

These two density dependent mechanisms can have profound effects upon the grouse and worm population and implications for control. Competition between individual worms for space, food or other resources will depend on current levels of infection, while the response of the host to the parasite will be a function of the cumulative exposure to infection[2]. Identifying the difference between these two mechanisms within a parasite-host system is not easy and cannot be determined readily from patterns of infection, since intensity and exposure will be correlated irrespective of the underlying mechanisms.

Experimental examination of the rate of reinfection may permit the dominant mechanism to be identified. In a system where competition for resources is the dominant density dependent mechanism, reinfection rates should be a simple function of current parasite intensity and will be similar to naive individuals. In contrast, a system where a host-mediated response produces the density dependent mechanism, rates of reinfection will be a function of past exposure; if parasite burdens were previously high, reinfection rates will be significantly lower when compared to naive individuals.

This chapter investigates two aspects of density dependent interactions in the red grouse-*T. tenuis* system. First, density dependent suppression of worm egg production is investigated. Second, comparative data on primary and secondary infections are examined to determine whether a density dependent response is a consequence of either a host-mediated response or worm competition.

## 26.2 Changes in worm egg counts with worm burdens

This section uses the same egg production data gathered in Chapter 25. Worm eggs were sampled from the caeca of shot grouse and counted using the McMaster egg counting technique. Intensity of worm infection was determined from the second caeca.

The intensity of infection and worm fecundity, measured as numbers of eggs per gram of caecal faeces (e.p.g.) were determined for a total of 422 grouse shot in August and September. Overall, egg production per worm did not decrease with worm burden[a], i.e. it was not density dependent.

Considering the adult grouse only, there was a significant decrease in the egg production per worm with intensity of infection, but no such relationship

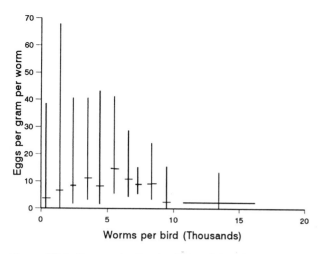

Figure 26.1. Egg production by *T. tenuis* in relation to intensity of worm infection. Points show mean ± 1 standard deviation, note the high degree of variation but an overall trend towards reduced egg production at high worm intensities.

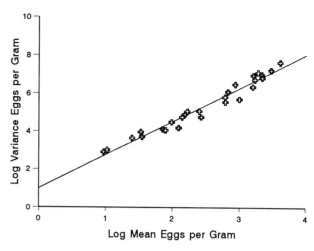

Figure 26.2. Day to day variability in egg production from individual grouse. (Variance, mean plot of egg production with best fit linear model) The slope of 1.76 indicates a high degree of variability.

was found for immature grouse[b]. This is perhaps not surprising since few immature grouse carry a heavy parasite infection, while 16 (5%) of the mature grouse carried worm infections greater than 10,000 worms per bird.

Overall, there is a general density dependent depression of egg production in adult grouse but, as with other helminth systems, a high variation in egg production (Figure 26.1).

### 26.3 Individual variation in egg production

Twenty-seven grouse were caught in spring, radio-tagged and followed during June in 1982 and 1983. Roost sites of radio-tagged grouse were pin-pointed at night and caecal material collected the following morning. Worm eggs per gram of caecal material were estimated for each site and geometric means and variance calculated for individual birds.

Consecutive daily collection of caecal material from individual grouse during June showed inherent variability in egg production. This can be examined in more detail by plotting the logarithm of the variance against the logarithm of the mean. This relationship from the 27 individuals was linear, with a slope of 1.76.[c] (Figure 26.2). If the day to day counts were randomly distributed this relationship would have a slope of one; the significantly steeper slope indicates high variability in egg production. In practical terms this means accurate measures of worm intensity cannot be made from egg counts.

One way of considering the usefulness of caecal egg counts as estimates of intensity of infections is to consider the relationship between eggs per gram in faeces and intensity of infection. If net egg output is directly proportional to intensity of worm infection

then a straight line passing through the origin would be expected. No such relationship is found for grouse (Figure 26.3), presumably because there is a tendency for individuals with high worm burdens to produce fewer eggs per worm.

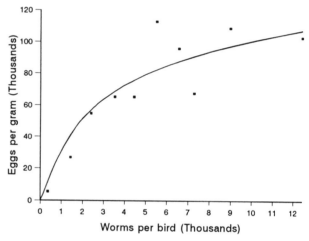

Figure 26.3. Worm egg production as a function of intensity of worm infection. Points show mean for data grouped into individual worm classes.

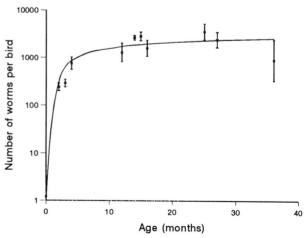

Figure 26.4. Age intensity curve for *T. tenuis* in red grouse. Points show mean and standard error of known aged birds collected from Gunnerside, North Yorkshire over a number of years.

## 26.4 Age intensity infection

As part of our long term study on red grouse, broods of grouse were located on the study area using trained pointing dogs. The dogs found individual chicks hiding in the heather when the chicks were two to 15 days of age and each was individually tagged using small numbered patagial wing tags. When tagged grouse were shot during subsequent shooting seasons, the age of the grouse at death was determined, the guts removed and intensity of worm infection estimated.

The age intensity curve for known age grouse shows a general increase in the intensity of infection with age (Figure 26.4). In many host-parasite systems such a relationship is often curved downwards as immunity develops in older birds and the parasites are rejected, this is known as a spontaneous cure curve. No signs of a spontaneous cure were found in this system.

## 26.5 Primary and secondary infections

From 12 August to the end of September, red grouse samples were collected from sporting estates in England and Scotland where a sample of adult grouse had been treated in the previous spring with an anthelmintic. The intensity of worm infections was determined for a sample of immature (3-4 months old), adult (> 15 months - a primary infection) and treated adult grouse (> 15 months - secondary infection). The sample of immature birds represented primary infections that had occurred in naive individuals over the preceding 3-4 months.

Grouse were dazzled at night, during March and early April, with a strong quartz-halogen lamp, caught in a net and then treated orally with Levamisole hydrochloride (NILVERM). Each bird was then individually tagged with a numbered patagial Quadtag; intensity of worm infection was estimated when birds were subsequently shot. With the co-operation of sporting estates, this procedure was replicated 15 times on grouse populations in North Yorkshire, Lancashire, Highland and Borders Regions. On one estate in Inverness-shire, a sample of several hundred grouse were treated in consecutive years from 1988 to 1990 and samples taken of birds treated both in the previous spring and in the preceding spring to determine whether treated individuals showed a continued increase in parasite infection.

Treated individuals represented a sample of individuals exposed to a secondary infection between April and the following August-September. The period of exposure was some six to 10 weeks longer than for the immature grouse, although the period of primary infection was included. If any density dependent response is host-mediated, then secondary infections will be an inverse function of previous parasite burdens and will be lower than primary infections. Alternatively, if the response is mediated through parasite competition for resources, then infection rate in primary and secondary infections will be similar and infection in secondary infections will not be an inverse function of previous intensity. Furthermore, secondary infections will continue to rise and a year later (i.e. 18 months after treatment) parasite burdens will be significantly greater than they were a year previously.

The intensity of secondary infections in adult grouse was associated with the intensity of primary infections in immature grouse. The relationship was not significantly different from the 1:1 line[d]. Obtaining levels of exposure from wild birds of known age was not possible within this system, although if a host-mediated response was important we could expect an association between levels of secondary infection and parasite intensity in untreated adult grouse. No such association was found[e], suggesting that rates of reinfection were not influenced by previous levels of infection.

These results show reinfection rates of treated individuals are not different from those of naive, primarily infected grouse. Parasite intensity in treated grouse continued to rise after treatment. Grouse collected 18 months after treatment carried significantly greater worm burdens than were carried by the same cohort of treated grouse only six months after treatment[f] (Table 26.1)

These data are not consistent with the hypothesis that a host-mediated response is limiting infection but they are consistent with the hypothesis that density dependent competition between parasites could suppress egg production.

153

Table 26.1. Geometric mean worm intensities in grouse sampled 18 months after treatment were significantly greater than in grouse sampled six months after treatment, showing reinfections continue to increase, a prediction consistent with the hypothesis of a low or non existent immunological response.

| | Period | Mean | Standard Deviation | N. |
|---|---|---|---|---|
| Treated spring 1989 Sampled autumn 1989 | 6 months | 790 | 2.41 | 151 |
| Treated spring 1989 Sampled autumn 1990 | 18 months | 1425 | 1.96 | 22 |
| Treated spring 1990 Sampled autumn 1990 | 6 months | 291 | 2.93 | 27 |

## 26.6 Discussion

Density dependent egg suppression of *T. tenuis* was observed in adult grouse and comparisons of rates of reinfection in treated grouse were consistent with the explanation that density dependence was a consequence of competition between parasites for resources rather than a host-mediated immune response. However, note that the reinfection experiments neither test specifically the nature of the mechanism generating density dependent egg production nor do they mutually exclude the possibility of a host-mediated response acting at the same time. The data simply indicate that a host-mediated response was not a dominant part of the system.

*Density dependent egg production*

As with many helminth systems, it is apparent that egg counts are poor measures of worm burdens due to both the high variability in egg production and the underlying density dependent suppression of egg production at high worm intensities. Egg count data could allow the qualitative division of individuals into those with high and low levels of infection, but quantitative assessment should be considered with great care.

The intensity dependent suppression of egg output occurred only in heavily infected individuals where there was presumably competition between individuals for either food or space. Density dependent suppression in fecundity is not uncommon in many parasite systems and has been recorded for all major human helminths. However, previous studies have shown that such depression can occur at low levels of infection, perhaps as a result of the hosts response to infection rather than competition between helminths.

*Mechanisms generating density dependent response:*

The age intensity curve in red grouse shows no evidence of a spontaneous cure to infections, unlike infections with the same trichostrongyle worm in other hosts including domestic chickens[4], grey partridge and quail[5]. The evidence from reinfection rates is consistent with the hypothesis that grouse produce a relatively poor immune response to this infection. The difference between grouse and other hosts is interesting and may be related to the small parasite community found in red grouse compared with other hosts.

While it is quite possible that density dependent egg suppression is a consequence of both an immune response by the host and competition between worms for resources, the evidence presented in this study would imply that competition was the major component of this response.

## 26.7 Summary

Density dependent suppression of egg production was found in adult but not immature grouse and only occurred at high worm intensities. Consecutive egg counts on individual wild grouse showed high variability in worm egg production and, in practical terms, this means that accurate estimates of worm intensity could not be made from faecal samples. Age intensity curves show no signs of self-cure and instead show a general increase with age. Reinfection rates of treated adults were not different from those of naive immature grouse and secondary infections continued to rise over a period of 18 months, consistent with the hypothesis that density dependent suppression in egg production is mediated through worm competition rather than a host-mediated response.

## 26.8 Notes

a. Egg production per worm did not decrease with worm burden, i.e. it was not density dependent: $r = -0.003$, $P > 0.05$, $N = 422$.

b. There was a significant decrease in per capita egg production with intensity of infection: $r = -0.157$, $P < 0.05$, $N = 299$ but no such relationship was for immature grouse: $r = -0.114$. $P > 0.05$, $N = 112$

c. This relationship from the 27 individuals was linear, with a slope of 1.76: $r = 0.98$, $N = 27$, $P < 0.001$,

d. The relationship was not significantly different from a 1:1 line: $F = 15.31$, $P > 0.10$

e. No association was found between old grouse and secondary levels of infection: $r = 0.228$, $P = 0.43$, NS

f. Grouse collected 18 months after treatment carried significantly greater worm burdens than the same cohort of treated grouse carried at 6 months after treatment: $t = 3.01$, $P < 0.001$.

## 26.9 References

1. Scott, J.A. (1936). The regularity of egg output of helminth infestations, with special reference to *Schistosoma mansoni. American Journal of Hygiene,* **27**, 155-175.

2. Anderson, R.M. (1986). The population dynamics and epidemiology of intestinal nematode infections. *Transactions of Royal Society of Tropical Medicine & Hygiene,* **80**, 686-696.

3. Anderson, R.M. & May, R.M. (1985). Herd immunity to helminth infection and implications for parasite control. *Nature (London),* **315**, 493-496.

4. Watson, H., Lee, D.L., & Hudson, P.J. (1988). Primary and secondary infections of the domestic chicken with *Trichostrongylus tenuis* (Nematoda), a parasite of red grouse, with observations on the effect of the caecal mucosa. *Parasitology,* **97**, 89-99.

5. Moore, J., Freehling, M. & Simberloff, D. (1986). Gastrointestinal helminths of the northern bobwhite in Florida: 1968 and 1983. *Journal of Wildlife Diseases* **22**, 497-501.

# CHAPTER 27

# THE EFFECTS OF THE TRICHOSTRONGYLE WORM ON GROUSE SURVIVAL AND BREEDING

**Worms reduce both the breeding production and survival of grouse and were an important casue of loss to the main study population.**

## 27.1 Introduction

Previous chapters have described aspects of the life cycle of the parasite and established:

(i) Grouse populations fluctuate in a cyclic manner
(ii) Parasites are aggregated within the grouse population but only to a low degree.
(iii) Parasite infections are density dependent and there are time delays in the system
(iv) Parasites do not appear to induce a host-mediated immune response to the infection.

These last three facts will allow parasite burdens to increase with the age of the grouse and the rate of infection to increase after a time delay with grouse density. If the parasite then has a direct effect on the grouse breeding and survival, this could be sufficient to generate population cycles. This is explored further in this chapter in two ways: first by examining whether mortality and losses from a study population increase with parasite burdens and second by reviewing experiments to determine if any correlation is one of cause and effect.

## 27.2 Population biology of red grouse

Intensive population studies were conducted from July 1979 to July 1989 on an area of 0.8km² of managed grouse moor, west of Gunnerside Ghyll, Swaledale, North Yorkshire. Analysis of the 107 years of bag record data from the estate produced a damped correlogram with a significant negative coefficient at half the cycle period of 4.7 years.

With the aid of trained pointing dogs, total counts of the study area were conducted in April to estimate breeding density, and again in July when chicks were seven weeks of age to estimate breeding production. In May of each year, nests of grouse were found using the dogs and clutch size and subsequent number hatched determined.

The population data were analysed using key factor analysis, the same technique described in detail in Chapter 8. Five periods of female loss were identified:

(i) hunting mortality $= k_0$,
(ii) overwinter loss $= k_1$,
(iii) reduction in clutch size through an inability to lay a maximum clutch (12) $= k_2$,
(iv) egg mortality $= k_3$,
(v) chick loss $= k_4$.

Overwinter loss included losses through natural mortality and also net loss through emigration and immigration.

Losses are expressed as k-values:

$$k_i = \text{Log}_{10}(N_i/N_{i+1})$$

where $N_i$ and $N_{i+1}$ are the number of females entering and the number surviving the ith period. Overall loss, $K_{TOT}$ was calculated as the sum of each loss $k_0$, $k_1$, $k_2$, $k_3$, $k_4$. The key factor that causes year to year changes in the population was identified by plotting each loss against the total loss and calculating regression coefficients (b), the submortality with the regression coefficient closest to unity accounts for the greatest year to year variation in total loss and is considered the key factor.

Changes in the size of the breeding population of hen grouse and the overall breeding success, measured as young per hen in July, are shown in Figure 27.1.

Regression analyses identified overwinter loss ($k_1$) as the key factor since this explained most of the variation in annual loss. This is perhaps not surprising as $k_1$ covered the greatest time period (Table 27.1, Figure 27.2). However, with the exception of shooting loss ($k_0$), regression coefficients between total loss and other losses ($k_1$ to $k_4$) were also significant (Table 27.1). There were no significant trends in the $k$ values during the period of study. Only $k_1$, overwinter loss, was correlated with grouse density immediately prior to the time the loss occurred.

Several of the k-values were correlated with each other. Overwinter loss ($k_1$) was positively correlated with each of the breeding losses; failure to lay a maximum clutch

**(a) Hen density**

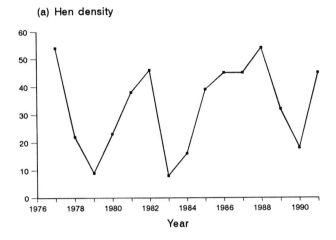

**(b) Breeding success**

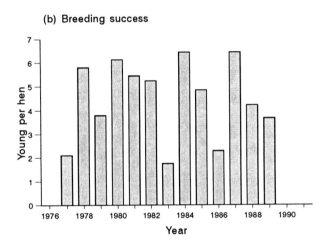

Figure 27.1. Changes in the size of the breeding population (a) and breeding success (b) of red grouse on the main study area.

Table 27.1. Correlation ($r$) and regression coefficients ($b$) between individual losses and total losses from the Gunnerside grouse population over 10 years. Significant coefficients ($P<0.05$) are indicated with an asterisk and $k_1$ considered the key factor with $b$ closest to unity.

| | | | | Losses | | |
|---|---|---|---|---|---|---|
| | | Value | $k_0$ | $k_1$ | $k_2$ | $k_3$ |
| Shooting: | $k_0$ | $r$ | – | | | |
| Winter: | $k_1$ | $r$ | .11 | – | | |
| Clutch: | $k_2$ | $r$ | .37 | .70* | – | |
| Egg: | $k_3$ | $r$ | .13 | .65* | .12 | |
| Chick: | $k_4$ | $r$ | .38 | .78* | .63* | – |
| Total | $K_{TOT}$ | $r$ | .38 | .93* | .75* | .82* |
| | $K_{TOT}$ | $b$ | .07 | .59 | .05 | .20 |

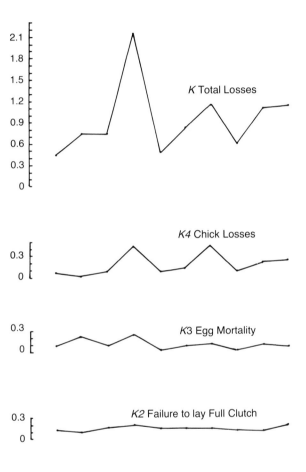

Figure 27.2. Year to year changes in mortality and losses from the Gunnerside study population expressed as k values. While winter loss ($k_1$) was the key factor, breeding losses ($k_2$, $k_3$ & $k_4$) were also associated with total loss (see Table 27.1).

157

$(k_2)$ was positively correlated with chick loss $(k_4)$ (Table 27.1). These associations between k-values may reflect some common factor affecting all losses.

Overwinter loss was the key factor that accounted for changes in the total loss from the population. Breeding losses, failure to lay a complete clutch, egg mortality and chick loss were also associated with total loss and not surprisingly were inter-correlated, suggesting a common cause may be influencing the various population processes.

### 27.3 Population losses and parasite burdens

Overwinter loss $(k_1)$ increased with both grouse density and the intensity of worm infection in adult grouse (determined during the subsequent shooting season and thus including the period of winter infection). Partial correlation analysis revealed that overwinter loss was more closely associated with parasite intensity when the effects of density were removed.

Both egg mortality $(k_3)$ and chick loss $(k_4)$ increased with the mean intensity of parasite infection

(Figure 27.3) while failure to lay a maximum clutch $(k_2)$ showed only a weak association with intensity of infection. While such correlations indicate that parasites could be a major cause of mortality in grouse they are not proof and were tested through parasite reduction experiments.

Table 27.2. Recovery of grouse either treated or untreated with an anthelmintic and subsequently shot in the following autumn Overall, treated grouse with reduced worm burdens survived better than grouse with natural levels of infection.

| Year | Treatment | Number | Number Shot | Number Not Shot | $P+$ |
|---|---|---|---|---|---|
| 82-83 | Treated | 15 | 7 | 8 | 0.107 |
| | Not Treated | 86 | 23 | 63 | |
| 83-84 | Treated | 93 | 38 | 55 | 0.048 |
| | Not Treated | 14 | 2 | 12 | |
| 88-89 | Treated | 65 | 5 | 60 | 0.104 |
| | Not Treated | 36 | 0 | 36 | |

Combined P value $<0.05*$

$+ P$ estimated from Fisher Exact Test.
*Individual probabilities combined by $X^2 = \sum 2 \log_e$

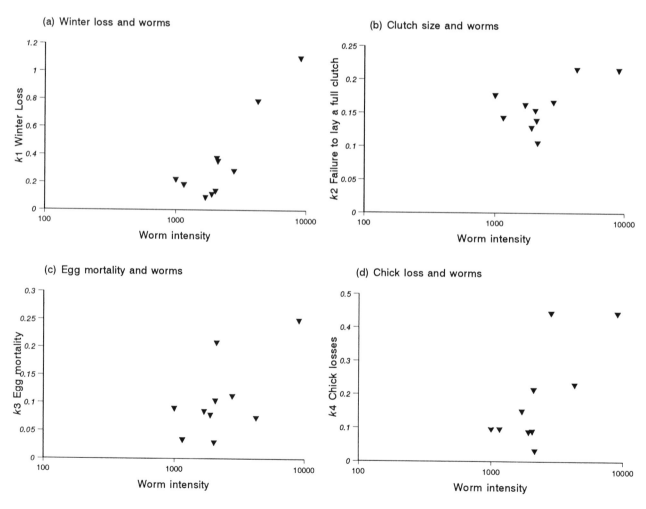

Figure 27.3. The relationship between losses from the Gunnerside population and intensity of worm infection in breeding adult grouse. Winter loss, egg mortality and chick losses all show a positive correlation ($P<0.05$) while failure to lay a full clutch shows a weak positive association ($0.1 > P > 0.05$).

## 27.4 Parasite reduction in grouse survival

Grouse were caught, tagged and treated in spring with the anthelmintic Levamisole Hydrochloride (NILVERM). Experiments were conducted 0.5km south of the main study area. Relative survival of treated and untreated birds was measured as the proportion of tagged birds that survived from the time of capture in early spring (February to April) through the breeding season to the shooting season. Most grouse found dead on the study area during field work carried high parasite burdens and died in spring (see Chapter 29); these would be classified as overwinter loss ($k_1$). Worm burdens for treated and untreated grouse were estimated when grouse were shot after 12 August and usually during August and September.

The relative survival of treated birds (from time of treatment to the shooting season) was significantly greater for grouse with reduced worm burdens (Table 27.2).

Table 27.3 Clutch size and hatching success of treated and untreated female grouse. In every year, treated birds consistently produced larger clutches with a greater hatching success. Values show mean ± 1 standard error and sample sizes in parenthesis.

| Year | Treated Females | Control Females | Significance |
|---|---|---|---|
| **(a) Clutch size** | | | |
| 1982 | 8.25 ± 0.62 (2) | 7.93 ± 0.36 (14) | NS |
| 1983 | 8.00 ± 0.34 913) | 5.28 ± 0.65 (11) | *** |
| 1984 | 8.80 ± 0.22 (15) | 7.59 ± 0.47 (22) | * |
| 1985 | 9.00 (2) | 8.00 ± 0.49 (10) | NS |
| 1986 | 8.67 ± 0.33 (3) | 7.61 ± 0.42 (23) | NS |
| 1987 | 8.40 ± 0.68 (5) | 7.90 ± 0.38 (10) | NS |
| 1988 | 10.4 ± 0.36 (11) | 8.31 ± 0.51 (16) | ** |
| 1989 | 8.25 ± 0.25 (4) | 6.86 ± 0.34 (7) | *** |
| **(b) Hatching Success** | | | |
| 1982 | 0.97 ± 0.02 (8) | 0.77 ± 0.09 (14) | NS |
| 1983 | 0.75 ± 0.11 (13) | 0.38 ± 0.13 (11) | ** |
| 1984 | 0.96 ± 0.02 (15) | 0.92 ± 0.24 (22) | NS |
| 1985 | 0.94 ± 0.06 (2) | 0.76 ± 0.12 (10) | NS |
| 1986 | 0.96 ± 0.04 (3) | 0.75 ± 0.08 (23) | NS |
| 1987 | 0.95 ± 0.05 (5) | 0.91 ± 0.03 (10) | NS |
| 1988 | 0.92 ± 0.05 (11) | 0.68 ± 0.09 (16) | ** |
| 1989 | 1.00 ± 0.00 (4) | 0.90 ± 0.04 (7) | * |

* Significance determined using t test, * = $P<0.05$, ** = $P<0.01$, *** = $P<0.001$

In Chapter 28 the effects of survival and breeding success on the population changes will be examined in detail but will require estimates of the effects of the parasites on the grouse. From the data presented in Figure 27.3, the slope of the relationship between female loss and worm burden provides an estimate of the instantaneous mortality rate induced by the parasite of $3*10^{-4}$ grouse worm$^{-1}$ y$^{-1}$ (S.E. = $5*/10^{-5}$).

## 27.5 Parasite effects on grouse breeding

Female grouse with experimentally reduced parasite burdens consistently produced larger clutches than untreated females, this increase was significant in four of eight years (Table 27.3a). Hatching success of treated females was significantly greater than controls in three of four years (Table 27.3b)

Overall, brood size was greater in each year of treatment. These results demonstrate that parasites reduce the breeding production of female red grouse and that differences are consistent between years (Figure 27.4). The experimental data provide a series of replicates from which the instantaneous rate of parasite induced reduction on grouse productivity can be estimated as $5*10^{-4}$ grouse worm$^{-1}$y$^{-1}$ (S.E. = $2*/10^{-5}$).

## 27.6 Management implications

The clear finding from this chapter is that the removal of parasites from individual grouse will increase both grouse breeding production and survival. While the techniques developed for catching and treating the grouse were developed principally for experimental purposes, the advantages are so clear that the technique has been developed and used as a management tool to reduce parasite burdens and increase overall productivity (see Chapter 29).

## 27.7 Summary

Ten years of intensive studies were conducted in northern England on red grouse and the parasitic trichostrongyle worm. Winter loss was the key factor explaining year to year changes in grouse numbers but

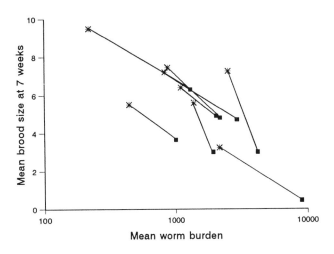

Figure 27.4. Brood size of treated (square) and untreated (star) female grouse when chicks were seven weeks of age in relation to mean worm intensity estimated five months after treatment. An increase in breeding production following treatment is shown. Standard errors omitted for clarity.

breeding losses were also important. Both winter and breeding losses were correlated with the level of parasite burden carried by the grouse. Experimental reductions in parasite burdens consistently increased breeding production and winter survival of grouse, thus demonstrating that parasites cause increased winter and breeding losses.

## 27.8 Notes

a. k1, overwinter loss, was correlated with grouse density immediately prior to the time the loss occurred, =0.651, $P<0.05$.

b. Overwinter loss (k1) increased with the intensity of worm infection in adult grouse; =0.883, $n=10$, $P<0.001$,

c. Partial correlation k1 versus intensity of infection with the effects of density removed =0.90, $P<0.01$, k1 versus Log10 female density with the effects of intensity of infection removed, =0.71, $P<0.05$.

d. k3 and intensity of infection in breeding grouse estimated during the subsequent shooting season, =0.63, $n=10$, $P<0.05$; k4 chick loss and intensity of infection =0.74, $n=10$, $P<0.02$. Failure to lay a maximum clutch (k2) and intensity of infection; =0.60, $0.1>P>0.05$, $n=10$.

## 27.9 References

1. Jenkins, D., Watson, A. & Miller, G.R. (1963). Population studies on red grouse *(Lagopus lagopus scoticus)*, in north east Scotland. *Journal of Animal Ecology,* **32**, 317-376.

# CHAPTER 28

# MODELLING THE INTERACTION OF GROUSE AND THE TRICHOSTRONGYLE WORM

**Parasites are aggregated with grouse, have a delay in development and reduce the survival and breeding production of the birds. Mathematical modelling demonstrates that these effects are sufficient to generate the population cycles in grouse numbers.**

## 28.1 Introduction

Three conditions that could destabilize grouse numbers and generate population cycles have been examined and identified in the last few chapters. These were:

(i) reduced breeding of grouse caused by the parasites

(ii) the parasites distributed with a low degree of aggregation within the grouse population,

(iii) time delays in parasite development and infection.

Given these findings the next question is to ask whether such effects are sufficient to generate the cyclic changes observed?. To answer this, we apply generalised mathematical models[1,2] which describe the fundamental aspects of the grouse-strongyle worm relationship. The details and mathematics of this work will not be presented here but are published elsewhere[3,4,5]. Much of this modelling was undertaken by Dr Andy Dobson of Princeton University.

## 28.2 Basic models

Two models were produced which describe the production and death rates of both the grouse and the parasite populations, and the flow rates between the different stages (Figure 28.1). Model 1 ignores the effects of larval arrestment but considers in detail the free-living larval stages of the parasite. Model 2 assumes the free-living larvae are relatively short-lived but includes details of the larvae when they enter a period of arrestment immediately after infecting a grouse. The model includes the data recorded in previous chapters to describe the distribution of parasites within the adult grouse population and the effects of the parasite on grouse breeding production and survival.

Model 2 considers a modification of the basic model by including a period of arrestment in larval development. Arrested development occurs in a number of parasite systems and has also been identified in this system, although the relative significance of this to grouse populations is not yet apparent. Arrested development occurs when a larva enters the host and does not develop immediately into an adult stage but remains as an inactive larva for a period. At arrested stages they have no effects on the grouse until they develop into adult worms. Since arrested larvae are present within the host, they will die if the grouse host dies, but since they are effectively dormant they have no discernible effect on grouse survival or breeding production. Although it is possible that only a proportion of larvae enter arrestment, in this model arrestment is considered an 'all or nothing' effect.

## 28.3 Dynamic properties of model and population cycles

If we consider both models in the absence of any parasite-induced effects on grouse breeding production, then neither parasite-induced host mortality, nor arrested larval development cause cyclic changes in the abundance of either the grouse or the worms (Figure 28.2). This is an important finding since it explains why earlier workers could not explain the cyclic fluctuations through the effects of parasites on grouse survival alone and why the effects of the parasite were ignored by some grouse researchers.

When the effects of the parasite on the breeding production of grouse are included in both models,

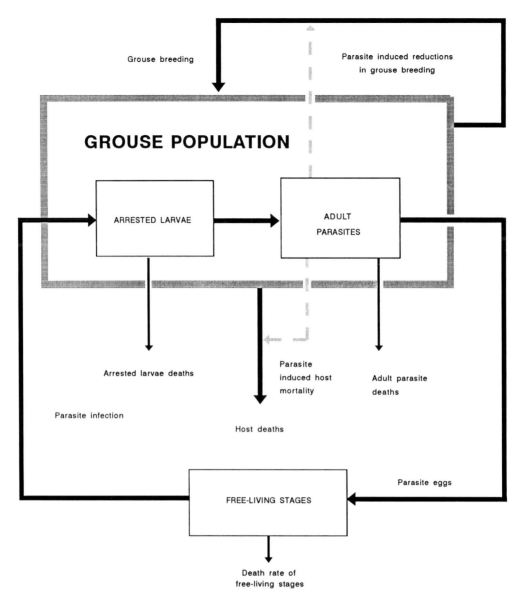

Figure 28.1. Schematic representation of the life cycle of the trichostrongyle worm in red grouse, illustrating the different birth, death and transmission rates occurring in the life cycle. Note that parasites can affect both host survival and breeding production.

then both grouse and parasites show cycles of abundance similar in period and amplitude to the type observed. Cycles can only be prevented by high levels of parasite aggregation or heavy mortality caused by the parasite, neither of which are characteristic of the grouse parasite system studied here.

In model 2, larval arrestment increases the tendency for grouse and parasite numbers to cycle but also increases the period of these cycles in comparison with model 1. Variations in cycle period between Scotland and England could be the result of greater levels of larval arrestment, a feature currently being examined.

## 28.4 Discussion

The application of these models to observed and experimental data collected on the grouse-parasite system suggests that the main interaction causing the sys-

tem to cycle is the effects of the parasite on grouse breeding success. The relatively low levels of parasite aggregation observed in the system further increase the tendency of the system to oscillate. This is not to say that parasites cause all population cycles.

Interactions with the parasitic nematode generate population cycles in red grouse through their time-delayed impact on grouse breeding production. Variations in cycle period between areas can be explained through changes in the propensity of larvae to arrest, and by changes in the growth rate of the grouse population. The period of the cycles will increase with the duration of larval arrestment and decrease with an increase in grouse clutch size.

## 28.5 Summary

The application of mathematical models to the find-

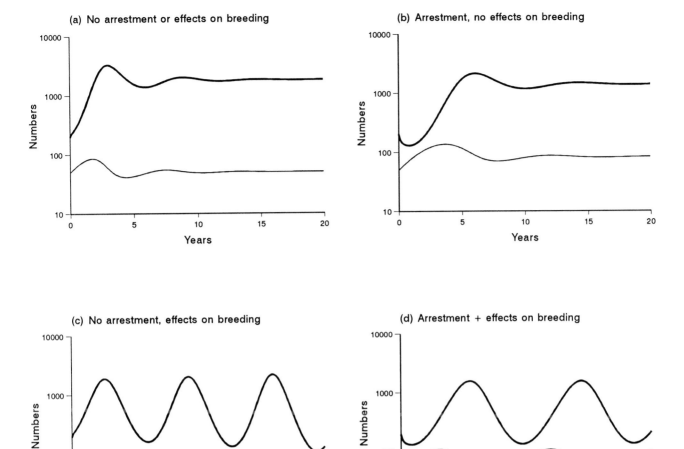

Figure 28.2. A comparison of the effects of larval arrestment and parasite-induced reduction in grouse production. In the top figures (a,b) the parasite has no effect on grouse breeding production, the figures on the left (a,c) correspond to a parasite with no arrested stages (Model 1), the figures on the right (b,d) depict the case where parasites arrest for 3 months (Model 2).

ings presented in earlier chapters found that neither the effects of parasites on grouse survival nor the presence of larval arrestment as a developmental time delay were sufficient to generate population cycles. However, population cycles were generated when the effects of parasites on the breeding production of grouse were included in the model. Arrestment did not generate population cycles but would tend to increase the periods of population cycles. In conclusion, the demonstrated effects of parasites on the breeding production of grouse are sufficient to generate cyclic changes in red grouse numbers.

## 28.6 References

1. Anderson, R.M. & May, R.M. (1978). Regulation and stability of nest-parasite interactions. I. Stabilising processes. *Journal of Animal Ecology*, **47**, 219-249.

2. May, R.M. & Anderson, R.M. (1978). Regulation and stability of nest-parasite interactions. II. Destabilising processes. *Journal of Animal Ecology*, **47**, 249-268.

3. Hudson, P.J., Dobson, A.P. & Newborn, D. (1985). Cyclic and non-cyclic populations of red grouse: a role for parasitism. Ecology and genetics of host-parasite interactions (Ed. by D. Rollinson & R.M Anderson). Academic Press, London.

4. Hudson, P.J. & Dobson, A.P. (1990). Red grouse population cycles and the populaiton dynamics of the caecal nematode, *Trichostrongylus tenuis*. *Journal of Animal Ecology* **61** 477-486

5. Dobson, A.P. & Hudson, P.J. (1992). Regulation and stability of a free-living host-parasite system, *Trichostrongylus tenuis* in red grouse. II. Population models. *Journal of Animal Ecology*, **61**, 487-498.

# CHAPTER 29

# NON-CYCLIC POPULATIONS & PARASITE BURDENS

**Some grouse populations do not cycle. These have lower worm burdens and tend to be in drier regions where the free-living stages of the parasite do not survive well.**

## 29.1 Introduction

In understanding population cycles in any animal species there are three questions that must be addressed

  (i) What causes the population cycles?
  (ii) Why does cycle period vary?
  (iii) Why do some populations not cycle?

The first two of these questions have been answered through the observations, experimental and modelling approaches described in the previous chapters.

The last question is the subject of this chapter: 'Why do some populations not cycle?'. Differences between cyclic and non-cyclic populations have already been addressed in Chapter 24. Cyclic populations tend to occur in areas of high rainfall and cool July temperatures. This chapter examines how such weather variables may influence the survival of free-living larvae and compares worm burdens from cyclic and non-cyclic populations to suggest that non-cyclic populations have low worm burdens.

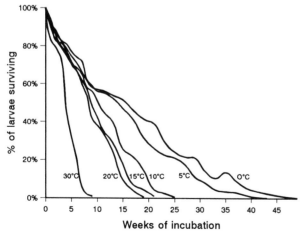

Figure 29.1. Survival of the free living third stage larvae in relation to variations in temperature. Larvae were kept in ovens at constant temperature and sampled consecutively (data collected by Dr H. Watson).

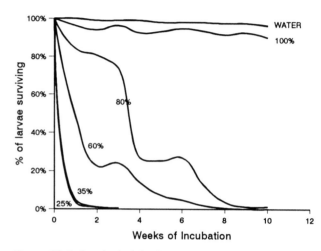

Figure 29.2. Survival of third stage free living larvae in relation to humidity (% relative humidity in laboratory samples), compared with larvae kept in water. Larvae exposed to low humidity showed reduced survival rates (data collected by Dr H. Watson).

## 29.2. Temperature, humidity and free-living larvae

In Chapter 24 it was apparent that population cycles did not occur in some grouse populations although the tendency to identify the presence of cycles increased with the duration of the time series and the area of the grouse moor. Excluding the shorter series and series from small grouse moors, two environmental factors tend to increase the tendency of populations to cycle: namely July temperature and days of rainfall. Cyclic populations tend to be in wetter and cooler areas than non-cyclic populations.

July temperature was identified as a variable that increases with infection rate between years but within one study area (Chapter 25), while variations between moors in average grouse bag are also associated with temperature but with higher bags on warmer moors. The temperature and the rainfall on the moors will influence parasites both directly and indirectly.

Laboratory experiments conducted jointly with Harold Watson and Professor Lee at Leeds University found

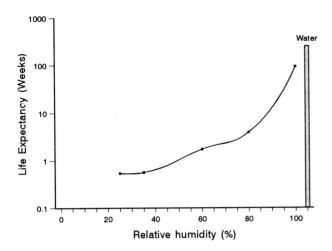

Figure 29.3. Life expectancy of larvae in relation to humidity; data extracted from Figure 29.2.

that survival of larvae was lower when temperatures were high (Figure 29.1) and when humidity was low (Figure 29.2). Humidity had a greater effect than temperature and reducing humidity from 100% to 80% had a dramatic effect on the life expectancy of the free living stages (Figure 29.3). Thus it would seem likely that during dry warm conditions, or on moors which are dry and warm during the summer period, survival of free-living stages may be reduced through the effects of drying out. This would reduce the infection rate of the parasites, so worm burdens would not build up in the grouse population, have adverse effects, and thus generate population cycles.

## 29.3 Worm burdens in cyclic and non-cyclic populations

Worm burdens from old grouse shot from non-cyclic grouse moors were lower than found on cyclic grouse moors[a] (Figure 29.4). On non-cyclic moors, just 3.6% of grouse inspected carried burdens greater than 4000 worms per bird, while from cyclic moors 24% of grouse carried burdens greater than 4000 worms per bird. A similar pattern was found for immature grouse[b].

## 29.4 Non-cyclic population data

The population data from the cyclic grouse moor in Chapter 27 showed clearly an increase in losses during the breeding season with level of worm infection in the adult grouse (Figure 27.3). No such relationship was found for the non-cyclic populations, mainly because parasite burdens did not reach a high level even when losses were high.

## 29.5 Discussion

Cyclic populations are located in areas with a relatively

high rainfall and cool periods during July. Evidence presented in this chapter shows that the survival of free living stages of the nematode parasite were reduced through a reduction in humidity and an increase in temperature, and that grouse shot from cyclic populations carried lower worm burdens. This suggests that on non-cyclic moors environmental variables may reduce the survival of the free-living stages, so leading to reduced rates of infection, low worm burdens in the grouse and only a small influence of the parasites on the survival and breeding success of the grouse. With low worm burdens and little effect on breeding production these grouse populations will not cycle.

The weather variables recorded in Chapter 24, and investigated in more detailed in this chapter, may not only have a direct effect but also an indirect effect on the survival of the larvae. Both the amount of rainfall and the temperature will influence the tendency of

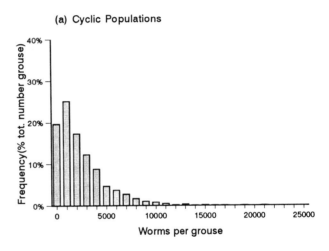

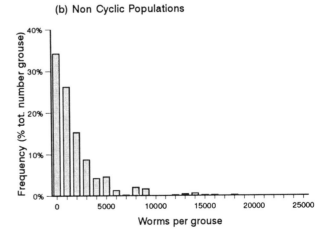

Figure 29.4. Worm burdens of adult grouse shot from (a) cyclic and (b) non-cyclic populations. Grouse from cyclic populations carry greater worm burdens than grouse from non-cyclic populations. It seems unlikely that parasites reach burdens high enough to have a significant influence on non-cyclic populations.

165

the moorland to develop peat. Only on areas with high rainfall and relatively low temperature will peat development occur and produce a damper environment than the freely drained heather moorland areas without major peat deposition.

### 29.6 Summary

Survival of free-living stages of the nematode parasite were greater in humid cool conditions, a factor known to be related to cyclic populations. Worm burdens in grouse were lower in non-cyclic populations and it is suggested that they were insufficient to have a significant effect on grouse populations. Weather variations may have both a direct effect on survival and infection of larvae and also an indirect effect on peat development and wetness of the habitat.

### 29.7 Notes

a. Grouse from cyclic moors have greater worm burdens, Goodness of fit $X^2 = 48.3$, d.f. $= 6$, $P < 0.0001$).

b. Young grouse from cyclic moors had greater worm burdens than from non-cyclic moors $X^2 = 9.21$, d.f. $= 2$, $P < 0.01$.

# CHAPTER 30

# THE TREATMENT OF PARASITIC INFECTIONS: MEDICATED GRIT AND DIRECT DOSING

**The effects of the parasites on grouse can be reduced through the application of medicated grit and by direct dosing.**

## 30.1 Introduction

Parasitic nematodes clearly have a detrimental effect on the breeding production of grouse and these effects coupled with aspects of the life cycle of the parasite are sufficient to generate cyclic fluctuations in grouse numbers.

This chapter describes two practical techniques for reducing the effects of the parasite on the grouse population. First the application of medicated grit and second the effects of direct dosing. Before considering medicated grit we will examine the use of grit in general by grouse.

## 30.2 Grit uptake and use by grouse

Heather is the principal component in the diet of grouse and yet is fibrous and difficult to digest. To aid physical digestion, the grouse ingest grit and pass it to the gizzard. Within the strong muscular wall and horny lining of the gizzard, the heather is milled to a mush and then passed to the lower gut for chemical digestion.

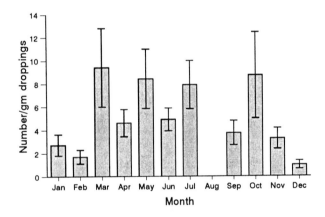

**(a) Number of grit pieces in droppings**

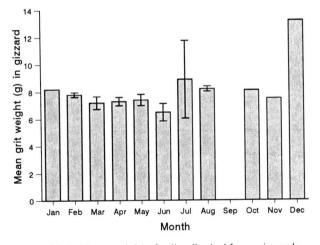

Figure 30.1. Mean weight of grit collected from gizzards of grouse during different months. Note there is little month to month variation. No samples collected in September.

**(b) Grit weight per gm of droppings**

Figure 30.2. Mean weight (a) and number of grit pieces (b) passed in grouse droppings collected during each month. Note the large variation between months.

167

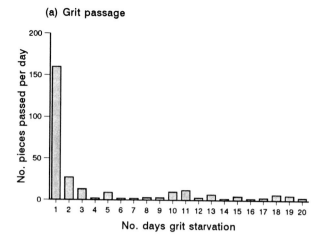

**(a) Grit passage**

**(b) Weight of grouse**

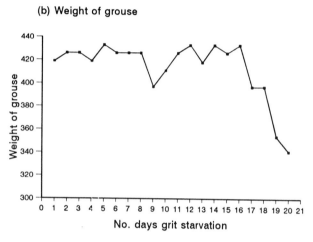

Figure 30.3. Changes in (a) grit passage and (b) weight of a captive grouse deprived of grit. Death was attributed to the loss of grit, a total of 258 pieces – about 50% of the grit present. (Source Hamand-Smith & Rastall, Grouse in Health and in Disease).

The quantity of grit in the gizzard varied between 350 and 1000 pieces but averaged about 500 pieces per bird and a total weight of about 8 grams (Figure 30.1). Grouse fed grit *ad lib* can pass in excess of 100 pieces per day in their fibrous droppings (20% of the gizzard contents) but this rate probably falls dramatically when grit is unavailable, for example during snowy conditions. By regularly collecting piles of droppings at roost sites each month and examining the number of pieces of grit passed, we found grouse pass about nine pieces per day in spring and seven in autumn (Figure 30.2a). This fluctuates greatly between months and is lowest in mid winter during snow conditions.

The grit within the gizzard shows a 10 fold variation in size, with some of the larger pieces weighing more than 0.06gms. (Figure 30.2b).

Grouse deprived of grit for long periods can lose condition and die, particularly during times of heavy

snow cover. Experiments on captive birds have shown that grouse can reduce their rate of grit uptake during periods when grit is not available but deprived birds can lose weight and may die (Figure 30.3).

**30.3 Medicated grit structure**

Many parasite control systems use an integrated programme, combining the techniques of direct treatment with sanitation and improved husbandry. While sanitation is clearly impractical for wild animals, indirect treatment where the drug is incorporated in the animals feed has been used in various systems, such as the control of gapes in pheasants. We have looked at the possibility of providing artificial feed for grouse and have tested a wide range of alternatives including oats, blackcurrants, raisins, feed blocks and even peanuts. Captive grouse will take a range of foodstuffs but wild grouse usually take artificial feed only under severe weather conditions. More recently some success has been achieved by applying oats and this is currently being investigated in more detail.

The only item artificially placed on the hill which is regularly taken by grouse is quartz grit. Strathclyde Chemicals of Johnstone, Glasgow (formerly Strathclyde Minerals of Barhead) have supplied grouse grit for many years and have developed a technique for coating grit with a kernel fat. By incorporating a drug within this fat (Figure 30.4. See opposite page 177.) the technology is now available for indirectly applying the drug to the grouse.

Table 30.1 Structure and use of grit taken by grouse compared to artificially available grit.

| Grit ingested: |
| --- |
| Average size in gizzard = 14 mgms |
| Range of size in gizzard = 1 to 530 mgms |
| **Grit passed:** |
| Average size passed by grouse = 4 mgms |
| **Grit available:** |
| Average size of Cornish grit sold = 20 mgms |
| Particle size: |
| <5.00 mm = 95% |
| <3.35 mm = 70% |
| <2.36 mm = 30% |
| <1.18 mm = 2% |

Trial production of medicated grit incorporating the anthelmintic fenbendazole (HOECHST) was used under veterinary prescription on a limited number of estates. Fenbendazole was used for four reasons:

(i) Fenbendazole is known to be safe to wildlife, even when taken in excess; sheep given 1000 times the recommended dose showed no ill effects.

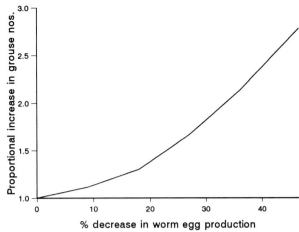

Figure 30.5. Predicted proportional increase in grouse numbers in relation to the proportional decrease in worm egg production caused by the application of medicated grit. This estimate was made from the model described in Chapter 28.

(ii) Fenbendazole is a broad spectrum anthelmintic known to be effective against eggs, adult and immature larval stages.

(iii) Fenbendazole is not water soluble and does not break down in light.

(iv) Fenbendazole has some effect even at very low concentrations but is particularly effective when given in split doses over a period of 15 days.

This last feature of Fenbendazole is of significance, since even low levels of drug application may reduce egg production of the worms and have a serious consequence for the grouse population. If we apply the model developed in previous chapters and ignore the effects of parasites on grouse breeding production, then even a slight decrease in egg production can reduce infection rate, reduce the effects of the parasite and increase the grouse population. While the application of this model includes a range of assumptions – and no firm conclusions should be drawn at this stage – it does indicate that if worm egg production is reduced by 30%, even with no direct effects on worm survival this would cause a significant increaSe in the grouse population (Figure 30.5).

To examine the effect of medicated grit on worm burdens, grit was placed on grouse moors in early spring when the snow cleared and we expected grit uptake to be high. Observations demonstrated that grouse visited and took the medicated grit. Of 50 piles monitored, 68% were used by grouse, 24% frequently. Worm burdens were monitored from the population when grouse were shot in the following autumn and compared with a neighbouring area where medicated grit was not used. The effect of treatment was very significant and overall reduced worm burdens by 44% (Figure 30.6). This appears highly successful since it is unlikely that all grouse took the medicated grit and the worm counts were conducted from a random sample of grouse five months after the medicated grit was used.

The possible disadvantage of medicated grit is that a low and frequent uptake of the anthelmintic could provide a strong selective pressure for the parasite to develop resistance to the drug. Resistance to Fenbendazole and other drugs has been recorded in other parasite systems. In the use of medicated grit the parasite is only exposed to the drug for a relatively short time of the year and if this system were coupled with the catch and treat method, resistance might not develop. At the current time there is no evidence of resistance in this parasite but this is a subject we are currently monitoring and investigating.

### 30.4 Direct chemotherapy: Catch and treat method

The catch and treat method to reduce worm burdens was developed principally as an experimental technique. Subsequently refined, it became possible to catch and treat large numbers of birds. Keepers on some grouse moors, both in the Scottish High-

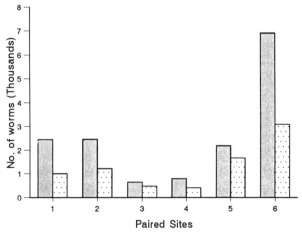

Figure 30.6. Mean worm burdens from paired moors in which one applied medicated grit and the second did not. The average percentage difference between treated and untreated moors was a 44% reduction.

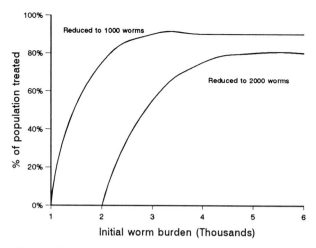

Figure 30.7. The predicted proportion of grouse that need to be treated to reduce worm burdens to 1000 worms and 2000 worms respectively. Usually more than 65% of the population would need to be treated to make a significant impact on the population.

lands and northern England can catch 50 birds per hour and in excess of 3000 birds per annum. Quite simply, grouse are caught at night and given a direct oral dose of a worming drug (anthelmintic) to reduce worm burdens. We have shown through experiments in Chapter 27 that this gives immediate relief and benefits to the treated birds.

The advantage of this technique is that it is highly cost effective and provides immediate relief for the bird. The disadvantages are that the effects of treatment provide few long lasting benefits and involve keepers working unsocial hours. Reinfection can occur soon after treatment and within a year the effects of the treatment on the worm population are probably quite small. To eradicate the parasite from the grouse population almost all the grouse would need to be treated during the winter months when infection had ceased. Even if the objective was to reduce the parasite burdens to a level where they were not having a significant impact, then at least 65% of the population would need to be treated (Figure 30.7). The sterling efforts of a few keepers have demonstrated that is possible to treat 40% of the population using this technique but it would seem very difficult to catch and treat as many as 65% of the grouse.

In summary, this technique is useful when a parasite outbreak is expected or has already started, since it provides immediate relief. On one occasion a keeper recorded a severe outbreak of trichostrongyle parasites in late March amongst his grouse population and quickly treated some of the remaining birds. The effects of the parasite on the grouse population were so large that the treated birds were the only adult birds found breeding on the area during the following summer.

### 30.5 Summary

Two techniques have been developed to reduce the worm burdens of red grouse and conseqeuntly improve breeding production and potential bag size. Medicated grit is coated with a kernel fat which incorporates the active anthelmintic Fenbendazole. Overall, medicated grit reduced worm burdens by 44% on areas were it was applied.

The direct catch and treat method provides immediate relief from parasites, although such effects are short-lived. Catch and treat is best applied when a severe outbreak of trichostrongylosis is expected, whereas the medicated grit can help to keep worm burdens at a low level and should be applied continuously.

# CHAPTER 31

# PARASITES AND PREDATION

**Predators and parasites both influence grouse numbers and may interact to reduce the tendency of grouse populations to cycle.**

## 31.1 Introduction

Like many ground nesting birds, red grouse are vulnerable to predation when incubating and show various adaptations to avoid capture. For most of the year, grouse emit scent which can be detected by a trained pointing dog at distances of up to 50 metres. Female grouse stop producing caecal faeces during the spring incubation period and dogs can only locate incubating females from a distance of less than 0.5 metres. This reduction in scent emission is associated with a change in the function of the bird's caeca that appears to be an adaptation to reduce detection.

The parasitic trichostrongyle worm is known to burrow deeply into the caecal mucosa causing disruption of the gut wall and internal bleeding. This pathology may hinder the control of scent emission and so increase the susceptibility of heavily infected incubating birds to mammalian predators that hunt by scent. In this chapter we investigate the interactions of predator, grouse and parasite by using observational data, a controlled experiment and modelling.

## 31.2 Parasite burdens in grouse shot and killed by predators

The main study was conducted on 17 km² of managed grouse moor in upper Swaledale, North Yorkshire, England. Regular visits were made to the study area and all dead grouse found were removed. Each corpse was carefully examined for any external cause of injury and in some instances skinned for signs of bite marks. During the study no grouse had died from 'accidents', since fence lines and overhead cables were absent. Each corpse was classed either as 'killed by predator' or, if there was no external injury, as 'found dead'. Careful examination allowed us to determine whether the grouse had struggled at death indicating predation, rather than death followed by scavenging of the corpse. Any grouse found during visits to other moors were treated in the same ways as those from the main study area. All corpses were brought back to the laboratory and, if the remains were in fit condition, the intensity of parasite infection was determined as described in Chapter 25.

Grouse killed by predators carried higher burdens of parasites than adult grouse shot in autumn, on both the main study area (Figure 31.1ᵃ) and in birds collected from all moors (Figure 31.2ᵃ). Furthermore, grouse found dead had higher levels of infection than grouse killed by predators on both the main study area (Figure 31.1ᵇ), and in the collections from all moors (Figure 31.2ᵇ). These results imply that grouse killed by predators tend to be heavily infected and thus vulnerable to predation.

Most of the grouse killed by predators were found during March (24%), April (29%) and May (26%), three to five months before the sample of shot birds were obtained. The parasite burdens of adult birds that are shot in the autumn reflect not only the worms that have passed the winter in the birds as adults and arrested larvae, but also the worms the bird have acquired during the summer infection period. As there is a period of parasite infection between the collection of the spring sample of birds found dead and the collection of shot birds in the autumn this creates a bias *against* a significant result. Despite this bias, shot birds still have lower parasite burdens than grouse killed by predators. We feel that the result underemphasises the impact of parasitism on the predation of grouse populations. Furthermore, comparisons within a year (1983) found that significantly more of the grouse killed by predators carried high intensities of parasite infection than the sample of shot birds (Figure 31.3c), demonstrating that predators selectively killed the heavily infected individuals from the population.

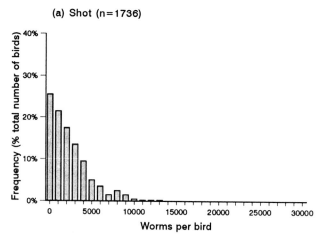

**(a) Shot (n=264)**

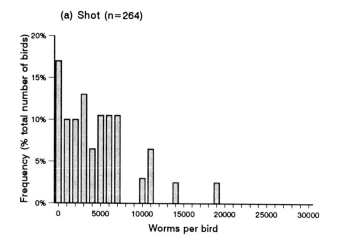

**(a) Shot (n=1736)**

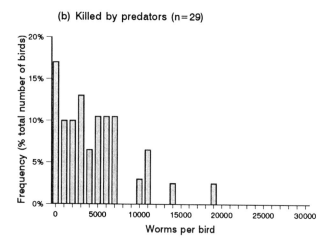

**(b) Killed by predators (n=29)**

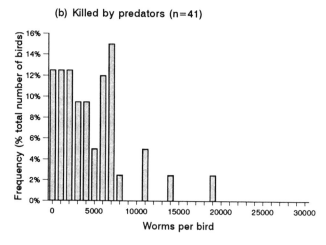

**(b) Killed by predators (n=41)**

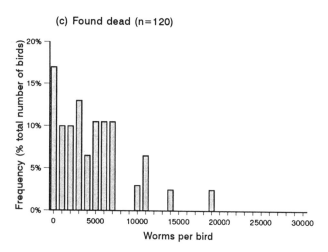

**(c) Found dead (n=120)**

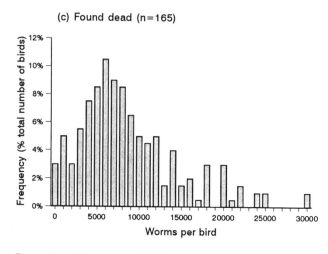

**(c) Found dead (n=165)**

Figure 31.1. Frequency distribution of worms per bird in grouse from the main study area between 1980 and 1984. (a) grouse shot, (b) grouse killed by predators, and (c) grouse found dead.

Figure 31.2. Frequency distribution of worms per bird in grouse from all study moors in the north of England: (a) grouse shot, (b) grouse killed by predators, (c) grouse found dead.

### 31.3 Parasites and intensity of predator control.

One of the main activities of keepers is to control the number of predators. In northern England, where crows are relatively scarce, foxes are considered by keepers to be the major predator of grouse. Interviews with keepers and estate managers were used to obtain information on the size and position of grouse moors and the numbers of keepers employed on each. The density of keepers was then determined by counting the numbers within 5km of the centre of each grouse moor and expressing this as the density of gamekeepers per 100km². On estates which employed more than one keeper the process was repeated for each keeper's beat and the average taken for the whole estate.

The density of keepers was determined for 44 of the 46 estates from which worm counts had been conducted. Keeper density ranged from 0 to 2.55 keepers 100km⁻² on these estates. These data were divided into one of five categories according to level of keeper density and are shown in Figure 31.4. There was a statistical difference between the observed distributions[d] and an increase in the frequency of birds with high worm burdens (> 5000 worms per bird) at high keeper density[d]. Furthermore, on those estates with samples from more than 40 birds there was a positive association between the proportion of birds with high parasite burdens (> 5000 worms per bird) and the intensity of predator control[e] measured as density of keepers 100km².

### 31.4 Worms and vulnerability to predation: an experiment

In the spring of 1983 and 1984, female grouse were located at night with strong quartz halogen lamps, dazzled and caught. In 1983 alternate females captured were given either 2mls Levamisole hydrochloride to reduce the infection of nematode parasites or 2mls water as a control. Female grouse were then fitted with a back-tab or radio-transmitter. In 1984 all female grouse caught were treated and

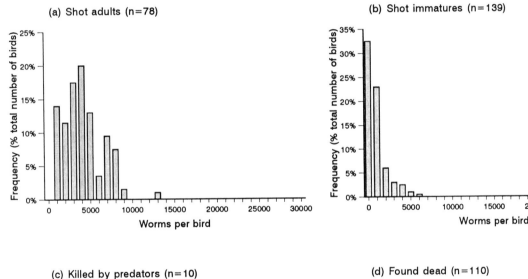

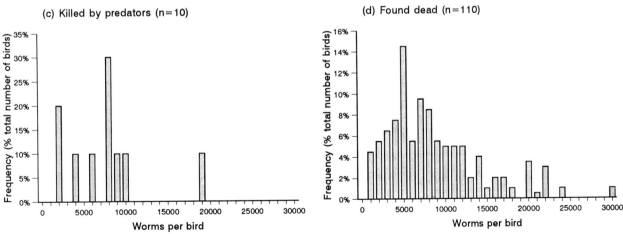

Figure 31.3. Frequency distribution of trichostrongyle worms in grouse from the main study area during 1983: (a) adult grouse shot, (b) immature grouse shot, (c) grouse killed by predators, (d) grouse found dead.

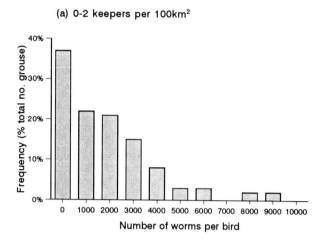

**(a) 0-2 keepers per 100km²**

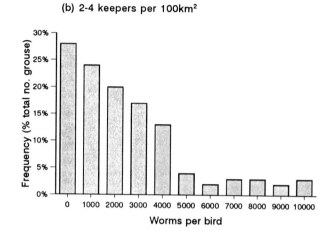

**(b) 2-4 keepers per 100km²**

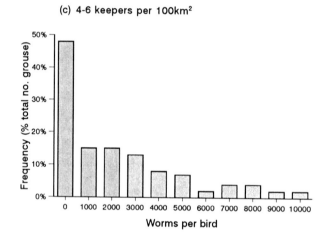

**(c) 4-6 keepers per 100km²**

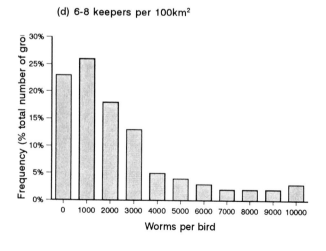

**(d) 6-8 keepers per 100km²**

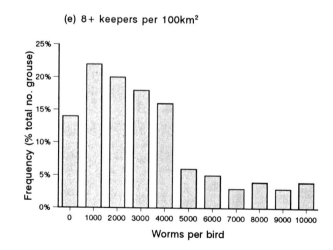

**(e) 8+ keepers per 100km²**

Figure 31.4. Frequency distribution of worms per bird from estates for varying intensities of predator control measured as the density of keepers within a 5km radius: (a) 0-0.5 keepers 100km⁻² (b) 0.5-1.0 keepers 100km⁻² (c) 1.0-1.5 keepers 100km⁻², (d) 1.5-2.0 keepers 100km⁻², (e) 2.0+ keepers 100km⁻².

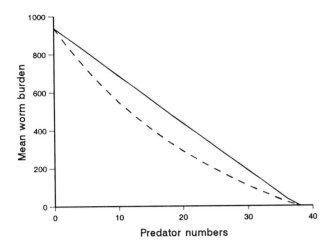

Figure 31.5. The relationships between mean parasite burden and predator density generated by the model for predators that do not selectively take heavily infected individuals (Model 1: upper line) and predators that selectively attack infected individuals (Model 2: lower line).

**(a) No arrestment**

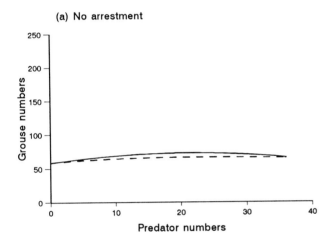

**(b) Four months arrestment**

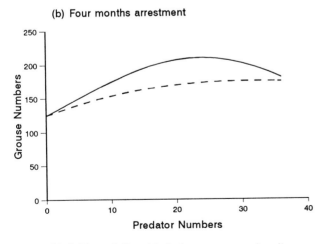

Figure 31.6. The relationship between grouse density and predator numbers for predators that do not selectively take heavily infected individuals (upper line) and predators that selectively take infected individuals (lower line). In (a) the parasites enter a very short period of arrestment; in (b) arrestment is more prolonged (4 months).

fitted with back tabs and untreated females were used as a comparative group.

The study area was divided into blocks and systematically searched by walking up and down each block with the dogs quartering the ground. Field observers located nests by inadvertently flushing an incubating female, whereas the dogs found the nests by scent; invariably such nests were well hidden from both the dogs and human observers. In 1983, when radio transmitters were fitted to both treated and untreated females, the general nesting area was located from the radio signal and then searched systematically with the dogs. While searching for radio tagged females, the observers were unaware whether the females were treated or control birds. Once the nest was located the content of each nest was checked and clutch size recorded.

Dogs that were trained to locate nests by scent were significantly better than humans at locating nests incubated by untreated control females with natural levels of infection[f] (Table 31.1). In contrast, there were no significant differences in the ability of humans or dogs to locate nests belonging to treated birds with reduced parasite burdens[f] (Table 31.1).

Table 31.1 Grouse nests found by dogs (scent) and random search (researchers) with respect to treatment of the female with anthelmintic to reduce parasite burdens

| Year | Treatment | Scent | Random |
|------|-----------|-------|--------|
| 1983 | | | |
| Treated | Low worm burdens | 6 | 7 |
| Untreated | High worm burdens | 37 | 10 |
| 1984 | | | |
| Treated | Low worm burdens | 9 | 7 |
| Untreated | High worm burdens | 29 | 7 |

### 31.5 Parasite intensity and size of caeca

The weight of grouse caeca was positively correlated with worm burdens for all adult female grouse examined[g]. This increase in caecal weight could be a response to damage caused by the worms to the structure of the caeca and consequently may interfere with scent emission.

### 31.6. Models of predation and parasitism

The mathematical models described in Chapter 28 can be modified to include the effects of predation on the grouse and consequent effects on the parasite population. The basic model used is the model 2 in Chapter 28, with the larvae entering a fixed period of arrestment. This model was extended and considered in two circumstances:

(i) The simplest case where the parasites have no effect on the vulnerability of their host to predation,
(ii) Where the susceptibility of the grouse to predation increases with parasite burden.

The consequences of adding predation to the model may be explored initially by examining the system at equilibrium i.e. when there is no change in host or parasite numbers. In both models the presence of predators reduces the mean parasite burden (Figure 31.5). If the parasites increase the susceptibility of hosts to predation, then larger reductions in parasite burden are produced since predators selectively remove the heavily infected individuals. In the absence of other mechanisms which may act to counter these effects, increased rates of predation may drive the parasites to extinction by pushing host density below the threshold for parasite establishment.

In the case where there is no selection of heavily infected individuals, the grouse population decreases as additional mortality due to predation is added to the system (Figure 31.6). In contrast, when predators selectively remove heavily infected individuals, then low levels of predation may actually lead to increases in the grouse population, particularly if the parasites arrest their development for a prolonged period. This counter-intuitive result is due to the predators selectively removing a greater proportion of the worm population than the host population, thus reducing the net impact of the parasite on the grouse population. This allows the grouse population to increase to a level determined by the combined effects of low predation and reduced parasitism. Further increases in the numbers of predators ultimately reduce the size of the grouse population and may drive the hosts below the threshold where they can sustain infection by the parasites.

The cyclic behaviour of grouse populations may also be influenced by predation; most importantly the presence of predators reduces the tendency of the host and parasite populations to cycle (Figure 31.7). This occurs

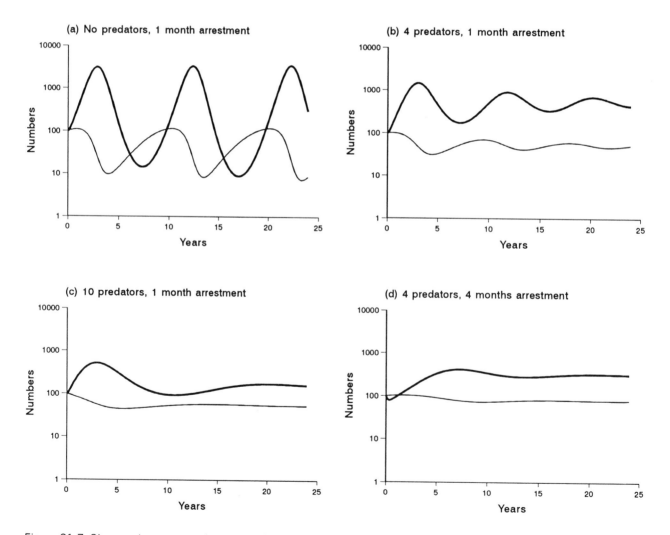

Figure 31.7. Changes in grouse and worm numbers for different levels of predation: (a) no predators, larval arrestment for one month; (b) four predators, larval arrestment for one month; (c) 10 predators, larval arrestment for one month; (d) four predators, larval arrestment for four months. In each figure the thick line shows host/grouse numbers, the thinner line gives mean burden of adult worms.

Clutch size, hatching success and chick survival are all reduced by the parasitic strongyle worm (Chapter 27).

Levels of strongyle worm infection can be determined from old grouse shot in autumn, although these levels tend to reflect the breeding performance of grouse in the preceding year rather than indicate what will happen in future years (Chapter 27).

The strongyle worm is more abundant in grouse on wet moors. Increases in levels of infection occur following periods of high grouse numbers (Chapter 29). *The Earl Peel*

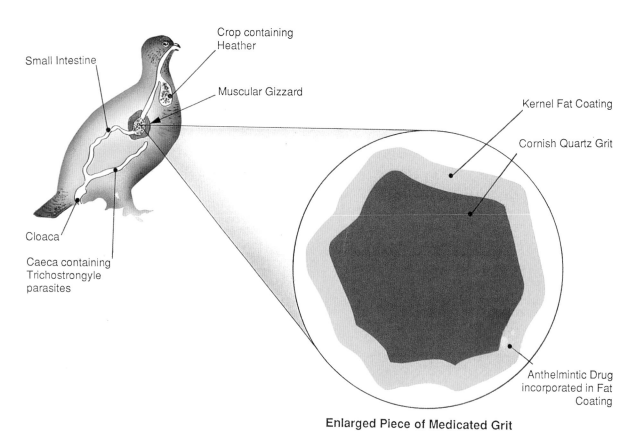

Figure 30.4. The structure of medicated grit which can be used to control the parasitic strongyle worm. Grouse ingest the grit which is coated with a kernel fat and incorporates a drug to kill the parasites (Chapter 30).

Direct dosing of grouse with an anthelmintic will reduce worm burdens and can be conducted on a large scale to control the strongyle worm when levels of infection are high (Chapter 30).

Setters and pointers were used to locate grouse nests. Dogs found it easier to find nests of heavily infected hens. Heavily infected grouse appear more susceptible to predators (Chapter 31).

principally because predators reduce parasite burdens by removing parasitized hosts from the population, this in turn reduces the delayed density dependent effects of the parasite on host survival and breeding, and suppresses the mechanism that generates the population cycles.

## 31.7 Discussion

An indirect impact of predators on the parasite population could have important consequences for the grouse population. Low levels of selective predation could reduce the effects of parasitism but higher levels will tend to wipe out these benefits quite quickly and result in reduced grouse density. During periods when grouse populations fall, this increased predation could result in longer cycles or even prevent grouse populations from cycling at all.

The model shows that parasite burdens, predation pressure and grouse density are closely linked. Changes in predation will influence both parasites and grouse densities irrespective of whether the predators act selectively or not. In this respect, the decrease in the proportion of birds with heavy infections on grouse estates with reduced numbers of keepers could reflect either the loss of heavily infected individuals through selective predation or simply reduced grouse densities resulting in reduced transmission rates and lower worm burdens. The results presented earlier in Sections 2 to 5 would suggest that in the absence of keepers, predation would keep grouse numbers at a low density, but when predators are controlled the grouse numbers rise and parasites become more important.

The control of natural enemies is one of the fundamental tenets of game management. Although traditional game management has concentrated on predators, the studies discussed here suggest that parasites may also be important in determining the productivity of game populations. Incorporating these interactions into management schemes for grouse is clearly a priority.

## 31.8 Summary

An extensive post-mortem survey of grouse revealed that birds killed by predators in spring and summer had significantly greater burdens of the nematode worm than grouse shot during the autumn. Furthermore, grouse killed by parasites carried greater worm burdens than grouse killed by predators. The proportion of grouse with high levels of parasite infection increased with the intensity of predator control as measured indirectly through keeper density. These observations suggest that predators selectively prey on heavily infected individuals.

Worm burdens were reduced experimentally in female grouse with an oral anthelmintic and nests of treated and untreated females were subsequently located either by research workers flushing incubating birds or by dogs trained to locate hens by scent. The dogs found significantly fewer of the treated than the control birds, suggesting that female grouse with large parasite burdens emit more scent and are more vulnerable to mammalian predation.

A modified mathematical model of the system is described which incorporates the effect of selective predation. Analysis of the model shows the importance of interactions between grouse, parasites and predators in determining the relative densities of each. When predation rate is low, selective predation will remove the heavily infected individuals from the population, leading to a reduction in the effects of the parasite on the grouse and an increase in the size of the grouse population.

## 31.9 Notes

a. Grouse killed by predators carried higher burdens of parasites than adult grouse shot in autumn on the main study area: $X^2 = 13.4$, $P<0.005$, d.f. = 3; and in birds collected from all moors: $X^2 = 22.5$, $P<0.001$, d.f. = 4.

b. Grouse found dead had higher levels of infection than grouse killed by predators on both the main study area: $X^2 = 13.3$, $p<0.005$, d.f. = 3; and in the collections from all moors: $X^2 = 20.7$, $P<0.001$, d.f. = 5

c. Comparisons within a year (1983) found that significantly more of the grouse killed by predators carried high intensities of parasite infection than shot birds: Fisher Exact Test, $P<0.05$.

d. There was a statistical difference between the observed distributions $X^2 = 1487.5$; $P<0.001$; d.f.. = 24, and an increase in the frequency of birds with high worm burdens at high keeper density: $r = 0.97$, $P<0.01$, d.f. = 3.

e. There was a positive association between the proportion of birds with high parasite burdens and the intensity of predator control: $r=0.57$, $P<0.02$, d.f.. = 15.

f. Dogs located nests better than humans where nests were incubated by untreated control females with natural levels of infection: 1983, $Z=-3.374$, $P=0.0004$; 1984, $Z=-3.872$, $P=0.0001$. There were no differences in the ability of humans or dogs to locate nests belonging to treated birds with reduced parasite burdens: $X^2 = 0.04$, $P>0.1$, d.f. = 1.

g. The weight of grouse caeca was positively correlated with worm burdens; $r = 0.60$, N = 208, $P<0.001$, d.f.. = 216.

# TICKS AND LOUPING ILL

# CHAPTER 32

# LIFE CYCLE OF THE SHEEP TICK AND INFESTATIONS ON GROUSE

**The sheep tick life cycle is described. Ticks are more abundant on grouse in areas with louping ill present.**

## 32.1 Introduction

Ticks and tick bourne diseases are a significant cause of stock mortality and financial loss throughout the world. In Britain, some moorland areas harbour populations of the sheep tick (*Ixodes ricinus*) which transmit a number of diseases among which is a viral infection that causes louping ill, and leads to serious losses to both the grouse and sheep industries.

Before describing in detail the distribution and prevalence of louping ill we will first consider the life cycle and abundance of the ticks. In general the ticks do little harm to their hosts other than take a small feed of blood and cause irritation, but the diseases they transmit are significant and would not persist if ticks were absent.

## 32.2 Life cycle of the sheep tick

The sheep tick has four distinct stages in its life cycle: the egg, larva, nymph and adult. Each of the active stages requires one blood meal from a host before moulting into the next stage. This life cycle is summarised in Figure 32.1 (opposite page 192 and typically takes three years with each of the active stages emerging, finding a host, feeding and moulting in each year. However, there may be variations within this life cycle from one area to the next and favourable conditions can result in a life cycle being completed in 18 months or in poor conditions as long as six years. Ticks emerge (rise) and seek (quest) for their hosts principally in spring although questing ticks can still be found on vegetation into late autumn. Within its lifetime the tick spends only about three weeks on the host; the remaining time is spent in the mat layer, the dead and decaying remains of vegetation which accumulate at the base of poorly grazed ground.

*Mating and egg laying:* Male ticks are about 2.5mm long, with a hard reddish-brown plate (shield) that almost covers the back. The females are larger and after a blood meal will swell to as much as 11mm long, but the shield is much smaller than the male's and confined to an area just behind the head. Adult ticks meet and mate on a host, either before or after the female has taken a blood meal.

After mating and feeding, the engorged female falls from the host and descends into the basal mat of the vegetation. If the mat is unsuitable she may move horizontally until cover is found but if no suitable mat layer is found she will dehydrate and die before oviposition. The number of eggs laid by the female is determined by the quantity of blood obtained during her last feed. The nourishment from the first part of the blood feed is directed towards extending the size of the body and the rest to the production of eggs. The time before egg laying commences is dependent on temperature but is usually of the order of two to five weeks. Egg laying can take about three weeks with an egg being laid every three to 12 minutes, but once again this depends on the ambient temperature and humidity.

Females usually lay about 2000 eggs but as many as 5000 have been recorded. As each egg leaves the vagina it is passed to a gland known as the Genes's organ (a gland unique to ticks) which covers the egg in a waxy protective layer. The eggs are deposited continuously and the waxy layer often leads to them sticking together as a large egg mass on the upper side of the tick.

*Questing behaviour:* Ticks are associated with areas of rough grazing, usually with the rough grasses *Nardus* (mat grass) and *Molinia* (purple moor grass), but they can also be found in bracken and heather. These species generally produce a thick mat layer in which the tick can survive. Areas of palatable grasses have little mat layer since grazing animals remove a large quantity of the seasons growth and by the end of the summer there is little dead vegetation to form a mat and a suitable tick habitat. The thick mat layer provides the pockets of high humidity essential for the survival of ticks from one stage to the next.

Survival of the larvae, nymphs and adults is dependent on the relative humidity (saturation deficit) experienced by the ticks. Ticks maintain their water balance when the relative humidity is 92% or more but below this level lose water through evaporation. The relative humidity of the mat layer is usually close to 100% throughout the year and the behaviour of the ticks in the mat is adapted to maintaining a careful water balance. If kept in 100% saturated air they tend to seek dryer conditions but as soon as they lose water they seek again the more humid conditions to maintain their water balance.

When ticks become active and commence questing for a host they crawl from the humid basal mat layer to the relatively dry tips of the growing vegetation where they lose water by evaporation. At a point, just before their water balance becomes critical the ticks move down to the mat layer and replenish their water supply before ascending the vegetation again. During their active period, female ticks will spend up to five periods of four to five days at the tips of the vegetation but the majority of the active period (three months) is spent in the basal mat layer replenishing the lost water.

The time spent questing on the vegetation will depend on the tick's rate of water loss, but the overall time limit available to find a host is influenced by the quantity of food reserves (lipids) remaining after the last feed. Nymphal ticks emerging in spring, all have high levels of lipid reserves which are slowly used up during the questing phase, the rate at which these are used being dependent on the climatic conditions, with a maximum survival time for nymphal questing ticks of about four months.

Most questing ticks on the vegetation are in a state of repose, positioned just below the tip or highest point of a piece of vegetation. The ticks sit with their legs tucked in, avoiding the direct rays of the sun and keeping out of the wind, a state which helps to reduce the rate of water loss. Vibration of the vegetation, as caused by a host walking through it, results in the ticks taking up a questing posture with legs outstretched in an attempt to contact and grasp the potential host.

Once on the host the ticks are stimulated to insert their mouthparts and suck blood by a combination of warmth and odour arising from the host. The sheep tick is indiscriminate in its taste of host and will parasitise most large mammals and birds, although the adult stages are generally only found on the larger mammals. A study in England estimated that between 94% and 99% of the tick population use sheep for their blood meals.

Ticks select areas of the host on which to feed; on sheep they generally avoid the long woollen areas of the back, rump, flank and withers and infest the head and legs and the comparatively bare axillary (arm pits) and inguinal (groin) regions. On grouse, nearly all larvae and nymphs are found around the eye or under the beak. This is partly because grouse chicks preen ticks from themselves and they are unable to reach these regions.

Seasonal activity: Ticks emerge and commence questing when the temperature exceeds 7°C in March and April and generally continue until September. The larvae tend to have a shorter period of activity, numbers increasing rapidly at the beginning of this period and finishing before August. Some researchers have paid a lot of attention to the fact that tick numbers appear to peak twice within a year, in spring and autumn. They believe the double peak is the norm and the single an aberrant exception to the rule.

The rate at which the ticks can develop from one stage to the next is dependent on when the ticks complete their feed of blood and on the ensuing climatic conditions. In some cases it is possible that ticks may feed

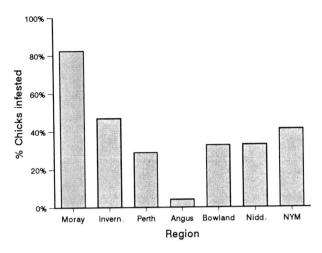

Figure 32.2. Variation in the prevalence of tick infestation on grouse chicks between regions. Regions are in a north to south order: NYM = North York Moors.

early in spring, develop into the next stage and commence questing for a host by autumn and so account for the double peak of activity. This second peak can also include ticks that fed in the previous autumn but were unable to complete their development until the following year and consequently did not become active until the autumn. In one site that exhibited a single peak of activity the sheep were not put to the hill until late in the season, so ticks were unable to obtain a host until late summer and presumably did not have time to feed and complete development until the following spring. As such the activity of ticks is a result of the interaction of host availability and climatic conditions.

## 32.3 Basic methods

Grouse broods and individual chicks were located on managed grouse moors using trained pointing dogs. Chicks were aged according to feather development, and the number of larvae and nymph ticks that were attached to the chick around the head was counted. Weight and wing-length measurements were also recorded.

Tick studies were concentrated at 5 major locations in northern England and Scotland:

1. North York Moors
2. Nidderdale, North Yorkshire
3. Bowland Fells
4. West Perthshire
5. Angus
6. Moray.

Some of the analysis presented here considers each chick as an independent sample. This is not strictly correct since the chicks within a brood tend to stay close together so if one chick is infested with ticks then the other chicks within the brood are also likely to be infested to the same extent.

## 32.4 Prevalence of ticks

The prevalence of tick infestation is defined here as the proportion of grouse which have at least one tick feeding, irrespective of the number of ticks per host. This varies greatly both between regions (Figure 32.2) and to a lesser extent between years (Figure 32.3).

The prevalence increases with the age of the chicks within the first two weeks of life and then stabilises over the next 10 days. While the pattern of this change in prevalence was essentially similar on moors with and those without louping ill (Figure 32.4, 32.5), in our study areas the moors with the louping ill reached a higher level of infestation (asymptote) than the study areas without louping ill.

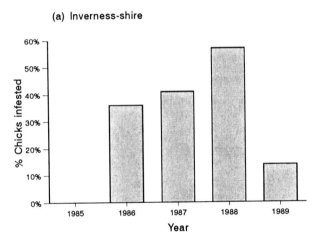

**(a) Inverness-shire**

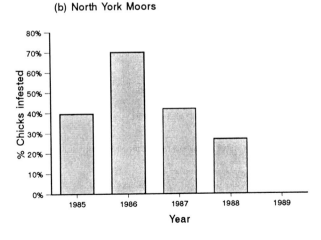

**(b) North York Moors**

Figure 32.3. Prevalence of ticks on grouse chicks between years from two study areas: (a) Inverness-shire and (b) North York Moors, showing year to year variation in levels of infestation.

181

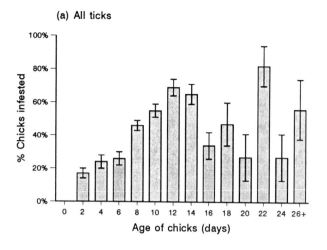

**(a) All ticks**

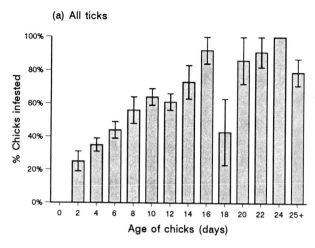

**(a) All ticks**

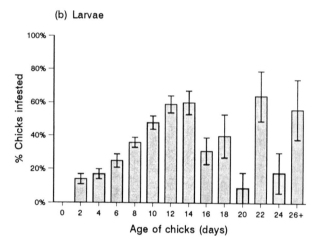

**(b) Larvae**

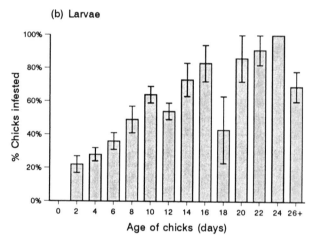

**(b) Larvae**

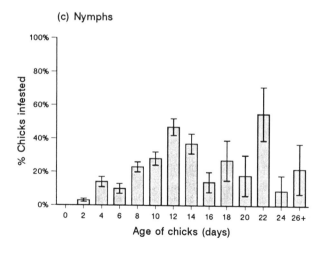

**(c) Nymphs**

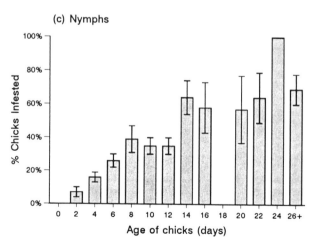

**(c) Nymphs**

Figure 32.4. Age prevalence curves for tick infestations on grouse chicks from grouse moors without louping ill; (a) all ticks, (b) larvae and (c) nymphs. The proportion infested reach a peak at 8-14 days of age.

Figure 32.5. Age prevalence curves for ticks on grouse chicks from populations where louping ill is known to be present. Greater levels of prevalence are reached in these populations than populations without louping ill.

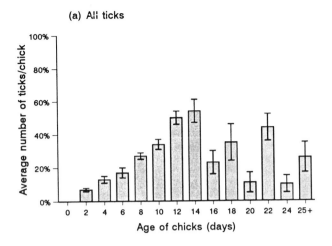

(a) All ticks

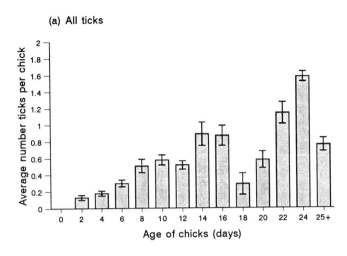

(a) All ticks

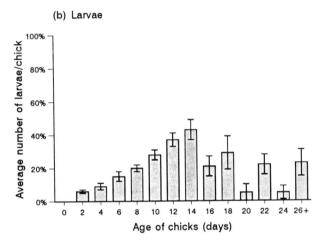

(b) Larvae

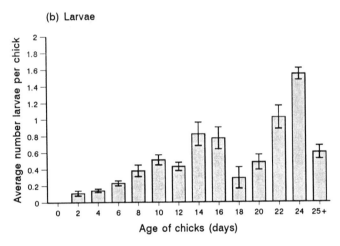

(b) Larvae

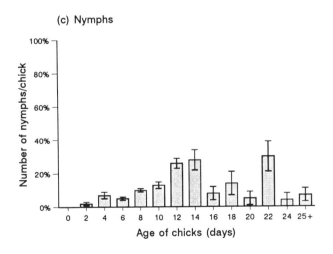

(c) Nymphs

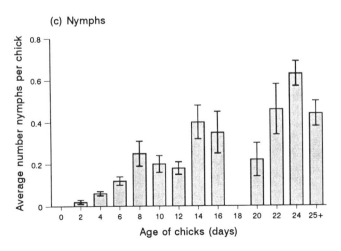

(c) Nymphs

Figure 32.6. Age intensity curves for ticks on grouse chicks from populations without louping ill; (a) all ticks; (b) larvae and (c) nymphs. As with prevalence, intensity of infestation reach a peak at 8·14 days of age.

Figure 32.7. Age intensity curves for tick infestations on grouse chicks from populations with louping ill known to be present. Intensity of infestation reached greater levels on moors with louping ill present.

183

## 32.5 Intensity of tick infestations

As with prevalence, the intensity of infestation increases with the age of the chicks over the first 8-14 days of life (Figure 32.6, 32.7). After this date, there may be a subsequent decline associated with the end of the tick rise but these data show a great deal of variation and are difficult to interpret clearly. Even so it is interesting to note that tick numbers reached a greater level on the moors with louping ill present.

The greater the number of infected ticks that bite the grouse, the greater the likelihood of a chick developing louping ill and the greater the contribution of grouse in sustaining the disease. The maintenance of the disease depends upon the average infection rate. When each infected individual gives rise, on average, to one other infected individual the disease will be maintained. This is known as the basic reproductive rate of the disease and depends on a number of features of the tick, virus and host life cycles. In particular transmission will be greater when there is a large number of ticks per grouse and by a high proportion of infected ticks. As such the presence or absence of louping ill will be influenced by the relative numbers of ticks to grouse.

## 32.6 Summary

The tick life cycle is described. Essentially ticks pass through four life stages: eggs, larvae, nymphs and adults. Larvae, nymphs and adult females require a blood meal to develop from one stage to the next but only larvae and nymphs obtain a blood meal from grouse. Prevalence and intensity of grouse chick infestation with larvae and nymphs increases with the age of the grouse chicks over the first eight to 14 days of life. While there is a great deal of variation in levels of tick infestation between regions the study areas recorded with louping ill tended to have greater levels of prevalence and abundance of ticks.

# CHAPTER 33

# PREVALENCE OF LOUPING ILL IN GROUSE POPULATIONS

**Louping ill causes high mortality in grouse and variations between years and places are associated with the abundance of ticks.**

## 33.1 Introduction

Louping ill is a disease of sheep and grouse characterised by tissues of the central nervous system and brain causing polioencephalomyeletis (inflammation of brain and nervous tissues). It is caused by a flavivirus transmitted between hosts by the sheep tick *Ixodes ricinus*. Diseased individuals exhibit nervous disorders, the obvious symptom being poor locomotion so sheep will stagger ('loup') and red grouse may be unable to walk or can loose control during flight.

Early field observers noted that the reproductive success of grouse in areas where ticks were abundant was frequently poor despite correct heather management and predator control. Moribund grouse taken from these populations were found to be infected with the louping ill virus in brain tissue. Subsequent studies in the field by James Duncan (Game Conservancy) and Dr Hugh Reid (Moredun Research Institute) demonstrated that louping ill was the cause of this mortality[1,2], while studies by ourselves in northern England showed that in areas where louping ill was absent but ticks were present, the ticks caused little mortality.

To understand the significance of louping ill to grouse populations in general and to understand the role of vaccination as a control method for reducing louping ill in both sheep and grouse, we initiated extensive sampling of grouse populations in different parts of the country. Such a survey over several years and from several localities would not have been possible without the kind co-operation of Dr Hugh Reid and colleagues at the Moredun Research Institute, Edinburgh.

## 33.2 Basic methods

Blood samples were collected from freshly shot grouse and serum was isolated from each sample by centrifugation. Sera were subsequently sent to the Moredun Research Institute for antibody assay using the Haemagglutination-Inhibiting Antibody test. Collection of field samples resulted in a certain amount of contamination from haemolysis (deterioration of blood cells), so only samples recording a positive response at a titre of 80 or more were taken as seropositive. The proportion of young and old birds found to be seropositive was estimated for a number of grouse moors and for some moors over a number of years.

## 33.3. Louping ill on moors

During the extensive survey of grouse moors conducted in 1979 and again in 1983, grouse moor owners were asked if ticks and louping ill were known to be present on their estate. Both have a wide distribution (Figure 33.1).

Levels of louping ill were determined for a series of grouse moors by examining the proportion of young and old grouse that proved to be seropositive. In some populations there was no significant variation between years in the proportions of old and young birds found to be seropositive[a] (Figure 33.2) so in this first analysis all samples from all years were combined.

Within some populations, a greater proportion of old grouse were seropositive to louping ill. This pattern was consistent between populations and the proportion of old grouse recorded as seropositive increased

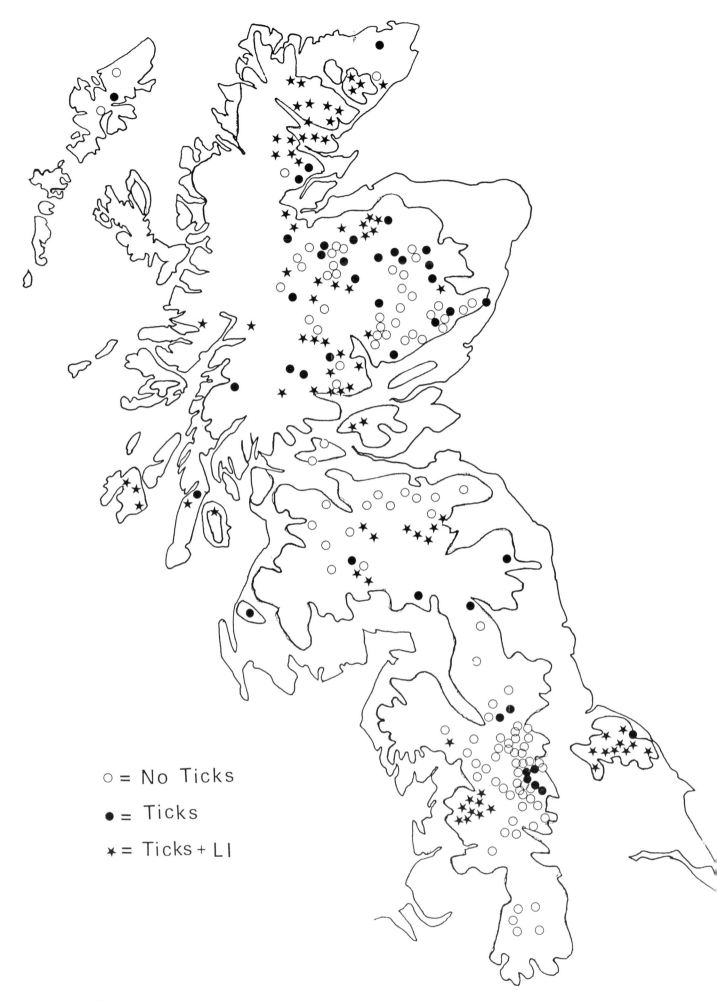

○ = No Ticks

● = Ticks

★ = Ticks + LI

Figure 33.1. Distribution of grouse moors recording the presence of ticks and ticks with louping ill (LI).

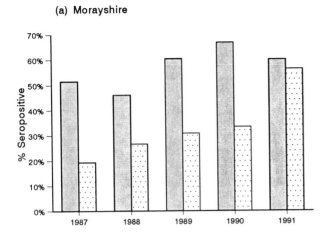

**(a) Morayshire**

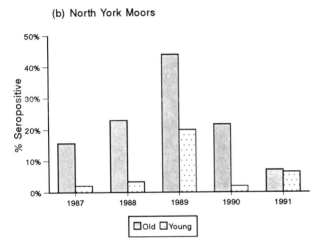

**(b) North York Moors**

Figure 33.2. Year to year changes in the proportion of young and old grouse seropositive to louping ill antibody from two populations in (a) Moray and (b) North York Moors.

with the proportion in young birds[c] (Figure 33.3). Within grouse populations there was no difference in the proportion of old cocks and old hens found to be seropositive[d].

The proportion of grouse seropositive varied between regions[b] with the greatest prevalence in parts of northern Scotland (Figure 33.4). Differences in the proportion seropositive between populations was not associated with aspects of sheep density or grouse density. On estates where prevalence was high the sheep stock tended to be vaccinated, this being a response by the farmers to try and alleviate the effects of the louping ill.

### 33.4. Variation in louping ill and tick abundance between estates

On six estates, the intensity of tick infestation on young grouse chicks was examined during the summer

months. Since tick burdens tend to increase during the first 8-10 days of life (Chapter 32) all results from chicks of less than 8 days were ignored and the intensity of tick infestation was compared with the proportion of young grouse recorded as seropositive. The proportion of young grouse seropositive to louping ill increased with the intensity of tick infestation[e] (Figure 33.5). Although such a relationship is dependent on one single outlying point, this finding agrees with later results and epidemiological knowledge of the system from which we would expect the relative abundance of ticks (ticks per grouse) to be important to the success of the virus.

### 33.5 Louping ill and chick survival

Analysis of population data (Chapter 8) has shown that breeding losses on grouse moors with louping ill present are larger than moors without louping ill.

Laboratory studies coupled with field experiments have shown quite clearly that grouse are highly susceptible to louping ill. In an experimental study of captive birds 79% of 37 experimentally infected young birds developed clinical signs of weakness and survived for only 6 days[1].

Comparative studies on grouse moors with ticks present and louping ill present indicated that ticks alone were not detrimental to chick survival but in areas with ticks and louping ill, chick survival was almost 50% lower (Table 33.1). In Speyside, field studies[1] found that infected chicks were more likely to die than uninfected chicks and overall chick survival was 89% lower on an area with ticks and louping ill compared with an area with few ticks and no louping ill.

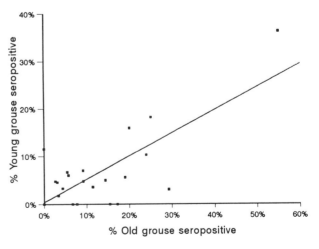

Figure 33.3. Relationship between proportion of young and proportion of old grouse seropositive to louping ill antibody. While the proportion of young increases with the proportion of old birds seropositive, the levels in old birds are consistently greater.

187

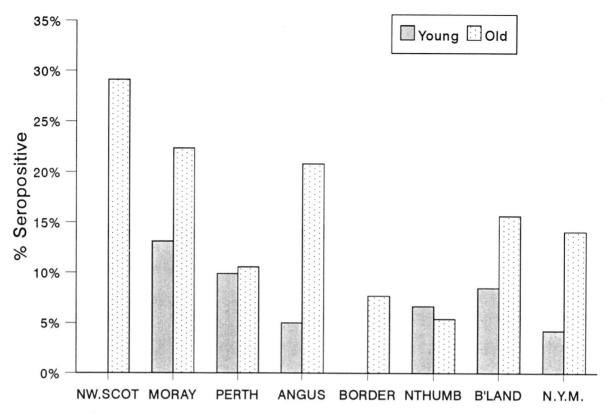

Figure 33.4. Variation in the proportion of grouse seropositive to louping ill antibody between regions. NYM = North York Moors.

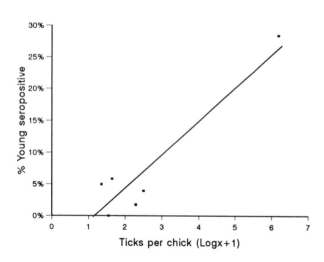

Figure 33.5. A comparison between populations of the proportion of young grouse seropositive and the average number of ticks recorded on chicks. Levels of louping ill were greater in areas where the tick levels were greater on the chicks, although such a relationship is dependent on a single outlying point.

Table 33.1 The effects of ticks and louping ill on the survival of grouse chicks, estimated from bag returns.

|  | Moors with: | | |
|  | No Ticks | Ticks | Ticks + LI |
| --- | --- | --- | --- |
| Number tagged | 345 | 343 | 467 |
| % shot | | 15.1% | 16.6% | 7.9% |

The late James Duncan conducted detailed studies on grouse, ticks and louping ill on some of the Moray study areas. He collected data on numbers of red grouse, breeding success and abundance of ticks as measured by the number of adult ticks on ewes living on the study areas. In general, each site shows an increase in grouse breeding losses during years of high tick abundance[a] and there is no difference between the different areas (Figure 33.6).

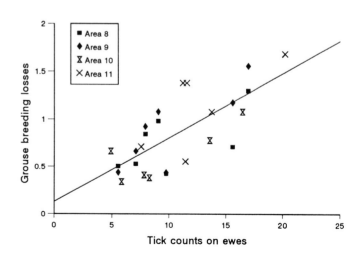

Figure 33.6. Breeding losses (log differences) of red grouse in relation to tick abundance from study areas in Moray, showing a general tendency for losses to be greater in years when ticks were abundant (data collected by James Duncan).

188

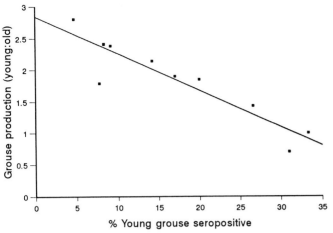

Figure 33.7. Grouse breeding production from different grouse populations in relation to proportion of young grouse subsequently found seropositive. The relationship implies that poor breeding is associated with high levels of louping ill infection. The slope of this line is close to a figure of 80% chick mortality.

In studies of captive birds, the presence of ticks did not influence the growth rate of chicks[3]. In studies of wild red grouse chicks, infected chicks weighed less than uninfected chicks[1].

In a comparison between study areas there is a negative relationship between the number of chicks counted in July and the proportion of young grouse that were seropositive (Figure 33.7). The slope of this line was consistent with a mortality rate of 80%. This is an interesting finding since it indicates that the mortality caused by the louping ill on the different populations has not resulted in increased immunity to the disease.

The strength of the immune response by the birds to the infection can be examined by the relative titre of the antibody detected through the HI test. The antibody titre was greater in old grouse than young grouse[f] (Figure 33.8), probably because the titre in the young birds represents the response to a primary infection, whereas in the adults the high titre reflects a secondary challenge of infection. There was no difference between old males and females in antibody titre[f].

### 33.6 Summary

Louping ill is a disease that causes high mortality in grouse but is only prevalent in certain parts of the distribution of grouse. The proportion of grouse seropositive to louping ill is usually greater in old than young grouse and while this varies consistently between populations some populations show little variation between years. Overwhelming evidence exists to demonstrate that louping ill causes serious mortality in young grouse chicks, with approximately 80% of infected chicks subsequently dying. The proportion of

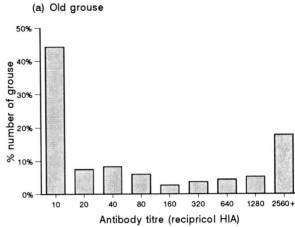

(a) Old grouse

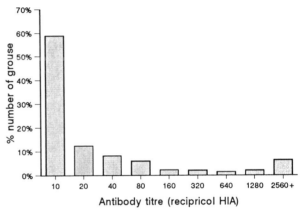

(b) Young grouse

Figure 33.8. Differences in the titre of antibody recorded from all old and young grouse. Generally antibody titre is greater in young grouse probably because young grouse have suffered recent infections of louping ill.

grouse seropositive was related to levels of tick infestation between populations. In comparisons within populations grouse breeding losses were associated with the levels of tick infestation on ewes.

189

## 33.7 Notes

a. There was no significant difference between years in the proportion of seropositive grouse for either young ($X^2 = 3.35$, d.f. = 3, $P = 0.341$) or old ($X2 = 2.21$, d.f. = 3, $P = 0.53$).

b. There was variation in the proportion of young grouse seropositive between moors ($X^2 = 301.3$, d.f. = 16, $P < 0.0001$)

c. The proportion of seropositive young grouse increased with the proportion of old seropositive, $r = 0.600$, d.f. = 20, $P < 0.001$.

d. There was no difference between the proportion of old males and old females that were seropositive at one site in Moray $X^2 = 0.06$, $P = 0.87$, d.f. = 1.

e. Proportion of seropositive young grouse was greater on moors with a greater intensity of ticks on chicks, $r = 0.942$, $P < 0.01$, d.f. = 4.

f. Young grouse carried higher titre levels than old grouse ($X^2 = 46.7$, d.f. = 8, $P < 0.001$) but there was no difference between old males and females ($X^2 = 8.61$, d.f. = 8, $P = 0.376$).

## 33.8 References

1. Reid, H.W., Duncan, J.S., Phillips, J.D.P., Moss, R. and Watson, A. (1978). Studies on louping ill virus (Flavivirus group) in wild red grouse (*Lagopus lagopus scoticus*). *Journal of Hygiene,* **81**, 321-329.

2. Duncan, J.S., Reid, H.W., Moss, R., Phillips, J.D.P., and Watson, A. (1979). Ticks, louping ill and red grouse on moors in Speyside, Scotland. *Journal of Wildlife Management*, **43**, 500-505.

# CHAPTER 34

# THE CONTROL OF LOUPING ILL

**Vaccination of sheep may remove louping ill from some grouse populations but this does not work on areas with high tick densities.**

## 34.1 Introduction

Many viral infections of humans and domestic stock are controlled through a vaccination or immunization programme. A vaccine against louping ill was developed during the 1970s but this caused problems during manufacture when a number of technical workers became infected. The vaccine was subsequently removed from the market and an attenuated vaccine developed which is still used to control the virus infection in sheep. In practice, farmers assume the adult ewes have developed their own immunity which they pass to their lambs through the colostrum and they vaccinate only the susceptible hogs and replacement ewes.

Ticks may feed on a wide range of hosts but only sheep and grouse produce viraemias which exceed the threshold necessary for transmission. Both the larvae and the nymphs feed on grouse but adult females are

rarely found. Since larvae only feed once, only an infected larva that moults into a nymph can infect a grouse, while both nymphs and adult females can infect sheep (Figure 34.1). The virus cannot be transmitted from an infected female tick to its eggs. While the vaccination of sheep was obviously developed to protect sheep, the removal of sheep as amplifiers of the disease may help to control the disease in secondary hosts such as the grouse. This chapter investigates epidemiological and control aspects of the disease through the application of models.

## 34.2 Epidemiological patterns within the system

Age-prevalence curves can provide information on a series of epidemiological measurements important for understanding how control mechanisms may operate. With viral infections like louping ill this is usually expressed as the proportion of individuals within the population that are seropositive with age. Some data were collected for this by Dr Hugh Reid and James Duncan. Subsequently, we obtained further information from the same study area when the grouse were older. The data describe what is generally observed for viral infections, an initial rise in the proportion seropositive with age to an asymptote (Figure 34.2).

*The Latent period* is the time from initial infection to when the virus reaches a concentration in the blood sufficient for it to be passed back to the tick; a point where the titre is $10^4$ platelets. In sheep this is approximately six days.

*The period of infectiousness* is the period that the virus concentration exceeds the threshold for transmission. For grouse this is probably in the region of five days.

Prevalence of infection in vectors is usually very low as a consequence of the short life expectancy of the

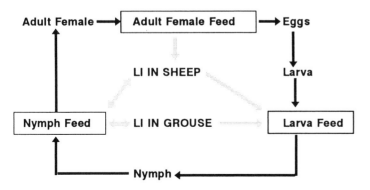

Figure 34.1. Schematic representation of tick life cycle and the flow of louping ill between hosts. Note that grouse can only receive louping ill from the nymph tick while sheep receive it from both nymph and adult.

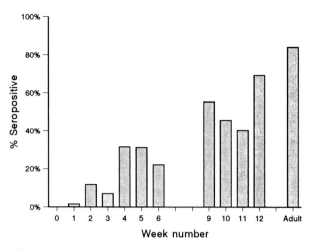

Figure 34.2 Age related changes in the proportion of seropositive grouse collected from a grouse moor in Moray. The first 6 weeks of data were collected by James Duncan & Hugh Reid and subsequent data in another year.

vector relative to the duration of infectiousness in the hosts. Estimates have placed this as low as one tick in every 1000 actually carrying the virus.

### 34.3 Principles of control

The success of a control programme is essentially dependent on the basic reproductive rate of the disease, a quantity known in epidemiological literature as $R$. This is the average number of new cases that arise from an infectious host, so when $R$ is 1 (the transmission threshold), each infectious individual gives rise, on average, to one other infectious individual and the disease is maintained. The object of a control programme is to reduce this value of $R$ to less than unity, so the prevalence of the disease falls and eventually become extinct. The lower the value of $R$ the quicker the disease will be eradicated.

The host population can be considered as a group of individuals which can be classified as susceptible, infectious or immune. The disease spreads through the population when infectious individuals pass the pathogen to susceptible individuals which then become infected and subsequently either die or become immune. The rate of spread of the disease depends on the structure of the host population but if most are immune, few infectious individuals pass the pathogen to the susceptible population. The aim of a vaccination programme is to take a proportion of the host population that are susceptible, make them immune and in so doing reducing the number of new infections. Mass immunization effectively reduces the size of the host population for the disease to spread through. Infectious individuals come into contact with immune individuals and the basic reproductive rate of the disease is reduced.

Not all individuals need to be vaccinated since a proportion of the susceptible hosts will fail to meet an infectious individual and they thus obtain protection from the 'herd immunity'. The proportion that needs to be vaccinated depends on the reproductive rate of the disease; the larger the value of $R$ the greater the proportion that needs vaccinating (this is $1-1/R$). Unfortunately this is frequently high, and most diseases require more than 90% of the host population to be vaccinated for successful eradication.

### 34.4 Modelling and the control of louping ill

The louping ill system is more complicated than a simple viral infection such as measles, where the disease is passed directly from an infectious host to a susceptible host. The louping ill system involves two hosts (grouse and sheep) and a vector (sheep tick). There are further complications since grouse mortality from the disease is greater than sheep mortality. Both nymphs and adult ticks may transmit the disease to sheep but since grouse are rarely bitten by adults, only nymphs can transmit the disease to grouse.

Despite these complications it is best to start with a simple description which we can understand and then to add the complications later. The basic model for a vector transmitted disease was developed by Ross at the turn of the century to describe the dynamics of malarial infection. It was extended and improved by MacDonald in the 1950s and then updated in the 1980s by Aron & May[1]. Essentially the mathematics of the system describe, through two equations, changes in the proportion of infected grouse and the proportion of infected ticks. Changes in the number of infected grouse depend on how frequently a single vector bites the host, the ratio of vectors to hosts and the survival of both vectors and infected hosts.

In this system, the basic reproductive rate of the disease is determined by the number of secondary hosts that subsequently become infectious, but it also depends on how long the host remains infectious, during which time susceptible vectors may also become infected and subsequently make further infectious bites themselves.

The maintenance of the disease depends on the average number of bites on grouse the tick makes during its lifetime that lead to the tick becoming infected. When this is high, then small changes in tick abundance will have little effect on the proportion of seropositive grouse and the disease will be stable and endemic. On the other hand when this value is small, then small changes in tick density are likely to result in substantial differences in the proportion of grouse

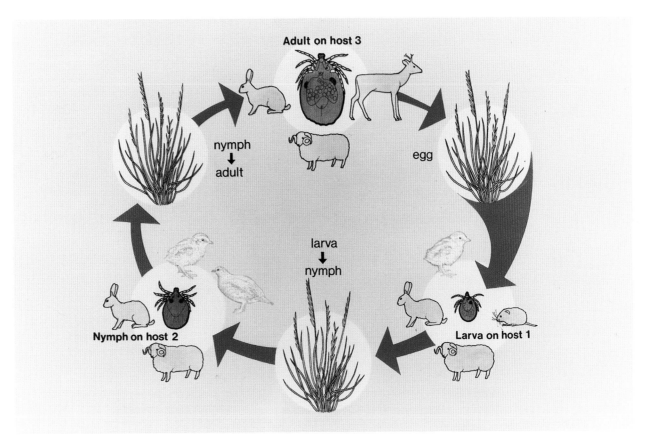

Figure 32.1. The life cycle of the sheep tick *Ixodes ricinus*. The tick feeds on hosts at three stages during its life cycle but since adults rarely occur on grouse only the nymph stage will transmit the virus that causes louping ill in grouse (Chapter 32).

Young grouse chick infested with ticks; most are concentrated around the eye and bill (Chapter 32).

A chick so heavily infested that the burden of ticks has caused the eye to close. This is not common but tick abundance tends to be greater on moors with louping ill (Chapter 33).

Fret marks on the wing of a grouse chick suffering from heavy infestation of ticks (Chapter 32).

Dipping and vaccinating sheep can help to control the disease louping ill in grouse but this does not benefit all grouse populations (Chapter 33).

To determine the level of louping ill in a grouse population, blood samples were taken during the shooting season and subsequently tested for antibody (Chapter 33).

infected and the disease will be unstable and epidemic in nature. In summary, the average number of bites made during a ticks lifetime that result in the tick becoming infected is a measure of the stability of the disease. When low the disease will be epidemic and when high the disease will be endemic. This is known as Macdonald's stability index.

Analysis of the data available for the louping ill system is scant, but based on a series of assumptions relating to age structure of parasites within the population, stability indices can be estimated. The interesting difference is that the Moray population studied exhibits a high stability index implying that here the disease is endemic (Table 34.1) . This is supported by the low coefficient of variation in the disease between years. In comparison the data from four other populations found a low stability index implying the diseases was epidemic and this was supported by the high coefficient of variation in the disease between years. Estimates of the basic reproductive rate for the disease suggest that in the Moray population this could be greater than unity and the grouse may play a significant role in maintaining the disease, although no firm conclusions can be drawn at the current time without more detailed information (Table 34.1).

Table 34.1 Stability values for louping ill estimated from epidemiological parameters and the variation in the year to year proportion of louping ill recorded in different grouse populations. The low variability and high stability index imply the disease is endemic on the Moray moor but may be an epidemic on other populations such as in the North York Moors.

| Population Region | Stability Index of LI | Variation in Annual LI | $R$ Basic Reproductive Rate of LI |
|---|---|---|---|
| N.Y.M.1 | 0.209 | 2.08 | 0.346 |
| N.Y.M.2 | 0.101 | 4 | 0.327 |
| Bowland | 0.357 | 1.50 | 0.327 |
| Angus | 0.270 | 4 | 0.248 |
| Moray | 1.617 | 0.135 | 1.355 |

This modelling approach is still a gross oversimplification, since the role of the sheep in the system is still ignored and the sheep can act as a reservoir host to generate an additional source of infection via the tick vectors to the grouse.

## 34.5 Vaccination and LI control

A vaccination programme should reduce the role of sheep as a reservoir host and in those populations where the value of R is less than one, lead to the elimination of louping ill in the grouse population. Knowledge of the system and the results presented here lead us to expect vaccination to have a significant effect on the level of louping ill in populations with low tick biting rates, in particular those in northern England, Perthshire and Angus. Conversely in the Moray populations the value of $R$ may be greater than one and vaccination would reduce louping ill in grouse, but this may not be sufficient to eliminate the disease since tick numbers are high. Vaccination will be beneficial in that it may well reduce the proportion of grouse infected but overall it would not be sufficient to eradicate louping ill totally even with the removal of the sheep population. Such conclusions are, of course, tentative but they provide a simple indication of the dynamics of the system.

The main difference between the Moray area and others is the high ratio of ticks to grouse, not necessarily the overall numbers. To reduce louping ill in this system would require further reduction in this ratio. Removal of alternative hosts such as hares, sheep, roe deer and goats may have a long term effect in reducing the size of the tick population but in the short term may actually increase the ratio of ticks to grouse and increase the problems of louping ill. Dipping sheep or reducing the number that successfully reach the grouse should have an additional effect.

## 34.6 Summary

This analysis and modelling exercise suggests that louping ill is essentially an epidemic disease on many grouse moors. It is probably sustained by amplification of the disease by some of the sheep and it may therefore be controlled by vaccination. In other areas such as on the Moray moors, the disease is endemic and constantly produces a high level of mortality. Sheep vaccination may help to reduce the prevalence in grouse but the high tick population will help to maintain the disease. In such circumstances the ratio of ticks to grouse is high and may well be sustained by alternative hosts such as hares, deer and goats. Removal of these hosts in the short term will increase and not decrease the ratio of ticks to grouse, but in the long term it may well reduce tick abundance and louping ill.

## 34.7 References

1. Aron, J.L. & May, R.M. (1982). The population dynamics of malaria. In: Population dynamics of infectious diseases (ed. R.M. Anderson), pp 139-179. Chapman and Hall, London.

# HEATHER LOSS AND RESTORATION TECHNIQUES

# CHAPTER 35

# THE LOSS AND MANAGEMENT OF HEATHER MOORLANDS

**Heather has been lost at a rapid rate, principally through overgrazing. Most of the effects of overgrazing occur during the winter months at sites for fothering sheep.**

## 35.1 Introduction

Conservationists, land managers and the Government are all concerned about the future of heather moorland in Britain's uplands. They remain one of the last undeveloped wildlife habitats in Britain and contain an animal community of international importance. A major component of the uplands is heather moorland: a semi-natural habitat that has been shaped and maintained through controlled grazing and burning and which provides the major habitat for grouse and a range of other upland bird species (Chapter 6). Sixteen moorland bird species are characteristically important to moorlands, eight of these are considered of international importance and were listed in Annex 1 of the EC Directive on the conservation of wild birds.

While there are a range of factors influencing the abundance of these upland birds, including pesticides, predation and persecution, the loss of the heather moorland habitat is a problem influencing the decline in at least half of these species, including grouse. Maintaining and restoring heather dominant vegetation is a priority both for those interested in conserving upland birds and in the production of grouse. More than 90% of the area of heather moorland lies in the hands of sporting estates which have traditionally maintained and managed this habitat through careful burning and grazing.

This chapter examines the loss of heather moorland and the impact of sheep grazing on areas of English and Scottish moorland currently managed as grouse moors. Areas already lost from grouse management are not included, although the relative loss of moorland through afforestation and overgrowing can be estimated from Table 35.1. Forestry now covers some 20% of the uplands, whereas bracken and moorland grasses comprise 40%, much of which has arisen through overgrazing and poor management.

Table 35.1 Upland vegetation classes (source: ITE and RSPB papers)

| Vegetation Class | Area (km²) | Percentage total of |
|---|---|---|
| Heather dominant vegetation | | |
| Heather/Bilberry | 14,384 | 33.2% |
| Heather/Cotton Grass | 2,098 | 7.2% |
| Subtotal | 17,482 | 41.4% |
| | | |
| Bracken | 1,322 | 3.0% |
| Rushes *(Juncus)* | 1,983 | 4.6% |
| Purple moor grass | 7,414 | 17.1% |
| Bent/wavy hair grass etc | 6,614 | 15.3% |
| Subtotal | 17,333 | 40.0% |
| | | |
| Forestry | 8,485 | 19.6% |
| | | |
| (Estimated grouse moor) | 16,880 | 39.0% |

## 35.2 Loss of heather moorland

Obtaining accurate measures of heather loss is not easy, although it is possible in places where comparable aerial photographs are available. Studies in Cumbria, the Peak District and the North York Moors have determined the rate of heather loss using this method. Heather loss is generally in the region of 1 to 4% per annum (Table 35.2). Although similar figures are not available for the Northern Pennines or the Borders, heather loss in these areas is probably at about the same rate.

195

Table 35.2. Loss of heather moorland in the North of England (source: NCC, North York Moors National Park, P.Anderson & D. Yalden[1]).

| Area | Habitat | Percentage loss per annum |
|---|---|---|
| Cumbria | Freely drained heather moorland | 4.0% |
| | Blanket bog | 0.4% |
| North Yorkshire Moors | Heather dominant moorland | 0.9% |
| Peak District | Heather dominant | 0.6% |
| | Heather co-dominant | 1.1% |

**(a) Sheep in England**

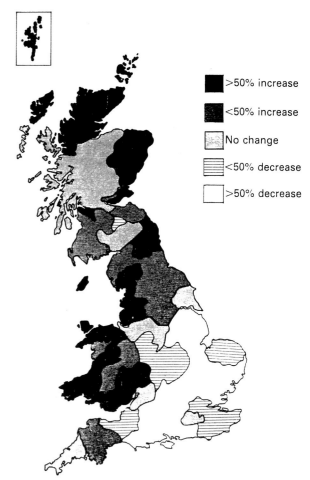

>50% increase
<50% increase
No change
<50% decrease
>50% decrease

Figure 35.2. Changes in the density of sheep on agricultural land 1875-1966 showing a large reduction in sheep in south east Britain and an incrase in upland areas (sources Sydes & Miller 1988; In: Ecological Change in the Uplands pp 323-337).

## 35.3 Overgrazing and stocking density

The most direct method of estimating sheep grazing pressure is to measure the percentage of the current season's vegetation growth taken by the grazing animal. Detailed studies by Sheila Grant and others at The Macaulay Land Use Research Institute (MLURI) have shown that where 40% of the seasons growth is grazed, there is a reduction in cover and standing crop. However, this does not reduce the production of new shoots or carbohydrate reserves. On the other hand, a grazing intensity which removes 80% of the current season's growth leads to a loss in carbohydrate reserves and shoot production, and so can be classified as overgrazing. Old heather and heather on wet ground is more sensitive, both to grazing and trampling, than are younger stands. Autumn grazing appears to have the greatest impact.

Quantitative information on grazing intensity does exist on a number of specific sites but a more extensive picture can only be achieved through examination of stocking rates and management procedures. Since the last war, changes in sheep density, winter feeding and shepherding have all caused an increase in grazing intensity on heather.

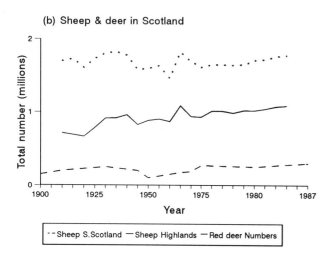

**(b) Sheep & deer in Scotland**

-- Sheep S.Scotland  — Sheep Highlands  — Red deer Numbers

Figure 35.1. Changes in numbers of sheep and deer in Britain. (a) The number of sheep reached a low following the harsh winter of 1947 but subsequently increased as sheep were moved from lowland to upland areas (see Figure 35.2). (b) Sheep numbers in Scotland have increased at a steady rate as have deer numbers, although the extent of these increase varies between areas.

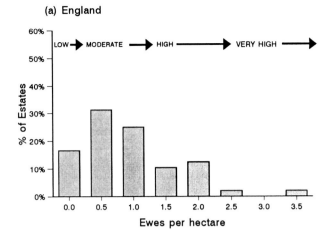

(a) England

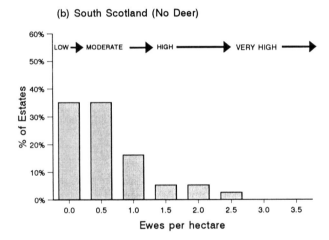

(b) South Scotland (No Deer)

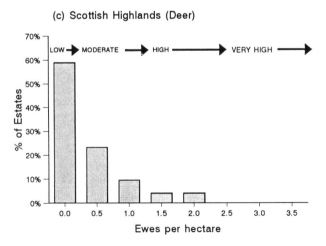

(c) Scottish Highlands (Deer)

Figure 35.3. Frequency distribution of grazing pressure on managed grouse moors in (a) England, (b) South Scotland (where deer are absent) and (c) Scottish Highland areas where deer are present. The proportion of moors with high sheep stocking levels was greater in England.

Within the last hundred years the size of the national sheep flock has fluctuated, but the sheep population is currently similar to that recorded a century ago (Figure 35.1). However, there has been a general shift away from sheep farming in the lowland areas and an increase in all upland areas (Figure 35.2). This higher stocking rate, coupled with the loss of good feeding ground to forestry and the increase in unpalatable vegetation such as bracken, has generally increased grazing pressure since the last war.

In Scotland the sheep population has increased only slightly, although grazing pressure has increased here through the loss of ground to forestry. Furthermore, the deer population is increasing at a rate similar to the rate of increase in sheep in northern England. Whether this has increased grazing pressure to the same extent is not clear from these figures. In our surveys, 39% of English grouse moors and 43% of Scottish moors recorded a recent increase in sheep stocking density.

As a rough guide to grazing pressure, one ewe to the hectare is usually considered the maximum stocking density to allow heather maintenance, although the actual figure will vary between 0.5 and 2.0 sheep per hectare (2.47 acres), according to the type of ground and the availability of other food. In our grouse moor surveys, 52% of English estates recorded a grazing pressure of more than one ewe to the hectare (Figure 35.3). Many of the English moors are commons, with the number of sheep limited through the Commons Registration Act 1965, although in reality some commoners ignore registration and carry more than the registered numbers. In a survey of stocking levels on registered commons of heather moorland in England, 25 provided details of actual stocking density compared with numbers registered. Of these, 20% recorded more sheep than were registered and in one instance there were four times as many sheep on the common.

In Scotland, sheep stocking rates are lower. Thirty per cent of estates without deer present stock at a rate greater than one ewe to the hectare. Evaluating the impact of herbivores on heather can be difficult where there are both deer and sheep present. Although sheep density is lower when deer are present (only 18% of estates carrying stocking rates greater than one ewe to the hectare), the majority of Highland estates are carrying between 0.15 and 0.30 deer per hectare.

### 35.4 Winter feeding and shepherding

Stocking rates cannot be used alone to estimate grazing intensity since such a measurement fails to take account of seasonal changes in the distribution pattern

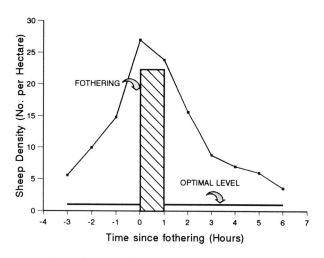

Figure 35.4. Average sheep density within 200 metres of fothering sites in relation to the time of fothering. Sheep density remained well above the optimal grazing level throughout the period and led to rapid localised destruction of the heather.

of sheep on the hill. Sheep are selective feeders. They graze on the palatable fescue and bent grasses when available, but switch to heather when these grasses are exhausted or have died back. Since heather is one of the few evergreens available on moorland and is usually exposed during snow cover, it forms a major part of the sheep's diet during autumn and winter. In our survey of sheep management on moorland areas, the majority of estates (80% of Scottish estates and 84% of English grouse moors) reported that sheep were kept on the hill during the winter months. Of those estates keeping sheep on the hill during the winter months the majority (80% in England and 75% in Scotland) provide supplementary feed in the form of hay, feed blocks or compounded feeds to maintain a high plane of nutrition before lambing. The action of winter feeding tends to concentrate stock within a limited areas and exacerbates the problems of trampling and grazing, particularly in areas of old woody heather.

To examine the influence of winter feeding on the distribution of sheep on heather moorland, we con-ducted a series of observations on five hefted flocks on a common in northern England. Here the sheep were fed in winter with a hay supplement. Farmers usually provided hay between 10 and 12am and spread it over an area of 0.1 hectare. There was a tendency for sheep to concentrate at the fothering point several hours before feeding (Figure 35.4) and remain at high densities even six hours after feeding. The area affected at each fothering site was 20 hectares. The major cause of heather loss in the short term is probably associated with the behaviour of sheep and the effects of sheep at fothering sites, although high stocking densities will obviously exacerbate the problem further.

In the past, concentration of sheep stock was prevented through the employment of a shepherd. Shepherds are rarely employed on English moorland since the sheep interests generally lie in the hands of owner-occupiers and tenant farmers. In Scotland, the absence of common ground and the history of sheep management has resulted in the employment of shepherds to care for the sheep owned by the estate. Here 70% of estates surveyed had a shepherd present.

## 35.5 Summary

Stocking density of sheep is particularly high on the blanket bogs of northern England and we can expect continued loss of heather if sheep numbers are not reduced. While most of Scotland does not carry the stocking density present in England, the increase in deer – coupled with the loss of grazing area – is causing problems.

Stocking density is only one component of the grazing problem and in general the damage caused is also influenced by the availability of alternative vegetation types and heather burning management. In this chapter we have indicated that localised overgrazing problems are often caused through winter feeding and shepherding practices, while a high stocking density simply exacerbates the problems.

## 35.6 References

1. Anderson, P. & Yalden, D.W. (1981). Increased sheep numbers and loss of heather moorland in the Peak District, England. *Biological Conservation*, **20**, 195-213.

# CHAPTER 36

# RESTORATION OF HEATHER ON OVERGRAZED AREAS.

**Restoring heather on overgrazed areas while maintaining sheep farming interests is an important conservation task. On areas with a viable heather root stock this can be achieved by altering grazing pressure. Areas without root stock need the production of a seed bank.**

## 36.1 Introduction

Large tracts of heather moorland have been lost or seriously damaged following periods of heavy grazing intensity. Restoring such areas for conservation and land use practices has become an important task, particularly at the current time when sheep farming has become less profitable and upland estates must diversify their activities. The challenge is to develop practical methods of restoring heather while maintaining sheep farming as a viable land use practice; and thus maintaining the multiple land use system in the uplands.

The simplest method for restoring heather is often to remove sheep and deer from the hill and wait for the heather to recover. This has been demonstrated on numerous occasions within the past 40 years through the construction of grazing enclosures. While sheep removal, or in some cases a reduction in numbers, may present an immediate solution, it is frequently impractical if only on financial grounds. Moreover, some habitats have reached the stage where the level of overgrazing has been too high for too long and ground dominated by rough grasses and bracken cannot be returned to heather moorland without significant management inputs.

To discover optimal management procedures for re-establishing heather moorland while maintaining conservation interests and sheep grazing, a series of trials was conducted. This chapter describes some of these trials and assesses the prescriptions required to return overgrazed areas to heather dominant sward. The objective is to develop such methods in a realistic manner where sheep farming can continue and encourage a multiple land use system on the area. At it's simplest,

heather can be restored either through a viable root stock or seed bank.

## 36.2 Hall Moor study area

Heather regeneration experiments were conducted on an area extending to 720ha (1800 acres) in Upper Swaledale in the Northern Pennines known as Hall Moor. The site lies at an altitude of between 480 to 672 metres (1575-2205 feet) with a rainfall of approximately 1800mm (71 inches) per annum. The peat depth varies from 15cm to 2 metres. At the outset less than 30% of the vegetation was heather. In some areas viable root stock is still present, while in other parts root stock is absent and only the remnants of a seed bed can be found. Local farmers tell how the area was once all heather but was killed over just a few years following a period of heavy grazing by cattle in the early part of the century. A more direct history of the vegetation changes can be established from an examination of pollen grains in different layers of the peat. Peat is deposited at a slow rate and as it accumulates so it stores the pollen grains that were abundant during that time. The pollen record provides an historic cross-section of vegetation changes and with estimates of peat accumulation these can be converted to a date format and so be used to establish changes in vegetation structure with time. Examination of core samples from the study area confirmed the anecdotal evidence of a dramatic decrease in the extent of heather at depths of 7.5cm and 5cm, corresponding with a loss of heather between 1877 and 1920 (Figure 36.1).

The study area was ring fenced in 1985 and additional fencing was erected to control stock movements and produce five experimental paddocks (Figure 36.2).

### 36.3 Heather restoration with a viable root stock

Sheep take relatively small amounts of heather during the summer months when grasses are abundant. They only switch their diet to the heather during the autumn and winter once the grasses die back or are exhausted. As such, a grazing regime with sheep on the hill during the summer but absent during autumn and winter should act to restrain the competitive grasses and to protect the summer growth of heather from winter grazing.

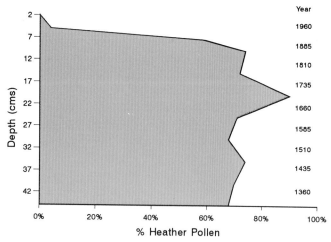

Figure 36.1. Percentage of heather pollen in core peat samples collected from Hall Moor. The proportion of pollen fell dramatically at a depth of peat coinciding with the turn of the century when black cattle were introduced onto the hill.

For the first two years, the prescription used on one of the paddocks was one ewe plus lamb-at-foot to 1.6 hectares from 1 May to 12 August. The results from the first two years indicated that grazing pressure could be increased on the area, so for the subsequent two years both grazing period and intensity were increased. The spring start was brought forward to 15 April to allow graziers to put the hogs returning from away-wintering straight onto the moor, and the autumn period extended so ewes were allowed to stay on the moor until the end of October. At this stage they were taken to richer in-bye fields prior to tupping. Lambs were weaned and removed from the area in August of all years.

Changes in the vegetation on the grazed area were compared to two control areas, one ungrazed and a second where grazing intensity remained high throughout the year. Vegetation was monitored using point transect techniques. At each of 26 permanently marked vegetation survey sites, vegetation was recorded over a 15 metre transect during August of each year. An eight pinned frame was pushed into the vegetation mat at a series of random points and the vegetation touching each pin was recorded. Sampling was repeated 32 times at each site to record a total of 256 points.

Average vegetation changes within the summer grazed plot showed an increase in the extent of heather by 33% (from 21% in 1988 to 28% in 1991). The ungrazed plots showed a greater increase of 81%, and the heavily grazed site no change in the extent of heather (Figure 36.4). During the vegetation survey on the heavy grazing site, no heather was recorded during the transects although heather was present, albeit in a poor way, on the study area. Removal of sheep during the winter months resulted in an increase in heather which was significant on both the areas with summer grazing and with no grazing.

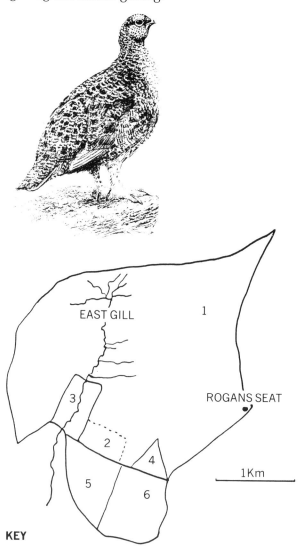

**KEY**

1 Out moor not drained but grazed.
2 Drained and not grazed.
3 Control high grazing pressure.
4 Control no grazing.
5 Drained and grazed
6 Not drained but grazed.

Figure 36.2. A map of Hall Moor study area showing the fence lines and paddocks used to manipulate grazing pressure.

Numbers of sheep have increased in upland areas. Even on estates carrying a reasonable density of sheep, overgrazing still occurs because sheep become concentrated at winter feeding sites (Chapter 35).

Heather at a winter feeding site damaged through excessive grazing and trampling (Chapter 35).

Burning areas with a coarse grass/heather mix may result in the grasses replacing the heather. In this instance purple moor grass (*Molinia*) has benefited from the heather being burnt (Chapter 35).

Concentrations of sheep and deer at feeding sites cause the rapid loss of heather. Such feeding sites should regularly be moved at least 250 metres (Chapter 35). *Les Stocker*

Coarse grasses will replace heather in areas where heather has been grazed heavily (Chapter 35).

The influence of grazing on heather. The area with heather present (right) has been grazed for a shorter period during the winter months (Chapter 35).

Large quantities of heather seed were collected from areas of burnt heather using an industrial vacuum cleaner (Chapter 36).

Heather seedling established on an overgrazed area. Heather can be re-established in areas without a seed bed given favourable conditions (Chapter 36).

Grass species and other low dominant species showed a 13% decrease on the summer grazed site and a 15.5% change on the ungrazed areas (Figure 36.3). Bilberry increased on both summer grazing and the lighter grazed site.

These sheep manipulation experiments demonstrate that heather can be recovered by maintaining a low sheep grazing pressure during the summer months and removing sheep during the winter months. In subsequent years this rate of heather recovery may well increase at a faster rate as the heather reaches dominance and starts to shade out the grass species. This was observed on parts of the study area where patches of heather had reached 61% of the vegetation cover.

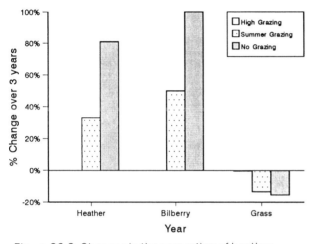

Figure 36.3. Changes in the proportion of heather, bilberry and grass species in the three paddocks with different grazing intensities. On areas with reduced grazing pressure the proportion of heather and bilberry increased, while grass levels fell There was no change on areas with high grazing pressure.

## 36.4 Establishing a heather seed bank.

Heather root stock is present on only a proportion of the study area. In some parts, root stock is absent and the removal or manipulation of sheep stock is unlikely to lead to a short term recovery of heather. To restore heather requires the stimulation or establishment of a heather seed bank.

*Identifying a seed bank:*

On one part of the study area known as Black Hill, examination of turf samples recorded root stock absent over 99.5% of the area. To examine whether heather seed was present, core samples of the top 50mm of soil underneath the grass root mat were taken at 25 localities. Samples were placed in individual trays in a green house and temperature maintained above

10°C for 24 weeks and the subsequent number of heather seedlings was recorded. Only four of the 25 samples produced heather seedlings and overall the samples averaged eight seedlings per square metre. In comparison, core samples taken from heather vegetation produced in excess of 2500 heather seedlings per square metre. These results show that Black Hill now carries insufficient dormant heather seed or viable root stock to allow natural heather regeneration.

Previous research on heather germination has shown that very few heather seedlings germinate under dark conditions such as occur under dense mature heather or grass. Research workers in the Netherlands have achieved remarkable success in re-establishing heather on heathland by removing the dense canopy of grass through turf stripping, thus enabling light to stimulate the heather seed to germinate. This method does, however, require the provision of a dormant heather seed bank.

*Establishing a seed bank:*

When a heather seed bank is absent and heather is to be restored seed must first be collected and the ground prepared for seed application.

While a number of seed collection techniques were attempted, initial trials indicated that the most effective method was to gather both seed and litter using an industrial vacuum cleaner. The greatest success was achieved on recently burnt areas with easy access to the litter layer during dry conditions. Even using a small capacity vacuum, one person could collect 100 kilograms of litter per day, and sufficient seed to cover an area of 800 square metres.

Before a seed bed can be established, the acid grass species must be removed and the soil exposed. Two techniques were tried. On one area, grasses were killed using the commercial broad range herbicide ROUND-UP (Monsanto) and on a second area the mat and grass layer was removed using a tractor and levelling blade. Seed was applied to each of these areas and onto an untreated control area at the rate of 120 grammes per square metre.

The scraped area produced 80 times more heather seedlings than the sprayed, area while no seedlings could be found on the untreated control in the initial year (Figure 36.5). In the following year the seedlings on the sprayed area were totally absent where the grass had recovered and swamped the heather seedlings while the seedlings on the scraped ground were still present, even if at lower numbers. While some seedlings died during the winter months, the

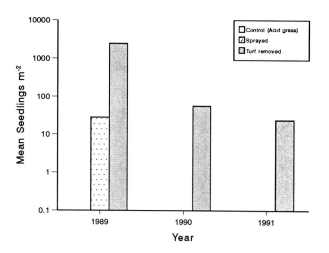

Figure 36.5. Heather seedling production and survival on untreated acid grass, sprayed acid grass and scraped areas. Only on scraped areas did seedlings establish and subsequently survive.

size of the surviving plants increased and provided a reasonable heather cover.

These results show that a seed bed can be established, although greater success is achieved when the ground preparation involves the physical removal of grasses and the mat layer.

### 36.5 Establishing a seed bank by planting seedlings

An alternative way to establish a seed bank is to introduce seedlings which will subsequently flower, produce seeds and establish a heather seed bed. This method involves preparation of the ground in the same way as for seed establishment, but instead of introducing seeds, heather plants are planted. Both techniques require sheep to be excluded from the plots, since they will pull the young heather seedlings.

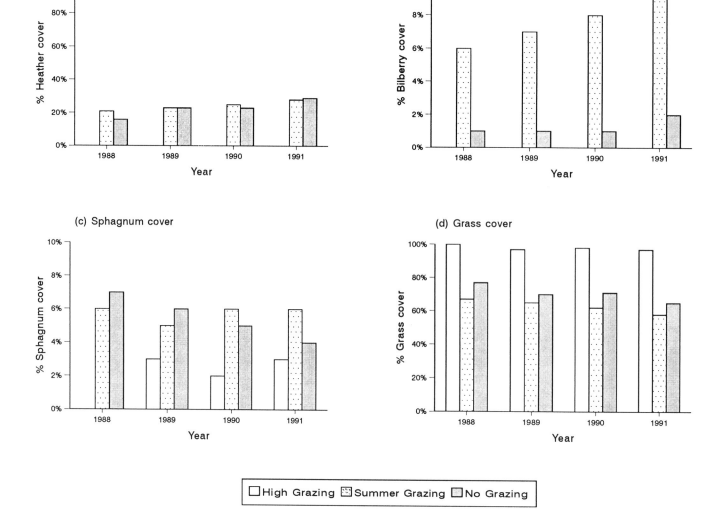

Figure 36.4. Extent of vegetation types in each of four years on Hall Moor in relation to grazing pressure.

Seed was gathered using the industrial vacuum cleaner and grown in a mixture of sand and peat in the greenhouse at a temperature of 10°C for seven months. Plants were acclimatised in spring by placing trays of seedlings outside. They were then planted in each of three prepared areas. Seedlings, transplanted in May onto the treated areas, survived the first summer and flowered. In the untreated control areas few seedlings were found and only 0.4% produced flowers, probably because many had died after being choked by the grasses. On the scraped area, 83% of plants produced flowers and 73% of the plants on the sprayed area produced flowers. Both groups produced about nine flower capsules per plant. Approximately 200 seeds per plant were produced, equivalent to 1800 seeds per square metre at the planting density of nine plants per square metre.

Autumn planting was also undertaken and the survival of both groups was recorded over the following year. Survival of both was 50% lower on the sprayed area than on the scraped area, with the seedlings planted in spring surviving better than those planted in autumn (Figure 36.6). Surprisingly, all plants suffered from high levels of tip removal by grouse during the winter of 90/91. Even so, planting into the scraped area was more productive than planting into sprayed grass.

These trials demonstrated that removing the turf by scraping and introducing heather seed or plants was a more effective technique than either no treatment or removing the grass with herbicide. Scraping does have limitations; it is costly, and great care is needed to avoid erosion when scraping large areas. To circumvent these problems we are currently developing a machine which will both prepare the ground and introduce seed or seedlings in a manner which would reduce the risk of erosion.

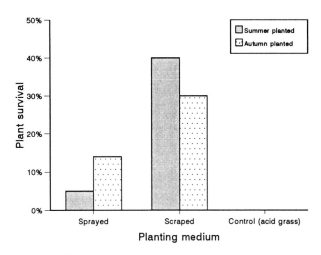

Figure 36.6. Annual survival of heather seedlings introduced onto sprayed, scraped and control areas in relaiton to the time of planting. Seedlings introduced to scraped areas in summer survived best.

Heather dominant moorland with both heather and grasses available is productive for a wider range of land uses than is acid grassland alone. The benefits to grouse production are obvious but at the same time extending the area of heather can improve winter feed for sheep and deer and increase the abundance of other moorland animals.

**36.6 Summary**

Heather restoration trials were conducted on Hall Moor, Swaledale on an area once dominated by heather but denuded through intensive cattle grazing. On areas with a root stock present, the rate of heather recovery was similar on the ungrazed area to the area with summer grazing (May 1 to August 12) at a stocking density of one ewe plus lamb to 1.6 hectares. Summer grazing may be considered beneficial since the sheep graze grasses during the summer months which may otherwise shade out the heather.

# CHAPTER 37

# COMPETITION FOR COTTON GRASS FLOWERS IN EARLY SPRING

**The nutritive value of immature cotton grass flower heads for sheep, deer and other moorland herbivores has long been recognised by shepherds. This chapter examines competition between grazing animals for this nutritional food source and the possibility that high stocking rates of sheep may limit its availability for grouse.**

### 37.1 Introduction

Cotton grass clearly obtains its name from the fluffy white cotton-like seed heads produced by the plant in late summer, although botanically the plant is neither related to cotton species nor is it a grass. Cotton grass is in fact a tussock forming sedge that abounds on wet moorland areas in the uplands of Britain. Two species are frequently recorded, the hare's tail cotton grass (*Eriophorum vaginatum*) and common cotton grass (*E. angustifolium*). The former has a single flowering spike within a tussock of finely splayed leaves whereas the latter species has broader, wine red leaves and has several flower spikes per stem. Throughout the rest of this chapter we refer to the hare's tail as cotton grass.

Cotton grass tussocks are believed to reach more then 100 years of age, the tussocks becoming larger on areas burnt or grazed heavily. The plant is specially adapted to living in acidic conditions and has developed ways of extracting and concentrating remarkable quantities of nutrients from the acidic, nutrient-poor soil. Phosphorous in particular is extracted and used to produce flowers in early spring, which are known locally as moss-crop or draw moss. These are an important source of nutrients for the herbivores since the flowers may be produced early in the season, sometimes under the snow and are often abundant before the heather has started to grow. Heather alone produces a poor nutrient base, particularly for the hen grouse, before growth has started in spring. Hence cotton grass provides an early and important source of nutrients to the pre-laying hen when collecting nutrients for egg laying and incubation. Sheep, deer and grouse selectively feed on the cotton grass flowers. On some moors the flowers themselves may be hard to find, but inspection of the droppings will reveal the remains of cotton grass flowers.

The flowers are nutritionally superior to most of the alternative feed on the hill and even equal to agricultural feed species (Figure 37.1). With such a high digestibility and nutrient content we can expect serious competition between the herbivores for the flowers, which may have an influence on egg production of red grouse.

### 37.2 Methods in assessing grazing impact on flower heads

The presence and abundance of cotton grass flowers was monitored on the Hall Moor study area in relation to the presence of sheep on four areas. First a control area with no grazing, second a lightly grazed area with one ewe and lamb to 1.8 hectares but with no winter

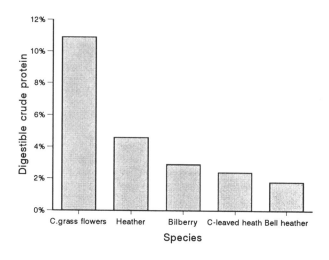

Figure 37.1. Digestible crude protein levels of various moorland plants, showing the relatively high level of cotton grass flowers in comparison with other moorland species.

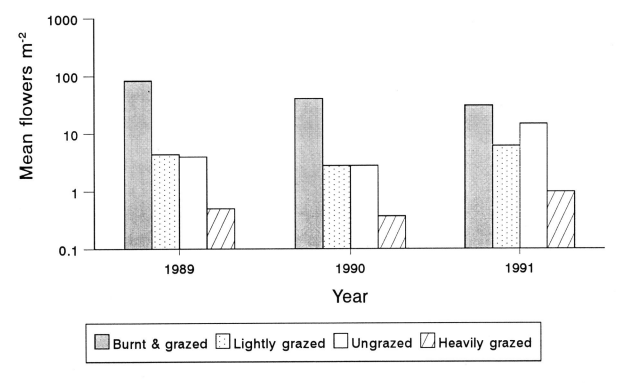

Figure 37.2. Cotton grass flower production on a burnt area and on areas with varying levels of grazing. Heavy sheep grazing reduces the number of flowers available for other herbivores, although burning may result in a short term flush of flowers.

grazing, third a heavily grazed area with a ewe and lamb to 0.5 hectares all the year round, and fourth a lightly grazed area as before but on an patch burnt in 1988 and monitored during the next three years.

### 37.3 Cotton grass seed head availability

The greatest abundance of flowers was recorded on the burnt area in the year after burning. This area carried a density of flowers 19 times greater than the control site, although the number of flower heads fell over subsequent years, presumably because the flush of nutrients released by the burning decreased (Figure 37.2).

The heavily grazed area had the lowest production in flower heads in every year, less than one flower head per m² per annum, while the lightly grazed site carried a density nine times higher in all years (Figure 37.2). All three sites increased in 1991, probably due to climatic changes.
High sheep stocking densities thus appear to reduce the availability of cotton grass flowers for other herbivores. Such an effect may have a detrimental result on the productivity of grouse, although neither clutch size measurements nor brood count data were available.

Burning of blanket bog is currently a contentious issue. On the one hand burning may act to destroy the deli-

cate upper layer of the peat and lead to serious erosion problems. On the other, farmers and moor managers may see a short term benefit it if results in a flush of cotton grass and other nutrient-rich flowers. However, before long term effects of burning can be established this study needs to continue.

### 37.4 Summary

The flowers of cotton grass form a highly nutritious source of protein utilised by female grouse in early spring during egg formation and laying. However, this food source is also used by other herbivores and controlled experiments demonstrate reduced numbers of flowers on areas with heavy sheep grazing. Burning areas of cotton grass can result in a flush of nutrients and invigorate the cotton grass, although this could also lead to erosion and damage to areas of blanket bog.

# CHAPTER 38

# THE ECOLOGICAL IMPACT OF MOORLAND DRAINAGE

**In the past 30 years, large areas of blanket bog and moorland in upland Britain have been drained by means of shallow open ditches commonly called grips. The benefits of drainage on blanket bog appear limited and yet may cause serious erosion.**

## 38.1 Introduction

During the 1970s, many areas of moorland were drained, encouraged by a 70% grant under the Common Agricultural Policy of the European Community. The grant aid was subsequently reduced to 60% in 1983, 30% in 1984 and to nil in 1985; presently there is no grant aid available for moorland drainage. The objective of most of this drainage was to reduce the water table and improve the growth of heather for grazing animals, principally sheep and grouse. The assumption was that since heather prefers to grow in dry conditions, drainage on blanket bog moorland would lower the water table and improve heather growth. This assumption has never been tested, although many hundreds of thousands of pounds have been given in grant aid for drainage. There are a number of anecdotal cases where heather growth has improved following drainage but many of these have been confounded with other changes in moor management and in particular changes in grazing intensity.

The effects of drainage on blanket bog moorland need quantifying. Stewart & Lance[1] have recently compared water tables and vegetation composition from blanket bog areas near drains. These effects and the effects of erosion by drainage were examined in an experimental way over a number of years as part of the Hall Moor Study.

With the aid of financial support from the Countryside Commission and technical assistance from the Institute of Fresh Water Ecology, a project was implemented to investigate the interaction of several moorland management practices. This factorial experiment became known as 'The Hall Moor Study'. Essentially, it examined the effects of drainage and grazing in a series of combinations to elucidate the effects of each factor and the combination of factors. This programme of research allowed several questions to be addressed:

i) Does drainage affect vegetation cover?
ii) Does drainage affect the water table?
iii) Is a significant amount of sediment lost into river systems as a result of drainage?

## 38.2 Methodology

To compare the effects of grazing with the effects of drainage, part of the Hall Moor Study area was divided into four paddocks, (Figure 36.2).

Two 10ha plots were drained in November 1987 by contractors with the remit to 'drain the area as they would for any client'. The drains were cut following contours, approximately 22 metres apart with a trapezoidal cross-profile: bottom width 300mm, top width 680mm, depth 360mm; with a side-wall angle of 28° and a cross-sectional area of 1764 cm².

The vegetation was surveyed on each of the areas using the 250 point survey technique described in Chapter 36. Each vegetation plot consisted of a 15 metre transect positioned across an open drain and sampled at various distances from the drain to determine how vegetation recovery varied with distance from the drain.

The water table was measured using a series of tubes (dip wells) inserted into the peat until they reached solid material. Each tube was 40mm in diameter with 6mm holes drilled every 5cm apart, designed to allow the passage of water from the water table into the tube. A stopper was fitted to the top of each tube to prevent rain entering and the depth of the water table below ground level was measured by means of lower-

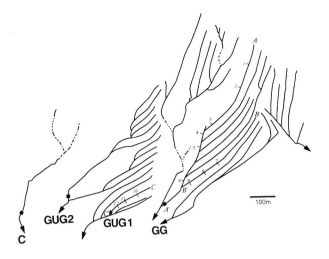

Figure 38.1. Map of drained areas showing the design of the drains, the location of the four sediment traps (solid squares) and the 12 points where drain profiles were taken. C is the control stream, GUG2 is the gripped and ungrazed site 2, GUG1 is the gripped and ungrazed site 1 and GG is the gripped and grazed area.

ing a line with a polystyrene float on the end down the tube until it reached the water table. A total of seven tubes were inserted across the line of a drain at progressively increasing distances from it. Four control transects were also placed 290 metres and 380 metres away on the opposite side of the watershed to act as controls. The wells were dipped every two weeks when the ground was not frozen from November 1988 to May 1991.

Sediment run off from the drains was collected in 4 large sediment traps. Three of the traps were sited at the bottom end of grips of varying length, with the fourth sited at the bottom of an existing stream as a control (Figure 38.1). The drains were cut into uniform terrain, with the resulting individual slopes varying little down their courses. The visual impact of the drainage was recorded with the aid of aerial photography before and after the drainage.

### 38.3. Drainage and vegetation cover

Heather increased on all four study plots but the greatest increase (17%) occurred in the areas with no drainage. The area grazed and drained increased by only 6% (Figure 38.2). This result would indicate that drainage alone does not influence the rate of increase in heather cover. Bilberry increased on all sites, with the greatest increase on the area not drained but grazed. The increase on the two areas which had been drained was lower. The increase in heather and bilberry was balanced by a loss in grasses, particularly cotton grasses.

### 38.4 Drainage and the water table

The assumption is frequently made that drainage will reduce the water table by increasing run-off and hence

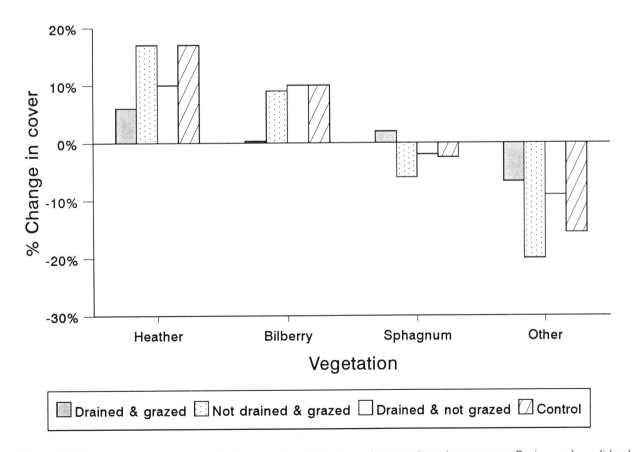

Figure 38.2 Percentage change in vegetation cover in relation to drainage and grazing pressure. Drainage alone did not influence vegetation change and on this study area did not increase heather cover.

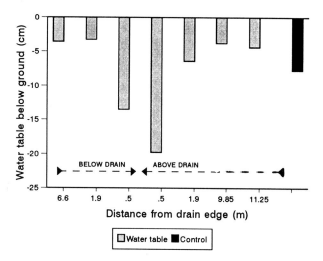

Figure 38.3. Water table depths above and below the drains. Only within 0.5 metres of the drain is there a significant effect of drainage on the water table.

creating a drier more productive environment. The water table measured in the dip wells was only significantly lower than the controls in wells within 0.5 metres of the drain, at greater distances there was no significant difference (Figure 38.3). The drains had a greater affect on the water table at the dip wells 0.5m. down hill from the drain than the comparable dip wells above the drain. This is presumably because the drain removes the water that would be running down the hill, but such effects are not significant when only 2 metres downhill of the drain.

These results demonstrate that the effect of drains on this site only reduced the water table within 0.5m. of the drain. Overall, this represents a 4.5% reduction in the water table (3% of the open ground) in a drainage system with drains set at 22 metre spacings. If the objective of a drainage system was to lower the water table over a large area of moorland the drains would have to be placed every 1 to 2 metres apart and effectively convert the moorland into a ploughed field. Such a system would be ridiculous and have no benefits to sheep, grouse or conservation.

## 38.5 Drainage and sediment run off

Drainage is known to cause erosion and although the extent of this problem has not been quantified there are some obvious examples of serious erosion of peatlands associated with drainage programmes. While excessive erosion is obvious, the amount of material removed from correctly placed drains has not been quantified in detail. This is an important problem since the removal of peaty soils could be ecologically damaging and destabilize large areas, while low and continual levels of sediment run off may reduce the

breeding production of trout and salmon in upland streams.

The direct impact of drainage on the size and shape of the drains was measured at regular intervals during the study. In the gripped and grazed system, 56% of the drain-length had cut into the mineral horizon, whilst in the gripped and not grazed system only 32% was affected. (The areas of exposed mineral horizon are apparent in aerial photographs as the light coloured areas in the drains). This apparent difference was probably not due to the effects of the sheep grazing but associated with the variation in peat depth between the two areas. In none of the drain runs did erosion increase regularly down the slope or where slopes steepened. Rather, deep erosion was localized and related to the presence of head-cuts in each drain. Overall, the erosion within each drain was large, with only 1.4% of the original drain not eroded on the areas surveyed (Figure 38.4).

The average cross-sectional area of the drains increased by 98% over a period of three years (Figure 38.5) although once again there was a great deal of variation between different parts of the drain. Furthermore, the peat erosion was not uniform throughout the year but tended to be greater during the autumn. The reason for this cannot be demonstrated from these results, although casual observations indicate that during the summer the drains frequently dry out, the peat cracks and when the first flush of rain comes in the autumn, the peat is lifted and carried down the drains. These larger lumps tend to settle out and be caught in the sediment traps while later in the winter and spring the finer sediment can be washed away in a fine suspension and not be caught by the traps.

Examination of changes in the cross-sectional area of the drain system provides estimates of the erosion in the two types of drain systems. In the short furrows coming straight down the hill (measurements at 10, 11 & 12), an average of 291kg of material were produced per metre of drain during the three years of this study and a total yield of 61 tonnes of sediment per drain. In the herring bone drain system, the 'feeder' drains (7,8 & 9) yielded 142kg of soil per metre of drain and a total amount of 369 tonnes of soil was collected. The main drain in the herring bone system (4, 5 & 6) produced 419kg per metre of drain and a total of 714 tonnes. These differences between the drain systems may reflect true differences in the rate of erosion but there are also large variations within each system. Nevertheless, it is not surprising that the main drain of the herring bone system carried the greatest erosion since this carried the largest quantity of water and material. We suspect it is the stony material brought

Flowers of cotton grass provide a rich source of protein for grouse and other herbivores in early spring (Chapter 37).

Cotton grass seed heads on an area of experimentally ungrazed moorland. Sheep and grouse will compete for the flowers in spring (Chapter 37).

Heather seedlings can be grown in a greenhouse and planted on the hill within a year to help restore heather (Chapter 36).

Drainage on experimental areas of upland blanket bog provided no substantial benefits to heather recovery but caused serious erosion (Chapter 38).

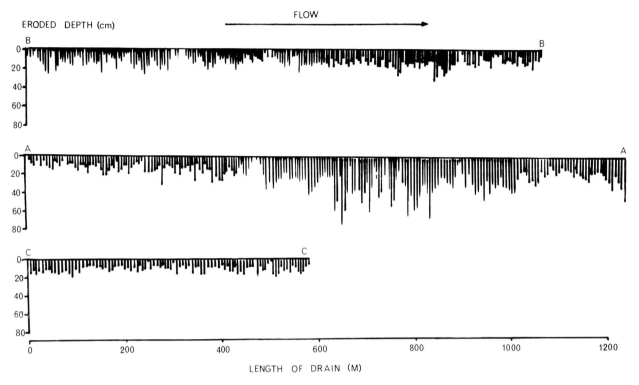

FLOW →

ERODED DEPTH (cm)

Figure 38.4. Erosion below original drain depth in three sections of a drain. In some parts of the drain the level had been reduced to nearly 80cm below the original base.

down the drains that causes some of the serious erosion.

From the information gathered we can make two estimates of the quantity of material removed by the drains during the first three years of drainage. First, the amount of material collected in the sediment traps during this time interval was approximately 7kg per metre of drain, this is a minimum estimate since it excludes the material that remains in suspension and is washed through the sediment traps. A second estimate of the quantity of material can be made from the increase in the cross-sectional area of the drain. As shown previously this ranges from 291 to 491kg per metre of drain, so an estimate of 300kg per metre of drain would seem reasonable. This second estimate is much greater than the first, but unlike the first includes all the fine material that would have been washed down through the traps. It is, however, estimated from only 12 sites (Figure 38.1). With a normal drainage system with drains at 22 metre intervals a square kilometre of moorland would carry approximately 45.5km of drains and produce 319 (minimum estimate) to 13,650 tonnes of material per square kilometre over the first three years. While these figures are very different they do reflect a large quantity of

material removed through erosion by drainage systems.

## 38.6 Conclusion

The evidence accumulated during this intensive study demonstrates that drainage of blanket bog has an insignificant effect on the water table and the recovery of heather vegetation. However from past observa-

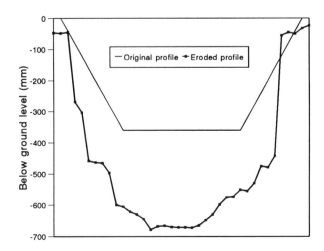

Figure 38.5. Average change in the profile of the drain three years after construction. Overall the cross-sectional area of the drain increased by 98%.

tions, drainage on moorland with lower rainfall may have a more positive effect in lowering the water table. The amount of material lost during the first three years since drainage has been large, and will continue to cause problems in the loss of substrate. It may also have repercussions further down the water system where sedimentation can be expected to have an influence on fish spawning beds.

## 38.7 Summary

The effects of drainage vegetation cover, water table and sediment loss were investigated on Hall Moor, an area of upland blanket bog in Swaledale. The drainage did not increase the extent of heather in the experimental plots. The water table was reduced within 0.5 metres of the drain but at greater distances there was no significant difference. The drains had a slightly greater effect on the water table down hill from the drains.

Drainage caused serious erosion and sediment run off. 56% of the drains cut into the mineral horizon on the gripped and grazed area and 32% on the gripped and ungrazed plot. The average cross-sectional area of the drains increased by 98% over a period of three years, although there was large variation between various parts of the drainage system. Peat erosion tended to be greatest in autumn. The amount of sediment produced by each drain varied between drains, with feeder drains producing 142kg per metre of drain and the main drain of a herring bone system yielding 419kg per metre. With a normal drainage system of 45.5km of drains $km^{-2}$ the estimates of sediment run off vary but range from a minimum of 319 to 13 650 tonnes of sediment $km^{-2}$ over the first three years.

## 38.8 References

1. Stewart A.J. & Lance, A.N. Effects of moor drainage on the hydrology and vegetation of northern Pennine blanket bog. *Journal of Applied Ecology*, **28**, 1105-1117

# APPENDICES

## APPENDIX 1:

# STATUS AND POTENTIAL OF RED GROUSE IN THE SPEY VALLEY

### A1.1. Introduction

This paper reviews the status and recent changes in numbers of red grouse on heather moorlands in the Spey valley. Numbers of grouse have fallen in recent years and as a consequence of reduced revenue from grouse shooting, a number of estates in the area have sold moorland for alternative forms of land use, such as afforestation. The loss of heather moorland is of concern both to conservationists and sporting interests; improved grouse stocks would provide important income for estates and help to prevent the sale of moorland to forestry, thus maintaining the heather-dominant habitat and its associated wildlife. Correlative evidence presented in this paper indicates that grouse numbers could be increased by additional management inputs, in particular the re-employment of moorland keepers.

### A1.2. Recent changes in grouse numbers within the Spey valley

The following analysis of grouse numbers is based on complete bag records obtained from 17 (of an estimated 32) sporting estates within Speyside. These tend to be the larger estates with a significant interest in grouse and deer production, and hence may reflect the more productive grouse moors in the area. In total, they represent 800km$^2$ of moorland where heather is the dominant vegetation.

Throughout the Highlands of Scotland there has been a general decline in grouse stocks since the mid-1970s. This decline is reflected in the bag records of grouse from moors in Speyside. The average number of red grouse shot has fallen from 23.5km$^2$ during the 1960s to 11.4km$^{-2}$ during the 1980s, although the extent of this decline varied greatly between estates and has generally been worst in Badenoch. Bag records are not a direct measure of grouse density, but there is a good correlation between August density and bag size, so that trends in bag records reflect changes in density.

### A1.3. Variations in grouse numbers within Speyside

Local variation in the average number of grouse shot is large. Currently, moors in the north-west of Speyside are producing the greatest bags and have shown the least decline. Most grouse moors in Speyside overlie relatively base-poor substrata, although there is a series of limestone outcrops west of Tomintoul. These outcrops are associated with one of the most productive grouse moors in the area and this moor harvested more grouse in the 1980s than it did during the 1960s. However, this is also one of the most intensively managed moors. It is perhaps significant that the most productive moor overlies the relatively poor quartz-feldspar-granulite and, because of this fact, there is no obvious correlation between soil type and numbers of grouse shot km$^{-2}$ in Speyside.

Previous studies on grouse have found correlations between grouse bags and the quality of underlying substrata when burning management is taken into account. However, in Chapter 4, no correlation was found between grouse numbers and substrata. A good correlation with keeper density and, in particular, the level of fox control was found.

Since the 1960s, the number of keepers employed on the 17 estates in Speyside has fallen from 39.5 to 21, a 47% fall in manpower involved in moorland management. In both the 1960s and the 1980s average grouse bags km$^{-2}$ were correlated with the density of keepers on an estate[a]. There was no significant difference between these regression lines[b], implying that reduced bags in the 1980s can be accounted for by the effects of the lower density of keepers.

The fall in the number of keepers in Speyside probably resulted from falling grouse numbers, rather than vice versa, and the tendency of upland estates to make keepers redundant when there were no grouse. It seems likely that a consequence of fewer keepers is that numbers of grouse have not recovered at a rate sufficient to allow the re-employment of keepers. The reason why numbers of grouse fell between 1974 and 1979 is not clear, although the breeding production of grouse (measured as the ratio of young to old birds shot) on the only estate in the area with sufficient records tended to be lower during the years when grouse numbers were falling[c]. The apparent cause of this reduced breeding production is not known, but may be influenced by poor spring weather and its effect on food quality.

An alternative explanation for the fall in grouse numbers is that there may have been a loss of suitable habitat for red grouse. While heavy grazing pressure from sheep and deer can cause the loss of heather moorland, and so of grouse habitat, this loss has not occurred on any large scale in Speyside.

**A1.4 Problems of reduced management**

The simple analysis presented in the previous section suggests that the current problem with grouse stocks in Speyside is simply a lack of keepers, and hence stems from reduced management inputs. Principal tasks of keepers include both the regular burning of the heather vegetation to produce a mosaic of different-aged heather stands[3] and the control of predators, in particular foxes and crows. Reduced numbers of keepers will result in both reduced burning and reduced predator control.

Recent studies in Speyside have found greater levels of grouse predation on areas with few grouse than on areas with higher densities of grouse. Signs of foxes, an important predator of grouse, were found five times more frequently on study areas in Speyside than on English moors. The number of grouse corpses found eaten by predators on the study areas between September and April represented 1% of the grouse population on the high-density moors in England, but 44% of the grouse population on the relatively low-density moors in Speyside. Winter losses on study areas in Speyside between October and April averaged 50%. They were only 35% on English moors and in a detailed study of grouse conducted in Glen Esk from 1956-61, when grouse density was relatively high, were 37%.

An additional problem within the Spey valley, not influenced by the level of keepering, is the presence of the tick-borne virus louping ill, which can reduce the survival of red grouse chicks[1]. Vaccination of sheep would be expected to reduce the prevalence of the virus in grouse, because grouse mortality due to the virus is too high for the grouse to maintain the virus in the absence of sheep. Some recent studies have not found this to be the case in Speyside (Section 8).

**A1.5 Potential for grouse in the Spey valley**

The decline in numbers of red grouse in the 1970s in other parts of the Highlands was associated with poor breeding, although the actual cause of this poor breeding is not known. Since the decline there has been a reduction in the number of keepers, and an associated increase in predation pressure. The correlative evidence presented here implies that average grouse density and harvest could return to the levels recorded in the 1960s by increasing the number of active moorland keepers and, in particular, the level of predator control during the winter months. The problem may be purely one of economics. With high overheads and high sporting rates, many estates cannot afford the additional keepers to improve grouse density, and the estates are caught in the downward spiral of fewer grouse and fewer keepers. In this respect, planning authorities should provide financial incentives (through reduced rates or the provision of grants and training courses) to improve keepering levels.

It should be stressed that the correlative data presented are not conclusive and need to be tested experimentally. Future researchers should aim to conduct such experiments and determine the precise needs of management to improve grouse numbers. The data available provide no indication of the cause of poor breeding during the years of decline, and it is possible that whatever this was could become a problem once more if grouse numbers increased. Hence, monitoring breeding production and the factors influencing it will be necessary. Nutrient loss from heather moorland may be significant, and further work is needed to evaluate its importance to grouse stocks.

Grouse shooting has traditionally been a major form of land use in the Spey Valley and the management activities associated with it can be considered complementary to sheep farming, tourism, deer stalking and conservation. Major conflicts with other forms of land use only occur when large areas of forestry are planted alongside grouse moors. The plantations influence the management activities of neighbouring estates by providing a refuge for predators of grouse, placing restrictions on heather burning activities and fragmenting the heather habitat. In the uplands associated with the Spey valley, planning authorities should give grouse management priority and encourage forestry planting away from hill land and at lower altitudes.

## A1.6 Summary

Examination of bag records from sporting estates in Speyside indicates that there has been a fall in numbers of grouse since 1974. Average numbers shot in the early 1980s were half what they were during the 1960s, yet the extent of the decline has varied and has generally been worst in the Badenoch district.

Changes in bag records were not related to underlying rock substrata but were correlated with the density of keepers employed. The relationship between keeper density and bag during the 1960s and the 1980s was not statistically different, indicating that the current lower levels are associated with reduced levels of keepering.

Reduced management inputs of burning and predator control may be influencing bag size, and there is evidence of relatively high losses due to predation during winter months. The correlation between bag and keeper density needs to be tested experimentally, and grouse breeding production needs to be monitored in case this falls once again. In the meantime, the reduction of sporting rates together with other financial incentives by local authorities could enable estates to employ more gamekeepers and so improve moorland management.

## A1.7 Notes

a. (1960s, $r = 71$, $P < 0.01$; 1980s, $r = 0.65$, $P < 0.01$)

b. ($F = 0.327$, $P = 0.48$)

c. (t test: $t = 1.73$, $P = 0.0505$).

## A1.8 References

1. Duncan, J.S., Reid, H.W., Moss, R., Phillips, J.D.C. & Watson, A. 1978. Ticks, louping ill and red grouse on moors in Speyside, Scotland. *Journal of Wildlife Management*, **42**, 500-505.

2. Jenkins, D., Watson, A. & Miller, G.R. 1963. Population studies on red grouse (*Lagopus lagopus scoticus*) in north-east Scotland. *Journal of Animal Ecology*, **32**, 317-376.

3. Watson, A. & Miller, G.R. 1976. *Grouse management.* Fordingbridge: Game Conservancy.

# RED GROUSE HOMING FOR 35 KILOMETRES

Red Grouse are generally considered sedentary. In a study in N.E. Scotland Jenkins et al[1] found that 97% of ringed cock grouse and 80% of hens were recovered (usually shot) within 1.5km of where they had been ringed; no cock was found more than 8km away, but one hen was found to have moved 42km. In our current studies of radio-tagged grouse in Speyside none moved more than 10km from the point of capture, even during snowy weather. However, there are casual observations of large scale grouse movements in the Badenoch District[2].

As part of an experiment, designed for another purpose, 43 grouse were caught at night on Flichity Moor, Strathnairn, Inverness-shire in March and April 1987 and taken within two hours to Ralia Moss, Speyside, Inverness-shire. This was a minimum distance of 35km from the north-west to the south-east corner of the Monadh Liath. All were tagged and some fitted with radio transmitters. On a number of occasions during the following four months we visited Flichity but heard no radio signal and saw no tagged grouse; we assumed the grouse had been unable to navigate back to Flichity before August 1987. However, on 12 April 1988 a cock was recaught within 1km of where he had originally been caught on 3 April 1987. Most displacement-release experiments have been done with long distance migrants but this example provides a substantial case of a relatively sedentary bird returning to its spring territory after displacement beyond its normal area of familiarity.

**References**

1. Jenkins, D., Watson, A. and Miller, G.R. (1963). Population Studies on Red Grouse *Lagopus lagopus scoticus* (Lath.) in North East Scotland. *Journal of Animal Ecology, 32*: 317-376

2. MacPherson, *The Field*, 24 August 1914.

# GROUSE SHOOTING IN SCOTLAND: ANALYSIS OF ITS IMPORTANCE TO THE ECONOMY AND ENVIRONMENT

James McGilvray and Roger Perman
Department of Economics
The University of Strathclyde

## A3.1 Introduction

At the end of May 1990, the Trustees of the Game Conservancy's Scottish Grouse Research Project, commissioned Professor James McGilvray and Mr. Roger Perman to undertake an economic research study of Scottish grouse moors.

Fieldwork for the project started in August 1990 and the final project report was completed in September 1991. This is a summary of the main results.

The objectives of the research were:

(1) to evaluate the economic significance of grouse shooting, including its impact on incomes and employment in Scotland;
(2) to assess the contribution of grouse shooting to conservation, recreation and the management of the Scottish countryside;
(3) to identify issues of importance to the future of grouse shooting and its role in Scotland's rural economy.

## A3.2 Methodology

Existing data on the income and expenditure of grouse shooting was limited so it was therefore necessary to collect primary data using a ten-page questionnaire, sent to 220 grouse moor owners or agents. A total of 87 usable returns (40%) were received and analysed, this response was sufficient to provide valid extrapolations for all Scottish moors. From this survey there was believed to be a total of 470 to 500 grouse moors with the best available estimate being 486.

## THE STRUCTURE OF SCOTTISH GROUSE SHOOTING

From the questionnaire replies and the previously existing data it was possible to draw up an estimate of grouse shooting activity in Scotland. The key data were:

| | |
|---|---|
| Total numbers of grouse moors in Scotland | 486 |
| Total acreage suitable for grouse shooting | 4.6 million acres |
| Average size of grouse moor | 9500 acres |

Number of days shooting (1989):

| | Let | Unlet |
|---|---|---|
| Driven shooting | 13 465 | 4312 |
| Walked up | 7558 | 5311 |
| Dogging | 1786 | 1232 |
| Total | 22 809 | 10 854 |

Average fee paid per brace for let shooting (1989)

| | |
|---|---|
| Driven shooting | £60.28 per brace |
| Walked up | £27.10 per brace |
| Dogging | £30.20 per brace |

Where grouse shooters came from in 1989;

| | |
|---|---|
| Scotland | 10% |
| Rest of UK | 50% |
| USA | 11% |
| Rest of World | 19% |

| | |
|---|---|
| Total annual bag for all Scottish grouse moors | 265 981 birds |

## A3.3 The economics of grouse shooting

*Direct Revenue, Costs and Investments:*

The questionnaire returns allowed estimates to be made of the revenues, costs and investments directly related to grouse shooting in Scotland.

Revenue, principally in the form of income from lettings, averaged £12 000 per moor in 1989, with a total for all Scotland of £5.83 million.

Direct costs were divided fairly evenly between expenditure on wages and on goods and services required for the provision of grouse shooting. Average outgoings were £20 000 per moor or £9.5 million for Scotland as a whole.

This means that in 1989 the average moor operated at a loss of nearly £8000. The total loss across all the moors in Scotland was £3.7 million.

In 1989, the average moor invested £3900 in habitat improvement and new equipment (Scottish total £1.9 million). This investment was in addition to the running costs outlined above.

*Direct Employment*

Employment connected with grouse shooting tends to be seasonal. In 1989, a total of 4578 persons found employment in activities related directly to grouse shooting. Many were not full time, but the man-hours involved can be calculated as the equivalent of 978 full time jobs.

*Indirect Economic Impact*

In addition to their direct expenditure on grouse shooting, moor owners and participants also spent money on additional services, equipment, accommodation, food, drink, travel, clothing, ammunition, gifts etc. This has an indirect impact on the economy of Scotland which would be absent without grouse shooting. A conservative estimate places this indirect expenditure at a total of £9.5 million in Scotland in 1989 and generated the equivalent of an additional 1345 full time jobs.

Adding these figures to the direct costs and employment generated, grouse shooting contributed a total of nearly £21 million to the Scottish Gross Domestic Product in 1989 and created the equivalent of 2323 full time jobs, often in remote rural areas in which alternative job opportunities are non-existent.

## A3.4 Grouse shooting and conservation

Information on the conservation impact of grouse shooting came from questionnaire replies and interviews with individuals. The views of conservation organisations were also sought.

Respondents argued strongly that these activities and the regeneration of heather, blaeberry and other flora, encourage heather growth at lower altitudes and enhance the presence and diversity of all forms of wildlife. Estates reported that their land management practices encouraged the presence of merlin, blackgame, blue hare and many small moorland birds. There was, however, a widespread opinion that increasing predator numbers were depressing grouse and other wildlife populations. Protected raptors in particular, were seen to be restricting red grouse and other wildlife.

The uses to which owners would put their moors in the absence of grouse shooting were:

| | |
|---|---|
| More intensive sheep stocking | 44% |
| Deer stalking | 24% |
| Forestry | 18% |
| Would/could not use in any other way | 14% |

The majority of experts would rank grouse shooting above forestry and more intensive sheep stocking in terms of beneficial environmental impacts. It is unclear how grouse shooting would compare with deer stalking or the reversion of grouse moor to wilderness.

## A3.5 The future of grouse shooting in Scotland

Survey data strongly suggest the demand for grouse shooting will exhibit moderate to strong growth in the foreseeable future. Much shooting is currently unlet, some because of the owner's preferences while in other cases it is a consequence of the moor not being beyond the threshold level of grouse density at which it can sustain commercial sport. A still greater number of estates feel unable to justify the large initial costs in rebuilding grouse potential — the realisable returns are too unpredictable.

Losses are incurred by 75% of Scottish grouse moors, and were grouse shooting regarded as purely commercial activity, this would be cause for concern.

Although some moors are managed as commercial enterprises, for the majority of owners their moors are a source of recreation for which they are prepared to pay. Commercial letting may be important in helping to defray expenses, and thus reduce the contribution which the owner has to make, but the activity itself is not governed by considerations of profit or loss. If it were, no more than a handful of moors would survive, since even among those which are profitable, few if any achieve commercially acceptable rates of return on capital.

Grouse moors can be thought of as providing recreational benefits in three ways. Firstly, paying participants enjoy the sport directly. Secondly, owners (and their friends and families) gain satisfaction both from the sport and through the pleasure which many of these persons clearly obtain from living and working in such locations. Thirdly, the wider public obtains recreational benefits (usually at a zero price) from access to moorland areas. It is expected that demand from this third category will increase. This may have an impact on grouse shooting because of disturbance. At present there is no system to compensate for such damage.

Grouse shooting as an activity is conspicuous in the absence of any positive incentive to pursue management practices that are judged to be environmentally sound and desired by the public at large. Indeed, the system of shooting rates serves to establish the opposite set of incentives in some respects. If a heather redevelopment programme is introduced and succeeds in raising grouse bags, the moor owner will often face a higher rates bill. The survey results show that, on average, 9% of grouse moor total costs are accounted for by these rates. But this understates their impact. A commercially successful moor operating a large grouse enterprise is unlikely to adjust its behaviour because of shooting rates, as the return attained by these moors will be significantly higher than the same land could achieve in other uses. But for smaller moors or those with a poorer management history, at or below the break-even position in terms of viability, behaviour can be affected very significantly. In some cases, owners have given up operating grouse moors altogether for this reason, whilst in many it appears to operate as if it were a tax on labour, reducing the effort devoted to moorland management.

We suggest that it would be desirable to introduce a fiscal mechanism that creates positive incentives to land owners to pursue objectives that are deemed to be in the wider public interest. Such a scheme would need to reward grouse moor owners in relation to

(a) the extent to which they encourage public access,

(b) the loss which they incur from sustaining populations of protected predators.

(c) the scale of their activities which are deemed to be of conservation benefit to the wider community.

Our impression is that a modest scale of incentive could have substantial effects. In the first instance, an appropriate vehicle could be remission of shooting rates in proportion to the extent to which the three objectives (a) to (c) are realised. Monitoring of the first two would be relatively straightforward, although we realise that matters will be less easy in regard to the third objective.

# APPENDIX 4

# PUBLICATIONS ON RED GROUSE BY THE GAME CONSERVANCY

## BOOKS:

1. Hudson, P.J. (1986). *The Red Grouse, The Biology and Management of a Wild Gamebird*. Game Conservancy, Fordingbridge.

2. Hudson, P.J. & Lovell, T.W.I. (1986). *Proceedings of the Third International Grouse Symposium*.

3. Hudson, P.J. (1987). *The Red Grouse - King of gamebirds*. Game Conservancy, Fordingbridge, 20pp.

4. Hudson, P.J. & Rands, M.W.R. (1988). *Ecology and Management of Gamebirds*. Blackwells Scientific Publications, Oxford. 263pp.

5. Lovell, T.W.I. & Hudson, P.J. (1989). *Proceedings of the Fourth International Grouse Symposium*.

## PRIMARY SCIENTIFIC PUBLICATIONS:

Hudson, P.J. (1982). Red grouse production and management in relation to tourism. In K.A. Hearn (ed) *Moorlands: Wildlife conservation, amenity and recreation*. 45-54.

Potts, G.R., Tapper, S.C. & Hudson, P.J. (1984). Population fluctuations in red grouse: analysis of bag records and a simulation model. *Journal of Animal Ecology*. **53**, 21-36.

Hudson, P.J. (1984). Some effects of sheep management on heather moorlands in the north of England. In D.Jenkins (ed) *The impact of agriculture on wildlife and semi-natural habitats*. Institute of Terrestrial Ecology Symposium No.13. 143-149.

Hudson, P.J. (1985). Harvesting red grouse in the north of England. In S. Beasom & S.F. Robinson (ed) *Game Harvest Management*. 319-326.

Hudson, P.J., Dobson, A.P. & Newborn, D.N. (1985). Cyclic and non-cyclic populations of red grouse: a role for parasitism? In D.Rollinson & R.M. Anderson (ed) *Ecology and genetics of host-parasite interactions* 79-89. Academic Press. London.

Hudson, P.J. & Watson, A. (1985). Exploited animals: The Red Grouse. *Biologist* **32**, 13-18.

Hudson, P.J. (1986). The effect of a parasitic nematode on the breeding production of red grouse. *Journal of Animal Ecology*. **55**, 85-94.

Hudson, P.J. (1986). Bracken and ticks on grouse moors in the north of England. In R. T. Smith (ed) *Bracken: Ecology, land use and control technology*. Parthenon Press.

Hudson, P.J. (1986). The effects of parasitic infections on the population fluctuations of red grouse in the north of England. In Hudson, P.J. & Lovell, T.W.I. *Proceedings of the Third International Grouse Symposium*.

Dobson, A.P. & Hudson, P.J. (1986). Parasites, diseases and the structure of ecological communities. *Trends in Ecology and Evolution*. **1**, 11-15.

Hudson, P.J. (1987). The environmental impact of bracken. *British Crop Protection Conference - Weeds 1987*. 285-290.

Hudson, P.J. & Newborn, D.N. (1987). The effect of the caecal threadworm (*Trichostrongylus tenuis*) on the population dynamics of red grouse. *The World Pheasant Association Journal*. **12**, 11-21.

Watson, H., Lee, D.L. & Hudson, P.J. (1987). The effect of *Trichostrongylus tenuis* on the caecal mucosa of young, old and anthelmintic treated wild red grouse *Lagopus lagopus scoticus*. *Parasitology*. **94**, 405-411.

Rands, M.R.W., Hudson, P.J. & Sotherton, N.W. (1988). Gamebirds, Ecology, Conservation and Agriculture. In P.J. Hudson & M.R.W. Rands (ed) *Ecology and Management of Gamebirds*. Blackwells Scientific Publications. 1-17.

Dobson, A.P., Carper, E.R. & Hudson, P.J. (1988). Population biology and life history variation of gamebirds. In P.J. Hudson & M.R.W. Rands (ed) *Ecology and Management of Gamebirds*. Blackwells Scientific Publications. 48-71.

Hudson, P.J. & Dobson, A.P. (1988). The ecology and control of parasites in gamebird populations. In P.J. Hudson & M.R.W. Rands (ed) *Ecology and Management of Gamebirds*. Blackwells Scientific Publications. 98-133.

Hudson, P.J. (1988). The status and potential of red grouse in the Spey valley. *The Management of the Spey Valley* (ed) D. Jenkins. 219-221.

Hudson, P.J. (1988). Spatial variations, patterns and management options in upland bird communities. *Ecological change in the uplands* (ed) M.B. Usher & D.B. Thompson. Blackwells Scientific Publications. 381-397.

Watson, H., Lee, D.L. & Hudson, P.J. (1988). Primary and secondary infections of the domestic chicken with *Trichostrongylus tenuis* (Nematoda), parasite of red grouse, with observations on the effect on the caecal mucosa. *Parasitology*. **97**, 89-99.

Hudson, P.J., Renton, J. and Dalby, G. (1988). Red grouse homing for 35 kilometres. *Scottish Birds*. **15**, 90-91.

Hudson, P.J. & Dobson, A.P. (1989). Population biology of *Trichostrongylus tenuis*, a parasite of economic importance for red grouse management. *Parasitology Today*. **5**, 283-291.

Hudson, P.J. (1990). Winter predation and the role of spacing behaviour in low density red grouse populations. In T.W.I. Lovell & P.J. Hudson (ed) *Proceedings of the Fourth International Grouse Symposium.*

Newborn, D.N. & Hudson, P.J. (1990) Distraction displays in red grouse. In T.W.I.Lovel & P.J. Hudson. (ed) *Proceedings of the Fourth International Grouse Symposium.*

Dobson, A.P. & Hudson, P.J. (1992). Macroparasites and host population dynamics. In M.J. Crawley (ed) *Natural enemies: the population biology of predation, parasites and diseases*. Blackwell Scientific Publications.

Hudson, P.J. & Newborn, D.N. (1990). Brood defence in a precocial species: variations in the distraction displays of red grouse *Lagopus lagopus scoticus*. *Animal Behaviour*. **40**, 254-261.

Hudson, P.J. & Dobson, A.P. (1990). The direct and indirect effects of the caecal nematode, *Trichostrongylus tenuis* on red grouse. In J.E. Loye & M. Zuk (ed) *Bird parasite interactions*. Oxford University Press. 49-68.

Hudson, P.J. & Dobson, A.P. (1990). The control of parasites in natural animal populations: nematode and virus infections of red grouse. In C.M.Perrins, J-D. Lebreton & G.J.M. Hirons (ed) *Bird Populations Studies: Their relevance to conservation and management*. Oxford University Press. 413-432.

Hudson, P.J. (1990). Population ecology of gamebird parasites. In *Proceedings of the XIXth International Union of Game Biologists*. 209-212.

Hudson, P.J. (1990). Herbivore management on ombrogenous mires and dry dwarf shrub heath. In Bragg, H. Ingram and R. Lindsay (ed) *Peatland ecosystems and man: An impact assessment.*

Hudson, P.J. & Dobson, A.P. (1990). Red grouse population cycles and the population dynamics of the caecal nematode, *Trichostrongylus tenuis*. *Red Grouse Population Processes (ed A. Lance & J. Lawton)*. 5-19.

Hudson, P.J. (1990). Territorial status in a low density grouse population: Preliminary observations and experiments. *Red Grouse Population Processes (ed A. Lance & J. Lawton)*. 5-19.

Moss, R. & Hudson, P.J. (1990). Changes in numbers of red grouse. In M. Whitby & S. Grant (ed) *Modelling Heather Management*. Department of Agricultural Economics and Food Marketing, University of Newcastle upon Tyne. 9-20.

Redpath, S.M.(1991). The impact of hen harriers on red grouse breeding success. *Journal of Applied Ecology*. **28**, 659-671

Hudson, P.J., Newborn, D.N. & Dobson, A.P. (1992). Regulation and stability of a free-living host-parasite system, *Trichostrongylus tenuis* in red grouse. I: Monitoring and parasite reduction experiments. *Journal of Animal Ecology*. **61**, 477-486

Dobson, A.P. & Hudson, P.J. (1992). Regulation and stability of a free-living host-parasite system, *Trichostrongylus tenuis* in red grouse. II: Population

models. *Journal of Animal Ecology*. **61**, 487-498.

Dobson, A.P. & Hudson, P.J. (1992). The population dynamics and control of the parasitic nematode *Trichostrongylus tenuis* in red grouse in the north of England. *Applied Population Biology* (ed) S.K. Jain & L. W. Botsford, 149-172. Kluer Academic Press.

Hudson, P.J., Dobson, A.P. & Newborn, D.N. (1992). Do parasites make prey vulnerable to predation? Red grouse and parasites. *Journal of Animal Ecology*, **61**,

Hudson, P.J. & Dobson, A.P. (in press). Population biology of Trichostrongylus. In M.E Scott & G. Smith (ed) *Parasitic Epidemiology*. Academic Press.

Redpath, S.M. Behavioural interactions betweeen hen harriers and their moorland prey. *Ornis Scandinavica*. **23**, 73-80.

## SECONDARY PUBLICATIONS:

Hudson, P.J. & Tapper, S.C. (1980). Grouse populations - do they cycle? *Game Conservancy Annual Review*. **11**, 17-23.

Hudson, P.J. (1981). The production of red grouse in 1980. *Game Conservancy Annual Review*. **12**, 59-62.

Hudson. P.J. (1982). Accumulation of strongyle worms in young grouse. *Game Conservancy Annual Review*. **13**, 102-104.

Hudson. P.J. (1983). Red grouse chicks & Insects. *Game Conservancy Annual Review*. **14**, 65-68.

Hudson, P.J. & Newborn, D.N. (1984). Strongylosis and grouse - its impact on production and future control measures. *Game Conservancy Annual Review*. **15**, 43-48.

Hudson, P.J. (1985). Population cycles in red grouse: do parasites play a role?. In *Population dynamics and epidemiology of Territorial Animals*. ITE Merlewood Report.

Hudson, P.J. (1985). Red grouse and gamekeepers in northern England. *Game Conservancy Annual Review*. **16**, 50-54.

Hudson, P.J. & Newborn, D.N. (1986) Grouse parasites and priorities for management. *Game Conservancy Annual Review*. **17**, 134-137.

Newborn, D.N. & Hudson, P.J. (1986). Scottish Grouse Research Project - initial findings. *Game Conservancy Annual Review*. **17**, 134-137.

Hudson, P.J. & Moore, P. (1987). Winter problems for Scottish grouse. *Game Conservancy Annual Review*. **18**, 146-150.

Newborn, D.N. & Hudson, P.J. (1987). Bracken and its importance on grouse moors in England. *Game Conservancy Annual Review*. **18**, 154-157.

Watson, H. & Hudson, P.J. (1988). The uptake of parasitic worms by red grouse. *Game Conservancy Annual Review*. **18**, 158-161.

Hudson, P.J. & Renton, J. (1988). What influences changes in grouse numbers? *Game Conservancy Annual Review*. **19**, 41-49.

Watson, H. & Hudson, P.J. (1988). The search for a new control method against trichostrongyle worms in red grouse: irradiated larvae. *Game Conservancy Annual Review.* **19**, 53-55.

Hudson, P.J. (1988). Louping ill vaccination, sheep and grouse. *Game Conservancy Annual Review.* **19**, 56-59.

Hudson, P.J. (1989). The Upland Research Group. *Game Conservancy Annual Review.* **20**, 110-111.

Hudson, P.J. and Newborn, D.N. (1989). The conservation of heather moorland. *Game Conservancy Annual Review.* **20**, 111-117.

Hudson, P.J. & Newborn, D.N. (1989). The environmental impact of bracken. *Game Conservancy Annual Review.* **20**, 117-119.

Hudson, P.J. & Newborn, D.N. (1989). Reducing the impact of parasites: the use of medicated grit. *Game Conservancy Annual Review.* **20**, 124-127.

Hudson, P.J., Renton, J. & Dalby, G. (1989). Winter losses and grouse predation in the Highlands of Scotland. *Game Conservancy Annual Review.* **20**, 127-131.

Redpath, S.M. & Hudson, P.J. (1989). Hen harriers and predation of grouse. *Game Conservancy Annual Review.* **20**, 131-133.

Hudson, P.J. (1990). Upland game conservation during the next decade. *Game Conservancy Annual Review.* **21**, 123-125.

Hudson, P.J., Renton, J. & Dalby, G. (1990). Territorial status and survival in a low density grouse population. *Game Conservancy Annual Review.* **21**, 126-127.

Hudson, P.J., Newborn, D.N. & Furrokh, I. (1990). Cycles in grouse numbers and the trichostrongyle parasite. *Game Conservancy Annual Review.* **21**, 129-132.

Newborn, D.N., Booth, F. & Hudson, P.J. (1990). Restoring heather dominant vegetation in the absence of a heather seed bed. *Game Conservancy Annual Review.* **21**, 129-132.

Hudson, P.J. (1991). Upland Ecology and research. *Game Conservancy Annual Review.* **22**, 148-151.

Hudson, P.J. (1992). The Red Grouse. BTO. *Breeding Atlas.*

Hudson, P.J. (1992). Research and Development. *Game Conservancy Annual Review.* **23**, 92-97.

Newborn, D.N. & Booth, F. (1992). The Ecological Impact of Moorland Drainage. *Game Conservancy Annual Review.* **23**, 106-109.

## GENERAL ARTICLES

Hudson, P.J. (1983). Predators and scent. *Shooting Times*, 28 July 1983.

Hudson, P.J. (1984). Keep ahead of the Game. *Farmers Weekly* 24 August 1984.

Hudson, P.J. (1984). The Irish Grouse problem. A view from across the water. *Shooting Times*, Irish Supplement. 1 November 1984.

Hudson, P.J. (1984). What do grouse do on a driving day? *Field & Countryside*. September 1984.

Hudson, P.J. (1985). Where have all the red grouse gone? *Field & Countryside*. March 1985.

Hudson, P.J. (1985). Miners, The Bishop of Durham and Grouse. *Field & Countryside*. April 1985.

Hudson, P.J. (1985). June - The glorious month for the grouse watcher. *Field & Countryside*. June 1985.

Hudson, P.J. (1985). The year of the grouse recovery ? *Shooting and Conservation*, August 1985.

Hudson, P.J. (1986). The Red Grouse. *Debretts diary* (1986).

Hudson, P.J. (1986). New techniques in grouse management. *Country Landowner*. August 1986.

Hudson, P.J. (1987). Scottish Gamebirds. *Scottish Bird News*. September 1987.

Hudson, P.J. (1987). Grouse - cause for concern? *Shooting Magazine*. July 1987.

Hudson, P.J. (1987). Sniffing it out - the relationship between parasites and grouse. *Shooting Times*.

Hudson, P.J. (1988). Scottish gamebirds: points of view. *Scottish Bird News*. March 1988.

Hudson, P.J. (1988). Grouse numbers - why were they good in 1987 and what will they be in 1988? *Shooting Times*. 12 May 1988.

Hudson, P.J. (1988). Medicated grit - the solution to grouse parasite problems. *Scottish Farmer*. 12 March 1988.

Hudson, P.J. (1988). Game For Conservation: The Uplands. *Shooting Times*.

Hudson, P.J. (1989) Not so glorious twelfth gets off to a quiet start. *Shooting Times*. 17 August 1989.

Redpath, S.M. & Hudson, P.J. (1989). Harriers and Grouse. *Shooting Times*. 13 July 1989.

Hudson, P.J. (1989). Grouse prospects. *The Shooting Life*. August 1989.

Hudson, P.J. (1990). Gripes with grouse. *Shooting*. August 1990.

Hudson, P.J. (1990). The red grouse shooting season. *Shooting Times*.

Hudson, P.J. (1991). Upland conservation. *Shooting Times*.

Newborn, D.N. (1991) Grouse prospects 1991. *Shooting Times*. August 1992.

Newborn, D.N. (1991) Scent emission in grouse. *Shooting Times*. September 1991.

Newborn, D.N. (1991). The 1991 Grouse Season. *Shooting Times*. October 1991.

# INDEX

A survey of the economics of grouse shooting in Scotland found the industry was worth a total of £21 million per annum (Appendix 3). *The Earl Peel*

Moorland owners invest capital to conserve heather moorland in the interests of grouse production (Appendix 3).